BOOKS BY PETER WYDEN

Day One

The Passionate War

Bay of Pigs

Peter Wyden
Day One

Before Hiroshima and After

Simon and Schuster   New York

Published by Simon and Schuster
A Division of Simon & Schuster, Inc.
Simon & Schuster Building
Rockefeller Center
1230 Avenue of the Americas
New York, New York 10020
SIMON AND SCHUSTER and colophon are registered trademarks
of Simon & Schuster, Inc.

Designed by Karolina Harris
Manufactured in the United States of America

Library of Congress Cataloging in Publication Data

Wyden, Peter.
Day one.

Bibliography: p.
Includes index.
1. Hiroshima-shi (Japan)—Bombardment, 1945.
2. Atomic bomb—History.   3. World War, 1939–1945—
Japan.   4. Japan—History—1912–1945.   I. Title.
D767.25.H6W93   1985   940.54′26   84-16060

ISBN: 0-671-46142-7

TO ADAM WYDEN

THE A-BOMB STORY
Some Principals

Leo Szilard had the idea first

Gen. Leslie R. Groves was overall boss

J. Robert Oppenheimer was scientific director

Norman F. Ramsey was senior scientist

Edward Teller wanted bigger bombs

President Truman ordered the bomb dropped

The "Little Boy" uranium bomb that hit Hiroshima

Shinzo Hamai, the mayor who brought Hiroshima back to life

Contents

Contents

Photo section follows page 247

Book Two   After the Bomb

Book One
Before the Bomb

One

The Surprise

The night was dark, the weather threatening. Standing tensely at the end of the runway, Dr. Norman F. Ramsey, a physicist from Columbia University, had watched the B-29 roar at him and lumber into the air as it edged toward the blackness of the Pacific. The round trip to Japan and back was 2800 miles, and since all bombers leaving Tinian in the Marianas had to be overloaded with fuel, there had been an epidemic of crashes on takeoff.

The plane that Ramsey watched carried the world's second atomic bomb, the pear-shaped "Fat Man" destined to be dropped on Nagasaki. If this B-29 had crashed as so many others had, Ramsey would not have witnessed a conventional explosion. He and much of Tinian would have evaporated.

Ramsey's relief was only momentary. His mission as chief scientist on the Tinian forward Air Force base had developed two complications that preoccupied him. Foremost in his mind was the figure fifty. Fifty. He had been instructed that fifty nuclear bombs might be required to force the surrender of the Japanese and end World War II. The dreaded alternative was an invasion of Japan against fanatical resistance.

15

Day One

Crashes on takeoff had not been anticipated by the A-bomb planners; if there were to be fifty drops, a nuclear disaster with enormous American casualties seemed "inevitable" to Ramsey.

The other unexpected turn of events had come to Ramsey's attention after the drop of the first atomic bomb, the sleek, blunt-nosed "Little Boy," on Hiroshima three days earlier.* The destruction of the city had drawn exuberant notices. "The greatest day in history," President Truman had called it. But on the short-wave radio in his air-conditioned bomb hut, Ramsey picked up an ominous note from the Tokyo frequency that "upset and puzzled" him very much.

Tokyo Rose, the English-speaking propagandist, announced that radiation injuries and illness were afflicting many survivors in Hiroshima. This was "quite a surprise" to chief scientist Ramsey. The effects of the bomb had been researched. No one had predicted such radiation problems. The bomb was behaving in a way that no one had expected.†

Ramsey was in a position to know this authoritatively because he had been chief of the Delivery Group back at Los Alamos, the government laboratory 7300 feet up on the breathtaking mesa in the remote New Mexico mountains. There, laboring frantically, passionately, he and some 4500 colleagues had unlocked atomic energy for the first time. And while everything behind the fences of their Tech Area had been wrapped in secrecy, Ramsey's Delivery Group had been most secret of all. Prohibited from discussing its work even at

* If the *Enola Gay,* the B-29 carrying the first bomb, had crashed on takeoff there would have been no nuclear explosion. It was a relatively primitive "gun-type" uranium bomb and was armed in flight. The more complicated plutonium bomb dropped on Nagasaki had to be fully armed before takeoff. Ramsey's alarm was amply justified because only one uranium bomb existed. Future bombs would be the plutonium type and they were about to be produced on an assembly-line basis.
† The attitudes and actions of Norman Ramsey are drawn from three interviews with the author in 1983 and 1984, when this elder statesman of science was chairman of the Board of Governors of the American Institute of Physics and a professor at Harvard University, and from the extensive recollections he dictated in 1960 for the Oral History Project at Columbia. The ignorance about the bomb that prevailed in 1945 was pinned down precisely in that history. As Ramsey explained it: "The people who made the decision to drop the bomb made it on the assumption that all casualties would be standard explosion casualties. . . . The region over which there would have been radiation injury was to be a much smaller one than the region of so-called 100% blast kill. . . . Any person with radiation damage would have been killed with a brick first."

16

meetings of the laboratory division heads, it reported to Dr. J. Robert Oppenheimer, the director.

It was the charismatic and oracular Oppenheimer who had prepared Ramsey for the dropping of fifty bombs, and "Oppie" was the ultimate authority on what the scientists called "the gadget." The 50-bomb estimate had seemed realistic. Each bomb was equivalent to about one week of bombing raids with conventional explosives. And while the making of the new weapon had posed, as Oppenheimer liked to phrase it, a "technically sweet problem," the bomb seemed to add nothing novel to warfare except escalated destructiveness. As Oppenheimer said, it merely made a "very big bang."

So when Oppie dispatched Ramsey, his most trusted senior physicist, to Tinian shortly after Hitler had been defeated and the war ended in Europe, Ramsey had expected routine duty. The two years at Los Alamos had been the most exciting adventure of the scientists' lives. But now, the problem solved, they were reduced to technicians. Their job was to keep dropping bombs without so much as a specific order from Washington, one after another, "as soon as made ready."

Ramsey had told his crew of nuclear specialists that they would serve a six-month tour of duty on the island. Their replacements for subsequent half-year stretches had already been designated.

The Tinian contingent had planned their personal lives to fit this timetable. One engineer had brought along hop seed in the belief that he would have ample leisure to brew his own beer. Ramsey, having left his pregnant wife behind in New Mexico, had bought no health insurance for his family. There would be plenty of time for his second child to be born in Los Alamos at government expense; the war seemed certain to continue for months. That was the plan. By the time of the second bomb drop on Nagasaki, a third bomb was about to leave Los Alamos for Tinian. Soon Ramsey was supposed to receive seven or more bombs per month.

Would the unexpected behavior of the weapon change the plan? Ramsey wondered. Nuclear explosions following takeoff crashes might be prevented by changes in the bomb design, and after he watched the hair-raising liftoff of the B-29 on August 9, Ramsey wrote Oppenheimer a long letter suggesting some modifications that he hoped would be adequate. But what about the unpredicted radiation dimension of the bomb? Ramsey had been the first American to learn that it released more than a very big bang, that it produced invisible aftereffects. And if this "upset" him, what would be the reaction in the United States?

It took a great deal to upset Ramsey. He was the most military of the civilian scientists—a six-footer, ramrod straight, endowed with an uninterruptable command voice, the son of a general. Before joining the Manhattan District bomb project he had served as consultant to the Secretary of War. Even Oppenheimer's boss, Major General Leslie R. Groves, the bulky bully who directed the $2 billion Manhattan effort, accepted this physicist, and there were only two or three scientists whom the general did not dismiss as dreamy tinkerers. How would Groves react to the surprising discovery that troubled Ramsey?

THE VIEW FROM WASHINGTON
ROOM 5121, WAR DEPARTMENT BUILDING, 21ST STREET AND VIRGINIA AVENUE 3:45 P.M., AUGUST 24, 1945

The telex message from Los Alamos changed General Groves's mood. Initially he had not been upset about the macabre news from Japan. He was annoyed. He thought the Japanese were bidding for international sympathy. But as the days went on, the alarm was not only spread by propagandists like Tokyo Rose. The Japanese news agency Domei reported that his bomb produced "uncanny effects . . . Even those who received minor burns and looked quite healthy at first, weakened after a few days for some unknown reason."

Finally, on August 24, Groves's staff in Los Alamos added a significant note to the chorus of worriers. Their telex said: "Project staff much concerned about Japanese broadcasts claiming murderous delayed radioactive effects at Hiroshima in view of (U.S.) press release that activity would be small."

This made the matter more legitimate to the general and he responded by telexing to Los Alamos a detailed summary of the Japanese broadcasts, adding that in his opinion the charges of radiation aftereffects were "hoax or propaganda." The laboratory leaders accepted this view. Their ranking radiation expert advised them that the complaints from Tokyo were "definitely a hoax because the data which the Japanese gave did not correspond to any experience known here."

Still, Groves realized that he could use more solid documentation to legitimize his bomb as an acceptable weapon of war. He could not afford to be condemned as the perpetrator of a new menace perhaps more inhuman than biological warfare. Were the Los Alamos doctors right when they said the Japanese complaints were nothing to worry about? Medical diagnoses could vary. The general decided to get a second opinion.

This time he turned to his Oak Ridge laboratory in Tennessee. At 9 a.m. on the 25th he was on the telephone to read excerpts of Tokyo newscasts to a medical colonel there, including one in which the commentator lamented the fate of "the living doomed to die of radio-activity."

"That's kind of crazy—a doctor like me can tell that," the colonel interrupted. "I would say this: I think it's good propaganda. The thing is these people got good and burned—good thermal burns."

"That's the feeling I have," said Groves. Then he cited a still more bothersome grievance. Tokyo radio claimed that those who "died mysteriously a few days after the atomic bomb blast were the victims of a phenomenon which is well known in the great radiation laboratories in America."

This increased further the indignation of the two officers, for the Americans did not know of any such phenomenon, and neither they nor the Japanese even remotely suspected that the disaster was not over; that in the ensuing months tens of thousands would die of essentially untreatable radiation poisoning; that thousands more would suffer for years from cancer, leukemia, mental retardation, chromosomal "aberrations," and other lingering abnormalities; and that forty years after the bombing of Hiroshima that city would still operate a 170-bed A-Bomb Hospital, ministering to victims of the catastrophe that Groves tried to dismiss as a "hoax."

The men who made the Bomb did not know what it was.

Two

Leo Szilard:
It Begins with Science Fiction

The father of the bomb was not Oppenheimer or Groves but Dr. Leo Szilard, and the idea of building such a device occurred to him as he waited for a red traffic light to change at an intersection of Southampton Row in London. Playfulness, not aggressive urges, led the short, plump, Hungarian-born physicist to visualize an atomic chain reaction as he ambled about the city in that golden September of 1933 pursuing his favorite pastimes: thinking and walking.

He had been exposed to the novel notion of superweapons the previous year while doing research at the Kaiser Wilhelm Institute in Berlin. But the first hint did not come to him in the laboratory. His professor, the revered Dr. Albert Einstein, had admired him as a genius "rich in ideas" ever since they collaborated on the invention of a new type of refrigerator, and Szilard drew his brainstorms for refrigerators, bombs, birth control devices, anything, from a hodge-podge of unconventional sources, including science fiction.

Just before he fled Hitler's Germany with all his belongings crammed into two suitcases, Szilard had relished a futuristic novel, *The World Set Free,* written by H. G. Wells in 1913. It prophesied a process of "atomic disintegration" that unleashed "limitless power" and led to global nuclear war. The conflict spread until two hundred cities lay shattered by the "unquenchable crimson conflagrations of the atomic bombs."

Szilard had all but forgotten this stimulating reading until he was

20

resettled in London and learned that Lord Rutherford, the discoverer of the atomic nucleus, addressing a meeting of scientists, had just dismissed atomic energy as "merest moonshine." Szilard recalled Wells's fantasy and his playfulness was piqued. Ernest Rutherford was director of the Cavendish Laboratory at Cambridge University, a shrine for physicists all over the world. A tall, commanding figure with a booming voice and a walrus mustache, Lord Rutherford represented authority. Szilard, thirty-five, distrusted authorities and their accepted wisdoms. He liked no sport better than to prove them wrong. He called on Rutherford and explained his idea of a chain reaction. The session ended badly. "I was thrown out of Rutherford's office," Szilard told the gregarious Dr. Edward Teller, another Hungarian refugee he had known since the days when both studied in Berlin.

Szilard reacted predictably to Rutherford's rebuff. "I assume that I became a scientist because in some ways I remained a child," he reminisced later. Like an uncontrollable youngster, he enjoyed playing with fire, and a small one would not do. When Rutherford scoffed at him in 1933, Szilard's urge to tinker with the universe had been pointing him toward biology, but the immensity of his chain reaction dream stopped his drift: "It was too exciting for me to leave it. So I decided not to go into biology as yet and to *play around* a little bit with physics." And whenever he found an exciting new toy to play around with, he would think and walk.

As the red light changed and Szilard crossed Southampton Row, it occurred to him that he needed to find one element that could be split by neutrons, sustain his chain reaction, and thereby liberate incredible amounts of energy. But the Greek word *atomos* meant anything that can't be split. Splitting the atom would mean dividing the presumably indivisible—and shattering accepted wisdom. No wonder Rutherford had brushed him off.

With enough money to live on for a year, Szilard withdrew to the Strand Palace Hotel. His room lacked a private bath, so until noon each day he lost himself in thought while soaking in the community tub off the corridor. In the afternoons he walked and pondered further. In the spring of 1934 he took out a patent describing how the chain reaction would work. Thoughtfully, he wanted it kept secret. He tried to assign it to the British War Office, but its experts did not share his excitement and could see "no reason to keep the specifications secret." Eventually the Admiralty cooperated on behalf of the Navy.

The splittable element, however, was still eluding him. Each of the 92 elements then known might have to be checked out. Szilard turned away from this "rather boring" drudgery. He detested routine. He tried to hire somebody to plod through the tedious screening; nobody was interested. It would require unplayful Germans to hit upon the elusive element, and Szilard would not start serious work on his atomic bomb until he had moved on to the United States. By then it was 1939, the year the world had been dreading, the year Hitler ignited World War II.

H. G. Wells could not have plotted more dramatic timing—nor cast a more credible messenger to deliver the crucial news that made the bomb practical.

The messenger was Dr. Niels Bohr, nicknamed the "Great Dane," and the news was that the atom had, incredibly, been split. Word of this event reached Bohr shortly after New Year's Day of 1939, just as his secretary and family were trying to hustle him out of his office in Copenhagen. Founder of the Institute for Theoretical Physics, Bohr had discovered the structure of the atom by extending the basic nuclear finding of Rutherford, his teacher and collaborator. Recognizable by his bearlike, rumpled bulk, his massive head and almost inaudible voice, Bohr had become, like Rutherford, a master teacher, a father figure of physicists everywhere, and his institute was another mecca of their profession.

Taking leave of his Danish headquarters to spend some months at the Institute for Advanced Study in Princeton, Bohr was running late, as usual. His office was a jumble of luggage. Because he sometimes missed ships and trains, his entourage was growing nervous when a staff physicist, Vienna-born Dr. Otto Frisch, burst in to spill a remarkable tale.

Frisch had spent Christmas with his aunt, Dr. Lise Meitner, a Jewish physicist from the Kaiser Wilhelm Institute in Berlin who had lately fled across the Dutch border and moved to Sweden. Calling at her rural boardinghouse near Göteborg, Frisch found her puzzling over a letter just in from Berlin. Dr. Otto Hahn, another student of

22

Rutherford's, who had been Meitner's collaborator for more than thirty years, was seeking her counsel about a bizarre experiment.

"Maybe you can suggest some amazing explanation," Hahn wrote.

Working with a new partner, he had bombarded uranium with neutrons. Unexpectedly, some of it had turned into a totally different element, barium. Could they conceivably have split the atom?

"We cannot yet bring ourselves to this conclusion which is at variance with all previous experience in nuclear physics," Hahn hedged in a report he had sent to a German science journal, *Die Naturwissenschaften*. He was in pain—his rheumatism was acting up—and he was worried. "Strange and deceptive accidents" might trap him into misinterpreting his results. Soon he might look like a fool, especially because he was only a "poor little chemist." Meitner had often teased him that he didn't really understand physics.

A tiny, birdlike spinster bursting with energy, Lise took her nephew on a walk through the snow. Otto put on skis to keep up with her. When he first studied Hahn's letter, he had told his aunt, "It's fantastic." Lise demurred, and eventually, perching on a fallen tree, she drew a dotted circle on the back of an envelope.

"Could it be this sort of thing?" she asked Frisch. It could and it was. Frisch rushed back to Copenhagen and asked a young biologist at Bohr's institute for the word that described the splitting of a cell. "Fission," said the biologist, and that was the phenomenon Frisch now explained to the departing Bohr.

The Great Dane interrupted almost immediately. "Oh, what idiots we all have been!" he exclaimed. He struck his forehead. "But this is wonderful. This is just the way it has to be!"

Having caught the *Drottningholm* with hardly a minute to spare, Bohr docked in New York on January 16. Frisch had handed him a sheaf of notes on the Hahn-Meitner calculations and Bohr worked out supporting figures on a blackboard that he managed to have installed in his stateroom. No question: the lock to limitless power had been pried open.

Euphoria over this breakthrough was tempered by Bohr's profound concern about the news sweeping Europe. Neville Chamberlain had sold out the western democracies in Munich. Hitler had gobbled up Czechoslovakia.

Day One

The antifascists were losing the civil war in Spain. The winds of war were ruffling the lives of everyone. The physicist Dr. Enrico Fermi and his wife, Laura, refugees from Italy, at the pier to welcome their old benefactor,* thought Bohr had aged markedly since they last saw him only months ago.

Bohr had promised to keep the fission news quiet as a matter of courtesy until Hahn's article appeared in print. Inevitably, after the Great Dane arrived in Princeton, the sensation leaked out to several insiders, among them another ingenious Hungarian refugee alumnus of the Kaiser Wilhelm Institute, Dr. Eugene P. Wigner. Like his other Berlin cronies, Leo Szilard and Edward Teller, Wigner, by then a physics professor at Princeton, would play a critical part in the making of the A-bomb.

So far the nuclear fan club was small. Soon Szilard would elevate it, in his mid-European imagery, to a "conspiracy," a Hungarian revolution. But not quite yet. Wigner, famous for his unfailing pessimism in political matters and for his equally relentless *politesse* toward everyone, was coming down with jaundice. Before checking into the hospital he passed Bohr's news to Szilard, who happened to be visiting Princeton but had to return to New York because of a severe cold.

Running a high fever and bundled up in the King's Crown Hotel on West 116th Street, opposite Columbia University, where he had attached himself as a freelance researcher without portfolio, Szilard alerted Lewis L. Strauss of the Wall Street investment house Kuhn, Loeb & Company.† The physicists at Princeton, he informed the financier, were reacting "like a stirred-up ant heap" to Hahn's "very sensational" and "entirely unexpected" experiment. Nuclear power might be possible and "unfortunately also perhaps atomic bombs." Szilard would keep in touch. He felt that Strauss's money and influence might come in handy soon.

Of the Hungarian triumvirate, only the energetic Teller was not

---

* Taking Bohr's advice, Fermi, whose wife was Jewish, had decided not to return to Mussolini's fascist Rome after traveling to Stockholm to collect the Nobel Prize. Instead, the Fermis settled in New Jersey. Fermi had also bombarded uranium but had not identified the fission phenomenon.
† In 1953 the haughty, widely disliked Strauss would become chairman of the Atomic Energy Commission.

ailing. His childhood limp never seemed to bother him.* He had moved to Washington and was professor of physics at George Washington University, five blocks west of the White House. He had been imported from Europe by an ambitious dean who was eager to overcome the university's reputation as the "G Street High School."

On Wednesday, January 25, Teller was completing arrangements for the fifth annual Washington Conference on Theoretical Physics when the phone rang in his brown-shingled little row house at 2610 Garfield Street off Connecticut Avenue. It was his co-host for the conference, Dr. George Gamow, a blond, Russian-born physicist affectionately known to students as "goofy Gamow" because he was so excitable. That morning he was more manic than ever.

"That Bohr has gone crazy," he exploded in his thick accent. "He says the uranium nucleus splits!"

In a lecture hall at George Washington University the next morning, some fifty senior scientists assembled to explore the scheduled conference topic, low-temperature physics. Instead Gamow announced a surprise speaker, Niels Bohr.† The Great Dane leaped to his feet, bounded up to the rostrum, and, his hands stuffed into his pockets, related Hahn's fission findings. His customary mumble made him inaudible to students crowding the standing room in the rear, but the scientists, straining to hear, reacted as if one of the Ten Commandments had been repealed.

Gamow excitedly began to cover the blackboard with figures. Teller, an alumnus of Bohr's institute, wondered aloud what would happen if fission released enough neutrons to start a chain reaction. His colleagues, too dazzled to think ahead, were more interested in confirming that fission actually liberated energy and, if so, how much. They did not mind cutting short the discussion when Teller reminded them that two reporters were present. The meeting was breaking up anyway. Many of the dignified conferees in their dark suits and white shirts were rushing to the doors. Fermi headed back to his new post at Columbia. The delegates from Johns Hopkins in nearby Baltimore

---

* His artificial left foot, the legacy of a streetcar accident in Budapest, resembled the handicap of Stanley Kubrick's 1964 movie villain Dr. Strangelove.
† Bohr had been released from his vow of confidentiality only minutes before. As the conference got under way, a reporter for Science Service handed him a copy of *Die Naturwissenschaften,* just arrived from Berlin. It contained Hahn's ground-breaking article.

had repeated Hahn's experiment by afternoon. Merle A. Tuve, another Bohr alumnus, dispatched a colleague up Connecticut Avenue to his laboratory at the Carnegie Institute's Department of Terrestrial Magnetism.

"Put a new filament in the particle accelerator," he instructed.

Shortly before midnight Bohr and Teller arrived to watch the fluttering green line on the screen of the oscilloscope attached to Tuve's accelerator. The laboratory was almost dark. Uranium was being bombarded by neutrons. "Here's another one!" Tuve would shout as the green line pulsed explosively to the top of the screen. Greatly excited, he joked that he could finally justify the expense of the accelerator. Bohr stood by, mesmerized and looking worried. It was dawn before the group broke up. Only Teller had considered the night's events almost anticlimactic. To him, as to most theoretical physicists, the act of discovery was more important than the confirmation delivered by the gadgets of the experimentalists.

The newspaper accounts of the meeting failed to make the front pages. The two press representatives were conservative science specialists from the *Washington Star* and Science Service and their stories promised little. They reported "new hope for releasing the enormous stores of energy within the atom." In some distant day the atom might fuel ocean liners. The reporters cautioned that nothing was imminent; so far the laboratory explosions were not even powerful enough to light a household lamp.

Within the science fraternity the excitement had barely begun. The physicist Dr. Luis W. Alvarez caught up with the Washington news stories as he relaxed in the campus barber shop at the University of California in Berkeley. He jumped up in mid-haircut and rushed to the Cyclotron Building. He had to reach one of his students, Philip Abelson, ahead of anyone else. Abelson had been working on an experiment similar to Hahn's and might get very upset. "Better lie down first," Alvarez began thoughtfully before he spilled the news. The shy and gentle Abelson did not recover his equilibrium for weeks.

In his office, Room 318 of Le Conte Hall, the Berkeley physics building, J. Robert Oppenheimer reacted to the news in a letter he wrote on January 28 to a colleague at the California Institute of Technology at Pasadena.

Oppie was very much the unworldly professor. His hair stood on end in a tall, fuzzy bush. His politics were stylishly radical; his mistress, his brother, and his sister-in-law were Communist Party members. He had no phone or radio and disdained newspapers. He had been building the Berkeley physics department into one of the country's finest and his students revered him slavishly. They imitated his fast but listing gait, his cutting wit, his taste for gourmet cuisine and wines, even the way he said, *"Ja, Ja,"* a remnant of his graduate-student days at Göttingen in Germany.

Like Bohr and Rutherford, he had made himself a master teacher, but no one could have guessed that this iconoclast would become the pivotal figure in translating Szilard's nuclear fantasy into hardware. Certainly not Oppenheimer himself. For the present he was as awed as everybody else.

"The U [uranium] business is unbelievable," he wrote his friend at Caltech.

Not literally. Already the men at Berkeley could taste what Oppenheimer later called the "technically sweet" problem: to make the bomb of bombs. Already Philip Morrison, one of his brightest graduate students, was at Oppenheimer's blackboard drawing a sketch of such a weapon. Fellow students were shouting suggestions from their seats. Leaning on his cane—he was crippled by polio— Morrison weighed some of the principal hurdles to be overcome: How much fissionable material would the bomb have to pack? Would it have to be too huge to be deliverable? And there were many more imponderables. "The neutrons," shouted someone. "You've got to show the neutrons!"* The neutrons, yes.

---

* Shortly afterward, Morrison wrote an article about his bomb and sent it to the *Saturday Evening Post*. It came back with a routine rejection slip. The *Post* editors were not ready for the new broom of warfare.

Three

Franklin D. Roosevelt:
The President Buys a "Bright Idea"
from His Favorite Jeremiah

The neutrons were preoccupying Leo Szilard when, barely recovered from his fever, he phoned Teller from Washington's Union Station. It was the day after Bohr had electrified their colleagues at George Washington University, and Teller was not surprised that his old crony was in town. Szilard loved to be unpredictable and rarely gave advance notice of his appearance.

"Teller, this is Szilard."

"Where are you?"

"At the station—could you come and get me?"

Teller and his wife Mici offered him one of their bedrooms, but Szilard declined after inspecting it. The bed was too hard. "I've tried to sleep in this bed before," he sniffed. "Where is the nearest hotel?"

The Tellers, accustomed to the eccentricities of their Budapest-Berlin-London compatriot, bedded him down in the nearby Wardman Park Hotel. They knew he was not the ideal house guest. Leo kept erratic late hours, preferred fatty or over-sweet delicatessen fare in drug stores and campus hangouts, and felt most at home with the impersonal bachelor comforts of hotels and university faculty clubs.*

Szilard was rounding up allies for his self-proclaimed nuclear conspiracy. The role suited him nicely. He used to tell friends he con-

---

* Until 1951, when he married his long-time Berlin friend Gertrud (Trude) Weiss, a medical doctor, Szilard lived out of suitcases and never kept an apartment or a car. He owned almost nothing but his clothes.

sidered himself a knight-errant, but this was an uncharacteristic understatement. He was a producer of spectaculars, a wire puller with a fine touch for casting, for props, and for financing. Teller, noisy, persuasive, and forward-looking in technical matters, was a qualified recruit. Quickly the two plotters agreed on their next step. To nail down the prospects for an A-bomb, they had to answer the crucial question: If neutrons produce fission, does fission produce the neutrons needed to release untold energy? Szilard promised to arrange the necessary experiment.

Back in the gloomy fourteen-story Pupin Physics Building at Columbia, Szilard encountered less enthusiasm. He wanted to enlist Enrico Fermi, the most brilliant physics experimenter in America—introverted, methodical, and egocentric. Fermi lived for physics. As he lectured before a blackboard his mouth sometimes turned white; he was so absorbed that he forgot he was holding chalk between his lips. Unhappily, he could not abide the tactless, clamorous Szilard and his freewheeling ways. The Fermi home in Leonia, New Jersey, was off limits to Leo. So Szilard dispatched a non-Hungarian emissary, Dr. Isidor I. Rabi,* a feisty little Russian-born physicist, to see Fermi. Rabi's judgment and no-nonsense manner were universally respected.

"What did Fermi say?" Szilard asked after Rabi confronted Fermi early in February.

"Fermi said, 'Nuts!' "

Mystified, Szilard asked Rabi to come along to Fermi's office.

"Szilard wants to know why you said 'Nuts,' " Rabi inquired.

Fermi said he meant that a neutron emission in the fission of uranium (and a resulting chain reaction) was only a remote possibility.

"What do you mean by 'remote possibility'?" asked Rabi.

"Well, ten percent," said Fermi.

Szilard never forgot Rabi's clincher: "Ten percent is not a remote possibility if it means we may die of it."

Driven by Rabi's alarm, Teller's Hungarian cheerleading, Wigner's

---

* Rabi would eventually win the Nobel Prize, as did Rutherford, Bohr, Hahn, Fermi, Wigner, Alvarez, and others who worked on the bomb, though not Szilard, Teller, or Oppenheimer. Ironically, Alfred Nobel, a Swedish armaments manufacturer and inventor of dynamite, had established the Prize because his work gave him a guilty conscience that drove him toward pacifism.

apocalyptic warnings of the Nazi menace, and his own mania for stage-managing the universe, Szilard decided to perform the crucial neutron experiment himself. This was a measure of his agitation, because he considered himself a brainstormer, not a laboratory tinkerer, and he hated to get his fingers dirty. He also needed space to work.

Jobless and with earnings of only $1000 the previous year, he had to look about for money to rent the required one gram of experimental radium. Financier Lewis Strauss did not respond to an overture for a contribution, so Szilard walked to the Upper Riverside Drive apartment of a friend, an inventor named Benjamin Liebowitz, borrowed $2000, and then obtained permission from Dr. George P. Pegram, dean of the Columbia Graduate Faculties, to set up temporary shop at the Pupin Laboratory. Pegram was unenthusiastic. Szilard felt the Columbia administrator considered the project "too fantastic to be entirely respectable."

The experiment delivered its verdict in late afternoon on March 2. On the seventh floor of the Pupin, Szilard had located an ionization chamber operated by Dr. Walter Zinn, a gentle former Canadian schoolteacher, who agreed to attend to the detail work. The necessary elements—uranium, radium, and beryllium—were in place. Szilard and Zinn watched the screen of a television tube. The laboratory was still. No one else was present when they threw the master switch. Flashes of light appeared on the screen and they knew instantly that they had made history: fast neutrons were being emitted in the fission of uranium. The bomb was possible.

Szilard watched the flashes for ten minutes, went home to the King's Crown Hotel, and phoned Teller.

An avid and noisy pianist, Teller was playing a Mozart sonata on his bargain-basement Steinway when the phone rang.

"I have found the neutrons," said Szilard in "code"—Hungarian.

When Fermi duplicated the Szilard-Zinn experiment with a different system but the same results, Szilard thought his conspiracy's money worries were over. It was time to inform the authorities in Washington; the government would surely finance further research. Szilard met with Fermi and Wigner in Pegram's office and on March 16, the day Hitler swallowed what was left of Czechoslovakia, the dean wrote a letter of introduction for Fermi to an admiral in the office of the Chief of Naval Operations.

Pegram's tone was relaxed. Fermi would be in Washington the next day anyway to lecture before the Philosophical Society, he wrote, which made him available to describe some new experiments to the Navy. This work suggested that uranium might be transformed into an explosive "a million times" more powerful than anything known. "My own feeling is that the probabilities are against this," Pegram concluded, "but my colleagues and I think that the bare possibility should not be disregarded."

This send-off yielded Fermi an hour with a military committee. Its members expressed mild interest in uranium as a new source of power for submarines. They promised the careful little scientist with the heavy Italian accent that they would "keep in contact"—and sent him home. Refugees were suspect. One of the committee's technical advisers called Merle Tuve at the Carnegie Institute and asked, "Who is this man Fermi? Is he a Fascist or what?"

At a gloomy meeting in Princeton the same week—it lasted until well past midnight—Szilard encountered more thoughtful doubts from a more meaningful authority: Niels Bohr. Surrounded by former Copenhagen disciples—Wigner, Teller, and others—Bohr judged that a bomb was impractical. "It can never be done unless you turn the whole United States into one huge factory," he cautioned the ebullient Teller.

Szilard, increasingly appalled by the likelihood that the Nazis would be quick to follow up on Hahn's work, pleaded that all further papers on nuclear progress produced by scientists in friendly countries should be voluntarily withheld from publication. The idea offended Bohr's spirit of free inquiry and he did not think everybody would cooperate.*

Szilard's concern over the alertness of Germany's scientists quickly proved justified. On April 24, a physical chemist in Hamburg, Paul Harteck, another trainee of Lord Rutherford, wrote Hitler's War

---

* Bohr was correct. Szilard, Victor F. Weisskopf, and other physicists cabled secrecy pleas to colleagues in Britain and France. Their campaign collapsed when they were turned down by Frederic Joliot-Curie in Paris, the son-in-law of Madame Eve Curie and the discoverer of artificial radioactivity.

Office in Berlin: "We take the liberty of calling your attention to the newest development in nuclear physics, which in our opinion, will probably make it possible to produce an explosive many orders of magnitude more powerful than conventional ones . . . That country which first makes use of it has an unsurpassable advantage over the others."

The letter was shown to the co-inventor of the Geiger counter, Professor Hans Geiger,* and his encouragement prompted immediate meetings at the ministerial level. The export of uranium was banned (Germany owned rich deposits in the Joachimsthal mines of newly occupied Czechoslovakia). In June, one of Hahn's close associates published a knowledgeable article in *Die Naturwissenschaften* describing a plausible way to produce a chain reaction and a "uranium machine." Szilard and his co-conspirators concluded that the secretive Nazis had to know much more than they were publishing. The refugee plotters were convinced that they were caught in a race that the United States Government had not yet even joined.

As New York's notorious heat and humidity slowed life for the summer (almost no air conditioning existed except in movie houses), Szilard launched another sortie to awaken official Washington. At a Princeton meeting of the American Physical Society, he approached a technical adviser of the Naval Research Laboratory and told him of a new uranium graphite system to sustain a chain reaction. Szilard had just finished designing it and the calculations looked excellent; even the cautious Wigner had said so. This time the government hid behind its red tape. When the Navy man wrote on July 10 that assistance was "almost impossible in light of the restrictions which are imposed on Government contracts for services," Szilard concluded that the military was not a likely source of research money.

Seasonal lassitude frustrated him severely. Fermi had left for summer school at the University of Michigan and his replies to Szilard's letters were cool. Dean Pegram reminded Szilard that it was summer; nothing could be accomplished toward the development of a graphite system until September or October.

Only Szilard and Wigner kept meeting and worrying. Distressed

* Geiger was yet another Rutherford disciple. He had worked with the master on the structure of the atom at Cambridge in 1911.

by the Nazi embargo on uranium, they thought of the enormous deposits in the Belgian Congo and decided that the Belgian Government should be warned against selling this scarce explosive to the Germans. Szilard recalled that his old Berlin teacher and collaborator Albert Einstein was a friend of the Queen of Belgium; the former Princess Elisabeth of Bavaria and the genius with the shaggy hairdo who gave the world the theory of relativity had played the violin together in a chamber music ensemble. Perhaps Einstein could be persuaded to write the Queen.

Szilard phoned Einstein's office in Princeton and learned that the great man was relaxing and sailing at a cottage owned by a Dr. Moore in Peconic, Long Island. Early one beautiful morning in July, Szilard and Wigner drove there in Wigner's Dodge coupe. For half an hour they hunted about, asking people for Dr. Moore's place. Nobody could direct them. When they were about to give up, Szilard asked a boy of seven or eight, "Say, do you know by any chance where Professor Einstein lives?" It was the right way to phrase the question. The boy had never heard of Dr. Moore but did know that Einstein lived on Old Grove Road. The gentle, elderly German refugee personified science for laymen everywhere.

Only physicists knew that Einstein, then sixty, had long isolated himself from the mainstream of his profession. His work on relativity dated back to 1905. He no longer looked at the science journals that arrived weekly in his home. "In Princeton they regard me as an old fool," he told a friend. So when Einstein, wearing an undershirt and rolled-up pants, ushered Szilard and Wigner onto Dr. Moore's screened-in porch and they began to talk in German around a wooden table, the great man was unaware of the excitement about a uranium chain reaction. "That never occurred to me," he admitted later.

When Szilard and Wigner briefed him, Einstein grasped the significance at once. Having been booed off the lecture platform in Germany, he also knew about the brutality of Nazis. Although he considered himself a pacifist, he was eager to help his visitors but reluctant to trouble the Belgian queen. He preferred to get in touch with a Belgian cabinet member of his acquaintance. Wigner, the worrier, questioned the propriety of approaching a foreign government. Einstein dictated a letter in German—Wigner, who took it down in longhand, marveled at how easily the old man's language flowed—and they all agreed to clear the text with the State Department.

The real problem—the difficulty of arousing interest in the United States Government—remained unresolved. "It will be a hard thing to put this across to the military mind," Einstein mused, which was precisely what troubled Szilard. The approach to the State Department seemed much too roundabout. He was like a man with an explosive special delivery letter and no post office.

Feeling too "green" to cope with official channels of communication, Szilard looked up another old Berlin friend, Gustav Stolper, an economist and former member of the German parliament. At least Stolper had been in politics. He had to know something about approaching politicians.

Stolper made an appointment for Szilard with an acquaintance, Dr. Alexander Sachs, an economist with the Lehman corporation at One William Street. The Russian-born Sachs had been chief economist for the National Recovery Administration in the early days of the New Deal. Supposedly he knew his way around Washington.

In Sachs, Szilard had found his postman at last. The Lehman vice president looked like the bespectacled little popular comedian Ed Wynn, "the perfect fool," but Sachs fancied himself a specialist in "prehistory." His sentences were endless and convoluted. His vocabulary was, to use one of his favorite words, "fantasticated." As a gloomily "Jeremiahesque observer" who "adumbrated" for "perduring" meanings, he already knew about fission from science journals and did not have to be sold on the significance of Szilard's mission.

Sachs proposed that Einstein write another letter. The subject was far too important for any government department. Sachs would deliver the message personally to President Franklin D. Roosevelt, to whom he had enjoyed access since he gave FDR advice on economics during the 1932 campaign. The President appreciated this entertaining "Jeremiah" who never sought publicity or a job. In those days before there were think tanks Sachs's futuristic long-distance vision was rare and valuable.

Delighted to agree that only the White House could help him, Szilard drafted a letter to Roosevelt, mailed it to Einstein, and asked for comments over the telephone. Einstein preferred another meeting. Wigner having fled the heat for the west coast, Szilard recruited

Teller to drive him back to Peconic in Edward's 1935 Plymouth. Wearing an old robe and slippers, Einstein served them tea and dictated a draft letter in German which Teller took down in longhand. It became the basis for two further drafts by Szilard, a short version and a longer one. Szilard had them typed on plain paper, dated them August 2, and mailed both to Einstein. He was unsure how long a letter the President might read ("How many pages does the fission of uranium rate?"). Einstein signed Szilard's longer version, his signature reflecting the old man's legendary modesty; it was barely larger than the typing.

The cautiously worded text promised nothing. It envisioned "extremely powerful bombs of a new type" but described their advent merely as "conceivable." These bombs, moreover, might "prove to be too heavy for transportation by air." Perhaps they would be deliverable only by ship. Einstein warned of the threat posed by nuclear experiments progressing at the Kaiser Wilhelm Institute in Berlin and urged the President to secure uranium supplies.

Szilard handed the letter to Sachs on August 15.* Nothing happened until October 11. Szilard's patience had never been more painfully tried. "Last week Wigner and I visited Dr. Sachs, who confessed that he is still sitting on your letter," he wrote to Einstein on October 3. "There is a distinct possibility that Sachs will be useless to us." Szilard and Wigner gave their mailman an ultimatum: Sachs would have only ten more days to act.

Sachs reminded the anxious Hungarians that it had not been an opportune time to tackle the President with a complex technical matter requiring careful deliberation. The era of tensions and threats was ending in these very days. The world was exploding. Hitler's tanks had rolled across the Polish frontier at dawn on September 1. On September 3, Britain and France had declared war on the Reich. Roosevelt had proclaimed a National Emergency on September 8 and was trying to persuade Congress to repeal the embargo on shipping arms abroad. Sachs shrewdly waited until the pressures of international crisis had eased somewhat and the President might devote a solid block of time to a speculative long-range problem.

Ushered into the President's second-floor White House study on

---

* On August 16 Szilard also asked the celebrated aviator Charles Lindbergh to act as middleman. Lindbergh never responded.

October 11, the eccentric little emissary from Leo Szilard carried a bulky load of books and papers. He knew he faced a difficult sale and did not want to fail. Decision makers, he well knew, were "punch-drunk with printer's ink." Technical material would have to enter the President's head "by way of the ear and not as a sort of mascara on the eye."

None too helpfully, Sachs began by reciting a long memorandum he had composed, detailing the roles of Hahn and Meitner and Szilard and Fermi and Wigner and Teller. He showed Roosevelt a 1938 book updating the history of science and Lord Rutherford's pioneering work on the structure of the atom. Only then did Sachs recite the first and last paragraphs of the letter Szilard had ghosted for Einstein, who was well known to FDR and had been an overnight guest at the White House.*

The President looked interested. Sachs did not have to tell him, as he sometimes did when Roosevelt grew bored with his long-winded presentations, that Sachs was paying for his trip from New York and would the President please pay attention. After about an hour, however, Roosevelt became distracted and indicated he was not convinced that the government should sponsor such a costly enterprise. The session was clearly ending, so Sachs asked whether he could come back the next day and the President invited him for breakfast.

Sachs's night was restless. He paced across his room in the Carlton Hotel. He took walks through Lafayette Park. How could he capture the President's imagination? At dawn he returned to his hotel, his strategy set. Wishing to do nothing that might distract him, he did not return to bed but dozed in a chair until his wake-up call sent him back to the White House.

"What bright idea do you have this morning?" Roosevelt asked cheerfully when Sachs was shown to the President's breakfast table.

"All I want to do is tell you a story," Sachs replied.

It was a long, elaborate tale, like all of Sachs's yarns. Its central

---

* After the war, speculation arose that the famous Einstein letter may have been superfluous because the scientists were already working toward the bomb, especially in England. Even Oppenheimer said that the letter "had very little effect." This ignored the fact that the scientists were communicating almost entirely with themselves and that the British lacked the means to mount the necessary enormous project. Einstein was the essential catalyst. Without his intervention the bomb probably wouldn't have been ready for use in World War II.

figure was Napoleon Bonaparte, and it dealt with Napoleon's eagerness to conquer England. When Robert Fulton, the American inventor of the steamboat, suggested that Napoleon commission a fleet of such vessels as an invasion force of unprecedented might, Napoleon brushed off these new weapons. Sachs then read to the President a recent prediction of a British physicist that the coming of atomic power was inevitable and that one could only hope man "will not use it exclusively in blowing up his next-door neighbor."

Roosevelt grinned and replied, "Alex, what you are after is to see that the Nazis don't blow us up."

"Precisely," said Sachs.

The President ordered a servant to bring a bottle of Napoleon brandy and two glasses were poured. The men sipped and FDR summoned his secretary, Brigadier General Edwin M. ("Pa") Watson. He handed Sachs's papers to Watson and said, "Pa, this requires action."

Despite this presidential green light, three years would pass before the bomb project moved beyond the exploratory stage, and the very first "action" meeting set the style for the frustrations that Szilard would endure.

Within a bureaucracy unacquainted with the potential of nuclear science, the bomb had become the orphan child of a newly formed Uranium Committee chaired by Dr. Lyman J. Briggs, an unassuming Hoosier who had been plodding up the civil service ladder for forty-three years, starting as a soil physicist for the Department of Agriculture. By 1939, the sixty-five-year-old Briggs was dozing through the twilight of his career as director of the Bureau of Standards. At meetings he had the disconcerting habit of closing his eyes. His accustomed associates were American-born and harbored no immodest designs on his slim budget. Strangers with exotic ideas spelled trouble, and the Hungarian triumvirate that dominated the meeting in his Connecticut Avenue office on October 21 was downright upsetting.*

Szilard stated his case for buying graphite to construct a system

---

* Szilard, Wigner, and Teller had been eager for Fermi to come. Fermi declined. Teller made a special trip from Washington to New York to persuade Enrico to change his mind. Fermi refused again. After the brushoff he had experienced in March, this prima donna had no wish to be humiliated by another committee.

for producing a chain reaction. Wigner and Teller spoke up in support. Briggs was impassive; so was the Navy ordnance expert, Commander Gilbert C. Hoover. The army representative, Colonel Keith F. Adamson, announced that he did not believe in complicated new inventions. When someone mentioned that 2.2 pounds of uranium might produce as powerful an explosion as 20,000 tons of TNT, the colonel remained unmoved. He said he had once stood right outside an ordnance depot when the whole place blew up, yet he was not even knocked down.

Teller brought up the subject of funding. Adamson asked, "How much money do you need?"

Szilard suggested $6000. Adamson launched into a lengthy lecture. It invariably required two wars, he said, before any new weapon proved itself. Besides, wars were won by the morale of troops, not by weapons. This was too much for Wigner. Though he was superpolite, he also had a sense of humor.* In his high-pitched voice he interjected that if weapons were of such small value, perhaps the army budget should be sharply trimmed.

"All right, all right, you'll get your money," snapped the angry colonel.

Even Szilard would have been floored if his crystal ball had revealed that the A-bomb project would require the then-unimaginable sum of two billion preinflation taxpayers' dollars.

---

* His notes to Szilard were often signed, "Wigwam."

Four

The Experimenters: What If the Entire Planet Were Set Afire?

Once the United States government had taken "action," as ordered by the President, no less, what happened was absolutely nothing. Briggs reported to Roosevelt that "if" a chain reaction were to be coaxed into reality this might "conceivably" eliminate the need for large batteries to power submarines, no more. But Szilard did not even hear this much from Washington.

The check for the $6000 promised by the Briggs committee did not arrive. Wigner and Teller returned to their teaching posts. Fermi worked on cosmic rays. Szilard's temporary permission to conduct experiments at Columbia had expired. His atomic war lay as dormant as the "phony war" phase that kept the European battlefronts quiet all that winter of 1939-40.

In his lonely room at the King's Crown Hotel, Szilard settled down to another depressing chore. "Under ordinary conditions I would naturally refund your loan from my private earnings," he wrote on December 24 to Benjamin Liebowitz, the inventor who had advanced him the $2000 for the crucial experiment with the neutrons. "Unfortunately, I have not earned anything this year, as I was tied up with this work on uranium." And the outlook for 1940 appeared glum. He asked that the loan be written off "as a bad debt."*

Fear of progress by the Nazis kept him at his one-man lobbying.

* In 1964, Szilard's widow learned that the debt had somehow been repaid after all.

The news from Berlin was unsettling. The director of the Kaiser Wilhelm Institute had been relieved of his duties because his Dutch citizenship made him ineligible for secret work. Shortly after he left Germany and became free to speak, word reached Szilard that a large section of the institute was being converted to uranium research.

It was time to reactivate his only potent weapon, Einstein. He went to see his old professor in Princeton and Einstein agreed to ask Sachs to nudge the President once more. Szilard told Einstein that he had devised another arm-twisting ploy to put pressure on the Washington authorities. He would submit an article to the *Physical Review* describing a graphite-uranium system that he felt certain would be chain-reacting. The article would be released only if the government refused to go ahead with the nuclear investigation in a reasonable time.* Szilard also saw to it that a copy of his manuscript was delivered to Washington by the very embarrassed Dean Pegram. Suddenly, on February 20, Briggs's promised $6000 arrived.

Sachs, finally realizing that his first approach to FDR had been "too academic," was also readily remobilized. The self-appointed Jeremiah transmitted another letter from Einstein to the President, dated March 7, warning that "interest in uranium has intensified in Germany." When the easygoing Pa Watson replied from the White House that the Briggs Committee recommended "the matter should rest in abeyance" pending further evaluation, Einstein wrote to FDR once more on April 25. Prompted by Szilard, he now urged formation of a separate organization to pursue "practical applications" of the atom with "greater speed and on a larger scale." Szilard had foreseen the need for what would become the Manhattan Project.

Pressured by Szilard's manipulations, Briggs told Sachs he would call another meeting of his Uranium Committee. Sachs and Dean Pegram would be invited.

"Well, what about Szilard and Fermi?" asked Sachs.

"Well, you know, these matters are secret," said Briggs, "and we did not think they should be included."

Sachs lost his temper, and so the two scientists were asked, after all, to participate in the discussion of their own secrets, even though they were not yet American citizens. Along with Wigner (who had become a citizen only lately) they were also appointed to a new

* Since Szilard's blackmail worked, the article was not published until 1978.

scientific subcommittee. Not for long. When the subcommittee met for the first time on June 13, Chairman Briggs announced that it would be disbanded that day. If the chain reaction failed to work, he explained, there might be a congressional investigation. In that event it would be embarrassing if funding had been recommended by anyone other than citizens of long standing.

Sounds of war, its phony phase quickly forgotten, seemed not to penetrate Briggs's ears. Hitler's April dash across Denmark and Norway was followed in May by the rush of his panzers through Holland and Belgium. The anachronistic fortifications of the Maginot Line were outflanked. The British had barely managed their humiliating evacuation at Dunkirk when all France surrendered to the hysterical dictator with the no longer amusing little mustache. The newspaper headlines turned more frightening each day—and still Briggs saw no need to speed up the atomic project or to spend significant money on it.

Szilard, seething, predicted all over the Columbia campus that Germany would win the war. Wigner wrote a very polite letter of resignation from the project. It was no consolation that Briggs's obsession with secrecy kept essential data from native-born scientists as well. When the Uranium Committee was enlarged—Szilard, Fermi and Teller were not invited—the newly added Yankee members were given the impression that they were working on a new power source for submarines, not bombs that could decide the war. And the treatment of refugees as outcasts humiliated the very men who were still doing the most to protect their adopted country.

The security agencies understood the émigrés least of all. Investigators swarmed after unconventional spirits like Szilard and stayed on the trail, spreading absurd accusations throughout the war years. "Mr. Szilard is said to be very pro-German and to have remarked on many occasions that he thinks the Germans will win the war," an Army intelligence report advised the Assistant Chief of Staff for war plans on October 1, 1940. "Reliable contacts among the faculty and authorities at Columbia University state they would not care to guarantee his discretion, integrity and loyalty to the United States."

Mindless gumshoeing led to grotesque "security" measures. Fermi and Szilard were specifically kept from knowledge of new experiments which their findings would have speeded up. Even the saintly

Einstein was distrusted. He was asked to assist with complicated theoretical questions that held up the purification of uranium, but the basic data needed to solve the problem was withheld from him. As a result, his scribbled notes were all but useless. He was nevertheless so careful to guard their confidentiality that he would not have them typed up.

"I do not feel that I ought to take him into confidence on the subject to the extent of showing just where this thing fits into the defense picture," Dr. Vannevar Bush explained to an associate,* and Bush was no timorous functionary like Briggs. Indeed, after June 1940, when Roosevelt appointed Bush, president of the prestigious Carnegie Institution, to direct all the government's science activities, Briggs's influence faded. Still, the counterproductive preoccupation with secrecy and the suspicion of "foreigners"—especially one as clamorous as Szilard—never abated, not even after their ideas became respectable.

In November, Columbia finally received a $40,000 contract to develop a Szilard-Fermi system for producing a chain reaction, and Szilard was given a place on the university payroll. His salary was $4000 a year, modest even then. But the atomic bomb project was no longer a one-man Hungarian band.

Bush—lean, tough, his New England twang matching the grizzled face of a sea captain—was a shrewd administrator and a scientist of scope, but he was juggling priorities for many defense projects. He judged that a usable bomb was "very remote," and his new deputy for nuclear projects, Dr. James B. Conant, president of Harvard University and a distinguished chemist, was even more pessimistic. Listening to the Uranium Committee's speculations that atomic power might revolutionize industry, Conant became annoyed.

"These fancies left me cold," he wrote later. Gravely worried about the way the war was going, he was interested only in projects

---

* Writing to Dr. Frank Aydelotte, who was director of the Institute for Advanced Study at Princeton and therefore Einstein's boss, Bush made it plain that his treatment of the old master was symptomatic of policy, not individual prejudice: "I very much wish that I could place the whole thing before him and take him fully into confidence, but this is utterly impossible in view of the attitude of people here in Washington . . ."

that would pay off in "months or, at most, a year or two." He was ready to write off plans for a nuclear bomb as irrelevant to national defense for the foreseeable future.

Neither Bush nor Conant knew that in England two refugees had already rendered the American pessimism obsolete. Otto Frisch, the nephew of Lise Meitner who had brought the fission news to Bohr, had escaped from Denmark and was now at the University of Birmingham working with his friend Dr. Rudolph Peierls. British authorities did not mind that the refugees puttered with nuclear research while the more trusted native talent pressed on with immediate military needs.

In the spring of 1940 Frisch and Peierls quite independently arrived at some novel calculations. The military significance was clear to them at once. But what to do? Like Szilard and his Hungarians, they cautiously questioned well-connected colleagues about likely contacts in Winston Churchill's government. The refugees wanted to make certain that their work would be "used by the right people" who "would get something done."

In due time Frisch and Peierls elicited polite official interest and drew up a memorandum that required a year to meander upward through the British bureaucracy. Their conclusions were stunning: Only five to ten kilograms of pure uranium would be needed for a bomb—not tons, perhaps as many as 100 tons, as the Americans had feared. Further analysis yielded a time estimate that met Conant's deadline. Churchill's men became convinced that a bomb could be readied in about two years—though not with the sparse finances and raw materials available in Britain.

Not until July 10, 1941, did an American physicist, returning from an unrelated mission to Britain, report to Bush in his office at Sixteenth and P streets in Washington with a sketchy preview of the British findings. A formal report arrived a few days later. Bush and Conant set about studying it, but the scientists in London, reeling from the aerial Battle of Britain and still pounded by Nazi fire raids, had grown impatient. They wanted action.

The most uninhibited of them, another Rutherford alumnus, Dr. Marcus E. L. Oliphant, cornered Briggs at the National Bureau of Standards in August and wondered out loud why they had received no American reaction. Briggs gazed down at his conference table, closed his eyes, and mumbled that he had not circulated the British report to the Uranium Committee because it was classified "top secret." The ebullient Australian-born Oliphant was appalled and said so vigorously.

Next he called on Bush and Conant and found them cordial but cool. By the time he met with Briggs's Uranium Committee he no longer felt bound by the rules of diplomacy. A forceful speaker, he made the word "bomb" reverberate around the room. He lectured the shocked Americans that they had no right to waste their time dreaming of power plants. Already the British had spent £50,000 ($200,000) on bomb research, more than the United States. In Oliphant's gross underestimate, making the bomb would cost $25,000,-000. Britain didn't have such resources to spare. The Americans absolutely had to get to work. The committee sat stunned.

Only at his next stop, the University of California at Berkeley, did the missionary from Britain hit pay dirt with an old friend, Dr. Ernest O. Lawrence. They were two of a kind: inspired technicians charged up with entrepreneurial zest. They liked practical results and knew how to promote them. The dapper, hyperenergetic Lawrence, a long-acknowledged technological genius—he had invented the cyclotron—escorted Oliphant through the eucalyptus groves on the hillside above San Francisco Bay, showing him the frame of the new 184-inch magnet being completed for his large laboratory and listening intently to Oliphant's recital of frustration. Upset that he had not been informed about the British findings earlier, Lawrence paced about in agitation and assured his friend that he would shake up his colleagues.

His opportunity came early in September, in the living room of Dr. Arthur Holly Compton on the University of Chicago campus. It had turned chilly early; a fire was roaring in the fireplace. A pompous personage with jutting jaw, deep-set dark eyes and stately carriage, Compton, dean of physical sciences, and a Nobel Prize winner, had been asked to review all nuclear work for the government. Lawrence and Conant were in town for the university's fiftieth anniversary festivities. Determined to win the reluctant Conant over, Lawrence spoke up for Oliphant's activist position on the bomb. He also thought that weapons could be fueled not only by uranium but by plutonium, a new element just discovered by two of his Berkeley colleagues.

Compton threw his considerable prestige behind Lawrence's enthusiasm. He was a man of very public piety. His father, sister, and brother-in-law were ministers and Arthur invoked God's name often in his classes and his social life. Of all the Americans who were by now aware that the radioactive genie could be released from its test tube, Compton was the most likely to harbor scruples. Yet the morality of the bomb did not trouble him. The Nazis did. He told Conant that he was much worried about their progress; they would not be pushing bomb research so hard unless they thought they would succeed.

That had become Conant's worry, too. The United States was not yet in the war, but its neutrality was by now a poorly disguised sham. And even the seemingly inevitable American involvement might not be enough to bring Hitler down. In June Nazi tanks had rolled into the Soviet Union in a surprise invasion, and they were now approaching Moscow. Control of all Europe was within Hitler's reach. Could a bomb be built in time to make any difference? Conant acted as if he still needed to be convinced.*

"Ernest, you say you are convinced of the importance of these fission bombs," Conant challenged. "Are you ready to devote the next several years of your life to getting them made?"

Lawrence sat up with a start. His eyes glazed. His mouth fell half open. He had been put on the spot, though only for a moment.

"If you tell me this is my job, I'll do it," Lawrence said. He too was dead certain that if the Germans made the bomb first, they would rule the world.

* By this time Conant was actually in favor of going ahead with the bomb. He was not only influenced by the British recommendations but by a "yes" vote from one of his own, Dr. George B. Kistiakowsky, an explosives expert whom Conant had asked to take a harder look at the nuclear realities. "Kisty," a boisterous Russian-born bachelor, was a brilliant chemist whom Conant had been proud to recruit for the Harvard faculty in the 1920s. Originally Kistiakowsky had been skeptical about the bomb. After some weeks of study, however, he assured Conant, "It can be made to work. I'm 100% sold." That Harvard judgment was good enough for Harvard's president. In 1944, Kistiakowsky became one of the most enthusiastic members of the team that built the bomb, but later he experienced other drastic changes of judgment. In the 1950s, his enthusiasm for nuclear destruction greatly tempered, he was President Eisenhower's science adviser. Eventually he worked for total disarmament as president of the Council for a Livable World.

Day One

. . .

In Szilard's anxious eyes American apprehensions were not nearly intense enough. His experiments with Fermi at Columbia were on too small a scale to advance the bomb by much. There was still no money to buy materials in significant quantities. No purified uranium was available. The uranium graphite system needed to be checked out, but construction had not yet begun on a reactor that could test a chain reaction on an adequate scale. Hitler's spearheads were twenty-five miles from the center of Moscow. What was Washington doing to advance the weapon that could win the war?

More than Szilard was told. Encouraged by the resolve of Conant, Compton, and Lawrence, Bush met with Roosevelt to ask for the crucial go-ahead. It was the morning of October 9, 1941, fully two years since Alexander Sachs had read the Einstein-Szilard letter to the President. Bush was delighted that Vice President Henry A. Wallace sat in at the White House meeting. When Wallace was Secretary of Agriculture he had shown a grasp of scientific problems, and Bush had shrewdly kept him informed about the bomb project.

FDR gave Bush all he asked for. Research and development was to be pushed to the limit. Financing was available from a presidential emergency fund. Top direction would rest with a new Section 1 of Bush's Office of Scientific Research and Development (OSRD). Henceforth the handful of Washington decision makers privy to the project would refer to it as "S-1."* At last the atomic foundling had a name.

Compton and Lawrence were meanwhile rounding up assessments of the bomb's feasibility. At Columbia, Fermi estimated that the critical mass (point of fission) for pure uranium might be as small as twenty kilograms or as much as two tons. At Harvard, Kistiakowsky thought the British estimate of the bomb's energy yield was too optimistic. At Princeton, Wigner, who had been coaxed back into the project, reconfirmed that a uranium-graphite pile would work. At Berkeley, J. Robert Oppenheimer, recruited by Lawrence to advise him and Compton on the theoretical physics, calculated that a hundred kilograms of pure uranium might be required for a weapon.

---

* Roosevelt specified that in addition to himself, Wallace, and Bush, no one except Conant, Secretary of War Henry L. Stimson, and Army Chief of Staff George C. Marshall was even to know of S-1's existence.

Bush agreed that a "fission bomb of superlatively destructive power" was possible; a cadre for the cast to produce it, though still scattered on college campuses across the country, was beginning to assemble.

Ready to take the next step, Bush asked Compton and Lawrence to meet him and Conant in the P Street office of OSRD on the morning of Saturday, December 6. There Compton was ordered to proceed with bomb design and Lawrence with uranium production. Lawrence announced that he "could" already produce substantially purified uranium 235 at the rate of one microgram per hour. Buoyed by this news, the others left for lunch at the Cosmos Club. Lawrence hurried to the airport and returned to Berkeley to convert his production projection into reality. He had carefully refrained from claiming that he "had" in fact turned out U-235 already. With luck, that would happen on Sunday, December 7.

All that day his physicists labored with him in the Old Radiation Laboratory. By evening the first sample micrograms of U-235—they were mere "faint green smudges"—appeared in the collection box of their calutron.* The scientists paused to absorb the radio news that Japanese carrier-based planes had swept down on Pearl Harbor in a surprise attack at 7:55 a.m. Hawaii time, destroyed most of the U.S. Pacific Fleet, and plunged the nation into war.

That night Lawrence was seized by a vague fear that something sudden and dreadful might also befall his very laboratory. A fence surrounded it, but there were as yet no patrolling guards. In the dark, Lawrence paced around the fence all night, guarding his domain, alone with his thoughts. Never gloomy for long, he visualized the miles of electromagnetic separation plants that would rise to purify uranium on a scale no one had ever dreamed of. Science was coming of age, science would be King.

Triumphant thoughts were far from the mind of Leo Szilard. In January 1942 he moved with his two suitcases into the University of Chicago's Quadrangle Faculty Club. Together with Fermi, Wig-

---

* The new device had been named by the promotion-minded Lawrence. "Cal" stood for California, "u" for the university. It was the world's largest mass spectrograph. To obtain parts for assembling it quickly, Lawrence had to dismantle one of his favorite cyclotrons.

ner, and hundreds of other scientists being rounded up under Arthur Compton's direction, he was at last supposed to prove by experiment that a large-scale self-sustaining chain reaction was possible. To disguise its real purpose, Compton christened his new creation the "Metallurgical Laboratory." He clustered it around Eckart Hall off 57th Street, the university building where, coincidentally, uranium 235 had been discovered.

Szilard and the rest of his crew were not inspired by this omen. Fear of the Germans gripped them hard. Fermi wondered which country he might escape to next. Wigner refused to let himself be fingerprinted. He was so sure the Germans would win the war that he did not wish to increase his risk of being tracked down and captured. Szilard complained bitterly to Vannevar Bush in Washington that their pace was too slow, the lines of command too confused. "Nobody can tell now whether we shall be ready before German bombs wipe out American cities," he wrote to the boss of all the many nuclear bosses on May 26.

Compton placed his bets on God. "Now is the time for faith," he wrote to Bush's deputy, Conant, who replied, "It isn't faith we need now, Arthur. It's works."

Compton dithered. He was a gentleman and harmony was more important to him than decisions. His senior staff began to wonder whether he would be boss at all if he did not so much *look* the part. "Even in private conversation with Compton I personally find it difficult to have an issue settled," Szilard complained in a memorandum he titled "What Is Wrong with Us?" Few guessed that Compton was simply frightened of the Germans too, and in June he recommended his own notion of important "works": a research program to develop "countermeasures" against Nazi A-bombs.

The action was shifting to California, Compton having deputized Oppenheimer to convene a brain trust of distinguished theoretical physicists. Nobody was designing a weapon yet, much less trying to construct one. Very little data was available that hadn't been known for more than two years. Only Szilard had his eye graphically on the future. "One has to visualize a world in which a lone airplane could appear over a big city like Chicago, drop his bomb, and thereby destroy the city in a single flash," he reminded his colleagues in one of the memoranda that poured from him during that season of his discontent.

In Oppenheimer, Compton had spotted a quick, organized mind. Perhaps it could sharpen at least the preliminary answers that were lacking. Precisely how much fissionable material was needed for a weapon? How "efficient" would the nuclear reaction be? What would be the destructive impact? What would the bomb look like? All summer Oppenheimer and his seven theoreticians wrestled with the imponderables in two attic rooms of Le Conte Hall on the Berkeley campus.

Filling in a security questionnaire, Oppie had lately admitted that he had been "a member of just about every Communist-front organization on the West Coast," and his political past would eventually come to stalk him like a ghost. But at Le Conte Hall security was still made of more primitive stuff. The windows of the thinkers' attic had been specially covered with steel netting. Oppenheimer was given the only key to the secure new lock. Since several of the conferees, including Oppenheimer, were chain smokers, fire was a bigger worry than treason. The next concern was not with Oppie's politics but with his arrogant personality.

One of the theoreticians, Dr. Hans A. Bethe, sturdy and deliberate, had detested Oppenheimer since their graduate-student days in Germany, when Oppie had nastily taxed Hans with a minor mathematical slip at an open meeting. Edward Teller, another of the conferees, had felt "overpowered" by Oppenheimer when Oppie plied him with too much hot talk and hot food in a Mexican restaurant during their first meeting some years before. Still another man in the smoky attic, Robert Serber, an imperturbable former Oppenheimer student, meek-looking but brilliant, wondered how his old professor could ride herd on such an assembly of prima donnas. Oppie had, after all, never administered anything.

All the skeptics were amazed. "Oppenheimer showed a refined, sure, informal touch," Teller remembered. And at first the chairman's task was not difficult. All the American and British research results were at hand, and the thinkers amiably agreed on the mechanics of the weapon and its explosion. The uranium core would be a sphere about eight inches thick. Assembly and detonation would have to occur in less than a millionth of a second. The pace of the meetings was relaxed; in deference to Teller's sleeping habits, they rarely convened before 11 a.m.

Suddenly, early in July, Teller detonated his private war on behalf of a new nightmare, the hydrogen bomb, soon called "the super." Some months ago, Teller told the group, he and Fermi had speculated at lunch about the incredible amounts of heat that would build up within an exploding fission bomb. Excited to be rummaging in the unknown, Teller had worked on this mystery privately and concluded that heavy hydrogen could be ignited by a nuclear explosion. A fusion weapon would become possible. It would be cheaper and infinitely more powerful than a fission bomb.

Oppenheimer and his colleagues were annoyed. They had a job to do and had not yet done it: to perfect plans for a fission bomb for the present war. A fusion bomb was a long way further up the road. Yet Teller was relentless. Acting as if the fission weapon was all but an accomplished fact, he injected the "super" into the discussions almost daily. It had become an obsession with him. Increasingly the others became impatient with the stream of his ideas. Teller was undeterred. Single-mindedly he kept calculating: What would happen when fission escalated into fusion?

Late in July he stopped Oppenheimer's show. Moving to their large blackboard, Teller demonstrated for the group his latest projections on the heat buildup. Oppenheimer and the others stared in silent shock. They were looking at a mathematical model for the end of the world. In a fusion explosion, the nitrogen in the atmosphere that surrounds the earth—and thereby the entire planet—might be set afire.

Oppenheimer suspended the sessions on the spot. He asked Hans Bethe to investigate Teller's figures rigorously and rushed to the phone to locate Compton. En route to a vacation at his lake cottage in Michigan, the stately director of the "Metlab" was picking up his key at the general store in Otsego when Oppie reached him, obviously distraught: "Found something very disturbing, dangerously disturbing . . . No, not to be mentioned over the telephone . . . Yes, we must see each other . . . Yes, immediately, without an hour's delay."

The next day Compton picked up Oppenheimer at the Otsego train station, drove him to a deserted beach, and listened to his apocalyptic story. He was horrified. If the heat question could not be disposed of, Compton ruled, the bomb project would have to be abandoned. His final verdict was worthy of a deity: "Better to be a slave under the Nazi heel than to draw down the final curtain on humanity."

The final curtain turned out to be premature—probably. Oppenheimer reconvened the meetings in Berkeley and Bethe reported that Teller's mathematics, while essentially accurate, had overlooked the heat that would be absorbed by radiation.

What about the end of the world?

"It couldn't happen," said Teller.

The others were not so certain. Eventually they computed the chances for Compton: three in a million. It seemed a reasonable risk to go ahead.

In Chicago, Compton faced still more decisions that would have daunted someone less solidly connected with heavenly authority. On a hot and humid evening some seventy Metlab group chiefs crowded into the commons room of Eckart Hall in near-rebellion. They wanted Compton not to hire the commercial contractor scheduled to construct a huge plant for uranium mass production.

Compton entered holding a Bible. Without introduction, he read from Judges 7:5-7 about the people whom God led to the water: "And the Lord said unto Gideon, By the three hundred men that lapped will I save you . . . and let all the other people go . . . ."

It was Compton's pious way of threatening his flock that only loyalists who supported private enterprise would be welcome to march in his atomic crusade.

On November 14 Compton showed that he could be resolute, even foolhardy, when cornered. With production deadlines crowding him hard, he announced at a meeting in Conant's Washington office that he would build the long-delayed chain-reacting pile on the doubles squash court under Stagg Field, the university stadium on Chicago's South Side. His tone was conversational, but Conant's face went white. The Army representative rushed to the phone. They were facing either the successful birth of the atomic age—or a catastrophic nuclear disaster within a packed metropolis.

Construction of a radiation-shielded pile building in the Argonne Forest 25 miles west of the city was hopelessly delayed by a strike,

Compton explained. Fermi, the project leader, had persuaded him with detailed calculations. The figures showed that there would be no runaway reaction releasing lethal amounts of radiation. Fermi also ruled out an explosion—at least on paper. As the potentially radioactive material built up in the pile, Fermi would allow the reaction to grow only very gradually. Theoretically there was no chance for the pile to go out of control. It was possible, however, that some new, unpredictable phenomenon might prove the figures wrong. Compton's team was groping in the unknown. They would be releasing vastly more nuclear energy than anyone had ever unleashed.

By protocol, Compton should have sought permission from Robert M. Hutchins, president of the university,* but he had felt that would be unfair. Hutchins could not evaluate the technology. Logically he could only say no and that would be wrong. So Compton was proceeding on his own. Conant and the Army could have stopped him at the November 14 meeting. They didn't. They felt the project was too far along. More delays were intolerable. It was already a full year past Pearl Harbor.

Construction of CP-1 (Chicago Pile No. 1) began on the squash courts near the corner of 57th Street and Ellis Avenue on November 16. Assisted by carefree high-school youngsters, the physicists were all but engulfed by blocks of graphite laboriously procured by Leo Szilard. Working in two shifts around the clock, the builders were kept warm by their labors. The outside temperature rarely went above 10 degrees Fahrenheit. There was snow on the ground and the stadium was unheated. Charcoal fires had produced too much smoke. The guards huddled outside in raccoon coats left over from the football days.

Szilard's graphite—he browbeat producers to purify it in quantity but never touched the stuff—was powdery, greasy, and pervasive. Stacks of this ultrarefined coal crowded corridors and stairwells. Its dust left the ground surface as slippery as a dance floor and seeped into the pores of the men and their lone woman colleague.† A black

---

* Stagg Field was available to the experimenters because Hutchins had abolished football at the university as inimical to education.
† Physicist Leona Wood met her husband to be, John Marshall, while both worked at the Metlab. They married in 1943.

haze hung in the air. More than 40,000 holes had to be machined into the bricks before they could be stacked onto the 8-by-8-foot cubical pile. Dullish brown uranium oxide, still scarce, was packed between the graphite as quickly as supplies arrived. Eventually the pile would top 16 feet, its 57 layers of graphite weighing 357 tons.

There were no plans or blueprints, only Fermi's mathematical projections which he refined from day to day. Sooner than planned, on Wednesday, December 2, so he decided, the pile would be high enough to go critical.

That morning Compton watched from the spectator balcony along with Szilard, Wigner, some forty other senior scientists, and Crawford M. Greenewalt of the DuPont Company, which was considering whether to become involved in plutonium production. Three young men perched on a platform above the pile. They were the suicide squad, ready to douse the pile with a cadmium salt solution if it went out of control.

Only one man was on the floor, George Weil, a young physicist who would slowly pull the last control rod. It was made of cadmium, a neutron sponge. Another rod hung suspended from the balcony rail. A project leader stood by with an ax. In case of emergency he would chop the rope so the rod would drop into the reactor and presumably stop the reaction.

"George will pull out his rod a little at a time," Fermi announced as if introducing a circus act. "We shall take measurements and verify that the pile will keep on acting as we have calculated." Thirteen feet of rod were in the pile.

"Go ahead, George," Fermi ordered at 10:37 a.m. Weil pulled the rod out one foot.

All eyes were on the recorder and the graph that measured the radiation. All breathing seemed to have stopped. Fermi grinned. The counter went clickety-clack, faster and faster and faster—and stopped where Fermi had said it would. Greenewalt's gasp was clearly heard.

Fermi ordered Weil's rod pulled another foot. And another. And another. At noon, nobody having indicated hunger pangs, Fermi, a man of steady habits, said, "Let's go to lunch."

In the afternoon the tense scene resumed.

"Another foot," said Fermi.

The clicking of the boron trifluoride counter increased.

"Eight, sixteen, twenty-four," called Leona Wood until the clicks turned into a roar too quick for her to decipher.

Everyone watched the graph's pen rise rapidly, then level off.

"Pull it out another foot," said Fermi at 3:20.

This time he turned to his anxious audience and said, "This will do it. Now the pile will chain react."

It did. The pen did not level off. Tension was at its peak. Nothing happened at all. After watching for 28 minutes, Fermi ordered "Zip in!" The pile was secured. The bomb project had crossed the line from the experimental to the production phase.

Wigner stepped up with a bottle of Chianti which he had held hidden behind his back. A small cheer went up. Everyone drank from paper cups. There was no toast.

Compton, pleased to see by Greenewalt's radiance that DuPont had been made a convert, called Conant in Washington. "Jim, you'll be interested to know that the Italian navigator has just landed in the new world."

Excited, Conant responded in Compton's unplanned code: "Were the natives friendly?"

"Everyone landed safe and happy!"

By then everybody had left the chill of the squash courts except Szilard and Fermi. As they stood in front of the reactor for which they would share a patent, Leo shook Enrico's hand. His eye as ever on the future, he told Fermi that this day would go down in history as a black mark against mankind.*

The same ambivalence would haunt many of the scientists: whenever they broke one of nature's barriers, they would know in their hearts that their personal triumph meant tragedy for everyone else on earth.

Certainly Szilard, the conscience of the innovators, felt this paradox every waking moment. Others felt no conflict at all. Mankind? They were not interested in anything so lofty, nor in long-range consequences. They only wanted to win the war.

What they needed now was an organizer and builder.

---

* By coincidence, December 2 had been declared a special day for Jewish mourning. The State Department had just announced that two million Jews had perished in concentration camps and that millions more were in imminent danger.

Five

Groves: "The Biggest Sonofabitch I've Ever Met"

Colonel Leslie R. Groves was in excellent spirits; he had just been offered a combat assignment overseas. Twenty-four years after he had graduated fourth in his class at West Point, his career would get the crucial boost he had been sweating out patiently in Nicaragua and other godforsaken outposts. For ten years he had been a lieutenant. At forty-six he was one of the Army's oldest colonels. Would he ever make general? As the engineer in charge of all military construction, he was completing his most visible job yet—the Pentagon, world's largest office building. But who remembered battles fought on construction lots? Combat command was what he needed badly.

On the morning of September 17, 1942, having testified before a congressional committee on a military housing bill, he ran into his gruff superior, Lieutenant General Brehon Somervell, in a corridor of the Capitol. Commanding all Army Services of Supply, the general would have to authorize Groves's overseas duty. Groves stopped to ask for his release, but Somervell refused.

"The Secretary of War has selected you for a very important assignment, and the President has approved the selection," he said.

Startled, Groves asked, "Where?"

"Washington."

"I don't want to stay in Washington."

"If you do the job right, it will win the war."

"Oh, that thing."

Groves felt crushed. While overseeing construction totaling $600 million a month, he had heard enough of the A-bomb project to know that it was not expected to cost $100 million altogether—a bad come-down for him. The news that he would immediately be promoted to brigadier general mollified him somewhat, but the same afternoon his worst suspicions were confirmed by an officer he had known since their days together in Nicaragua, Lieutenant Colonel Kenneth D. Nichols.

Uninspired but punctilious, the pale-faced Nichols had ranked fifth at West Point, had studied in Berlin, and held a Ph.D. in engineering. Lately he had helped to run the Army end of the A-bomb project, known as Manhattan Engineer District.* He considered Groves "the biggest sonofabitch I've ever met" and did not mind that Groves was "horrified" when Nichols told him the truth about the state of the nuclear effort. Vital uranium supplies had not been acquired. Acquisitions of plant sites were in abeyance. Production equipment was not coming through. The scientists' ideas were based far too much on theories and dreams. They didn't even know whether plutonium was a solid, a gas, or an electric substance. "The whole endeavor," Groves concluded, "was founded on possibilities rather than probabilities."

That same afternoon the pear-shaped Groves stormed into Vannevar Bush's office on P Street. Bush, though well aware that the atomic project badly needed a tough, decisive boss, was appalled to meet this brusque, very fat officer,† whose temper was as bristly as his mustache. Tact was not among his caller's well-concealed assets.

"What do you think of him?" Bush was asked on the phone afterward by Somervell's chief of staff.

"He looks too aggressive."

"He is, but we thought that quality of his was what we needed most. Groves is a go-getter; he gets things done."

"I'm afraid he may have trouble with the scientists," said Bush. And in a doleful memorandum to another insider, Harvey H. Bundy,

* So named because its first office happened to be in New York.
† Fluctuating with his attempts at dieting, Groves's weight remained one of the best-kept confidences of the bomb project. Guesses ranged between 250 and 300 pounds. Among the secrets in his office safe were pound boxes of chocolate creams and turtles which his staff was expected to keep replenished.

special assistant to Secretary of War Henry L. Stimson, Bush added: "I fear we are in the soup."

Knowledge of Groves's background would have unnerved Bush further. As the youngest son of a Presbyterian Army chaplain whose gospel preached hard work and harsh discipline, Leslie (called Dick as a boy) learned repression early. The lowest frivolity permitted in his home was studying the *World Almanac*. Nobody was allowed to play baseball or anything else on the Sabbath; Dick stayed in the house bent over books. At eleven, he worked at picking walnuts. Chaplain Groves disapproved of smoking, drinking, profanity, and wasting time. So would the son.

In the Army, Leslie Groves earned a reputation for bullying and for needing to assert his authority. He enjoyed humiliating people in front of their peers. "Here, get this dry-cleaned," he told Nichols, by then his deputy, and he took off his tunic while a meeting of scientists watched. Many contemporaries who did not hate Groves feared him. His simplistic black-and-white values, which he liked to explain in terms of baseball rules and ethics, were ridiculed as naïve.*

If few claimed to like Groves, absolutely nobody considered him incompetent or lazy. Nichols felt the pace at once. Before the end of Groves's first day on the job, he ordered Nichols to get hold of a supply of uranium. By lucky coincidence, the Manhattan District office had just received a tip that a Belgian company, the Union Minière du Haut-Katanga, might own some of the scarce metal that had first started Leo Szilard fretting when he turned to Einstein for help three years before.

Wearing civilian clothes, Nichols appeared in the Belgian firm's New York office the next day, September 18. The elderly managing director, Edgar Sengier, had been alerted by French and British scientists about the strategic importance of uranium as early as 1939 and had firmly sided with the Allies in the war. Having tried three times to interest the State Department in his ore, Sengier had grown impatient with the U. S. Government.

---

* Groves enjoyed reading other people's correspondence, including the letters in the lovelorn column "Mary Haworth's Mail," but he was easily shocked by human frailty. When one of his wartime secret mail drops flushed up an explicit love note, his secretary kept it away from the general. She considered it unfit for his eyes.

When Nichols inquired about uranium, Sengier asked for his identification and then demanded: "Do you have authority to buy?"

"I have more authority, I'm sure, than you have uranium to sell."

"Good, then let's make a deal, Colonel."

To Nichols' amazement, Sengier disclosed that he had ordered 1250 tons of rich ore shipped to the United States for safekeeping almost three years earlier. Some 2000 steel drums full of it, more than $2 million worth, were stored a short ferry ride away in a Staten Island warehouse.

"I want to start hauling that uranium away tomorrow," said Nichols. In longhand, they drew up an eight-sentence agreement on a yellow pad. The price was $1.60 a pound, the bottom market quotation. In twenty-four hours Groves had broken the first of the atomic project's many bottlenecks.

His debut before the policy makers of the S-1 project came on September 23, the day of his official promotion to general. His measure would be taken by the intimidating personage affectionately known to intimates as "the Colonel": the gaunt, deliberate Secretary of War, Henry L. Stimson, seventy-five, colonel of artillery in World War I, Secretary of State under President Hoover, and ranking Republican in the Democratic war cabinet of Franklin D. Roosevelt.* Seated around the conference table of Stimson's enormous office in the E-Wing of the Pentagon were Bush, Conant, and Generals Marshall and Somervell, along with other advisers. All were much senior to Groves. Stimson proposed forming a new committee of seven or nine to supervise S-1. Groves, who detested any committee he couldn't appoint himself, objected; the group would be too large for efficiency. As soon as Stimson agreed to a committee of four (Bush, Conant, Groves, and a Navy admiral) the new brigadier general executed a daring maneuver.

"May I be excused?" he asked, rising and glancing at his watch. "I've got to get out of here if you're through talking. I don't want to miss my train to Tennessee."

At Oak Ridge the next morning he gave the go-ahead for the construction of the uranium separation plant that would ultimately cost

---

* Nobody's rank impressed Stimson. Once he waved a bony finger at FDR and admonished: "Don't dissemble with me, Franklin!"

$544 million and employ 85,000 people. The project had been delayed by indecision for months. When Groves returned to Washington, General Somervell told him that Stimson had been impressed by his abrupt exit. "You made me look like a million dollars," Somervell said. "I'd told them that if you were put in charge, things would really start moving!"

Not for long. Pressing on to Chicago on October 5, Groves found himself stopped cold. Arthur Holly Compton picked him up at the train and proudly showed off the Metlab, its staff grown to 1200. Groves thought Compton was too theatrical and ever after called him "Arthur Hollywood" behind his back. Meeting Szilard for the first time, Groves decided to engage him in a debate about the merits of various reactor cooling systems. It was the opening gun for a feud of epic intensity, a Hatfield-McCoy duel that would outlast the war.

Then, in Eckart Hall that afternoon, Groves felt hit "with the impact of a pile driver." It was his first exposure to physicists at work. Fifteen of the most senior men, including three Nobel laureates, took turns scribbling near-illegible equations on a blackboard. They were demonstrating once again how much fissionable material one bomb would require. It all looked entirely too casual and messy to Groves. His engineer's mind-set tolerated only precision. Physics was Greek to the general; his math being adequate, however, he pointed out to the scientist at the blackboard that one figure was copied incorrectly on the next line. The lecturer cheerfully conceded the error and erased it with a finger, leaving Groves shaken.

When a final figure was produced, the general asked how accurate it was. The scientists estimated that it was correct to a factor of ten. Groves being unfamiliar with this terminology, it was explained to him that the true figure might be from ten times less to ten times more. He considered this as "idiotic" as telling a wedding caterer to have food ready for between ten and ten thousand guests.

"How do you expect me, if I need so many bombs per month, to build a factory based on your vague figures?" he demanded. "Shall we design for, say, three bombs a month, or for three-tenths of a bomb or for thirty bombs?"

The scientists had no answer to this reasonable question. Not content to leave them to their embarrassment, Groves decided to let them know that he felt very much their equal, Nobel Prizes and Ph.D.s notwithstanding.

"I had ten years of formal education after I entered college," he lectured. "Ten years in which I just studied. I didn't have to make a living or give time to teaching. I just studied. That would be the equivalent of about two Ph.D.s, wouldn't it?"

Szilard voiced his indignation at this insensitivity the moment Groves left: "You see what I told you? How can you work with people like that?"

Asking himself the same question, Groves lectured Compton privately. "You scientists don't have any discipline," he barked. Compton countered mildly that discipline was not a useful tool in advanced research. It would test all his faith, he told himself, to spend the war as a buffer between the scientific and the military mind.

At Berkeley, Groves's next stop in the tour of his embryonic domain, Ernest Lawrence—blond, blue-eyed, boyish-looking and tanned—attempted a smooth selling job. "We're going straight to Radiation Hill, General, you're going to have a surprise!" he boomed, and drove Groves from the station to the campus at breakneck speed, careening around corners without slowing down, his face constantly turning toward the petrified general. There was too much theory at Chicago, he told Groves. "Out here you'll see [uranium] separation actually going on!"

The actuality was hardly cheering. The Calutron was still grinding out green smears of U-235, mere micrograms and only 30 percent pure. The staff physicists were as chagrined by Groves's technical ignorance as their colleagues had been in Chicago. Lawrence kept herding the general along, talking fast. Like a child needing to show off a new toy, the scientist felt sure he could impress the big man from Washington with the huge new 184-inch cyclotron.

"You've never seen such a magnet," he exclaimed. "It's the largest in the world! Come, I'll show you!"

Lawrence tugged Groves to within nose length of the machine. "Look through here, General. See that arc? It's that arc going around that makes the separation!"

Groves asked how long it took to get a separation. Fourteen to twenty-four hours, said Lawrence. How long were the machine's runs? Ten to fifteen minutes. How much U-235 winds up in the collection baskets?

"Well, actually, we don't get any sizable separation," Lawrence confessed. "I mean, not yet. This is still all experimental, you see."

Groves saw. He decided that Lawrence and his people would benefit from one of his G.I. pep talks and told the assembled staff to work harder. Turning to Lawrence, he concluded, "Professor Lawrence, you'd better do a good job. Your reputation depends on it!"

The ensuing silence was profound. Nobody patronized Ernest Orlando Lawrence, the Nobel Prize winner for 1939. Lawrence responded by taking the general to lunch at Trader Vic's, where he looked him in the eye: "General Groves, you know, with respect to what you said to me—my reputation is already made. It's *your* reputation that depends on this project."

Groves swallowed this indisputable logic and made his peace with Lawrence. It was not difficult. The general appreciated Lawrence's confident attitude and candor, and, like most bullies, he enjoyed meeting his match. He was also shrewd enough to admit to himself how desperately he depended on the scientists and their knowledge, no matter how depressingly vague. He needed answers, and, walking again with Lawrence down the laboratory's Cubicle Row, he zeroed in once more on the green smears of separated uranium.

"How pure will it have to be?" he wanted to know.

Lawrence, the experimentalist, could not say. That was a question for a theoretician. He suggested asking Oppenheimer.

Getting off the elevator on the third floor of Le Conte Hall on October 8 and heading for Oppie's office, Groves met his match again. And more. The meeting was a mismatch of two worlds and the contrasts were grotesque.

Grove was the provincial clergyman's boy, Oppenheimer the coddled scion of a wealthy Jewish importer from New York's elegant Riverside Drive.

Groves the eleven-year-old field hand . . . Oppenheimer the precocious genius who, at the same age, prattled Greek and delivered a scientific paper before the New York Mineralogical Club.

Day One

Groves the puritanical West Pointer . . . Oppenheimer the arrogant recluse who sailed his own 28-foot sloop at eighteen, graduated summa cum laude from Harvard in three years, studied at the Cavendish, at Leyden and Göttingen, was fluent in German and French and taught himself Sanskrit for fun.

Groves the archconservative . . . Oppenheimer the radical who donated one-tenth of his pay to the Communist cause for the Spanish Civil War.

Groves the engineer who lived by blueprints . . . Oppenheimer the dreamer dabbling in theories.

Here was Groves, the obese bully, his uniform ballooning at the midriff, meeting Oppenheimer, the fragile six-footer with a 28-inch waist, weighing 128 pounds and hating fat people . . . the non-smoker and near-teetotaler facing the five-packs-a-day man who turned martini mixing into a rite . . . the Washington politician-general seeking common ground with the intellectual Californian who could not abide newspapers . . . these two personalities could not have been less alike.

Destined to misunderstand each other or worse, they were nevertheless to become one of history's oddest couples. Without their leadership the A-bomb project would require two other eccentrics of equally diverse talents—or bog down in unending delays, perhaps failure.

Their relationship clicked because they needed each other; both were shrewd enough to recognize this and both could therefore tolerate accommodations that taxed them to their respective limits.

Their historic encounter in Le Conte Hall was low key. Groves was groping for specifics that he could shape into factories and bombs. Oppenheimer, still a freelance floater at the age of thirty-eight, was one of the few senior physicists not yet tied up in full-time war work. Groves needed someone who would help him catapult his troublesome scientists off their "fannies" (the general's prissy word). Oppenheimer was setting himself up to be caught for a top spot so that he too could join what he called, in the terminology of his Communist friends, "the people's war."

Groves asked about the behavior of the volatile neutrons. To this and other inquiries Oppenheimer responded crisply, without jargon and without pushing any pet ideas. Groves complimented him on his clarity and cool analytical skills. Oppenheimer was engagingly modest. "There are no experts," he said. "The field is too new." Groves decided to keep an eye on this fellow.

People conversant with the growing Oppenheimer legend would have been dumbfounded by this show of gentility. They thought of Oppie as a flamboyant actor. Students who flocked to his seminars, sometimes volunteering to take the same course twice, wanted not only to be touched by his erudition but to witness the lightning performance of his mind and, after classes, to hear their role model read Plato aloud in the original Greek. When he received a dual appointment for Caltech as well as Berkeley, presiding half of each year in each place, his disciples kept packing up and following their Pied Piper.

Lieutenant Colonel John Lansdale, Jr., Groves's military counterintelligence chief, beginning to delve into Oppenheimer's past, diagnosed that Oppie had "a need to dazzle." Frank Oppenheimer, the younger brother, admired the way everything Robert did (nobody ever called him "Bob"*) became somehow "special"; ducking off a country road to urinate, Oppie would emerge from the bushes bearing a flower. He was always a spectacle, often a charmer.

In his youth his brilliance had at times been a handicap. His professors suspected that he asked certain questions only to show off his knowledge. Students not quick enough to track his mind were cut down by Oppie's cruel put-downs. Whenever he was not loved but feared, he drifted into melancholia. It was a recurring symptom.

Earlier, he had outgrown extended episodes of physical and mental illnesses that would have overwhelmed anyone less determined to find himself. Twice he had to pause for months of convalescence, hiking and riding in the New Mexico mountains: once after a bout with colitis, again following five months in bed with tuberculosis. While studying at Cambridge, he despaired about inadequate progress in his studies; he nearly strangled a friendly fellow student and hovered at "the point of bumping myself off."

A psychiatrist diagnosed dementia praecox. According to the prognosis, treatment would do more damage than good.†

* The nickname "Oppie" started as "Oppje" when he studied at the University of Leyden. Oppenheimer hated both names.
† Now obsolete, the term was synonymous with schizophrenia, then considered hopeless.

Day One

Remarkably, by the time Oppenheimer offered his mind to Groves, the struggles for health had left no overt reminders except for a mild, persistent cough. Like any sensitive actor, Oppie had adjusted to accommodate his audiences. The general was obviously a perfectionistic egomaniac, but he possessed the power to dispense jobs and unlimited funds. Nothing mattered more. So all during the war Oppie treated Groves with unfailing deference. Isidor Rabi said, "Oppenheimer handled him beautifully, and it wasn't always easy." Even privately Oppie never called the general anything worse than "his Nibs." The old arrogance exploded less frequently. His charm blossomed with his increasing stability and teaching success. His hair was cropped very short. His ambition grew.

He had enjoyed watching how his powers of organization and persuasion maneuvered such disparate talents as Edward Teller and Hans Bethe through the Berkeley committee investigations the previous summer. Lawrence's many successes had left him envious. And, for the first time, he had assumed the conventional responsibilities of a husband and father. The bachelor who had camped without telephone or radio in an apartment on Shasta Road had transformed himself into a family man earning $1200 a month and occupying an impressive residence at 1 Eagle Hill in the Berkeley Hills. The home overlooked the bridges sweeping across San Francisco Bay.

These changes reassured the watchful Groves but they jarred Oppenheimer. From 1936 to 1939 his chaotic private life had revolved around Jean Tatlock, a tall, slender dark-haired beauty, the daughter of a Berkeley professor. She was working for her doctorate in psychology and, as a member of the Communist Party, had no trouble opening up Robert's heart and checkbook on behalf of its campaigns for underdog causes.

The couple's love life was anguished. Robert worshiped Jean and showered her with costly gifts. Twice they were on the brink of marriage. Each time Jean could not make the commitment. She would torture Robert for months with tales of other men. A manic depressive, she had been in psychoanalysis and repeatedly reentered psychiatric treatment. Ultimately she broke off the affair.

Within months, at a Pasadena garden party, Oppenheimer picked up another "injured bird" (his term): Katherine Puening Harrison, research fellow in biology, born in Germany, a first cousin once removed of General Wilhelm Keitel, Hitler's army chief of staff. Kitty's first marriage, to a musician who was a drug addict, had been annulled. Her second husband, a Dartmouth graduate and son of an investment banker, had become a Communist union organizer and died fighting in Spain with the Abraham Lincoln Battalion. During this marriage Kitty, whose I.Q. was 196, typed letters for the Communist Party and lived in squalor on welfare in Youngstown, Ohio. Barely launched on her third marriage, to a British physician doing cancer research in a Los Angeles hospital, she encountered Oppie and immediately fell in love, this time for life.

Men were often taken with the bright, hard-drinking Kitty. Women feared or hated her, or both. They found her dictatorial, mean, and, well, very odd. Not conventionally attractive, she exuded sexuality in the style of Jeanne Moreau. Her candor and determination were astonishing. "Gotta get the semen out of this," she informed a female drinking companion while shaking out her nightgown. Sitting on the floor with a bottle of whiskey, she told another confidante that she had deliberately allowed herself to become pregnant so Oppie would marry her. Their son Peter was born six and a half months later, the divorce and wedding having taken place in Nevada on the same day. The baby was nicknamed "Pronto" for his alacrity.

Many shocked friends of Oppenheimer's could never fathom what attracted him to Kitty, and over the years the union remained as lively a topic for amateur analysis as his compatibility with Groves. Both collaborations rested, in fact, on a neat meshing of needs and neuroses. Groves would make Oppie famous. Kitty supplied domestic tranquility, a home operated with Prussian punctilio, and slavish devotion. If her ethereal Robert suddenly wanted to build atomic bombs—a secret that sounded so improbable when he first mentioned it that she broke out in disbelieving laughter—she would direct her considerable cunning to the support of this new ambition.

Robert's plans were explicit. He thought the project needed a unified separate laboratory to focus exclusively on the weapon itself: working out unknowns of its explosion, designing it, building it, testing and using it on the enemy in time to end this war, not the next one. The director's job would suit him. Officiating as the director's wife and hostess would delight Kitty and bolster her self-importance. But would Groves ever hand such a plum to the likes of Oppie?

Remembering his Berkeley session with Oppenheimer as one of the few tolerable experiences of his dismaying inspection swing, Groves wired Oppie to come to Chicago. From there they would travel east together aboard the Twentieth Century Limited and have another talk. The general liked working in the privacy of trains. With his tiny Colt automatic tucked into his trouser pocket—it was a .32 caliber on a .25-caliber frame—he felt secure. Nichols and another colonel were jammed into the same tiny roomette. Nobody was comfortable, but they had plenty of time for an uninterrupted exploration of the bedeviled project's bottlenecks.

The morale of the physicists was terrible, Oppenheimer warned. Scattered from coast to coast (in addition to laboratories at Berkeley and Chicago, another operation was still alive at Columbia and smaller projects languished elsewhere), they lacked a sense of direction. To build and test ordnance, actually to experiment with explosives, an isolated and remote proving ground was essential. The best mix of the best skills could be concentrated in one place and tightly controlled there. Now was the time to start up such a place. Constructing the first A-bomb entailed so many unknowns that the leaders could not wait for delivery of fissionable material. All programs had to run concurrently.

Groves responded favorably. He had been thinking along the same lines. The scheme was practical and would save their most precious asset: time. And isolation would help preserve secrecy. The general called it "compartmentalization" and was obsessed with it because he thought it insured protection not only against spies but against the proclivities of the scientists. They talked too much, especially to each other. He had never seen so many people waste so much time talking. Each should stick to his own job and keep quiet. If senior men in a laboratory had to communicate with each other to avoid redundant work, that made sense. But Groves would never let his infantile charges "establish a great university where they discuss their new ideas and try to learn more from each other." He thought of them privately as "crackpots" and proposed to humor them no more than the Army catered to riflemen.

Oppenheimer did not argue with Groves during the eight-hour conference. He even agreed cheerfully that the scientists should wear uniforms and become subject to military discipline. Pleased at the prospect of turning into an officer himself, he shortly reported to San Francisco's Presidio for his Army physical. The doctors called him fit to become a lieutenant colonel although he was twenty-seven pounds under his ideal weight. His "chronic" cough did not trouble them because his TB had not recurred since 1930.

Though Oppenheimer had designed the new bomb laboratory, now code-named "Project Y," Groves was not about to make him director. "No one" with whom he talked "showed any great enthusiasm" for Oppie, and he felt the same way himself. The other atomic laboratories were headed by Nobel Prize winners; Project Y needed equal prestige. Unfortunately, Oppenheimer had never concentrated on one subject at sufficient depth to be considered for a Nobel. The director's position called for an experimental physicist, not a theoretician, another strike against Robert. It required strong administrative experience; Oppie had none.

Groves pursued his recruiting chore with his usual diligence, knowing that natural candidates such as Rabi were already indispensable in other defense work, notably radar. The general considered Lawrence ideal for Project Y but knew he could not be spared at Berkeley. Lawrence suggested Dr. Edwin McMillan, the co-discoverer of plutonium; Groves thought him too young. Compton, who was needed in Chicago, suggested Dr. Carl Anderson, a Nobel Prize winner who turned the job down as insufficiently prestigious. Oppenheimer proposed Dr. Wolfgang Panofsky of Caltech. Groves found Panofsky too irrepressible and theoretical-minded. So why not Oppenheimer?

Bush and Conant were unenthusiastic to the end. Compton and Lawrence voiced reservations about Oppie's leadership qualifications. Groves ended the hunt with a characteristic pronouncement: "Find me another Ernest Lawrence, and we'll appoint him. But where do you find such a man? With Oppenheimer we at least have a first-rate theoretician and an extremely brilliant mind. As for the administration, *I* will see that it works!"

Having settled on the man, they had to find the right place to put him.

Oppenheimer and Edwin McMillan arrived in Jemez Springs, New Mexico, on November 16 to meet a colonel from the Corps of Engineers who had been site hunting for more than a month. It was cold and cloudy. Jemez Springs, a dark, deep canyon in the 11,000-foot Jemez mountain range, consisted of a resort hotel and a few empty buildings. It was the spot the colonel had picked for Project Y because it fit the specifications of his assignment.

The place had to be at least 200 miles away from the West Coast because Groves feared "the ever-present threat of Japanese interference." It was to be isolated so that the general's gossipy scientists would not mingle with curious civilians and could experiment with explosives without risk to anyone but themselves. The project had to be accessible by rail and air and Jemez Springs was only about 50 miles north of an excellent transportation center, Albuquerque.

The canyon could hold a laboratory with a population originally estimated at 265, including support personnel.* And there were almost no locals who would have to be evicted.

Oppenheimer, who had loved this countryside since the days of his convalescence from TB, and who spent summers at a ranch in the area, hated Jemez Springs. The canyon was too deep; the lack of sunshine would be depressing. Groves, who joined the group shortly, vetoed the site for a more practical reason. "This will never do," he snapped, grouchy because his arm had fallen asleep en route. Jemez Springs was too hemmed in for any expansion. Any engineer knew that infant projects tended to grow as inevitably as infant humans.

"I don't want to waste the day," he said to Oppenheimer. "Let's look some more. Do you have any idea where we might find something?"

"Well, we can go back to Albuquerque by way of the Los Alamos

---

* Oppenheimer then visualized a nucleus of six scientists and their families, supported by technicians and other service auxiliaries—a revealing indication of his innocence about the complexity of his mission. By the end of November 1942, the projected population was 600. In 1945, Project Y employed 5000. Construction costs were originally estimated at $300,000, but by the end of the project's first year $7.5 million had been spent.

Ranch School, and you might be interested in that," Oppie said. "It's about 55 miles from my ranch over a very rough trail. We've often ridden across by horse, so I know the place."*

In late afternoon the military sedan with the four men pulled up at Fuller Lodge, the large, rustic main house of the school. It was an exclusive institution for toughening up sons of affluent families from all over the country at $3500 per year. Unheated, expensive, it was ailing financially because of the war. As Groves and his companions stepped out of their car the students and their masters, wearing shorts, were playing soccer in light, drizzly snow.

Groves liked the location at once. They were not far below timberline, surveying a gigantic green mesa, the cone of a long-extinct volcano. The views of the Jemez Mountains and of the Sangre de Cristo (Blood of Christ) range 40 miles away and reaching to 13,000 feet, were breathtaking. The men bent over maps and spoke to no one from the school. Its log cabins would be a useful nucleus for housing to come. Water would be a problem. The only road—it led to Santa Fe, about 30 miles southeast—was dreadful, even by local standards, but Groves paced it critically for about half an hour and pronounced it fixable.

The search party left for Albuquerque in excellent cheer. They had found everything they had come for: space, seclusion, and accessibility to satisfy Groves, and a magnificent setting with a fairly temperate year-round climate to lure prima donna scientists out of the comforts of their nests in the cities. Not least, Oppenheimer and Groves had hit upon a style, a splendor that spelled possibilities. If an ultimate weapon was within reach of achievement, this mesa with its limitless views and ageless peaks seemed an inspired birthplace.

Groves telephoned Washington that evening to start acquisition proceedings. The school's owners were pleased to sell out. On November 23 the paperwork was under way. The first of 3000 construction men moved in by the end of the year.

---

* In 1950 Oppenheimer disclosed that Los Alamos had been his secret choice for the project's location all along. His passion for New Mexico went back to 1928, when he first leased his dude ranch. He bought it after World War II. It was near the tiny settlement of Cowles, 9000 feet up, and lacked electricity. He named it Perro Caliente because he exclaimed, "Hot dog!" when he first saw it.

Day One

. . .

When would bomb production begin? President Roosevelt, authorizing the spending of $400 million in December, was anxious for an answer. Vannevar Bush and his advisers trod cautiously. On the basis of Groves's estimates, they considered production unlikely before June 1, 1944. January 1, 1945, was a slightly more realistic target. The first half of 1945 looked like a "good" possibility. Would they beat the schedule of the Germans? Bush told Roosevelt that he had no way of knowing. He was not optimistic. "It is quite possible that Germany is ahead of us," he said, and certainly the scientists continued to think so. In Chicago, the ever nervous Eugene Wigner received a message smuggled out of Germany by an old friend, a German physicist knowledgeable about the Nazi bomb project. It urged the Americans to hurry up if they wanted to be first with an atomic weapon.

And Oppenheimer was the key.

Six

J. Robert Oppenheimer:
A Grave Question Of Loyalty

Oppenheimer the actor felt comfortable in his role as a radical. His friends and critics on the Berkeley campus observed how effectively Jean Tatlock had pierced his cultural isolation and stirred his social conscience. Newspapers were delivered to his home, including the Communist Party organ the *People's World*. Friends returning from Russia with frightening accounts of Stalin's bloody purges were shocked by Oppenheimer's disbelief. His regular checks for Spanish Republican refugees—$100 a month or more—were collected personally by Party functionaries. Ernest Lawrence furiously wiped clean a blackboard at the Radiation Laboratory on which Oppie had announced a meeting about the Spanish Civil War, and when a waiter in a restaurant ridiculed the Spanish Loyalists Oppenheimer threw a plate of spaghetti at him.

Some of his adoptive causes crowded in from close to home. The experiences of Jewish relatives who had escaped from Nazi Germany drove him to "smouldering fury." His graduate students' despair at finding jobs in the lingering Great Depression kept him up long into the night addressing envelopes for the local teachers' union, of which he was secretary. And then Kitty's past caught up with her—and with him. It was a pleasant surprise for both.

Kitty had been open with her new husband about her passion for her second spouse, Joe Dallett, the strapping, handsome Youngstown steel organizer who died in Spain. He and Kitty had been planning

71

a reunion when word reached her in Paris of his death. The messenger was his close friend Steve Nelson, a burly former coal miner from Pittsburgh, the commissar of the Abraham Lincoln Battalion and a graduate of Moscow's Lenin School of Party leadership. Nelson had just been invalided out of Spain and showed great kindness to the distraught Kitty.

"Good guys," was Oppie's judgment about Dallett and Nelson.

Shortly after Pearl Harbor, Nelson happened to settle in Oakland as the local boss of the Communist Party, and one night he and Oppie were both speakers at a meeting to raise money for Spanish refugees. Afterward Robert went up to him and announced with a smile, "I'm going to marry a friend of yours, Steve!" Nelson looked startled. "I'm going to marry Kitty."

Nelson was delighted. He admired Robert's Byronic looks, his encyclopedic memory, and the precision tooling of his language. It flowed "as if the words were written out ahead of time." Oppie claimed that he had read all three volumes of Marx's *Das Kapital* on a three-day train ride and Steve was awed; he had never even mastered the first of the books. It was natural for the Nelsons and the Oppenheimers to become friendly and they visited each other until Robert moved to Los Alamos. He said his work was secret, but there was never a hint that Steve's interest in him was more than social.

Early in 1943 the Oppenheimers' sociability brought about a fleeting encounter at which a distressing hint of espionage *was* dropped. The incident would haunt Robert for the rest of his life. Kitty and Robert had asked Haakon Chevalier and his wife for dinner. When Oppie went to the kitchen to mix his famous ultradry, frigid vodka martinis—they were stirred, never shaken—Haakon followed him. He was a close friend, a charming, cultivated professor of Romance languages at Berkeley, president of the teachers' union. Though he was no outstanding intellect, his translations of André Malraux and a book on Anatole France had brought him a respectable academic reputation.

Chevalier told Oppie that he had had a visit from George C. Eltenton of the nearby Shell Development Company laboratory. A haughty British engineer whom Oppenheimer disliked, Eltenton had spent five years in the Soviet Union. In California he had become active in the teachers' union. His ties with the Soviets remained excellent. In some embarrassment, Chevalier dropped startling news. Eltenton had informed him that he could secretly transmit technical information to Russia.

Was Chevalier hinting that Oppenheimer might wish to hand over secret information? Or was he simply alerting Oppie that he had become a target for such a proposition? The question was never fully settled. But there was no doubt about Oppenheimer's response. He rejected the idea with some heat. He felt "friendly" to the idea of sharing atomic information with the Soviets, he said, but only through official channels, not illegitimately via "the back door."

Cozy feelings for the Russians were not evidence of disloyalty at the time. General Groves, who was paranoid about all foreigners, would have been happy not even to share information with the British. But most Americans admired the courage of their Russian allies. During the winter of 1942-43 the Soviets had fought an epic house-to-house struggle for Stalingrad, finally routing the Germans and inflicting 300,000 casualties.

The Soviet government was getting arms from America but not the "cooperation" in scientific matters "which it felt it deserved." That had been the argument offered to Eltenton by the professional spy who set the approach to Oppenheimer in motion: Peter Ivanov, the Soviet vice consul in San Francisco. Convinced that the situation was of a "critical nature," Eltenton had felt "free in conscience" to approach Chevalier and had suggested that Haakon in turn approach Robert. Ivanov had assured him, so Eltenton told Chevalier, that secret data would be "safely" transmitted to Russian channels through "photo reproduction."

Oppenheimer decided not to mention Chevalier's approach to anyone, so Groves did not learn of it for months. Yet nobody had to convince the general that his beloved bomb project was an all too real target of spies. As early as October 10, 1942, he had learned that Oppenheimer was being fingered as a potential Communist agent. An FBI report, "monitored through a microphone-telephone technical installation," informed Groves of a meeting held by Steve

Nelson at Communist Party headquarters in Oakland with two other men. One remained unidentified. The other was a young researcher at Ernest Lawrence's Radiation Laboratory.

The scientist told Nelson that an important new weapon was under development at the laboratory. Steve then brought up an unnamed scientist who "used to be active but was inactive." He was "considered a Red" but "the Government lets him remain because he was good in the scientific field." Cautiously Steve added that this man had worked for the teachers' union and for Spain and "could not cover up his past." The agents concluded that the subject of the meeting could only be Oppenheimer. Did he have secret dealings with Nelson?

Then Groves was handed an intelligence plum that left him with no further doubt: an espionage conspiracy had taken shape. The spies, though amateurs, had learned critical secrets. The extent of their knowledge was frightening, but there was also news to relieve the general's mind: the conspirators had already given up on their key target, Oppenheimer. That much was clear from a talk Nelson had in March 1943 with a local scientist named "Joe." They met after 1:30 a.m. in the tiny Oakland bungalow that Steve had bought with a down payment of $1500. Agents were able to record the long dialogue almost verbatim although both men spoke in whispers throughout.*

This time explicit intelligence information was passed. Oppenheimer and his group were working on a highly secret revolutionary explosive, Joe told Steve. The project was about to be removed to a remote section of the country. Hundreds of millions of dollars were being "poured" into it. Joe revealed the key elements. "The material is uranium, a radioactive substance, you know," he explained, and

---

* The transcript ran 27 pages. *See* file entitled "Lansdale (investigative)," National Archives, Modern Military Branch. "Joe" was subsequently identified as a former Oppenheimer student, Joseph W. Weinberg, a Communist who allegedly sold atomic secrets during much of the war. Weinberg was held in contempt by Federal District Court for refusing to answer questions in a federal grand jury investigation of espionage activities. The court subsequently upheld his right against self-incrimination and dismissed the contempt charges. After the war Nelson was tried for sedition and acquitted. In his 1981 autobiography he maintained that the charges of atomic spying were "pretty hokey stuff, backed up only with the false testimony of FBI agents and informers." He still insisted: "I had no knowledge of what kind of technical work these young physicists were engaged in."

proceeded to dictate to Steve a technical formula of more than 150 words dealing with its separation. He also transmitted the current official thinking of the Manhattan Project's time schedule, and he mentioned Oppenheimer by name: "Oppie, for instance, thinks that it might take as long as a year and a half."

Steve asked Joe to dig for further information and told him not to worry about whether the Soviets could use it in building a bomb of their own. "It's not up to us to decide that they can't do it," Steve said. He also instructed Joe in the rudiments of conduct as a spy. Joe was to stop all drinking. He was to turn in his Party dues book. From now on he was never to talk about the project except outside while walking or swimming. But there were no instructions concerning Oppenheimer.

"I was quite intimate with the guy," Nelson told Joe. "There was a personal relationship because his wife used to be the wife of my best friend who was killed in Spain. I know her very well." Oppenheimer only wanted "to make a name for himself—unquestionably," Steve said. Unfortunately, that was also what his wife wanted for him. "To my sorrow his wife is influencing him in the wrong direction."

As Groves could deduce from the transcript of this conversation, Kitty was moving her husband toward an approved goal of capitalism—success—and away from communism with its tacky clerical chores in Youngstown, Ohio. But Groves's greatest satisfaction came from Nelson's worst disappointment: the loss of Oppie himself to the Communist cause.

"He's just not a Marxist," Steve mourned to Joe.

Yet for the director of a supersecret weapons project, Oppenheimer was, as Groves was about to learn to *his* sorrow, curiously lacking in judgment. On June 12, after a day of business on the Berkeley campus, Oppie visited his former fiancée Jean Tatlock. Groves's security agents trailed him to her apartment on Telegraph Hill in San Francisco. For four years Oppenheimer had seen Jean only on open social occasions, usually with Kitty present. In the spring Jean had sent word that she was desperate to see him again. He did not go. Lately, so faculty friends told him, she was once more in psychiatric treatment, extremely unhappy and getting worse.

At the 1954 government hearings that resulted in the revocation of his security clearance, Oppenheimer was asked, "Did you find out why she had to see you?"

"Because she was still in love with me."

"Was she a Communist at that time?"

"We didn't even talk about it."

He spent the night. Agents kept watch outside.* In the morning Tatlock drove him to his flight for New Mexico. He never saw her again—and eventually she committed suicide.

In the face of crises piling up all around him, Groves was making a point of not relying on summaries of the many reports about Oppenheimer. He read all documents in their voluminous original versions. He trusted no security man, not even someone he held in as high regard as Lieutenant Colonel Boris T. Pash, chief of the Counterintelligence Branch, Western Defense Command. The professorial-looking Pash took pride in having broken open the Communist infiltration of Lawrence's Radiation Laboratory and had never trusted Oppenheimer. The Tatlock episode further inflamed his suspicions.

Late in June, Pash suggested in a memorandum to the Pentagon that the Communist Party might be maneuvering to divorce Oppenheimer "officially" but that the separation would not be real: "There is a possibility of his developing a scientific work to a certain extent, then turning it over to the Party, perhaps through an intermediary." The colonel recommended that Oppenheimer be "removed completely from the project and dismissed from employment by the U.S. Government."

Groves would not have it. He needed Oppenheimer, and anyway the man already knew far too much to be jettisoned gracefully. The surveillance system that was in place would continue a tight watch on him and keep Groves in absolute control. While the general trusted nobody, his egomania allowed him at least to trust his own judgment about men, which over the years did indeed prove superb.

* In his meticulously researched 1981 book, *J. Robert Oppenheimer—Shatterer of Worlds,* Peter Goodchild reported: "There seems a strong possibility that they managed to bug the meeting electronically, and two people described to me how the couple talked for a long while in the living room before retiring to the bedroom."

Besides, he *liked* Oppenheimer. One of his secretaries, Anne Wilson, thought the general had something of a crush on Oppie, for Groves once told her: "He has the bluest eyes you've ever seen and they look right through you." What could a mere intelligence man like Pash read in a man's eyes?

On July 20, Groves dictated his edict to the security people: "It is desired that clearance be issued for the employment of Julius Robert Oppenheimer without delay, irrespective of information which you have concerning Mr. Oppenheimer. He is absolutely essential to the project."

Something else moved Groves to trust this strange creature from another world. The general explained the affinity best when he was asked why he habitually offered sensitive information to Oppie that he withheld from other top scientists.

"Maybe," he said, "because Dr. Oppenheimer agreed with me."

Since Leo Szilard never saw fit to agree with Groves about anything, the warfare between these two stubborn giants, the establishmentarian and the provocateur, inevitably escalated as the list of charges grew on both sides. Szilard no longer muttered behind the general's back. He was openly rebellious. He argued that the general's compartmentalization policy aided the Nazis by delaying the project's work and that Groves was leading the country into a calamitous postwar arms race by failing to deal with the international implications of the bomb. And the worst outrage: It seemed that the general was trying to steal Szilard's patents for the government, particularly the one for the initial reactor in the Chicago stadium.

Easily bored, unable to concentrate on routine tasks, Szilard churned about the Chicago Metlab like a whirlwind—precisely the kind of uncontrolled spirit Groves could not abide. Roaming the corridors—for a while he also occupied a particular perch near the cafeteria from which he intercepted and buttonholed people—Leo peppered the other scientists with unsolicited (usually perceptive) suggestions for their work. Friends mused that he should be stored frozen in suspended animation and awakened periodically so that his latest crop of ideas could be harvested.

While his air of command became so notorious that critics—and even friends like Eugene Wigner—called him "the general," Szilard's energies were not fully absorbed by keeping only the Chicago laboratory in an uproar. He left the project on mysterious private missions, often to Washington, maintaining his contacts, challenging, scheming, but always carefully within the bounds of security rules.

Compton was kept scampering like a fireman trying to diffuse the fallout from Szilard's broadsides to Vannevar Bush; Leo's paper tide went on leapfrogging official channels, forever gushing criticism, cosmic and petty. Even the cleaning women at the Quadrangle Club branded Szilard impossible; a complaint reached Compton's office that Leo was too lazy or absent-minded to flush his toilet. "That's what maids do," he said.

Groves reacted like the proverbial bull seeing red. For Stimson's signature, the general drafted a letter to the Attorney General declaring it "essential to the prosecution of the war" that Szilard be interned for the duration. When Stimson refused to entertain this idea, the general asked Compton simply to fire Szilard. Quietly in sympathy with much of Szilard's thinking, Compton asked Wigner for advice. Wigner said he would quit if Szilard was discharged. Since Wigner was essential for the design of new reactors for massive factory production of uranium and plutonium, the idea was dropped.

In the protracted controversy over Szilard's patents, money was only the most visible issue. The man who dreamed up the A-bomb wanted $750,000. Groves considered this a despicable holdup attempt and ordered the clearance of Szilard's patent attorney revoked. It was another duel of wills. Originally conciliatory in the negotiations, Szilard had switched tactics by 1943. His recalcitrance intensified as his dissatisfaction with the bomb project mounted. As if taunting Groves, he kept offering to sign an agreement only to back off and conjure up new complications. To avoid potential legal challenges, he had himself removed from the government payroll. Patience exhausted, Groves ordered Szilard to sign or leave the project. Whereupon Szilard gave just enough ground to stay on.*

Groves never forgave Szilard these time-consuming guerrilla maneuvers and never let up on efforts to discredit this pesty foreigner,

* He agreed to a nominal price for the reactor design, $25,000 plus $15,417.60 in expenses, but kept refusing until after the war to sign a final agreement.

preferably by catching him in an indiscreet or disloyal offense. But the pickings of constant surveillance remained a source of frustration for the general's swarm of Counter Intelligence Corps agents (known as "creeps") throughout the war.*

Reporting to CIC headquarters, Room 2D655 in the Pentagon, on June 19, 1943, to acquaint himself with findings of his colleagues in Chicago and New York, Special Agent W. L. McFatridge read their observations and summarized them in his notes: "The surveillance reports indicate that Subject is of Jewish extraction, has a fondness for delicacies and frequently makes purchases in delicatessen stores, usually eats his breakfast in drug stores and other meals in restaurants, walks a great deal when he cannot secure a taxi, usually is shaved in a barber shop, speaks occasionally in a foreign tongue, and associates mostly with people of Jewish extraction. He is inclined to be rather absent minded and eccentric, and will start out a door, turn around and come back . . ."

For three days McFatridge and five other agents followed Szilard around Washington as he met with such friends as Rabi, Wigner, and Lewis Strauss. Typical entries from their log—

1 p.m., June 21: "Subject alighted from the taxicab at the Wardman Park Hotel and entered the lobby. He was observed pacing up and down the full length of the lobby for approximately 20 minutes. He later purchased a paper and sat down in the lobby but did not appear to be reading it."

9:55 p.m., June 21: "Subject entered the Wardman Park Pharmacy where he proceeded to read a newspaper and ordered what appeared to be grapefruit juice and a sandwich."

Agent McFatridge's negative findings were limited to his annoyance at Szilard's absent-mindedness. "On one occasion he got off the elevator a short distance from his room, entered the room, came out in the hall about five minutes later and asked the maid where the elevator was located," he reported. "It was found necessary to cover all possible exits to insure not losing him."

Groves was not appeased. "The investigation of Szilard should be continued despite the barrenness of the results," he ordered in a

---

* Eventually 485 of these operatives were at work.

memo to his security force. "One letter or phone call once in three months would be sufficient to pass vital information."

Oppenheimer, meanwhile, was becoming a more promising subject for the general's investigators. Visiting the security officer in Durant Hall on the Berkeley campus in late August, Oppenheimer, on getting up to leave, casually volunteered a surprise blockbuster: he had heard a rumor, he said, about a British engineer at Shell, George C. Eltenton. The man was supposed to be able to supply classified data to the Soviet Consulate. The security men should keep an eye on him. Oppenheimer did not name himself or Haakon Chevalier.

Colonel Pash eagerly took up the chase at a follow-up meeting with Oppenheimer at Durant Hall the next day. A hidden tape machine recorded every word. Feigning deference ("I don't mean to take too much of your time"), Pash solicited details about any contacts with the Soviet Consulate. After some sparring, Oppenheimer told an involved story. Its substance: two of his close associates at Los Alamos had been approached, he claimed, by "a member of the faculty" at Berkeley. Pash wanted the name of that contact. Oppenheimer refused to cooperate further.

"To go any further would involve people who ought not to be involved in this," he told Pash.*

"Well, we appreciate it and the best of luck," lied Pash. To him, the worst fears about Oppenheimer now stood confirmed, and on September 2 he received support from the security chief in Los Alamos, Captain Peer de Silva, a West Pointer of twenty-six, suave and handsome in the movie-hero stereotype of the day. "Oppenheimer either must be incredibly naive and almost childlike in his sense of reality, or he himself is extremely clever or disloyal," de Silva wrote. "The former possibility is not borne out in the opinion of the officers who have spoken with him at length."

His conclusion was sweeping and unequivocal: "J. R. Oppenheimer is playing a key part in the attempts of the Soviet Union to

---

* At the 1954 security hearings this was correctly labeled "a cock and bull story." Asked why he lied, Oppenheimer—turning white and rubbing his hands between his knees—responded from the witness chair: "Because I was an idiot." Nothing resembling espionage was ever traced to Oppenheimer. But, trying to protect his friend Chevalier, he had become guilty of monumentally bad judgment.

secure, by espionage, highly secret information which is vital to the security of the United States."

Pash forwarded this memo to the Pentagon with approving comments and another shot of his own at Oppie: "The only undivided loyalty he can give is to science."

The Pash and de Silva verdicts were still en route to Groves's desk when the general shared a sixteen-hour train ride with his security chief, Colonel Lansdale, and Oppenheimer. They talked about Robert's interview with Pash. Groves asked for the name of the "contact." Oppenheimer now said he would reveal it, but only if directly ordered to do so by Groves. The general decided not to press the issue. Neither he nor Lansdale believed Oppenheimer was a security risk. And if Oppie felt he was mistrusted, he might in the future hold back such useful information as he had volunteered about Eltenton.

Disquieting news kept arriving from Berkeley. On September 6 a message from George Weinberg was intercepted: "Dear A: Please don't make any contact with me, and pass this message to S and B, only don't mention any names." Could Oppenheimer possibly have tipped off his ex-student Weinberg that Groves's "creeps" were on to him?

It was time for Lansdale to interrogate Oppenheimer, and he did so for more than two hours on September 12 in Groves's austere, high-ceilinged office, Room 5121 on the fifth floor of the War Department at 21st Street and Virginia Avenue. The ventilating louvers were sealed, the two big safes locked. The two adjoining desks were normally occupied by Groves and his executive assistant, Mrs. Jean O'Leary, a pretty young widow whom Groves trusted enough to have her listen in and take notes on all his telephone conversations. Oppenheimer and Lansdale were alone except for the microphone hidden in the general's desk.

Lansdale had taken Oppenheimer's measure earlier, at Los Alamos, but had spent more time with Kitty. She fascinated him. "She hates me and everything I stand for," he first decided with good reason. He was a self-confessed "hidebound" Republican, a feisty thirty-year-old trial lawyer from Cleveland with a country drawl and a leathery face. He bossed the hated "creeps" who read all Los Alamos mail and listened to all telephones. He placed agents in the Santa Fe hotels as room clerks and he was not above offering a secretary $100 a month extra for spying on her boss—if the boss was Oppenheimer.*

Lansdale enjoyed fencing with Kitty: "She was trying to rope me, just as I was trying to rope her." She was "at once very frail and very strong." He wanted to convince her that he wanted to evaluate Oppenheimer fairly. It was obvious that he was making progress with Kitty when she offered him a martini. ("Not the kind to serve tea," he concluded from her handling of the drink.)

A Harvard Law School graduate, Lansdale brought sophistication and common sense to chores he considered essential yet "nasty." He was another of Groves's superior personnel choices. To him, a Communist quite simply was "anyone more loyal to Russia than to the United States." He was convinced that Oppenheimer did not fit this mold, and as Kitty spoke to him fiercely he could see, as Steve Nelson had seen, that she was the government's perfect ally, the best barrier against her husband's immature but dangerous flirtations with the Party.

"I became convinced that in him she had an attachment stronger than Communism, that his future meant more to her than Communism," he summarized later. "She saw he must have no far-left connections. No one could have guarded him better. She was going to provide us as good security as anyone could get."

With the Germans at this point believed to be running "far ahead" in the race for the bomb, Lansdale was, as he later recalled, under a "very terrible feeling of pressure" when he faced Oppenheimer in Groves's office. Worried about the Weinberg connection, Lansdale was "pretty fed up" with Oppie's resistance. He and Groves had agreed that they now absolutely had to have the name of the contact with the Soviet Consulate.

Lansdale tried every lure he knew. "You're probably the most intelligent man I ever met," he flattered Oppenheimer. "I think that you can give us an enormous amount of help."

He hinted that he already knew the name he needed most but that he wanted it confirmed. When this got him nowhere, he went on, "I want that name and I want to ask you pointblank if you'll give it to me. If you won't, OK, no hard feelings."

"I feel that I should not give it," said Oppenheimer. "I don't mean

* The secretary, Anne Wilson, turned Lansdale down indignantly.

that I don't hope that if he's still operating that you find it. I devoutly do. But I would just bet dollars to doughnuts that he isn't still operating."

Lansdale asked about a variety of names, ostensibly to discuss Party memberships.

"How about Haakon Chevalier?" he inquired.

"Is he a member of the Party?" parried Oppenheimer.

"I don't know," said Lansdale.

"He's a member of the faculty and I know him well. I wouldn't be surprised if he were a member. He is quite a red . . ."

No sensitive information was developed in the long meeting, even though Lansdale could hardly have been more reassuring. "I've made up my mind that you, yourself, are OK," he said, "or otherwise I wouldn't be talking to you like this, see?"

"I'd better be—that's all I've got to say," replied the director of the Los Alamos laboratory.

On a visit to the laboratory Groves finally ordered Oppenheimer to give him the name of the contact. Oppenheimer named Chevalier.* It was the last development in the great Oppenheimer spy case until the security hearings of 1954. The distinguished suspect was in the clear. But he was operating in anything but a vacuum.

---

* Nothing happened as a result of the disclosure except that Chevalier was denied clearance for an innocuous job with the Office of War Information. Oppenheimer insisted later that he had informed Groves that he had been Chevalier's contact. Chevalier—as well as author Peter Goodchild, who examined relevant records—concluded that Oppenheimer, the perennial darling of liberals, was guilty of implicating his friend but not himself.

Seven

The Enemy: The Race Widens

The German counterparts of the American insiders were bothered by inhibitions about the morality of the bomb but thought they knew a way out of their dilemma.

Their work was moving smoothly. By September 1941 they saw "the open road ahead." Their first atomic pile was operating and they were producing uranium metal at the rate of one ton per month. But they knew that they faced stupendous obstacles. The science adviser to Hitler's military high command was ridiculing their efforts and wanted all their "atomic poppycock" stopped. Their raw material requirements would be immense, quite possibly prohibitive. Without a supreme effort, a workable bomb would be many years distant.

The principal scientists at the Kaiser Wilhelm Institute agreed that they had reached a crossroads. They could push their bomb project to the utmost or tinker along routinely. The decision was up to still another Nobel laureate, Werner Heisenberg, who at the age of nineteen had been a favorite student of Niels Bohr in Copenhagen; recently he had taken over the directorship of the institute.

Though Heisenberg was a loyal German, he devised a scheme by which the physicists of the world might relieve their collective consciences and stop an atomic arms race before it got started in earnest. He would let Britain and the United States know that he would not finish a German bomb in time for this war. Then the scientists on the other side could slow down as well and the world would be safe. His old mentor Bohr was back in Nazi-occupied Copenhagen. He would be the ideal middleman to deliver the German peace message to the west.

One chilly October evening Bohr and Heisenberg went walking in the darkness of the park near the Carlsberg brewery in the Danish capital. Both knew that Bohr was under surveillance so they were on edge. The old warmth between them was missing. Bohr suspected that his former student was a Nazi agent trying to find out about nuclear progress in the West. Heisenberg feared that whatever he said would get back to Germany and place his life in "immediate danger."

Elaborately circumspect, Heisenberg asked whether Bohr thought it was "right" for physicists to work on the "uranium problem" in view of the implications for warfare.

The question obviously frightened Bohr. "Do you really think that uranium fission could be used to construct weapons?" he counter-questioned.

"I know this is possible in principle," Heisenberg replied, "but it would require a terrific technical effort. One can only hope that it cannot be realized in this war."

Shocked, Bohr inferred that the Germans were well on the way to perfecting the bomb and he eventually conveyed this conclusion to the Allies. Heisenberg was upset because his old teacher had seemed to misunderstand him but could think of nothing to break the impasse. In effect, his peace mission had exacerbated Allied fears of German competition.

Since Allied military intelligence could find out nothing of value, the Americans remained unaware that the Germans were faltering. In the Helmholtz lecture room of the Harnack House, the headquarters of the Kaiser Wilhelm Institute in suburban Berlin-Dahlem, Werner Heisenberg briefed Munitions Minister Albert Speer on June 4, 1942. It was a most secret and solemn occasion. Heisenberg brought along Otto Hahn and other authorities. Speer was escorted by military and technical advisers, including Professor Ferdy Porsche, the Volkswagen designer.

Heisenberg explained in clinical detail how an atomic bomb could be assembled with uranium or plutonium. Field Marshal Erhard Milch, Hermann Goering's deputy, inquired how large an explosive charge would flatten a major city. "As large as a pineapple," Heisenberg replied, indicating the size with his hands. The Americans might have a bomb in two years, he said, but Germany lacked the resources to compete with such an all-out effort. Hahn noted in his diary that Speer approved some helpful construction projects, such as a special air-raid shelter for Heisenberg's first large uranium reactor. But when the Reichsminister briefed Hitler about the conference the Führer made no move to speed up the project. He was placing his bets on guided missiles.

On December 22, little more than a week after Fermi and Szilard had demonstrated their self-sustaining chain reaction in Chicago, Dr. Yoshio Nishina took the first solid step to enter Japan in the competition for the atomic bomb: he summoned one of his researchers, Dr. Masashi Takeuchi, into his long, narrow corner office on the second floor of Building No. 37 at the Riken Institute in northwest Tokyo.

Riken had been at the heart of Japanese research in physics and chemistry since 1917. The Nuclear Research Laboratory had been founded in 1935 by Nishina, a warm, round-faced professor-administrator of fifty-two, affectionately known as *Oyabun,* the old man. Like the scientific leaders of the American and German A-bomb projects, Nishina had apprenticed in the finest European laboratories: from 1921 and 1922 with Rutherford at the Cavendish, from 1923 to 1928 with Niels Bohr in Copenhagen. He was also a close friend of Ernest Lawrence, who helped him build Japan's first cyclotron and hosted a happy sukiyaki dinner for Nishina in San Francisco not long before Pearl Harbor.

Nishina had grown fond of the West. He never stopped working on his English; his unabridged 1935 Webster's International Dictionary was a fixture on its wooden stand near his desk. Japan's war against America struck him as "insane." To one of his researchers he confided, "Any fool knows the power and might of the United States." But he was a patriot too. "We are all aboard a sinking ship," he said, "we must do what we can to save it."

Such outspokenness was rare for him; Nishina was a judicious and very private person. He had been noncommittal when the Japanese Army first requested him, in April 1941, to investigate the feasibility of an A-bomb. There seemed to be no urgency, and almost nothing was done until July 18, 1942, when a policy meeting was called. This time the Navy asked him to chair a committee of eleven senior scientists to report on the weapon at a further meeting in the Suikosha, a naval officers' club at Shiba Park in Tokyo.

The conferees, impressed by the American embargo on exports of uranium and radium, felt certain that a major effort was under way in the United States, but they doubted that even the Americans could finish building a weapon for this war. "You college professors are apt to be too conservative," scolded a Navy captain, and he asked the scientists to work as systematically as the Navy built battleships. But where would uranium come from? None existed in Japan. Perhaps some deposits could be found in Burma. This seemed likely to one aged professor; he knew of a promising "wrinkle" in the Burmese earth.

Nishina said little. The committee concluded that it would take Japan at least a decade to produce a bomb. The Navy lost interest, but then the war began to go badly for the Japanese. They lost the Battle of Midway. The terrible fighting on Guadalcanal was going against them. "We must do everything we can for our country," a discouraged Nishina had told his staff when it celebrated the first anniversary of Pearl Harbor. The Army had shown renewed interest in an A-bomb. Suddenly it wanted the weapon in two years.

Nishina decided to hand the crucial assignment, uranium separation, to Takeuchi, and his rank-conscious staff wondered why. Takeuchi, thirty-three, was not close to Nishina and not one of the ranking or senior men. He was an authority on cosmic rays, not a nuclear physicist. A gangling figure whose little head was perched at an angle above a very long neck, he had an ingratiating dimpled smile. He looked like an inquisitive chicken and was not noted for dynamic creativity.

Takeuchi also wondered why he was singled out for such an important assignment. It puzzled him considerably. He knew it would be an "epochal" job and did not think it could be done in two years. Nishina indicated gently that he did not tend to think so either. That certainly was discouraging. Takeuchi thought for a moment he would

try to decline the job and stay with his cosmic rays; he felt he be-
longed there. Then he considered further: even if he could not help
make a bomb, perhaps he could become a pioneer of a new industrial
revolution fueled by nuclear energy. The thought cheered him and
he told Nishina he would do his utmost. Nishina never told anyone
why he picked this gentle soul for such rugged work.

Another gentle soul had by that time been diligently at work for
more than a year to help still another group of competitors joining
the race for the A-bomb: the Russians. Their helper was an unassuming, bookish German physicist, Dr. Klaus Fuchs. His motives
were political, his value to the Soviets beyond measure. Yet to become one of history's most effective spies required no effort from
him whatever.

Professor Rudolf Peierls at Birmingham University drew Fuchs
into nuclear research in the spring of 1941 with the worthiest intention. Having convinced the Churchill government that the bomb was
a practical idea, Peierls and his colleague Otto R. Frisch needed help
with complex mathematical calculations. Peierls and Fuchs had met
when Fuchs was a physics student at Bristol University. Peierls had
been impressed by Fuchs's research papers and had heard that the
Bristol professors thought highly of this colorless twenty-nine-year-
old German refugee. Fuchs looked like the perfect man for the job
of precision drudgery in Birmingham at £275 a year.

Peierls knew that Fuchs, the son of a Lutheran minister, had fled
Germany as soon as Hitler came to power in 1933. He did not know
that Fuchs had been an active youth leader of the Communist Party
in his home town, Kiel, and had once been beaten and thrown into
a river by a Nazi street gang. In 1934 this crucial bit of personal
history from a Gestapo report had been volunteered by the German
consul in Bristol to the chief constable of that city, but since its
source was tainted the report was discounted then and again later,
when Fuchs was cleared to work with classified information. If anything, it confirmed that Fuchs was no Nazi.

Peierls was delighted with his new assistant. Fuchs was meticulous
and absolutely reliable in his work. His reports were precise, well
written, and always on time. He learned quickly, worked long hours
into the night, and was eager to take on unexpected emergency as-

signments. Eyes hidden behind thick spectacles (he was very near-sighted), the lean, somewhat lost-looking Klaus was the sort of gem treasured by all bosses: the man who lived for his work. Peierls invited Fuchs to live in his home, and for two years his family cared for Klaus, sewing on his buttons and providing him with some social life.

Although Fuchs displayed no interest in politics, his basic loyalties had remained very much alive. "I had complete confidence in Russian policy, and I believed that the Western Allies deliberately allowed Russia and Germany to fight each other to the death," he confessed a decade later. "I therefore had no hesitation in giving all the information I had . . ."

It was simple for him. A Communist acquaintance put him in touch with a man Fuchs would know only as "Alexander." He was Simon Davidovich Kremer, secretary to the Soviet Military Attaché in London. At least four times in 1941 and 1942 Fuchs met Kremer and handed him detailed reports he had written describing the progress of the British atomic project, code-named "Tube Alloys." Sometimes Fuchs brought along carbon copies of the reports he had written for Peierls. The meetings were concluded quickly at crowded bus stops or on quiet residential streets, always on weekends or in the evenings so Fuchs would lose no time from his work.

After Kremer left for other duties, Fuchs passed his papers to a German Jewish refugee, a housewife he knew as "Sonya," until, in late November of 1943, it was time for him, too, to depart to a new post: to continue his work under the auspices of General Groves in the United States.

The Russians were slow to follow up on Fuchs's extraordinary luck. Not until the early summer of 1942 was Igor Vasilevich Kurchatov called to Moscow and given the assignment to build an atomic bomb. Before then the Soviets could not afford to act upon their intelligence reports on atomic weapons research from Fuchs and other sources in Britain and Germany. Many of their laboratories lay heavily damaged or destroyed by Hitler's invasion and the fighting to push the Nazis back. Physicists were in the military or assigned to tasks for the country's immediate survival.

Kurchatov, tall, broad-shouldered, the most knowledgeable of their younger nuclear physicists—he had just turned forty—had been equipping naval vessels with coils to demagnetize them and protect them from German mines. During a recent bout with pneumonia he had developed mild heart trouble and had grown a huge beard shaped like a flaring spade; friends began to call him "the Beard."

While Kurchatov felt cheered to be returning to physics, he harbored doubts about his new assignment. Unlike more ambitious Soviet administrators, he took pride in his frugality. The bomb would be hideously expensive. Could it be achieved in time to pay off in this war? Was it even right to divert manpower and raw materials to it when the war required a supreme effort? He proceeded with deliberation.

By the spring of 1943 only twenty of his old colleagues were temporarily settled in the Seismological Institute on Pyzhevski Lane. They arrived with no more than one small suitcase each, having abandoned their books, their papers, and most clothes in evacuations or air raids. Oppenheimer and his friends would have been struck by the *déjà vu* of the Russians' ruminations.* The Kurchatov team deplored that they lacked even a microgram of pure uranium. Their ideas for building a nuclear pile varied widely and provoked heated arguments. A new cyclotron had to be constructed; laboriously, orders for parts were parceled out among several factories.

Progress was slow, equipment desperately short, and they had only one mechanic, yet already Kurchatov was running out of space. He took over a deserted building of the Institute of Inorganic Chemistry on Big Kaluga Street and armed guards appeared for the first time. He had synopses prepared of papers that Szilard, Bohr, and Joliot-Curie had published before the curtain of censorship descended. On Pyzhevski Lane he ran staff seminars, much as Oppenheimer had, to determine what avenues to the bomb looked least forbidding.

In midsummer, suddenly, the leisurely pace changed. The government's alarm over the nuclear competition had increased. Orders arrived to push the project to the utmost. This time the word came from the nation's highest authority: the Central Committee of the Communist Party, the voice of Joseph Stalin. He was determined not to lag behind America, where Oppenheimer had set a furious pace.

* At no time during the war did the West suspect that the Soviets were at work on an A-bomb.

Part 2
Building the Bomb

Part 2

Building the Bomb

Eight

Los Alamos I:
The Lure of the Magic Mountain

Dr. Robert R. Wilson put down the telephone receiver and turned to his wife, Jane. "My God," he said, awed, "Robert Oppenheimer is coming to visit!"

It was right after Christmas 1942 at Princeton University. Already recognized, at twenty-eight, as one of the country's most imaginative physicists, Wilson directed a team that was separating uranium with a machine of his invention. It worked, though not efficiently enough to be practical. A fiercely independent one-time cowboy from the town of Frontier, Wyoming, Wilson, whose bristly hair and scrappy temper reminded people of a porcupine, had respected Oppenheimer since graduate student days at Berkeley. His old professor's surprise visitation at this time portended action.

Over dinner, Oppenheimer unfolded an epic sales pitch. He wanted the Wilsons to resettle with him in a New Mexico mountaintop laboratory of bewitching beauty. They would all but vanish there because the project was cocooned in secrecy. It would win the war. Mrs. Wilson asked about the salary. "Don't worry," Oppenheimer exclaimed without further explanation, "you'll be rich!" Wilson wilted under Oppie's romantic vision. He had just finished reading Thomas Mann's novel *The Magic Mountain* and found the similarities striking.

"I almost expected, empathetically, to come down with tuberculosis," he remembered later.

Day One

He accepted immediately, and almost all of his team of forty were persuaded by Oppenheimer to move west with him. They brought along a formidable dowry: a cyclotron that they negotiated away from Harvard by posing as an Army medical team.* Privately Oppenheimer was his snotty old self, even about an acquisition of talent on such a sweeping scale. "I bought them as a job lot at Princeton," he sneered to one of his deputies.

For Wilson and the other scientists being courted by actor/salesman Oppenheimer, the spell cast by the Los Alamos Mountain was usually irresistible. Rushing from campus to campus Oppie first recruited the most prestigious researchers so that their names would become magnets for lesser stars. Hans Bethe, Edward Teller, and other ranking theoreticians of the first Le Conte Hall study group joined up early. The great Isidor Rabi, busy perfecting radar at M.I.T., would make himself available as Oppie's senior consultant. Enrico Fermi would shuttle in from Chicago as often as his commitments there permitted and would eventually settle in Los Alamos too.

Preaching with "mystical earnestness," Oppenheimer captured the imagination of his prospects. The scenery. The outdoor recreation. The best men. Unlimited resources. It would be "one large family" fighting "the people's war." And always, overridingly, the Lorelei of the "technically sweet" problem beckoned. Who could resist the dare to leap for the big breakthrough, to create the hitherto impossible?†

When Oppenheimer encountered doubts, he usually found ways to still them. One physicist wondered whether his bicycle would be usable in the mountains. Oppie said it took only half an hour by bike to the Rio Grande, neglecting to mention that the road went downhill so steeply that the return trip required three hours.

---

* Groves insisted that the cyclotron "theft" succeeded as a wily ruse. "We certainly fooled them up there at Harvard," he told Wilson, who had reason to suspect that President Conant had cleared the deal with his university colleagues.

† Although Groves wanted Oppenheimer not to reveal the project's objective to prospective recruits, the general's obsession with secrecy was no great handicap. Key men like Robert Wilson had passed security muster earlier. And for most of the science community, Groves's secret lay surprisingly open anyway. Even a standard textbook, *Applied Nuclear Physics,* reported in 1942: "The separation of uranium isotopes in quantity lots is now being attempted in several places. If the reader wakes some morning to read in his newspaper that half the United States was blown into the sea overnight he can rest assured that someone, somewhere, succeeded."

Szilard, the Chicago Cassandra, was one of the few who remained unmoved by Oppie's campaign. Leo and Robert were not *simpático* and the isolation of the mesa offended the delicatessen patron and urban cosmopolite in Szilard. "Nobody could think straight in a place like that," he told friends at the Metlab. "Everybody who goes there will go crazy."

Wilson had meanwhile developed second thoughts over a more immediate threat to the scientists' sanity: the limitations of the military mind. Crisscrossing the country on missions with Oppenheimer to get Los Alamos rolling, he argued that it was a rotten idea for the scientists to join the army. What would happen if arbitrary orders from above were "nonsensical"? And what scientists ever got first-class results by following instructions unquestioningly?

With "a faraway look in his eyes," Oppenheimer, the incipient lieutenant colonel—he had already ordered his uniforms—countered that this war was different from any other. He dressed it up as an idealistic "indigenous upsurge" for freedom and against fascism. His language reminded Wilson of the old radical slogans for labor unions and Spain, freshly dusted off on behalf of patriotism. Wilson, who had been apolitical at Berkeley, more a follower of Ernest Lawrence, the redblood, than of Oppenheimer, the mollycoddle, was distressed by the sloganizing.

"I thought he had a screw loose somewhere," he reminisced later.

So did others who were also badly needed for the project. Two of the most influential, Rabi and Dr. Robert F. Bacher, had already worked with the military and experienced it as inhibiting. Scientists needed to be independent. They had to question judgments. Openness to trial and error, not rigidity, had to be encouraged. At a February meeting in Oppenheimer's room at the Waldorf-Astoria Hotel in New York, Wilson was delighted to hear Rabi and Bacher tell Robert they would not join an army regime.

Groves backed down. The scientists would remain civilians. Groves consoled himself by noting that Oppenheimer's men would have looked ridiculous in uniform, especially if they were to try saluting. Wilson was happy. He detested Groves and once walked out on a meeting after the general had made a particularly odious remark.

Oppenheimer's innocence about administration and the "plumbing" of laboratory experimentation was the next hurdle Wilson confronted on the way to his Magic Mountain. By early March of 1943 Oppie had been pressured into tossing off an organization chart. The projected staff population had been revised upward to a more realistic 1500. But when Wilson traveled to Los Alamos to move the Harvard cyclotron into its new home, the X Building, the chaos on the mesa appalled him. There was no evidence of any planning. He fled to Chicago to team up with Dr. John H. Manley, an experimental physicist whom Oppenheimer had also deputized to shape up Los Alamos. Manley was equally upset at Oppie's indecisiveness. Together they descended on their director at Berkeley and badgered him for an entire day.

What personnel should arrive at Los Alamos at which stage? Who would be responsible for what? What were the priorities? Wilson and Manley, hammering away, found out that almost nothing had been settled.

Traditionally Oppenheimer's daytime affairs spilled over to his elegant Eagle Hill home in the evening. At a party that night Wilson and Manley were exposed to the usual heady amalgam of smoke, martinis ceremoniously mixed by the master, gourmet food in fastidiously tiny portions, and the conversation of sophisticated guests. Oblivious to social niceties, Wilson and Manley kept pressuring their host; he had to appreciate the urgency of technical decisions that were crying to be made.

They kept up their assault until Oppenheimer exploded in a "tantrum." With four-letter words he dismissed his visitors as meddlers and their worries as unimportant. Wilson and Manley were aghast, unaware that they were merely breathing the temporary dust of another Oppenheimer personality transformation. The insecure professor who once frightened students with his bite and then mellowed to convert them into camp followers, the olympian intellectual who disdained the troubles of the world only to turn radical activist, was making himself over once again. This time he was becoming a manager, especially of difficult people.

Starting March 15 his pork-pie hat and crumpled suit bobbed up all over the Los Alamos construction site. Makeshift order slowly emerged. Barracks-style laboratories were rising in the fenced-in "Tech" area. Scientists were checking trucks in and out and sleeping on the porch of Fuller Lodge. Communications with the outside world were limited to one noisy telephone line maintained by the Forest Service. This time Oppie was making a universe.

It opened for business April 15 in the Main Tech complex on the mesa, now called "The Hill," with some fifty scientists assembling for three days of briefings. Groves dispensed limp handshakes and a rude sendoff. He reminded his flock that if *they* failed it would be *he* who would have to stand before a congressional committee to justify their squandering of his money.

He had been talked out of antiparachutist training for the scientists and would not require Oppenheimer to impose total compartmentalization within Los Alamos. And already Groves had reason to feel morose about these defeats. As if to rub it in, the orientation sessions were exactly the kind of all-disclosing talkfests that made the general feel he was sponsoring picnics for gossips and spies.

For the role of briefer Oppenheimer cast a surprising but ingenious choice: Dr. Robert Serber, another of his former Berkeley students, later his teaching assistant. Serber was a wispy, insignificant-looking figure with a low, uncertain voice that kept stumbling over words, but he was known to everyone in the room as a brilliant theoretician. His personality intimidated no one. He was not controversial. He liked everybody, even Groves. His mastery of the subject was total and he had no pet schemes to push. Nothing jarred his serenity, not the carpenters still hammering in the hallways, not Manley's whispered admonition to Oppie (which Oppie transmitted in a whisper to Serber) that he must never refer to a "bomb." Even within the family, the proper term was "gadget."

Bumbling along on what he called his primer, the tiny Serber laid out mountainous problems. Uranium would eventually be supplied by the manufacturing plant at Oak Ridge, plutonium by another factory going up at Hanford, Washington. It might take them as long as two years to produce sufficient raw materials for a "critical mass" that would hopefully be large enough to yield a nuclear explosion. About the behavior of uranium—especially its neutrons—much was still unknown. As for plutonium, no one there had ever seen even a sample of it.

But since not a day was to be lost, the Los Alamos group was to go ahead with the construction of the bomb on the basis of calculations alone—just theory. Serber said that the radiation of a uranium bomb would kill every living thing within a radius of 1000 yards. This was not considered shocking because blast effects would kill everything within 2000 yards.

To detonate a critical mass too slowly would cause a fizzle. A modified artillery gun inside the bomb casing would therefore fire a lump of uranium onto a spherical uranium target at 2000 feet per second. Given perfect timing, the impact of one subcritical mass on the other should produce a nuclear explosion. The kill effects of a plutonium bomb should be greater but so would the construction difficulties.

Throughout Serber's presentation, Oppenheimer could see how his insistence on not compartmentalizing Los Alamos was helping his work. Excited whispers in the audience told him that the men were pleased to be taken into management's confidence. When Oppenheimer invited them to talk back freely, physicists, then chemists, and finally ordnance experts offered contributions. And it was a very young ordnance man who triggered what would be the most innovative creative burst in all the life of the Manhattan Project. He told the group that they should not work toward an explosion, as everyone kept saying. "Explosion" meant pounding apart. They wanted "implosion," which meant driving together.

That word hit Dr. Seth H. Neddermeyer hard. He was a scrawny, tall physicist, still another former student of Oppenheimer, who had recruited Neddermeyer during a walk on the grounds of the National Bureau of Standards where he had long been doing research that bored him. As he listened to Serber's lecture, Neddermeyer, a cold cigar butt clenched between his teeth, had become restless. His mind was forming images of uranium and plutonium spheres being squeezed so hard from all sides at once that they turned soft. He had hit on an entirely fresh configuration for the bomb, and as soon as he heard the word "implosion" he raised his hand.

At thirty-six Neddermeyer was considerably older than most of his new colleagues, but he was shy, a poor speaker and a worse salesman. Groping for words to make his vague visions plausible, he proposed that while a gun would do its compressing in one dimension, two or three dimensions would work better. Fissionable material should be compressed by exploding a layer of TNT wrapped around it. The explosive would not have to travel as far as with the gun method and bombs could be made to work with less of the scarce fissionable materials.

Not one man in the room believed him. Neddermeyer's bomb could never work unless uncounted simultaneous explosions could be marshaled to produce a symmetrically converging shock wave of fantastic uniformity and power. Nothing like it had ever been attempted or thought about.* Oppenheimer questioned Neddermeyer skeptically. Other senior physicists poured more and more objections into the ensuing sharp debate. The comments of the ordnance experts were the most scathing. Discovering that Neddermeyer had no background in explosives, they found polite ways to tell him he was crazy.

Oppenheimer was not so sure. They would go ahead with the gun for uranium and plutonium, but he did not think they could afford to ignore the implosion possibility entirely. Once the briefings had ended he called the dejected Neddermeyer into his modest 10-by-15-foot corner office on the second floor of the sprawling wooden Tech-1 Building and told him without enthusiasm: "This will have to be looked into." Oppie looked tired and seemed lost in the special chair he had had imported from his Berkeley office because it protected his delicate back. The rest of the setting reflected wartime austerity: thin, creaky wooden flooring, blackboards along the walls, and no pictures.

Implosion, Oppenheimer mused, looked too intricate to be brought off in time to affect the war, yet Neddermeyer should feel free to prove otherwise. "Use as many men and as much equipment as you can," instructed Oppenheimer, the newly minted administrator. Neddermeyer, still having trouble administering even his own thoughts, walked out with a new title: Group Leader, Ordnance Division, Section E-5, Implosion Experimentation.

"If you can do it," Oppenheimer cracked, grinning, "I'll give you a bottle of whiskey."

And still Groves opposed the free flow of ideas. The success of Serber's lectures encouraged Oppenheimer to authorize a weekly colloquium to keep his staff informed. Groves reacted with alarm. Even

* The very word "implosion" remained classified "secret" until six years after the war.

within the confines of an isolated project, he insisted, some barriers must stay up. Oppenheimer said that sensitive information should go to anyone whose work might profit from it. It would speed the project. Also, scientists would guard more rigorously against leaks if they knew the significance of what they were doing. Oppie wanted to treat them like adults, Groves like naughty children. The two compromised. The colloquia continued but with somewhat restricted attendance.*

The schism between the power blocs—Oppenheimer described the scientists as "us" and the military as "them"—became a fixture in his thinking. It was an unending struggle, with Oppenheimer employing Gandhi-like tactics and even slapstick humor. After Groves complained that Oppenheimer's trusty pork-pie hat made him too identifiable for supposed enemies, Robert received the general in his office wearing full Indian headdress—and the subject of hats was dropped. Robert Wilson and the other scientists noted, however, that Oppie was careful to remember that the general had the power to fire him at any time.

"Yes, General . . . yes, General," the Wilsons heard Oppie intone into the phone when Groves called during a dinner party at the Oppenheimers' house on "Bathtub Row."† For the benefit of the guests, Robert's obsequiousness was punctuated by smirks that he flashed in their direction.

Wilson felt happily caught up in the Oppenheimer charisma. Like almost everyone else on The Hill, he became the boss's devoted lieutenant, gladly subservient to such an extraordinary mind. "Oppenheimer stretched me," he recalled later. "His style, the poetic vision

---

* Groves's security phobia kept even his deputy, Colonel Nichols, out of Los Alamos until near the end of the war. When Nichols was finally admitted for a visit, the general instructed the laboratory staff not to "tell him too much." There was another reason why Groves did not want his right hand at Los Alamos to know what his left hand was doing at Oak Ridge. He wanted each laboratory to think it was a bottleneck holding up progress at the other. He thought this would encourage competition and greater speed. Instead, the senior scientists discovered what the general was up to and became enraged.

† Only the most senior men and their families could be accommodated in the former homes of Ranch School faculty, and these had bathtubs. The new Army barracks, apartments, and dormitories for everyone else had only showers. A bathtub was the supreme status symbol at Los Alamos. Teller languished without one, to his great disgust.

of what we were doing, inflamed me. In his presence, I became more intelligent, more intense, more prescient, more poetic myself."

Arriving at Los Alamos as a stereotypically laconic frontier personality, Wilson, to his wife's amazement, turned articulate, positively bubbling. Always a slow reader, he tried to imitate Oppie's speed at absorbing print: "When he handed me a letter I would glance at it and hand it back prepared to discuss the nuances of it minutely." Away from the great man's presence, Wilson found it difficult later to reconstruct what had been decided. "No matter," he explained. "The tone had been established. I would know how to invent what it was that had to be done."

Edward Teller did not enjoy the tone of Los Alamos. He felt bottled up, not stretched. He had come primarily to work on the Super, his baby, the hydrogen bomb. He assumed he would be his own boss and expected that the academic-style free-for-all of the brainstorming sessions back at Le Conte Hall would continue.

From the start, he felt betrayed by Oppenheimer. The goal-oriented discipline of the mesa offended him, particularly since its goal was not his. Oppenheimer's troops were obsessed with the uranium and plutonium bombs, which failed to challenge Teller sufficiently. Oppie's "psychological finesse" with the staff he found "deeply repulsive." Like his friend Szilard in Chicago, Teller staged a one-man mutiny.*

"It was a shock to work in a machine-like organization," he remembered later. "I refused. It was not my style." It was not his style, in short, to accept any boss.

Oppenheimer assigned Teller to Hans Bethe, director of the Theoretical Division. Teller and Bethe had been great friends, but the division was a sizable enterprise—eventually it included eighty people—and Bethe, a friendly, patient man, was too busy for Teller's frequent interruptions about the hydrogen bomb and his fertile flow of novel ideas, most of them irrelevant to the A-bomb. Cornered,

---

* Both men were memorialized in a mock prayer that made the rounds in both laboratories: "Lord, deliver us from our enemies without and our Hungarians within." Many other similarities existed between the two men's personalities. Both were convivial, childishly impulsive, disdainful of detail, and they were insatiable sugarholics. Teller's addiction to chocolate was legendary.

Bethe finally hauled out a large pocket watch and frowned at it conspicuously.

Teller was insulted. Bethe had turned too Prussian. The division was "overorganized." The calculations about Neddermeyer's implosion theory that Bethe assigned to him in ever larger volume were beneath his talents. Petty calculations could be relegated to others. Teller had come to think and to think big.

His disagreements with Oppenheimer were numerous and as complex as these two mental giants themselves. Some concerned only style. Oppie was too glib for Teller, and he encouraged others to be glib. "You had to do anything in order to avoid looking foolish," said Teller. "You had to talk as though you know, whether you know or don't know." Other differences between them were deeply political. Teller thought that Oppie surrounded himself with too many liberal ideologues and that he resisted Groves and the military too much.

Oppenheimer, thinking that Teller was too valuable to lose, coddled him like a superstar. Once a week he met with him alone, a privilege otherwise granted only to division heads. He relieved Teller of routine duties with Bethe but did not stop all investigations of the H-bomb. At the Tuesday evening colloquia, his patience was tried by Teller's frequent challenges of his authority and by Teller's greatest technical weakness—sloppy, sometimes wildly sloppy, mathematics—but he rarely responded with one of his nasty wisecracks. (When he did so on one occasion, Teller did not respond with his normal high-pitched giggle but turned white and gave a convulsive start.) Cleverly Oppie countered Teller's distrust with a gesture of trust. He asked Teller to greet and brief all new staff arrivals, a chore of high visibility that Teller enjoyed.

And so this rebel, whose cause was his own, wandered about the mesa at his uneven gait, working only on what he liked and pouring his frustrations into his old Steinway, which he played as late as three in the morning, much to the consternation of neighbors. Less psychological finesse from Oppenheimer could have broken either Teller's spirit or that of the entire laboratory.

Nine

Los Alamos II:
Crisis on the Mesa

In the depths of a canyon off Oppenheimer's mesa, Seth Nedder-meyer celebrated Independence Day, July 4, 1942, by blasting pieces of steel piping into the air. He hoped he could begin to prove the practicality of an implosion bomb by making his metal cylinders collapse evenly. But no matter how he adjusted his explosives and equipment as the weeks went by, the cylinders he retrieved were uselessly twisted, and when he reported on the experiment at one of Oppie's seminars he again faced derision.

"It stinks," said Dr. Richard P. Feynman from a back row. It was an indignity predictable from this flamboyant theoretician of Robert Wilson's Princeton group;* he was twenty-five and acquiring a reputation as the project's comedian. More crushing was the verdict of Captain William Parsons, the dignified, nearly bald career Navy officer picked by Vannevar Bush and General Groves to head the Ordnance Division. "I question Dr. Neddermeyer's seriousness," said "Deke" Parsons, a rank-conscious resident of "Bathtub Row." Descending untypically to a quip, the captain scoffed that Neddermeyer would next try to implode a can of beer without spilling the beer.

Oppenheimer, still following no more than a hunch, did not join the prevailing view that implosion was a preposterous dream. Neither did Edward Teller, who discussed it with Dr. John von Neumann, a

---

* In 1965 Feynman would win the Nobel Prize for discoveries in quantum mechanics.

witty, plump fellow Hungarian whom Teller had met in Budapest in 1925 and whom Oppenheimer had also known since student days in Europe.

The gregarious "Johnny" von Neumann, a mathematician, a computer pioneer, and the founder of game theory, was one regular visitor-consultant at Los Alamos whom nobody hesitated to call a "genius."* Applying his famous mathematical acrobatics to Neddermeyer's problems, he calculated that implosion was indeed feasible and that it would require less of the precious fissionable material than the gun method. Unfortunately, he found a hitch: the symmetry of the shock wave could not vary by more than 5 percent. This meant that a vast new range of experiments and computations would have to be mastered. Neddermeyer, the lone-wolf tinkerer, was not accustomed to operating on such a scale and had resisted Oppenheimer's instructions to expand his team to the limit. Seth had chosen to plod on with six men.

"Use more men and move faster," Oppenheimer told him.

"I'm no operator," Neddermeyer demurred. "Never was."

A complex crisis was building. It would last for more than a year and endanger the entire bomb project. As it gained in intensity, Oppenheimer changed. The arrogance of his youth returned and Neddermeyer was his first victim. He patronized Neddermeyer, then bullied him. "Oppenheimer lit into me," Neddermeyer remembered. "From my point of view he was an intellectual snob. He could cut you cold and humiliate you right into the ground. On the other hand, I could irritate him."

Neddermeyer *was* irritating. He continued to muddle along at the pedantic pace of an academic researcher. He would not bend with pressure. It was not his way to rush and he had no ambition to become an executive. He did cherish his independence, which further infuriated his immediate chief, Deke Parsons, a conservative nuts-and-bolts technocrat who supervised him closely, remained wedded to the "good old gun" method, and suffered Neddermeyer as a vague bumbler. "The two never agreed about anything," said one senior scientist who had to work with both.

---

* At the age of six von Neumann could divide one eight-digit number into another entirely in his head.

Personality conflicts were not the only dimension of the developing crisis. More fundamental was the staggering difficulty of producing even tiny quantities of usable uranium and plutonium. Groves's riverboat gamble in plunging ahead to build the half-billion-dollar Oak Ridge plant was paying off, but only up to a frustrating point. The factory began operating in August 1943 but kept breaking down. The black powder that it eked out contained only 15 percent pure uranium 235. Oppenheimer was told he could count on enough uranium for just one bomb by mid-1945.

At least it was a bomb sure to work, for in November Robert Wilson's cyclotron group reported final good news about the one crucial property of U-235 that had remained in doubt. Nearly all its neutrons were emitted in less than a thousand millionth of a second. That meant the gun method would work fast enough for a uranium bomb. But since nobody believed that a single bomb—without at least the enforceable threat of more to come—could win the war, the plutonium bomb suddenly assumed supreme importance.

In another wild toss of his dice, Groves had begun in March to build his second city from the group up, this one in the wilderness of Hanford, Washington, to produce plutonium 239. Fermi and Wigner in Chicago were designing its reactors. Some 45,000 freezing, badly housed construction workers, deploying 11,000 pieces of machinery, were rushing this plant to completion. For once, Wigner overcame his congenital pessimism. He assured Oppenheimer that the eventual output of plutonium would be "almost unlimited." With the gun method and a plutonium supply assured, it seemed that time and the Germans were the only obstacles left.

To the scientists acquainted with the skills of Werner Heisenberg, Otto Hahn, and other German nuclear researchers, the Nazi threat was becoming acute. Leo Szilard and others suggested elaborate espionage schemes, even, half-facetiously, the kidnaping of Heisenberg during a lecture trip to Switzerland. If the Germans were not yet about to perfect a bomb, they might have devised ways to dump dangerous quantities of radioactivity on American cities; they might even drop an entire reactor. Dr. Harold C. Urey, the discoverer of heavy water and another of Groves's Nobel Prize winners, became so alarmed while working at Columbia on uranium separation in the summer of 1943 that he urged Groves to warn the American public of a possible atomic attack.

The general would rather have slit his throat than talk in public about nuclear warfare, but the possibility of German atomic attacks worried him. He warned General Marshall that Americans might have to withstand "punishing blows" from "large quantities" of radioactive materials, and he sent Geiger counters "under highest secrecy" to the Manhattan District offices in Washington, New York, Boston, Chicago, and San Francisco. Military officers in those cities were instructed in the instruments' use. Scientists were on standby orders to "proceed to the scene of suspected radioactive attack," including the sections of Britain where General Dwight D. Eisenhower's Allied troops were massing for the invasion of the Continent.

At Arthur Compton's Metlab some of the scientists had convinced themselves that Hitler had singled out Chicago for atomic attack. The most likely time, they calculated, would be Christmas 1943. Several men sent their families to the country. Compton, himself apprehensive, was not critical of their precautions.

Christmas having passed peacefully, Compton and his staff thought that the Nazis planned a nuclear New Year's surprise. Dr. Norman Hilberry, Compton's principal assistant, decided not to go to bed New Year's Eve until well past midnight. In case of a radioactive emergency with the troops in England, it was his assignment to dispatch a group of scientists to Europe aboard Air Force planes standing by at the Chicago airport, and he did not want to be asleep until it was daylight in Britain.

Hilberry and his wife were about to retire when the ring of the phone broke the stillness of their Chicago apartment. The phone was at the end of a long hallway. Hilberry had never sprinted down that hall so quickly. He was certain that a nuclear attack was on. He picked up the phone. There was a long silence. Then an unknown voice slurred: "Happy New Year!"

As D-Day for the invasion neared, Groves went to see Chief of Staff General George C. Marshall and urged that General Eisenhower be informed of the "terrifying effects" of radioactive fallout.* Mar-

---

* The deadliness of radioactive materials became known within months after Wilhelm Röntgen discovered X-rays in 1895. But only after the Hiroshima

shall agreed that Groves should send one of his officers to England
to brief Eisenhower personally. Following this visitation, Ike's chief
surgeon distributed two discreetly worded directives on May 3, 1944.
Administrative Memo No. 60 announced an investigation into "several instances of fogged and blackened photographic and X-ray film."
Further such occurrences were to be reported at once. To preserve
secrecy and avoid a scare, the most likely cause of unexplained film
exposure, radiation, was not mentioned. Memo No. 58 asked all
medical personnel to report any cases of a debilitating but supposedly
"mild disease of unknown etiology" whose "most constant and reliable sign" was leukopenia, a drastic loss of white cells in the blood—
a prime radiation symptom.

Groves's own most terrifying nightmare was the still mysterious
status of the Nazi atomic effort. Determined to smash it and capture
the scientists in charge, he organized an investigative team to advance with the Allied front-line troops and track down the German
laboratories without wasting one moment. The top-secret mission
was called "Alsos" (Greek for "grove") and was headed by Boris T.
Pash, the same intelligence colonel whose enthusiasm for undercover
work had enabled him, back in California, to finger Oppenheimer as
a Soviet spy.

The colonel was again tracking ominous clues. British intelligence
had heard of a Swiss scientist working in an abandoned spinning mill
in Bisingen, a village in the Black Forest, on an explosive "a thousand times more powerful than TNT." American censors had intercepted a letter from a prisoner of war assigned to a secret research
laboratory at Hechingen, three miles to the north. Allen Dulles, chief
of the Bern mission of the Office of Strategic Services, reported that
the great Werner Heisenberg had moved to the same town. Hechingen had been declared a *"Sperrgebiet."** Pash was also told that
some of the huge bunkers built along the French coast might shelter
atomic warheads.

---

bombing did it gradually became apparent how small a dosage could cause illness or death, and that radiation could remain dormant in the human body for
years before turning fatal.
* Groves and his men did not know that Hechingen had been declared a
"restricted zone" for no military reasons; it had simply received all the civilian
bombing refugees it could handle.

On August 25 the intrepid Pash in his jeep rode into Paris behind the first five French tanks liberating the jubilant city. Four times the colonel and his four companions were forced back by sniper fire, but that evening they drank champagne from laboratory beakers at the Collège de France with the leading French nuclear physicist, Joliot-Curie, who told them he knew little of the Germans' efforts but thought they were making no real headway.

Groves did not believe him. Files just captured in Brussels showed huge quantities of refined Belgian uranium flowing into Germany, 140 tons between January and May of 1943 alone. And records seized in Paris revealed that the Germans had confiscated all French stocks of the radioactive metal thorium, a possible alternate for uranium for which there was almost no commercial use. The Americans still did not realize why they found it so difficult to uncover solid evidence of a large Nazi nuclear project: they were looking for something that did not exist.

This gratifying solution of their five-year riddle emerged—at least on paper—in early December in newly liberated Strasbourg. This time the investigation was headed by Dutch-born Dr. Samuel Goudsmit—hawk-nosed, warm and witty. An old friend of Oppenheimer's, he had become scientific director of Alsos because of a unique combination of qualifications. He was an outstanding nuclear physicist; he spoke several languages; he seemed to have been friendly with everybody in European science, including Werner Heisenberg, who had been his house guest at the University of Michigan before the war; and since Goudsmit had not been connected with the bomb project before, he could reveal no technical secrets if he was captured.

In the wing of a Strasbourg hospital an Alsos team found a nuclear physics laboratory with seven physicists and chemists who tried to pose as physicians and arrogantly refused to talk about their work. But they had been remarkably sloppy about their papers. As the Germans shelled the city, Goudsmit, by the light of candles and a gas lamp, pored over files and correspondence that added up to an inside picture of the entire German A-bomb effort.

Letters from scientists within Germany complained in clinical detail about their headaches. In a wastebasket Goudsmit found the draft of a letter to Heisenberg criticizing the disappointing progress of the German uranium pile. No question remained in Goudsmit's mind: the enemy was still puzzled by bottlenecks that Groves's men had eliminated two years earlier.

Pleased by the implications of his success as a scientific detective, Goudsmit said to one of his military associates, "If the Germans don't have the bomb, then we don't need to use ours."

"You don't know Groves," said the officer. "If we have such a weapon, then we'll use it."

At Los Alamos, Groves's defenses against espionage created exactly the impression he desired. Senior scientists were assigned bodyguards and fake names (Fermi became Farmer, Wigner was Wagner). Driver's licenses were made out to numbers, not names. Phone lines were known to be monitored and none existed outside the Tech area. Mail came and went only to Box 1663, Santa Fe. All conversation outside the Tech area was so conscientiously self-censored that even ranking wives like Mrs. Fermi, almost unbelievably, had no idea what their husbands were working on.

Ever eager to placate Groves, Oppenheimer loyally fell in with the security drill. Although he could never learn to operate the recording device on his phone and eventually tore it out in disgust, he dispatched little Robert Serber as a counterspy to the La Fonda Hotel in Santa Fe to spread phony tales about the project. (Unlike the scientists whom Serber briefed at the initial Los Alamos work session, the bar patrons showed no interest.)

Nobody suspected that the real danger would come not from outside the project but from a Trojan horse within.

Along with his mentor, Professor Peierls, and other British scientists newly assigned to help Groves and Oppenheimer, Stalin's spy, Klaus Fuchs, arrived in the United States on the troopship *Andes* in early December 1943, and was first stationed in New York to work with the group at Columbia University on uranium separation.

His instructions from his Soviet contact in Britain, "Sonya," had been precise and he followed them exactly. On the specified Saturday in January 1944 he appeared at a street corner on the Lower East Side with a tennis ball in his left hand. A man wearing gloves and carrying a book with a green binding and another pair of gloves met him, introduced himself as "Raymond," and took him by taxi to a restaurant on lower Third Avenue, where Fuchs handed over his latest data.

He had at least four more meetings in New York with "Raymond," who was Harry Gold, a flabby, sad-looking biochemist, born Heinrich Golodnitsky in Switzerland. In March they met for less than a minute on Madison Avenue; in mid-June in Woodside, Queens; in late June near Brooklyn's Borough Hall; in mid-July they got together at 96th Street and Central Park West and strolled through Central Park for an hour and a half, talking shop.

During these encounters Fuchs passed along packages of typed and handwritten papers disclosing plans for the design of the uranium bomb and the Oak Ridge production plant. He outlined the timing and scale of Groves's entire program. And he answered questions that Gold transmitted from his Russian contact, Anatoli A. Yakovlev, the Russian vice consul in New York, known to Gold as "John." The Soviets were so delighted with Gold's goodies that they referred to him as "the candy man," but when the little chemist offered Fuchs $1500 for one delivery Klaus flatly rejected the money.

For the next rendezvous, scheduled at the Brooklyn Museum of Art, the punctilious Fuchs failed to appear. Nor did he keep an alternative date set for Central Park West. Greatly disturbed, Gold went to Klaus's apartment house at 128 West 77th Street. The doorman knew only that Fuchs had left. Yakovlev tracked down Fuchs's sister Kristel in Cambridge, Massachusetts. Gold went to see her and explained that he was a friend of Klaus. Kristel said that her security-conscious brother had told her no more than that he was going "somewhere in the Southwest." Not until 1945 would Fuchs choose to reveal to the Russians that he was working at Los Alamos.

Realizing that he was trailing the western powers and needed to expand operations again, Kurchatov, "The Beard" in Moscow, went shopping for a Los Alamos laboratory of his own. He rejected more and bigger buildings within the capital. "The city is too confining," he said. He thought his "Laboratory No. 2," eventually named the Atomic Energy Institute, would grow greatly but at a rate he could not yet predict.

In mid-1943 he decided on Khodysenkoe Field, a large abandoned artillery and machine-gun practice range beyond the belt-line railroad, half a mile from the Moscow River. He and his staff—they still numbered less than fifty, including the furnace attendant—moved into an unfinished three-story brick building of the Institute of Traumatic Medicine at the edge of a potato field.

By spring of 1944 the new laboratory building was barely completed and still mostly unfurnished. The cyclotron on the first floor was unfinished. By summer two rifles were firing at each other on the second floor in an experiment to model the gun method of bomb assembly. By fall columns of graphite were being stacked up in two army tents below Kurchatov's office window, but the black bricks were still too impure to produce a chain reaction. It all added up to a slow, rudimentary effort and the Beard was running more than three years behind the Allies. New word from his man Fuchs would help.

Oppenheimer was also running aground. The realization of imminent disaster dawned in slow stages. Early in 1944, analysis of the first plutonium 239 samples revealed traces of another isotope as well, plutonium 240. Its properties could abort a gun-method bomb. The gun might trigger a premature "predetonation." More experiments on more samples revealed the disturbing presence of even more PU-240 than originally suspected.

On July 11 Oppenheimer advised Conant of the worst: the gun method was useless for plutonium. It was not fast enough and would be certain to cause a fizzle. In Chicago, Arthur Compton turned white when he heard the news. In Washington, the normally easygoing Conant called the situation "desperate" and went into emergency deliberations with Groves.

The conclusion was obvious. Neddermeyer's faster implosion process absolutely *had* to be made to work, no matter what effort it took.

With morale on the mesa at a low and still dropping, Oppenheimer decided on a drastic reorganization of the entire laboratory. Neddermeyer was shunted aside to putter with details. Parsons was moved off to put the finishing touches on the gun-method bomb and to get it ready for a combat drop once sufficient uranium was accumulated. (The captain was furious. At one of Oppenheimer's meetings Groves had bawled him out so severely for resisting Neddermeyer that he worried about his career. He was married to an admiral's ambitious daughter and pushing hard for promotion.)

Von Neumann and Peierls conceived explosive lenses that they hoped would achieve the symmetry required for implosion. Rudimentary IBM computers were imported and employed by Dick Feynman* to cope with the flood of new calculations. More metallurgists and other specialists were recruited from across the country. In addition, the Army called in 200 (later 400) engineers and draftsmen from its ranks to fashion hardware nobody had ever seen before.

And then Oppenheimer had to persuade Groves to swallow yet another dose of bedevilment. Unlike the uranium bomb, the plutonium gadget would incorporate so many unknowns that it would have to undergo a full-scale field test—of itself an unprecedented, high-risk enterprise, and so complex that planning for it would have to start at once. Groves agreed most reluctantly. He did not wish to waste a microgram of plutonium—or one day's time from the bomb delivery schedule he had given Secretary of War Stimson.

To supervise the high-explosives component of the frantic new implosion program Oppenheimer brought in George Kistiakowsky, the Russian-born explosives expert from Harvard. Hard-driving and volatile, "Kisty" enjoyed drink and practical jokes and was the best brain in the country for making implosion work. His experience told him not to be optimistic, however. Highly organized, he prepared a day-by-day schedule of his desired progress. His last entry, for the end of 1944, read: "The test of the gadget failed. Project staff resumes frantic work. Kistiakowsky goes nuts and is locked up!"

Though no one worried about Kisty's equilibrium, intimates did become concerned about Oppie's state. His weight dropped to a cadaverous 116 pounds. After a stretch of puffing mostly on a pipe he went back to chain-smoking cigarettes. Sleeping became such a problem that he had to take Seconal nightly. And as the laboratory's crisis deepened, the melancholy and self-doubts of his youth again began to haunt the man whose "psychological finesse" had alienated Edward Teller.

Most colleagues could not discern Oppenheimer's personal crisis.

---

* Feynman understood the machines so thoroughly that he could also repair them. In his spare time he teased the security people by opening the safes of Edward Teller and other colleagues.

For a party game in Oppie's home, each scientist was asked to name a person whom he'd rather be, and nobody remarked on the emotional significance of Oppie's selection: Enrico Fermi, so cool, uncomplicated, untroubled, so beyond challenge.*

Colleagues continued to admire Oppenheimer extravagantly and, with the exception of Teller, were forgiving of his trespasses. They did not mind when he nodded or shook his head in response to a question that a questioner had not yet finished asking. They marveled at him as "the master of the synopsis" who needed only a few minutes to summarize every relevant detail of a two-hour meeting and point the group toward the next task. They shrugged when he publicly insulted a physicist for the gaucherie of ordering steak well done. They smiled indulgently when he was too vain to leave the privacy of his house while recovering from the unsightly aftereffects of chicken pox. His four-letter language was considered amusing, and when he absent-mindedly drove his car through the security gate and a guard shot at his tires, the story circulated that Oppie backed up and handed the guard a dollar, thinking he was driving across the Bay Bridge at Berkeley.

Only the strongest personalities could deflect the director from his agenda of the moment. Norman Ramsey managed to stay his own course by never venturing into Oppenheimer's presence without a set of explicit notes. He feared that without these he might take his leave from the boss without bringing up what he had come for.

But Robert F. Bacher saw the boss with his act down. Oppenheimer had asked the sturdy, unflappable Cornell professor to head the newly formed Gadget Division, which was to conduct the implosion experiments and design the plutonium bomb. Bacher was also a key man on the new Cowpunchers' Committee, set up to ride herd on the overall implosion effort. Oppie took him for daily walks around the mesa. Often they walked and talked for two hours with Oppenheimer pouring out his anguish. The project had become too

---

* Because of the infallibility of his pronouncements, Fermi was called "the Pope." When Teller informed a group lunching at Fuller Lodge that Fermi would make his first appearance at Los Alamos the following week, mathematician Stanislaw Ulam intoned the Latin announcement that follows the white smoke signal from the College of Cardinals in the Vatican signifying the election of a new pope. Johnny von Neumann explained the reference and everyone at the table applauded.

complicated. He did not think he could coax it to success. Bacher was alarmed. He had known Robert since the 1920s and had never seen him so despondent.

The women in his life did not help. In January 1944 he was visibly upset and went walking alone among the pines after word came that Jean Tatlock, the woman who had radicalized him, had swallowed sleeping pills and then plunged her head deep into the full bathtub in her San Francisco apartment.

Kitty stepped up her already copious drinking and became an ogre in the eyes of the Los Alamos wives. Even the courtly Hans Bethe called her "a bitch, but an elegant bitch." Official entertaining bored her; she left it to the socially adept Mrs. Parsons. But Kitty bristled with rank consciousness and her tactlessness was notorious. "My guests are more important than yours," she wrote in a note to her neighbor, Elsie McMillan, when she removed a chicken from the McMillan refrigerator. "Let's measure hips," she challenged another wife—and fetched her tape measure to show off her figure.

Her relationship with Robert became, if anything, more dependent. "Love you!" she would call out to him at a party and throw him an adoring look which he acknowledged with the studied graciousness of royalty. Privately too Kitty became more possessive. She accused Robert of having affairs with other women, especially his secretaries, and she engineered the breakup of some of his prewar social relationships with colleagues.

How could the proud and elegant Robert tolerate the embarrassing Kitty? Preoccupation with this perennial topic led to few satisfactory answers and much psychologizing among couples at Los Alamos. They treated Kitty gently, like a mental case who wielded considerable power. Robert's associates admired his patience with her disruptive antics and felt sorry for him during her frequent absences, especially when she left the mesa for a month to stay with her parents, seemingly on the edge of an emotional breakdown.

Robert's treatment of his children elicited stronger feelings. To a considerable extent the youngsters were raised, as was then customary among rich European families, by a German maid ("a regular tyrant," said Oppie's sister-in-law). With the second child, Katherine (Toni), born during the first year at Los Alamos, Robert's apparent need to reject his own turned bizarre. When Kitty was away and he

114

called on the friends who were looking after Toni, Robert did not ask to see the baby, and when she was brought out he never touched her. Eventually he wanted to offer Toni to friends for adoption, which appalled even Kitty.*

Just when the laboratory's uncertainties loomed more forbidding than the surrounding mountain ranges, the most potent possible morale booster made his entrance on the mesa: Niels Bohr, the Great Dane, alias Nicholas Baker for security purposes. His many former students and associates greeted him excitedly as "Uncle Nick," and his appearance suggested the benediction of a father figure. "Somehow he seemed the embodiment of wisdom," remembers the mathematician Stan Ulam. "If Bohr was there, it would have to work," said Bernard J. O'Keefe, a junior engineer. "He made the enterprise, which often looked so macabre, seem hopeful," Oppenheimer said later.

In special danger because he was half Jewish, Bohr had been smuggled out of Nazi Denmark to neutral Sweden on a fishing boat. He had made his way to London in the bomb bay of a British Mosquito bomber, where he passed out because the helmet with its oxygen attachment was too small for his leonine head. In Washington he had bemused General Groves with his bumbling ways and absentminded jaywalking. "Here's Niels Bohr coming to see me again," Groves said when the screeching of brakes and the whistles of patrolmen announced a commotion under his office window. He put up with the annoying professor only because he wanted to be able to say that "everything possible had been done to get the best men."

In the train compartment en route to Los Alamos, where Bohr, between missions to Washington and London, would spend much of 1944, Groves was all but bent out of shape by his efforts to make out the great man's mumbling about the future political implications of the weapon that Bohr called "the bum." Greeting the limping general, Oppenheimer asked why he was so stiff. Groves said, "I've been listening to Bohr."

Oppenheimer and his lieutenants listened even more avidly to Bohr, because he possessed the power both to understand and to uplift. Bohr had scope. "Is it big enough?" was his first question to

---

* Toni committed suicide in 1977 after an unhappy love affair.

Oppenheimer when he was shown through the sprawl of the expanding project. The Great Dane was given an office where he appeared each morning with the eight-o'clock whistle. He sat in on meetings and offered solutions to such technical riddles as the initiator for the detonation of the implosion weapon.

Quickly Bohr became one of them. He counseled and cheered Oppie, who revered him. He went hiking and skiing with the Fermis, surprising them with his agility. He regaled the Peierls family, old friends, with jokes. He met and eluded his first skunk. But his key contribution came on the loftiest level during nights of discussions with Oppenheimer and other admirers. Pacing the noisy floorboards, Bohr showed them the future as a benign prophet. He calmed them, especially Oppenheimer, who was moved by Bohr's "high hope that the outcome would be good, and that in this role of objectivity, friendliness and cooperation, incarnate in science, would play a helpful part; all this was something we wished very much to believe."

And they did believe. Another Bohr disciple, Victor Weisskopf, Hans Bethe's Viennese mainstay in the Theoretical Division, remembered: "Every great and deep difficulty bears in itself its own solution, and therefore the greater the hardship, the greater would be the reward that would come out of it. This we learned from him."

Bohr's built-in solution excited his listeners beyond measure. He hoped to persuade Roosevelt and Churchill to listen to him. He wanted them to tell Stalin about the bomb quickly and to make an offer to share its control. Openness would be the one way to short-circuit polarization between the two great powers, to defuse future power struggles throughout the world, and to avoid an atomic arms race.

The vision was breathtaking, and in January 1944 Bohr boarded the Santa Fe Railroad for Washington. He had plans.

Part 3

The Policy Makers Fumble

Ten

Niels Bohr:
Failure of a Prophet

President Roosevelt was shocked but managed not to show it. Despite his instructions that nobody in Washington was to know of the S-1 project except a very limited handful of the highest policy makers, Supreme Court Justice Felix Frankfurter had come to the White House to talk about international control of the bomb. The Justice referred to it only as "X" and clearly did not know the technical details, but he had learned enough about the weapon to cause him grave concern about its future impact on world affairs.

His source had been Niels Bohr, he told the President. They had first met at Oxford University in the early 1930s—Frankfurter had been the George Eastman visiting professor there—and had talked of their friendship with the great Lord Rutherford. Recently they had renewed acquaintances at a tea party in the Danish Legation. Frankfurter had had no trouble guessing the mission that had brought Bohr to America. The Justice, formerly dean of the Harvard Law School, happened to be the country's most illustrious busybody. He seemed to know everyone and had gotten wind of the bomb project's existence through scientist friends. Bohr, aware that Frankfurter was a confidant of FDR, was delighted to accept an invitation to lunch in the Justice's chambers. He had fortuitously run into the ideal listener for his scheme: a pipeline into the White House.

With both men anxious not to violate secrets, the lunch conversation at the Supreme Court in late January began with some awkward fencing. The Justice broached the subject with a "very oblique reference" to "X," to test whether Bohr was really knowledgeable. The professor began to reply "in an innocent remote way," but it quickly became clear what both were talking about. Bohr explained how the atom's energy could become an instrument of peace and plenty rather than a permanent threat of war: "X might be one of the greatest boons to mankind or might become the greatest disaster." Bohr considered it unlikely that the Germans could make a bomb in time and they were certain to be defeated. The Russians were the real danger. Frankfurter promised he would try to get the President interested in Bohr's plan to approach them.

It was not hard. Once Roosevelt became reconciled to Frankfurter's knowledge of the bomb, he admitted to being "worried to death" about its control. They talked for an hour and a half, although Frankfurter two or three times indicated his readiness to leave.

The Justice said it might be "disastrous if Russia should learn on her own about X, rather than that the existence of X should be utilized by this country and Great Britain as a means of exploring the possibility of effective international arrangements with Russia." He also told the President that Bohr believed "it would not be too difficult" for the Russians to find out on their own how to make the bomb.

The President asked Frankfurter to arrange for Bohr to see him at the White House. Meanwhile, Bohr should "tell our friends in London" that FDR was "anxious to explore ways for achieving proper safeguards in relation to X." Frankfurter was delighted. The President had been "plainly impressed." Bohr would have a listener in the White House.

Bohr received the news from Frankfurter when he returned in March from another trip to Los Alamos. Excited at being called upon to exert his influence in the highest affairs of state, the Great Dane called on Lord Halifax, the British Ambassador in Washington. The usually somber Halifax became equally aroused and deemed FDR's message of such importance that he asked Bohr to deliver it to Churchill in person.

Shortly after arriving in London, Bohr received a startling invitation. Peter Kapitza, a Russian physicist and a friend since the days when both worked with Lord Rutherford at Cambridge, wrote from Moscow asking him to settle in Russia with his family and pursue "scientific work." Bohr submitted his long and "deepfelt"—but negative—reply to the British Secret Service for clearance. When he delivered his letter to the Russian Embassy and talked with the Soviet Counselor, he came away with the impression that the Russians knew of the American and British work on the bomb and that they wanted him to help with the Soviet nuclear effort. Bohr would have found most receptive listeners in Moscow.

Unhappily, Churchill, his designated listener in London, was set from the start to shut his ears to Bohr. Lord Halifax had alerted Sir John Anderson, the British Government's principal science manager and a member of the War Cabinet, who had transmitted and endorsed the sense of Bohr's views in a memorandum to the Prime Minister. Churchill had "peppered" it with negative comments. At the end he had scrawled, "I do not agree." He absolutely refused to say a word to the Russians about the bomb. He even rejected Anderson's request to brief his own War Cabinet.

Furiously involved in planning the invasion of Europe, only three weeks away, Churchill grumpily agreed to see Bohr at 10 Downing Street on May 16. He had heard of Kapitza's letter and was suspicious of Bohr's contacts with the Russians. Bohr, mistaking the courage of the Prime Minister's ringing speeches for political imagination, held the highest hopes. Anderson worried that "Bohr's mild, philosophical vagueness of expression and his inarticulate whisper may prevent his making the desperately preoccupied Prime Minister understand him," and he so informed Lord Cherwell, Churchill's personal science adviser, who would sit in on the meeting.

Anderson was right and Cherwell complicated the communications problem. Mumbling, as usual, Bohr wanted to build up his argument step by step, as he had proceeded with Frankfurter, Halifax, and Anderson. But Churchill quickly grew impatient. When Cherwell put in a remark on an extraneous subject, he inadvertently set off an argument with Churchill that took up most of the half-hour allotted to Bohr, who sat by silently. He was never given time to make his case for sharing atomic information with the Russians; or to mention that Roosevelt had personally told him he would welcome British suggestions for international control of atomic energy; or, perhaps most important, to emphasize that he did not wish to share any information until after a safe control mechanism was in place.

Leaving, Bohr inquired whether he might send the Prime Minister a memorandum developing these points.

"It will be an honor for me to receive a letter from you," replied Churchill, greatly annoyed that his time had been wasted, "but not about politics."

Much more than the meeting of two minds had been at stake. A course was set for decades to come. It was one of the few truly fateful turning points in history. A breakthrough toward disarmament had been possible for a moment. The opportunity to avoid the outbreak of an arms race had been missed. No better chance would ever come again.

Bohr did not give up. On his return to Washington he reported his galling experience to Frankfurter, who hurried to tell Roosevelt about it. FDR responded with one of his characteristic gestures: he threw his head back and laughed. He knew what happened to people who tried to reason with Winston in one of his bellicose moods. FDR still wanted to listen to Bohr. To prevent another misadventure, he asked to see a memorandum from the professor in preparation for their meeting.

Washington was insufferably hot and humid in those late June days. The temperature exceeded 90 degrees by 10 a.m. and very few buildings were air-conditioned. In his hotel room, Bohr paced and dictated his memorandum to Aage, his scientist son. The father revised and kept revising. The son typed and retyped. The seven-page memorandum that went to the White House on July 3 was styled in Bohr's convoluted prose, but its reasoning was acute.

It called for "most urgent attention" to the proposition that possession of the bomb was meaningless: "Unless, indeed, some agreement about the control of the use of the new active materials can be obtained in due time, any temporary advantage, however great, may be outweighed by a perpetual menace to human security." The reward for action would be priceless: "Without impeding the immediate military objectives, an initiative, aiming at forestalling a fateful competition, should serve to uproot any cause of distrust between the

powers on whose harmonious collaboration the fate of coming generations will depend."

On August 26 Bohr was ushered into the President's Oval Office,
and neither the ambiance nor the substance of their meeting could
have differed more radically from the professor's encounter with
Churchill. The invasion of Normandy had turned into a triumph;
Allied forces had broken out of the beachheads and just liberated
Paris. The President was relaxed, cheerful, and seemed to have unlimited time. Smiling expansively behind his gadget-laden desk, he
welcomed Bohr with a sweep of his famous cigarette holder. No one
else was present.

Grinning mischievously, FDR said he had heard about the fiasco
with Churchill; Winston was sometimes hard to handle but even his
notoriously resistant stands against Stalin could sometimes be
changed. The President told several amusing stories of his successful
mediation between the two unfriendly allies during the summit conference at Teheran. Bohr felt like an insider.

The President claimed to share Bohr's optimism about the future
of atomic energy. He appeared to agree that the Russians should be
approached and told a story to illustrate his belief that Stalin was a
realist; the Russian dictator was certain to understand the atomic
stakes. FDR would discuss the matter with Churchill at their meeting
in Quebec, scheduled for September.

Bohr had been told of FDR's charm and his ability to make visitors think he agreed with them when he disagreed or had not yet
made up his mind. But the Great Dane thought that on this occasion
the President had been too explicit to be misunderstood in the
course of their seventy-five-minute conference. Bohr was elated. He
had reached the ear of the world's most powerful listener. The "fateful competition" of an armaments race, the scourge that would afflict
generations, seemed avoidable.

Perhaps the statesmen should authorize the scientists to make the
first approach to the Russians. These feelers would commit the statesmen to nothing. On September 7 Bohr wrote the President a follow-up letter with this additional suggestion. He also drafted a letter
to his Russian contact, Kapitza, and held himself in readiness to go
to Moscow to open negotiations.

He underestimated Churchill's stubbornness. The Quebec meetings having concluded, as the Prime Minister phrased it, in a "blaze of friendship," he and FDR closeted themselves in a small, stuffy room at the Roosevelt estate in Hyde Park, New York, on Monday, September 18, to talk about the bomb. The outcome was a 127-word *aide-mémoire* rejecting Bohr's suggestion for an early attempt to control atomic energy and also casting doubt, for the first time, on whether the bomb should be used in the war at all.

"The matter should be regarded as of the utmost secrecy," it said, "but when a 'bomb' is finally available, it might perhaps, after mature consideration, be used against the Japanese, who should be warned that this bombardment will continue until they surrender."

Moreover, Churchill had turned Roosevelt so violently against Bohr and his works that, suddenly, the Great Dane had been branded as a most dangerous character.* "Inquiries should be made regarding the activities of Professor Bohr and steps taken to ensure that he is responsible for no leakage of information, particularly to the Russians," the memorandum concluded.

On his return to England, Churchill further expressed his fixation against Bohr in a memorandum to Lord Cherwell, the science adviser. "The President and I are much worried about Professor Bohr," he railed. "How did he come into the business? He is a great advocate of publicity. He made an unauthorized disclosure to Justice Frankfurter who startled the President by telling him he knew all the details. He said he is in close correspondence with a Russian professor, an old friend of his in Russia to whom he has written about the matter and may be writing still. The Russian professor has urged him to go to Russia in order to discuss matters. What is this all about? It seems to me Bohr ought to be confined or at any rate made to see that he is very near the edge of mortal crimes."†

---

* How Churchill accomplished FDR's dramatic turnabout remained cloaked in secrecy. The *aide-mémoire* itself did not turn up until after Roosevelt's death; it had been misfiled with naval papers. In 1963, Oppenheimer told the historian Alice Kimball Smith that he believed the Hyde Park decision was based on "a substantial if not total misunderstanding of what Bohr was after." In particular, the statesmen did not seem to realize that Bohr, that most deliberate of men, envisioned agreement on verifiable safeguards *prior* to any disclosure of sensitive information.

† Nothing came of all this. Halifax and Cherwell came to Bohr's defense because both "felt strongly that the great P.J. [Panjandrum Churchill] was barking up an imaginary tree."

. . .

Roosevelt never received Bohr again but sent him to see Vannevar Bush. Bohr was dismayed, but he had in fact made inroads in the single-mindedness that had pervaded the pursuit of the bomb regardless of consequences. The President had come to realize the need for some explicit policy on the use of the bomb in the war and its control afterward. On Friday, September 22, he summoned Bush to the White House, and after the science adviser had assured him that Bohr was reliable the President mused about the future of S-1. Should the bomb be dropped on the Japanese outright or tested in the United States and held in reserve as a threat?

Bush allowed that this required careful discussion. It was the first time the bomb was being appraised as a political as well as a military weapon.

What about postwar controls? Lord Cherwell being present, Bush did not feel free to tell the President that he had come to agree with Bohr. He and Conant had been thinking along the same lines: the Russians would have to be kept from developing the bomb secretly and, perhaps twenty years hence, becoming tempted to trigger a catastrophic conflict. International control was the best answer. Instead of speaking out, Bush offered to tell Secretary of War Stimson that the President would like to discuss these subjects with him.

When Bush called on Stimson at the Pentagon the following Monday, the Secretary was not optimistic about holding Roosevelt's attention long enough for a discussion in depth on S-1. The President was visibly ailing, possibly failing. Stimson would try. Bush took a closer look at Stimson, who had just turned seventy-eight and was running the greatest war effort in world history. The Secretary looked frail and tired. Bush suggested that he and Conant draft some brief proposals for Stimson to take to FDR. Stimson accepted eagerly.

Only five days later, on September 30, 1944, Bush and Conant sent Stimson three documents predigested for an exhausted Secretary and a mortally ill President. One argued the case for international controls in detail. The second did the same but briefly. The third was a covering letter reducing all the policy questions to a few sentences for Stimson to take in at a glance.

The Bush-Conant analysis was remarkably prescient. The bomb would be ready before August 1, 1945, but any nation with good scientific and technical resources could overtake the United States and Britain in three or four years. Attempting to protect security through secrecy would be useless. Controls on raw materials would be unworkable. All but the military and manufacturing details of the bomb should be disclosed as soon as its feasibility was demonstrated. Echoing Bohr's advice, Bush and Conant proposed free interchange of all scientific information through an international organization whose technical staff should have access to all laboratories, military establishments, and industrial plants in the world.

A first use of the bomb against a city was excluded in this scenario. A "demonstration" was to precede a military drop. "This demonstration might be over enemy territory, or in our own country," Bush and Conant proposed, "with subsequent notice to Japan that the [nuclear] materials would be used against the Japanese mainland unless surrender was forthcoming."

In December, the concept of a demonstration was fleshed out further for Roosevelt by the ubiquitous Alexander Sachs, who had kept on churning out more of his exercises in "prehistory" since he first briefed FDR about the bomb in 1939. Sachs broke down the introduction of atomic power into two initial stages: first a "test" to make certain that the bomb worked, then a "rehearsal demonstration" to show off its violence.

The key provisions of his scenario outlined a careful step-by-step procedure: "Following a successful test, there should be arranged (a) a rehearsal demonstration before a body including internationally recognized scientists from all Allied countries and, in addition, neutral countries, supplemented by representatives of the major (religious) faiths; (b) that a report on the nature and the portent of the atomic weapon be prepared by the scientists and other representative figures; (c) that thereafter a warning be issued by the United States and its allies in the Project to our major enemies in the war, Germany and Japan, that atomic bombing would be applied to a selected area within a designated time limit for the evacuation of human and animal life, and, finally (d) in the wake of such realization of the efficacy of atomic bombing an ultimatum demand for immediate surrender by the enemies be issued . . ."*

* The quotation is from the summary Sachs prepared for the Pentagon after the war. The original memorandum was lost or destroyed, evidently in the White House.

According to Sachs, the President, exhausted from campaigning for an unprecedented third term, "nodded his agreement" to these proposals. Sachs also recalled that the President was becoming "yonderly minded"; FDR's sentences were punctuated by lengthening pauses during which the President acted detached to the point of seeming not to be present.

The momentous events of the ensuing months left little time for planning the future of the bomb. The Germans made a surprise lunge to stave off defeat with a winter offensive that turned into the Battle of the Bulge. The Russians aggravated Roosevelt and Churchill with their aggressiveness at the Yalta Conference in February 1945. The United Nations was scheduled to be founded in San Francisco, starting in April, and Bush recommended to FDR that it be authorized to police nuclear activities throughout the world. But Stimson, the key action figure, did little to follow up about S-1.

"I only wish he had the vigor of youth when he is so badly needed," Bush said to Conant.

Shortly before noon on Thursday, March 15, the President finally called Stimson and asked him for lunch at the White House. The Secretary explained that the bomb was expected to be ready for testing in midsummer. Decisions were waiting to be made about its use and future control. Stimson explained the opposing schools of thought. Groves and the military wanted secrecy to continue. Bush and Conant favored free interchange of nuclear information and unrestricted access to laboratories around the world. Policy on these matters had to be settled by the time the bomb was ready for use, Stimson advised. The President agreed but did nothing. The Secretary never saw him again.

Bohr, meanwhile, had been working on yet another memorandum to the President. So diligently did he apply the lessons he had learned from his touchy excursions into high politics that he even fended off an offer of aid from his friend, the great—but too impractical—Albert Einstein.* Bohr knew he needed advice from clever politicians and therefore consulted Frankfurter and Halifax.

---

* Prompted by an old friend, a refugee scientist connected with the Metlab in Chicago, Einstein wrote Bohr on December 12, 1944, to suggest, remarkably, the very concept Bohr had urged on Roosevelt three months earlier: that the

Day One

On April 12, the gangling, spare Ambassador and the little Justice sought privacy by walking through Rock Creek Park, the pretty wooded ravine in northwest Washington. They reviewed the problem point by point. Who should take Bohr's new appeal to the President? How should Russian cooperation be secured and then managed?

It was a warm, almost cloudless spring day, and as they started to leave the park the peaceful scene was pierced by the sudden tolling of church bells. The ringing continued and grew until it seemed to fill the air all around them. People stopped to speak to others. Some froze where they stood, some started running, some wept. Frankfurter and Halifax stopped and listened to the circulating news. The President had died while resting at Warm Springs, Georgia.

"Odd, wasn't it," Frankfurter wrote Halifax later, "that our dear friend should have died the very time you and I were pooling our forebodings?"

The man with the vibrant laughter and the dancing cigarette holder had been listening to the forebodings of many voices on the bomb. Bohr the gentle scientist. Churchill the egomaniac Russophobe. Frankfurter the meddling humanist. Bush the agile science policy adviser. Sachs the outside braintruster. If Roosevelt had determined in his mind what he was going to do about his private forebodings on the bomb, he had told no one. And it no longer mattered. Whoever wanted to influence the nuclear future would have to gain the ear of his successor.

---

ranking scientists of the leading powers, including Kapitza in Russia, band together to avoid what Einstein called "a secret technical arms race." Einstein urged Bohr: "These men should bring combined pressure on the political leaders in their countries in order to bring about an internationalization of military power." On December 22, Bohr visited Einstein in Princeton and assured him, without mentioning details, that "the responsible statesmen in America and England were fully aware" of the dangers and opportunities created by the bomb, whereupon Einstein abandoned his efforts.

Eleven

Harry S. Truman: "A Little Boy on a Toboggan"

Admiral William D. Leahy walked into the Oval Office of the White House on the new President's first day in office, April 13, 1945, just as Harry S. Truman sat down in Roosevelt's chair. To Leahy, the chief White House military adviser, Truman looked as if he were only trying out the seat. He rolled back and forth on the coasters. Finally he rolled forward with a sigh to face the desk that had been swept clear of FDR's memorabilia. When Leahy placed a high stack of urgent papers before him, the papers with their problems assumed an incongruous dimension. They looked bigger than the thirty-third President behind FDR's desk.

Nobody could have filled Roosevelt's chair. He had been President for twelve years, longer than anyone. Revered as the smiling father figure who took the nation by the hand and led it out of the Great Depression, cursed as a dictator—"that man in the White House"—he personified the innovation and the cunning that held a generation in his spell. And he had had time, time to mature, time to prepare for the job. When FDR was Assistant Secretary of the Navy, Truman had been plowing the family acres near Independence, Missouri.

During Roosevelt's lifetime, Truman had told friends that he had quite deliberately expelled from his mind any thought that fate might force him to succeed to the chair of this exalted figure. Even after FDR's death, so he wrote to Mrs. Roosevelt, the bespectacled, neatly attired former senator continued to think of the deceased leader as

129

The President. So did everyone else. When Eleanor Roosevelt entered the East Room of the White House for FDR's funeral service, all dignitaries rose. Nobody stood for poor Harry Truman, for whom there had been no time to learn the job, for whom time had run out.

Greeting reporters at the Capitol, many of them old friends from his Senate days, he asked for commiseration with his lot. "Boys," he beseeched, "if you ever pray, pray for me now." Yet the most heartfelt prayers could hardly overcome Truman's most crippling handicaps. In later years he would be admired for his initiatives, his pluck, and the sign on his desk saying "The buck stops here." On entering office he understood that he needed to appear decisive, but his self-confidence was as low as his ignorance was great.

His experience in foreign affairs had remained nearly nil over the years.* Roosevelt had assigned only inconsequential errands to Vice President Truman and had told him not a thing about the bomb. Earlier, it had taken just a word over the phone from Jean O'Leary, Groves's assistant, to shoo away staff investigators for Truman's Senate committee from the doors of the Hanford atomic project, where they had turned up scenting excessive expenditures.

The bomb entered Truman's life swiftly; he had barely taken the oath of office. His swearing-in ceremony, at 7:09 p.m. on April 12, had lasted only a trifle more than one minute. The first cabinet meeting followed immediately. It was perfunctory; Truman was not close to Roosevelt's advisers. Silently, all filed out of the room except for the aged Secretary of War. Stimson asked to speak to Truman about "a most urgent matter" and briefly sketched the "immense project" that would give the country "a new explosive of almost unbelievable power."

Stimson remained so vague that the new President was understandably "puzzled." The next day his old Senate crony James F. Byrnes

* The dangers facing the nation while a new President learns his job are little understood. For a superbly trained newcomer like Roosevelt, most recently the Governor of New York, the honeymoon phase produced the sensational "hundred days" of New Deal reform legislation. For John F. Kennedy, inexperience was a root cause for his approving the disastrous invasion of Cuba at the Bay of Pigs. Truman was quickly intimidated by the onslaught of his unaccustomed burdens. "On my first full day as President I did more reading than I thought I ever could," he remembered.

dropped by and filled in some of the less subtle details.* The bomb could "destroy the whole world," conceded Jimmy Byrnes, but he felt cheerful about it on the whole. He recognized the diplomatic potential of the weapon for blackmail. It would be handy if the United States wanted to throw its weight around. Truman remembered his saying, "It might well put us in a position to dictate our own terms at the end of the war." Byrnes exercised much influence on the lonely President in those early days, especially about the Russians, who had begun communizing Poland in violation of the Yalta agreements; the President would need to stand up to these obstreperous people.

"I saw him daily, giving him what help I could," Byrnes recalled too modestly. Grateful and impressed, Truman asked Byrnes to become Secretary of State.† And when Vyacheslav Molotov called at the White House on the afternoon of April 23, Truman demonstrated his notoriously short temper for the Soviet Foreign Minister and gave him hell. Agreements had to be observed mutually, snapped the President; "a one-way street" would not be tolerated.

"I've never been talked to like that in my life," Molotov protested.

"Carry out your agreements and you won't get talked to like that," said Truman, feeling Byrnes's oats.

Stimson was meanwhile spending nearly three days closeted with his closest advisers, preparing at last to brief the President fully on the bomb and its implications. In the final week of April the decision-making apparatus was still stuck where Stimson and Roosevelt had abandoned it after their last meeting, in mid-March; it hung in limbo. The test of the bomb was expected in less than three months. Nobody had decided whether the bomb should be used if it worked, and if so, how and where. The alternative to its combat use—an invasion of Japan—looked dreadful. General Marshall had come up with

---

* Byrnes had known about the bomb project since FDR had taken him into his confidence in 1943, but only seven congressional leaders of both parties were informed. Stimson briefed them in 1944 and revealed that the enormous appropriations were hidden in the War Department budget under "expediting production."

† A diligent student of history, Truman wanted Byrnes for more than the management of foreign affairs. With the vice presidency vacant, the Secretary of State would be first in line to succeed to the presidency. Truman recalled: "At this time I regarded Byrnes as the man best qualified."

a highly speculative prediction of 500,000 to possibly more than a million American casualties "if conventional weapons only were used."

To assist with his workload on S-1, Stimson had summoned two long-time intimates. The punctilious Harvey H. Bundy had been his Assistant Secretary of State during the Hoover days. The easygoing George L. Harrison, president of the New York Life Insurance Company, had known Stimson since World War I and had preceded Bundy as law clerk to Supreme Court Justice Oliver Wendell Holmes. As anonymous, convention-bound establishmentarians, Bundy and Harrison worshiped "the Colonel"; rarely disagreed with their austere leader; tended his papers on the bomb; and controlled the traffic to their chief's overloaded ear. They were his musketeers, but they were not ciphers. Given Stimson's physical frailties, the astute Groves, for one, often found it politic to deal with the influential Bundy instead.

Even with the aid of such loyal troops, it was difficult for Stimson to focus on the bomb for three days straight. Migraine headaches and intestinal complaints often kept him awake during these climactic months of his career. A good night's sleep was cause for jubilant entries in his diary. General Marshall tried to deal with him only during the mornings because in the afternoons the Secretary was usually sleepy. But Stimson carried on gamely, sometimes walking with a cane, always with all three buttons of his suit coat fastened, as if braced for a strong wind. Frequently he fled Washington for extended rests at Highhold, his estate on Long Island.

While Stimson did not try to predict how the new administration might decide to deal with the bomb, he was deeply troubled. His personal chemistry with its principals was not propitious. Byrnes thought the old gentleman was *passé*. Truman, still a farmer when Stimson served President William Howard Taft as Secretary of War from 1911 to 1913, probably sensed that the Colonel did not like him. They had not got along well in the past. "Truman is a nuisance and pretty untrustworthy man," the Secretary had written in his diary the previous year, after he finally had to exert the full power of his status to keep Senator Truman from snooping through the atomic laboratories. "He talks smoothly but acts meanly."

As a former trial lawyer and district attorney in New York, Stimson had long accepted "the need for infinite pains in preparation," and the 700-word memorandum he took to the White House at noon on April 25 received his infinite care. He wanted the President to enter the decision-making process knowledgeably. After all, Truman still knew almost nothing about the issues posed by the bomb, yet he could order the S-1 project's direction changed at will.

The staging of the meeting received equally delicate attention. Marshall absented himself, saying that the press would become too curious if he were to appear with both Stimson and Groves. Though it was not known whether the reporters suspected what the bulky General Groves was doing, Stimson decided to enter the President's office alone. The general was spirited to the west wing of the White House through a back door and underground passages and was ushered into the meeting a few minutes later.

Truman read Stimson's memorandum on the spot. "Within four months," it began, "we shall in all probability have completed the most terrible weapon ever known in human history, one bomb which could destroy a whole city." And that would be only the opening act of the nuclear drama. Stimson weighed the new technology against "the world in its present state of moral advancement" and warned: "Modern civilization might be completely destroyed."

The American monopoly could not last, the Secretary predicted, "although probably the only nation which could enter into production within the next few years is Russia." International control of the weapon would be exceedingly difficult: "No system of control heretofore considered would be adequate to control this menace." Yet "the question of sharing it with other nations and, if shared, upon what terms, becomes a primary question of our foreign relations."

Stimson did not touch at all on the issue of using the bomb against Japan. Much less did he question whether such a drop was wise or necessary. He did not mention the option of a nonviolent demonstration. He stopped short of advocating international control. He offered no steps toward a postwar policy. He also did not allude to a problem that was placing blinders on all the President's advisers and rendered their discussions sterile: the widening communications gap between the technicians and the policy makers.

The unique new technical and operational problems arising from the bomb had grown so complex that the two sides were not speaking the same language. "Don't tell me all this," Stimson had begged

Groves when the general tried to brief him that month. "I don't understand a word you're saying!" General Marshall, widely admired for his intellect, had started to steep himself in papers on S-1 but sent them all back after three hours because he could not penetrate them.

For the first time in history decision makers had become so helplessly dependent on the arcane wisdom of specialists that they could no longer inject relevant questions. So no one asked before or during Truman's briefing whether anything other than the scope of the bomb's destructiveness was unique about it, and the 24-page report that Groves handed the President after he had finished reading the Stimson memorandum was also silent about a unique qualitative characteristic of the weapon, *radioactivity,* never before used in warfare.

Groves limited himself to unsophisticated background facts and impending scheduling. Early in July, Oppenheimer should be able to test an implosion weapon at Alamogordo, New Mexico. About August 1, the first gun-type bomb, called Little Boy, should be ready and would need no test. A second implosion bomb, called Fat Man, should be ready that month. A special Air Force unit was in training and would by then be capable of dropping the bombs.

Truman was becoming impatient. Stimson and Groves had trouble persuading him to finish reading the general's report. Repeatedly the President put it down and said, "I don't like to read papers." The visitors managed to urge him on. Stimson argued, "Well, we can't tell you this in any more concise language. This is a big project."

The President raised not one question at any time during the 45-minute session. To advise on the "various questions" about the handling of the bomb, he approved the appointment of an *ad hoc* Interim Committee. Stimson would be chairman but Byrnes, as the President's personal representative, would have a powerful voice. The issue of using the bomb during the war was not addressed at all during the President's briefing.

No doubt frightened by the potential casualties of an invasion and eager to shorten the war, Truman was not about to commit domestic political suicide and leave unused a $2-billion bomb that could save American lives. Besides, the revered FDR was not known to have considered any action other than using the bomb. And so Truman told Stimson and Groves to continue on their current course, as if the unrestricted use of the bomb had been national policy determined by Roosevelt. Nobody pointed out that FDR had left behind no policy at all.

The slide toward the bomb's use was now in motion. Truman's position was set. "He was like a little boy on a toboggan," Groves said with his usual tactlessness after the war.

Part 4

Dealing with the Doubts

Twelve

The Scientists: First Reservations

Unaware of Bohr's explorations, Leo Szilard, the restless Chicago prophet, had also been maneuvering for a hearing from Roosevelt to exert pressure on behalf of much the same arguments. Trailed by Groves's security agents, he went to Princeton on March 25, 1945, to enlist the help of Einstein, just as he had turned to his old collaborator in 1939, and Einstein handed him a letter of introduction to FDR.

"[Dr. Szilard] now is greatly concerned about the lack of adequate contact between scientists who are doing this [secret nuclear] work and those members of your cabinet who are responsible for formulating policy," Einstein wrote. Fearing that a direct approach to the President would fail, Szilard sent Einstein's letter to Mrs. Roosevelt, who gave him an appointment at the White House for May 8.

Unlike Bohr, who spoke only for his conscience, Szilard represented an aroused constituency within Arthur Compton's Metlab. With most of their war work completed, the Chicago scientists were gravely engrossed in concern about the future. They could spare more time for contemplation than the bomb makers of Los Alamos, and Szilard kept stirring up their fears with memos and discussions.

His thinking had changed greatly since the 1930s. Starting out as a childlike tinkerer "playing around" with physics, he had been converted by the Nazi menace into a carping, abrasive critic who hounded Bush to speed up the bomb project. Only a demonstration of the bomb's "destructive power [that] has deeply penetrated the mind of the public" would do. Such a demonstration could not be the mere muscle flexing envisioned by Bush. Only bombs that "have actually been used in this war" would Szilard consider convincing.

Even some of his adherents found Leo's gyrations hard to follow. "He was a wild man," said Hans Bethe.

Bush handled the wild man gingerly. He wanted no trouble from his worried charges in Chicago. In March the busy science czar set aside an entire day in his P Street office to listen to Leo's complaints. Alienated by Szilard's gossipy private intelligence system, his cantankerous manner, and his insistence on raking over obsolete grievances of earlier years, Bush listened patiently and tried to placate Szilard by assuring him he might feel different if he knew of secret moves being pursued outside Chicago—secrets that Bush could not share with him.*

Writing Bush off as a bureaucrat with a closed mind, Szilard cultivated his Chicago power base. He circulated a 13-page memorandum asking the Metlab staff to consider "collective action." His ideas kept revolving and by spring of 1945 he had turned himself into a dove. When the Russians captured Berlin on May 2, the international situation had taken a new turn. What were the implications of using the bomb against Japan, then a second-rate power with no nuclear capability?†

To prepare himself for a meeting with Roosevelt, Szilard unfolded ferocious intellectual activity along more technical and sophisticated lines than Bohr had marshaled. In a lengthy draft memorandum he prophesied new dangers still mortifying the world forty years later: a highly urbanized United States was more vulnerable to atomic destruction than Russia with its fewer large population centers; atomic competition between the two powers could invite a preventive war; for international controls "to be effective, it would be necessary that our agents and the agents of Great Britain move freely around in

---

* "I think Szilard is interested primarily in building a record on the basis of which to make a 'stink' after the war is over," Conant told Bush.
† General Groves and other bomb advocates later charged that Szilard and his European fellow refugees lost interest in the bomb as soon as the charred remains of their personal nemesis, Hitler, were found in Berlin. But Szilard argued that the scientists' original enthusiasm for the bomb had been motivated by self-defense—the specific fear of a Nazi bomb.

Russia"; the Russians would have to be strong-armed, perhaps even tricked, into cooperation.

A further memorandum destined for Roosevelt warned: "Perhaps the greatest immediate danger which faces us is the probability that our 'demonstration' of atomic bombs will precipitate a race in the production of these devices between the United States and Russia."

Prepared to be scolded again for wildcatting outside official channels, Szilard showed his presidential briefing materials to Compton in the director's office, Room 208 in Eckart Hall. The Metlab chief read them with care and, to Szilard's astonishment, said, "I hope that you will get the President to read this." Elated, Szilard went back to his own office. Within five minutes, Norman Hilberry, Compton's assistant, came in and reported a flash that had just come over the radio: President Roosevelt was dead.

Hunting for the ear of the new President, Harry S. Truman, a product of Democratic boss Tom Pendergast in Kansas City, Szilard discovered a young Metlab mathematician who had worked for the Pendergast machine to earn his way through graduate school. Together they traveled to Kansas City and three days later Szilard had an appointment at the White House. He showed Truman's appointments secretary a revised version of the memorandum he had prepared for Roosevelt and was told that the President would like him to see James F. Byrnes the next day, May 28, in Spartanburg, South Carolina.

Joined by two Metlab colleagues to buttress his credibility as spokesman of the Chicago scientists, Szilard took the night train south, again trailed by Groves's agents. He was mystified. Why would the President want him to see an old southern politician? He knew that Byrnes, sixty-six, had long been a friend of Truman in the same exclusive club, the United States Senate, and that his record in public service was awesome. Byrnes had been a Supreme Court Justice, and when Roosevelt called him away from the court to place him in charge of war mobilization he had given "Jimmy" the unofficial title of "Assistant President." But almost nobody knew that the natty, purse-lipped Byrnes, at the moment briefly a private citizen, was soon to be named Secretary of State and had been aware of it for more than a month.

Day One

In his Spartanburg home Byrnes read the memo that Szilard had intended for Roosevelt, but it took the visitors only a few minutes to discern that the ex-Justice would be difficult to influence on nuclear issues.

Szilard suggested that Russia might soon become an atomic power. Byrnes replied, "General Groves tells me there is no uranium in Russia." Szilard informed the ex-Justice that while Russia's supply of rich ore from Czechoslovakia might be limited, it was bound to possess considerable low-grade ore, which was almost as useful.

When Szilard proposed that the United States refrain from testing its bomb and give the Russians the impression that the project had not succeeded, ex-Senator Byrnes asked, "How would you get Congress to appropriate money for atomic energy research if you do not show results for the money which has been spent already?" He brought up his own earthier concern about the Russians—their expansion in Eastern Europe, including Szilard's native Hungary—and suggested that a demonstration of the bomb and American military power might make the Soviets more manageable.

Szilard was "completely flabbergasted." He thought that bomb rattling would greatly frighten and antagonize the Russians. And how could he communicate with this South Carolina politician mired in conventional thinking, unaware that the atom was about to revolutionize the world?

"Well, you come from Hungary," the future Secretary of State drawled on, "you would not want Russians to stay in Hungary indefinitely."

Szilard's "sense of proportion" was outraged. How could he be expected to worry about little Hungary when the bombing of Japan might start an atomic arms race that could destroy the United States and Russia? He reflected that the world would have been better off if he had become an American politician and Byrnes a Hungarian physicist; "there would then have been no atomic bomb and no danger of an arms race."

Just as Churchill found Bohr offensive and could not be bothered to comprehend the world as seen through a scientist's prisms, so Byrnes turned on Szilard with distaste. The politicians and the scientists were polarizing into two camps, each speaking its own language.

And in Szilard's case, his personality was not helpful. Byrnes found him too aggressive. "His general demeanor and his desire to participate in policy making made an unfavorable impression on me," he wrote later. To Edward Teller he complained that Szilard was "a terrible man" who dared to tell him what to do; scientists should know their place, the laboratory.

Wanting nevertheless to find some common ground, Byrnes asked Szilard what he thought of Oppenheimer. Szilard expressed admiration. Byrnes then asked one of the other scientists whether he would feel reassured to know that the following week Oppenheimer would meet in Washington with a new top policy-making group just summoned into existence by Secretary of War Stimson, the Interim Committee.* The scientist said Oppenheimer's participation would make him feel "far more comfortable." Outmaneuvered by Byrnes, Szilard fell silent.

Before going back to Chicago, he stopped in Washington and saw Oppenheimer, who was in town to meet with the committee. Szilard told Oppie that he thought it "would be a very serious mistake" to drop the bomb on Japanese cities and thereby alert the Russians to its power.

Oppenheimer disagreed. "The atomic bomb is shit," he said.

"What do you mean by that?" asked the amazed Szilard.

"Well, this is a weapon which has no military significance," Oppenheimer asserted with all the authority of a newly anointed military expert. "It will make a big bang—a very big bang—but it is not a weapon which is useful in war." Perhaps he meant that the sweep and inhumanity of its destructiveness would make it, like gas warfare, unacceptable once its potency had been shown; perhaps he simply wanted to get rid of Szilard. Oppie did add that the Russians should not be taken by surprise; they should be told about the bomb and that the United States intended to drop it on Japanese cities.

Szilard considered this form of communication with the Russians reasonable but incomplete. The Russians had to be brought around so they would cooperate in the postwar control of the bomb. This would require careful moves explicitly directed toward that end.

---

* By giving the group this innocuous name, Stimson sought to reassure Congress that the group was temporary and would not invade legislative turf.

Oppenheimer, unconvinced, asked, "Don't you think that if we tell the Russians what we intend to do and then use the bomb in Japan, the Russians will understand it?"

"They'll understand it only too well," said Szilard, meaning that they would feel threatened. Szilard also understood something else: unlike most of his Chicago colleagues, Oppenheimer seemed to have developed a stake in the use of force. He had become committed to the very big bang. Just as Byrnes wanted to justify the expense of the bomb project to Congress, Oppie wanted to hit the Japanese and show off his sweet achievement.

On his return to Chicago, Szilard found the Metlab in uproar. One of his fellow visitors to Spartanburg, the popular Dr. Walter Bartky, later vice president of the University of Chicago, had been summoned and dressed down by Groves. Infuriated by Bartky's failure to repent, the general had demanded an explanation of the unauthorized mission from the usually conciliatory Compton, who fired back a vigorous four-page secret memorandum spelling out the root causes of the scientists' near-rebellion.

"I believe the reason for their action is that their responsibility to the nation is prior to and broader than their responsibility to the Army," Compton argued. "Having first conceived the idea, then having persuaded the nation to undertake its development, and finally having successfully made the new powers available for use, the scientists cannot be satisfied to remain without assurance that all possible is being done to insure their wise application."

Compton made clear that he considered the scientists' clamor reasonable: "They have had little assurance that serious consideration of [the atom's] broader implications is being given by those in a position to guide national policy. The scientists will be held responsible, both by the public and by their own consciences . . ."

The gentle Compton even permitted himself an attack on the Secretary of State for failing to explain the atomic dilemma to the founding conference of the United Nations, the prospective policeman of international nuclear control. "His appreciation was so limited as possibly to serve as a hazard to the country's welfare," Compton charged. He blamed Groves, who had briefed the State Department for the U.N. talks.

Dealing with the Doubts

Still another statesman among the scientists, Dr. James Franck, was influencing Compton powerfully all along. Like Bohr and Szilard, Franck was a European refugee (he was from Germany) whose conscience caused him to fret not only about the competence of his own war work but about its consequences. A Nobel laureate in 1925, he had been one of Oppenheimer's teachers at Göttingen.* Perpetually mournful-looking, Franck was retiring and unpretentious. His colleagues considered him something of a saint and called him "Pa." While he did not seek personal influence, he had been the very first scientist to think of leaping beyond normal channels to question atomic policy at the top of the government.

Indeed, Compton had been able to persuade Franck to take charge of the Metlab's chemistry section in 1942 only by agreeing to an extraordinary condition: if the bomb were to become ready before another nation had also developed it, Franck would be permitted to present his views about its use to someone at the highest policy-making level. With President Roosevelt dead and the war in Europe about to end, the time had come for Compton to redeem his promise.

Unaware of Bohr's earlier efforts with Churchill and FDR, Franck composed a seven-page memorandum summarizing the ideas circulating at the Metlab: Political leaders needed to realize that atomic power would make traditional competition between nations obsolete ("The future war has an entirely different and a thousand times more sinister aspect than the war which is fought now"); the scientists were confronted with an "intolerable" conflict "between our conscience as citizens and human beings and our loyalty to the oath of secrecy."

Though the Franck manifesto contained nothing new, it conveyed the sense of isolation and despair besetting the atomic pioneers of the Metlab.

Nobody paid attention. In violation of Groves's rules, Compton took Franck to Washington and arranged a breakfast meeting at the Wardman Park Hotel with his old friend Henry A. Wallace.† The former Vice President was now Secretary of Commerce. He had to

---

* During a lecture tour to Berkeley years later, Franck was cut down by Oppenheimer's arrogance. At a seminar, Oppie derided a question raised by his gentle old professor as "foolish."

† No doubt Compton and Franck would have been aghast if they had known one of Groves's ultimate (and never declassified) secrets: for about two years the general had some of the Vice President's meetings bugged.

rush off to other engagements and, at any rate, had no voice in foreign or military matters. After a brief discussion Franck presented Wallace with his memorandum. It wound up in the files of Vannevar Bush.

Disappointed, Compton decided on another effort to crash through the Washington sound barrier set up by Groves. He formed a committee of Metlab scientists to conduct a full study of the bomb's political and social implications. Franck was appointed chairman. Perhaps someone in Washington would pay attention the next time. The Chicagoans were agreed: no cause so vital could be abandoned at so seminal a time in history. And on Oppenheimer's mesa, reservations were also being heard.

Thirteen

A Harmless Demonstration of the Bomb: Death of an Option

Bundled up in his mackinaw, Robert Wilson trudged through the snow and posted notices all over the Tech Area laboratories of Los Alamos. The young group leader who had been recruited by Oppenheimer together with his Princeton team was calling a meeting in "X Building," the cyclotron lab, for an unprecedented discussion. His topic: "The Impact of the Gadget on Civilization." He knew nothing of the agitation in Chicago.

Talks with Niels Bohr, whom he revered as the conscience of the physicists, had stirred Wilson's own conscience. Bohr was communicating only with a handful of leaders. Wilson thought that more of the bomb builders should be giving thought to the morality of what they were constructing.

As soon as Oppenheimer spotted Wilson's announcements he called him into the director's office and asked him to cancel the meeting. Surprised, Wilson asked why. The security people wouldn't like it, said Oppie. Wilson, the unreconstructed frontiersman from Wyoming, asked why it mattered whether the security people liked it or not. Oppie, taken off guard, reacted to this ingenuousness as if he had been jarred by a "bombshell." Wilson was startled; he couldn't understand why Oppenheimer should be so apprehensive about what the security people thought about a nonmilitary subject.* To hell with them. He was going ahead with his meeting, he said.

* Oppenheimer displayed considerable sensitivity about the concerns of Groves and his security people throughout the war. Only Kitty knew why. In later

Day One

Fewer than fifty scientists appeared for it in their heavy winter gear—an unimpressive turnout—but Oppenheimer came, which of itself turned the gathering into an occasion. Wilson was delighted to see their leader. His presence "added a certain tone to any meeting."

For this meeting Oppenheimer added a negative tone, but he injected it with so much cheer and finesse that nobody seemed to notice or care that their activism was being squelched.

The questions Wilson raised for the group were cosmic. Why were they working on the bomb at all when the defeat of the Germans was at hand? Was it morally right to continue? How would this "terrible object" change the world?

Oppenheimer broke in quickly with an ingenious—and wholly imaginary—scenario. The United Nations was going to be organized in a few months, he noted. It would be crucial for the bomb to be demonstrated beforehand. The results would be made public, or so Oppenheimer seemed to take for granted. People around the world would learn of its unimaginable destructive potential. They would be so awed that the statesmen would ban it forever. But if the bomb did not become a reality soon, the wily military would keep its existence secret until the next war and unleash it then. Therefore it was vital that the men at Los Alamos continue to work as hard as they could.

These visions appealed to Wilson and his conferees. Satisfied, they scattered into the cold. No further group discussions questioned the dedication of Los Alamos, and the unreality surrounding that cold night would linger. Wilson would not remember the date of the meeting, not even the month; or who, besides Oppenheimer, attended; or why none of the participants talked of ways to demonstrate the bomb harmlessly but convincingly.

And these failures were the least of what burdened him in later years. Why did he never consider walking away from the bomb, not even after the Germans were defeated? Why were they all acting "as automatons"? Why did he never call another meeting to examine the impact of their gadget more closely? "It simply was not in the air,"

---

years, when Oppie's colleagues learned that, as Wilson put it, the government "had so much on him," they came to understand what a convenient hold Groves possessed on Oppie to insure his good behavior. In 1945, Wilson believed that Oppie was trying to keep *him* from getting in trouble with security.

Dealing with the Doubts

Wilson remembered. "Our life was directed to do one thing, it was as though we'd been programmed to do that."

But the drive to build the bomb came also from within the scientists' souls. "We were the heroes of our epic," Wilson wrote, "and there was no turning back."

So he worked seven days a week and into the night, until he "would nearly drop," going home just for a few hours of sleep, unswervingly "directed" to do that one thing. Why? Was everyone in the Los Alamos mountains going "crazy," as Szilard had predicted when the lab was organized? Was it that each one, certainly Wilson, considered himself "an Oppenheimer man" doing Oppenheimer's will?

Perhaps they were just being human. "To have asked us to pull back at that moment," Wilson reflected, "would have been as unrealistic and unfair as it would be to ask a pugilist to sense intellectually the exact moment his opponent has weakened to the point where he will eventually lose, and then to have the responsibility of stopping the fight just at that point."

Yet the issue of the bomb's overwhelming power—and of the moral rights to unleash that power—would not stay quiescent. Doubts bobbed up all over Los Alamos throughout the spring and summer of 1945, never in a coherent way, always in fleeting, isolated private encounters, like occasional bubbles percolating in water kept slightly below the boiling point. And as the founding conference of the United Nations passed without the bomb being ready, and the race grew more frenzied to get the weapon to work in time to make its weight felt at the Big Three conference in Potsdam in mid-July, the issue narrowed to one word: demonstration.

In his office, Oppenheimer brought it up with his old friend and confidant Bob Bacher, that steady hand, now associate director of the lab. Even General Groves trusted Bacher and had okayed him as Oppie's liaison with the Metlab. Inevitably Bacher brought word of the unrest in Chicago and how Leo Szilard, James Franck, and their friends argued that the bomb was not needed to win the war. "How do we know?" Oppenheimer asked Bacher. The question answered itself. Nobody knew, and it seemed improper for the scientists to pose as experts on the subject.

Though it was Oppenheimer who mentioned the possibility of demonstrating the bomb harmlessly for the Japanese before using it in earnest, he did it lightly, as if this question also answered itself. There was no discussion. As Bacher summed up their conclusion: "Once you know how to make the bomb it's not your business to figure out how not to use it." Modesty was uncommon with Oppie, but Bacher did not question his friend's motives.

When the crusty little Isidor Rabi settled down in Oppie's office for one of his periodic consultations—he invariably arrived in the desert country with umbrella and galoshes regardless of season—Oppenheimer contemplated the demonstration option with this senior adviser. Unlike Bacher, Rabi was no mere colleague. He was six years older than Oppie, already a relatively senior man when both did research in Hamburg in the 1920s. More worldly than Robert, Rabi coped better with the émigré scientists ("Oppie needed me to deal with the Hungarians"). And since he had an office in Washington, Rabi had also cultivated an understanding of the decision makers, particularly Groves, whom he dismissed as a "buffoon" and a "malaprop."

Rabi was convinced that the war was over, the Japanese as good as defeated. The United States should have relaxed in anticipation of their collapse. But it would have been stupid wishful thinking to expect the new President to sit back. Rabi could sense the determination in Washington to fight the Orientals: "They were not people one loves."

On the other extreme, the "Europeans" in Chicago were hopelessly "sentimental." They had no "feeling for the war." They were not earthy pragmatists like Rabi, who said proudly of himself: "I think with my hands." Szilard was brilliant but he scattered his ideas all over the place and didn't follow through on them; there were far too many of them anyway. It was hard to take Leo seriously. Compton was a weakling. To sway him one had only to appeal to his vanity.

Rabi's view was equally jaundiced about any attempt to sway the Japanese with a demonstration. He saw no way to shake them with such a maneuver. "This is absurd," he snapped at Oppenheimer. Why give away the element of surprise? It would be empty "fireworks." Only the destruction of a town would be "incontrovertible."

Who would evaluate a demonstration? The Emperor? He would never understand that new principles of physics had been mobilized. His warlords? They would suspect a ruse. The entire business was not worth serious analysis.*

Dr. Kenneth Bainbridge, the Harvard physicist in charge of the Trinity test at Alamogordo, approached Oppenheimer with an idea for demonstrating at least the bomb's blast effects so that the bomb builders could educate themselves. Bainbridge wanted to erect some buildings along radii expanding from the Ground Zero point of his desert site. Even this very limited demonstration was vetoed. Oppenheimer told Bainbridge that he had taken up the suggestion with Groves and that the general did not want to endanger security by importing civilian construction workers to the test area just to add a frill to the desired big bang.

By mid-June the demonstration alternative was corridor conversation throughout the Tech Area. Interest was building in developing methods to make the idea viable. Someone might have galvanized this desultory groping into an organized investigation. No one did so, but in the privacy of his office Oppenheimer was willing to listen to such individual soul searchers as Robert Wilson.

Oppenheimer told his young cyclotron group leader that he was serving on a panel making recommendations on the use of the bomb; the last chance for making suggestions was imminent. Wilson asked:

"Why not invite some Japanese observers to Trinity?"

"What if it's a dud?" countered Oppenheimer.

"Well, we could kill 'em all," said Wilson, not meaning it. He was venting his frustration at his inability to solve the problem reasonably

---

* Serious analysis was precisely what the demonstration option never received. In 1975, Rabi said, "You would have to have built a model town to make a realistic demonstration." In 1983, at eighty-five, Rabi could, forgivably, not be certain whether the concept of a model town had entered his 1945 discussion with Oppenheimer. In any event, an entire town would have been more than necessary—and at the same time not enough—to demonstrate the bomb convincingly. A few structures strategically placed around widening radii would have sufficed to display the blast effects. To demonstrate long-term radiation, a considerable number of large laboratory animals would have been required. Time would have been needed to stage all this effectively—time that the decision makers felt they could not spare if American war casualties were to be minimized.

and was aghast that such bloodthirsty—and pointless—words had come out of his mouth.

Talk of a demonstration would not subside. Outside his office, Bob Bacher was intercepted by one of his most thoughtful young physicists, Volney Wilson. An associate of Compton at the University of Chicago before the war, Wilson had originally had scruples about joining the S-1 project. He started at the Metlab only after he felt that a German A-bomb was a real threat. Now transferred to Los Alamos, Wilson proposed that with Germany defeated, the laboratory stop working on the bomb altogether.

Bacher said that would be dangerous; another Hitler might some day pick up where they stopped. It was vital to demonstrate the potency of the bomb. Whereupon Wilson proposed a spectacular international display before a gala audience. They should build a model city and invite all the world leaders, including Stalin, to watch one bomb destroy that city. Briefed by Oppenheimer, Bacher indicated that no such idea would win official approval but assured him that Oppie, whose judgment was considered trustworthy by all, was participating in the decision making.

The two men in charge of planning the actual bomb drop went so far as to mull over some of the technical problems that would turn any nonmilitary demonstration over Japanese territory into a complicated business.

Although Norman F. Ramsey was in many ways the most military of the scientists, he liked the demonstration concept. And he was highly knowledgeable. Ramsey served on the hush-hush Target Committee and directed the Delivery Group, whose work was the most secret of Los Alamos secrets.

With his boss, Deke Parsons, the Navy captain who was Oppenheimer's chief weapons specialist, Ramsey considered exploding the bomb over the sacred Mount Fujiyama or Tokyo Bay. The results would not be sufficiently impressive, they decided. (They were conducting their private deliberations prior to Trinity; that test demonstrated the overpowering visual impact of a nuclear explosion for the first time.)

Dealing with the Doubts

The mass destruction of buildings might impress the Japanese, but if they were given a warning in time to evacuate a city, their fighter planes might lie in wait and shoot down the plane carrying the bomb; Japan was too far from the nearest American base to provide fighter cover.

Ramsey was interested in protecting the moral stature of the United States, but how far could one carry one's concerns over spiritual values while young men were dying in the war? "You don't want to have extra people die to make yourself feel good," he said later. Extra people would also die as a result of the delay inevitably caused just by making arrangements for a demonstration, even if the end of the war were to be postponed by only a couple of weeks.

Finally Ramsey decided that his explorations were doomed anyway. A demonstration was not practical because it was not "saleable." The subject did not even enjoy "official recognition" within Los Alamos. How could high levels of the government be convinced that such a risky and time-consuming step was worth trying? The official climate was not right for it and that was that.

It would have been impossible to persuade the military to take the issue seriously. The physicist Philip Morrison discovered this by stopping an Air Force colonel of his acquaintance in the hallway of the administration building to urge that the Japanese be given a warning of an imminent bomb drop.

"You're not flying the airplane," said the colonel icily, which shamed the normally very vocal Morrison into permanent silence on the subject.

Beyond the Los Alamos and Chicago atomic enclaves the demonstration notion found isolated advocates as well. In Washington it was briefly championed by Szilard's old friend Lewis L. Strauss, the Wall Street financier, who had become an admiral on the staff of Navy Secretary James V. Forrestal. Strauss had once visited a large forest of cryptomeria trees at Nikko, a village not far from Tokyo. They were very tall trees with large boles, much like American redwoods. An atomic blast, he told Forrestal, "would lay the trees out in wind-rows from the center of the explosion in all directions as though they were matchsticks and of course set them afire in the center . . . A demonstration of this sort would prove to the Japanese that we could destroy any of their cities at will."

The admiral later recalled that "Forrestal agreed wholeheartedly with the recommendation," but no record exists that the Secretary communicated Strauss's thought to Secretary Stimson or President Truman.

One appeal did reach the top. It was the most emotional antibomb protest of the time and it came from a lone, lowly soul without contacts at the major laboratories: Oswald C. Brewster, a warmhearted, temperamental engineer for a Manhattan District contractor, the Kellex Corporation in New York. "Owl" Brewster, who had helped with early work on uranium isotope separation, had changed his mind about the bomb after Germany was defeated. His friends noticed that he had become greatly upset, but he would not say why. On May 24, he addressed a 3000-word letter to the President; a Manhattan Project security agent delivered it to Washington, where it wound up in Stimson's hands.

"This thing must not be permitted on earth," Brewster wrote. "We must not be the most hated and feared people on earth, however good our intent may be." He urged a demonstration before any combat use in Japan. "I beg of you, sir, not to pass this off because I happen to be an unknown, without influence or name in the public eye. . . . There surely are men in this country to whom you could turn, asking them to study this problem."

Stimson was much taken with Owl Brewster's torment; it reflected his own. He urged General Marshall to read "this remarkable document" and share "the impress of its logic." The Secretary then took the unusual further step of delivering the letter to Truman himself. Records show that it was returned from the White House on June 2 with no indication of any presidential reaction; it had become just another paper for the files.

In Berkeley, Mark Oliphant, the British emissary whose disgust at the lethargy of the original Uranium Committee had shaken his friend Ernest Lawrence into hurrying the bomb project along in 1942, had returned to sound the alarm once more. This time Oliphant transmitted his moral reservations about a surprise drop of the bomb. The two friends chatted about it privately but often—first casually, then with some urgency.

Oliphant had talked to another old friend and hero, Niels Bohr, in Washington and come away with qualms. The elegant, business-like Lawrence—ostensibly no soft touch for a proposal to muffle the bang of what he had helped to build—agreed that a demonstration was an idea to be pushed. It was in line with his own thinking.

"The bomb will never be dropped on people," he had told a Berkeley colleague earlier in the war. "As soon as we get it, we'll use it only to dictate terms of peace."

His talks with Oliphant did not address the problem beyond speculating whether it would help to have a bomb "blow the top off" Mount Fujiyama. But the value of the concept remained lodged in Lawrence's head. He would pull it out later and place it before the people who counted.

But the demonstration idea was dead. Oppenheimer would see to its burial in Washington.

Fourteen

The Interim Committee: Ten Fateful Minutes at Lunch

Secretary of War Stimson arrived at his Pentagon office relatively early on May 31—at 8:40 a.m. He was not enjoying the pleasantly warm, cloudless day. As so often, he confided to his diary that he was "feeling bum after a bad night," weighed down by lethargy. By 10 a.m. he would nevertheless have to steel himself for a most important confrontation. His S-1 Interim Committee—whose very existence was secret—was scheduled to meet for the first time with its new scientific advisory group: Oppenheimer, Compton, Fermi, and Lawrence.

Stimson had assembled an extensive agenda ("I prepared for the meeting as carefully as I could"), but, like his initial briefing memorandum for President Truman, the list of topics failed to reflect plain reality. It did not mention the most pressing questions facing the policy makers: whether in fact to use the bomb in the war, and, if so, whether first to stage a peaceful demonstration in the hope that it, along with fearful conventional bombings and the declining Japanese fortunes of war, might persuade the enemy to surrender.

For the regular committee members,* these curious omissions from Stimson's program would come as no surprise. They had al-

---

* Stimson was chairman, Harrison his alternate. Byrnes was the President's personal representative. The other members were: Bush, Conant, Under Secretary of the Navy Ralph A. Bard, Assistant Secretary of State William L. Clayton, and Karl T. Compton, president of the Massachusetts Institute of Technology (and Arthur Compton's brother). Groves enjoyed permanent guest privileges. General Marshall and others attended occasionally.

ready met three times, taking up such routine items as the atomic partnership with the British and the text of the press release that the President might issue after the bomb's initial stateside test, scheduled for July 4, "if the thing got out of hand." Only one question provoked "vehement" discussion. Bush and Conant estimated it would take the Russians four years to build a bomb; Groves predicted twenty years. Neither Stimson nor anybody on the committee or in the Secretary's office considered that Soviet postwar cooperation might become more difficult to obtain unless the Russians were assured of international control before the bomb was dropped on Japan. And nobody brought up the possibility that a surprise drop might create a moral liability for the United States.

Impressed by the bomb's overwhelming cost, hardened to the terrible enemy casualties routinely inflicted by American fire raids, and frightened by the potential bloodshed of an invasion of Japan, now scheduled for November 12, the committee plodded on under the unspoken assumption that the bomb was a conventional legitimate weapon; that war-weary American voters would want it used promptly; that its drop would soften up the Russians at the negotiating table and jolt the Japanese into a quick surrender.

Under General Groves's watchful eye, the group invested all its time in secondary issues.* Groves was pleased. To him, dropping the bomb was not in question. Only the possibility of delay haunted him. As he said after the war, "The best way I can think of to have delayed the project would have been to start discussing throughout the project: 'Shall we use the bomb or not when we get it?' " Instead he silently applauded the mounting momentum for unquestioned use of the bomb and, in internal discussions, ridiculed the notion of a peaceful demonstration because it would dissipate the surprise element as well as a key sting of the weapon: its enormous shock value.

* The Interim Committee was another intriguing demonstration of "Groupthink." The term was coined in 1965 by Irving L. Janis, professor of psychology at Yale University. He applied it to historical events that went out of control: the bombing of Pearl Harbor, the escalation of the Vietnam war, the invasion of Cuba at the Bay of Pigs. Janis showed how leaders, when under pressure and cut off by secrecy restrictions from relevant information, can turn themselves into a blinded herd and gallop off in the wrong direction. Janis was not alone with his interpretation. Elting E. Morison, Secretary Stimson's biographer, had become convinced by 1960 that Stimson and his inner circle were "moved, without perhaps a full awareness, toward a predictable conclusion by the *inertia* [emphasis added] developed in a human system."

Reservations did bubble under the committee's placid surface, but not strongly. One member, Navy Under Secretary Ralph A. Bard, was becoming concerned about using the bomb without warning but did not press the issue. In a 42-page memorandum that Arthur Compton submitted to the committee three days before its May 31 meeting, the Metlab director called the question of the bomb's use "first in point of urgency," but Stimson and the committee continued to behave as if it had been settled and required no discussion.

Ever the diplomat, Compton had allowed in his memo that "This whole question may have received the broad study it demands," but during the morning session on May 31—sixteen men were seated around the conference table in Stimson's office—he saw no evidence of any study, either past or anticipated. "It seemed to be a foregone conclusion that the bomb would be used," Compton recalled later.

Stimson's introductory rhetoric elevated the bomb onto a high level. He wanted to impress on Oppenheimer and the other members of the Science Panel that he "did not regard it as a new weapon but as a revolutionary change in the relations of man to the universe" and "that we were looking at this like statesmen and not like merely soldiers anxious to win the war at any cost." The bomb must not become "a Frankenstein which would eat us up."

The ensuing discussion was less lofty and once again remarkable for what was not said. Compton sketched the future of nuclear weaponry, including the hydrogen bomb, which, so Oppenheimer added, would require not much more than three years to develop. Oppenheimer predicted that the first bombs would pack an explosive force of 2000 to 20,000 tons of TNT, the later models up to 100,000,000 tons. The figures sparked no discussion. Neither did Oppenheimer's estimate that 20,000 people* would be killed in an A-bomb attack on a city.

A lively debate on how to deal with the Russians took up much of the morning. Bush and Conant stuck by their earlier guesses that it would take the Russians four years to build a bomb. Compton guessed six years. Groves repeated his prediction of twenty years. Oppenheimer, drawing on Bohr's thoughts during their talks in Los Alamos, suggested that the United States feel out the Russians about joining

---

* This extremely low estimate assumed that much of the population would have been able to seek shelter.

in a system of international controls. They should be approached without being told details of progress already achieved in this country, but the contact should be sought promptly. "If we were to offer to exchange information before the bomb was actually used, our moral position would be greatly strengthened," he said.

The word "moral" had finally been dropped into the discussion, if only in a very limited context: the timing of the bomb's combat use. At no time did Oppenheimer, Compton, Fermi, or Lawrence speak up during the meeting to inform the Interim Committee of the grave moral doubts tormenting many of the scientists in Chicago and a few of those in Los Alamos.

The climate around the table was, at any rate, not suitable for non-belligerent attitudes. General Marshall, that civilized warrior, discovered this when he agreed with Oppenheimer. The Russians should not be prejudged, Marshall argued. Their apparently uncooperative stance reflected their feelings of insecurity. Why not allow two prominent Soviet scientists to witness the bomb test scheduled for Alamogordo, New Mexico, next month?*

Jimmy Byrnes, the President's man, who had said little up to this point, intervened sharply. If the United States were to give information to the Russians even in the most general terms, he insisted, they would demand admission into the American-British atomic partnership. Bush noted that even the British had never been given blueprints of the American plants. Byrnes was adamant. He wanted secrecy and utmost speed in production and research efforts to insure that the United States stayed ahead and dominant in the nuclear

* Only two days earlier, on May 29, the thoughtful Marshall had tried to impress on Stimson the importance of "warning" the Japanese prior to a military bomb drop. The occasion was a meeting in the Secretary's office with Assistant Secretary of War John J. McCloy, who made a memorandum of Marshall's statement which the general later approved: "General Marshall said he thought these weapons might first be used against straight military objectives such as a large naval installation and then if no complete result was derived from the effect of that, he thought we ought to designate a number of large manufacturing areas from which people would be warned to leave—telling the Japanese that we intended to destroy such centers. There would be no individual designations so that the Japs would not know exactly where we were to hit—a number should be named and the hit should follow shortly after." Marshall emphasized the moral value of giving the Japanese advance notice. "Every effort should be made to keep our record of warning clear," the memorandum specified. "We must offset by such warning methods the opprobrium which might follow from an ill-considered employment of such force."

field. No objections were heard and Marshall's suggestion was quickly dropped.

At about 1:20 p.m. everyone in the group except Marshall adjourned for lunch to a dining room across the hall from Stimson's office. The conferees were split up among four tables, making general discussion impossible. R. Gordon Arneson, an army lieutenant who worked in Bundy's office and maintained meticulous minutes of all the Interim Committee's formal sessions, took no notes.* Yet at one of those tables, accommodating Stimson, Byrnes, Oppenheimer, Lawrence, Groves, and possibly others, the option of harmlessly demonstrating the first atomic bomb for the Japanese received the only top-level attention it would ever get.

As Lawrence remembered it, Byrnes asked him to elaborate on a proposal for such a demonstration which Lawrence said he had briefly offered during the morning session.† No one subsequently questioned that the ensuing luncheon discussion was superficial, totally negative, took up no more than ten minutes, and meandered along as if nobody had ever thought about a demonstration before.

Compton later reconstructed the table thoughts this way: "If a bomb were exploded in Japan with previous notice, the Japanese air power was still adequate to give serious interference. An atomic bomb was an intricate device, still in the developmental stage . . . If during the final adjustments of the bomb the Japanese defenders should attack, a faulty move might easily result in some kind of failure. Such an end to an advertised demonstration of power would be much worse than if the attempt had not been made."

Only one bomb would be available at first, as Compton summarized the discussion, and what if it were a dud? And more: "If the test were made on some neutral territory, it was hard to believe that Japan's determined and fanatical military men would be impressed.

---

* After the war Arneson became adviser on nuclear problems to Secretary of State Dean Acheson.
† Recollections of this luncheon conversation differ somewhat. Although the minutes of the morning meeting contain no reference to such a proposal by Lawrence, he reconstructed the luncheon discussion in a letter to a friend, a science historian, on August 17, 1945. Only one other eyewitness account exists. In his 1963 memoirs, *Atomic Quest,* Compton recalled that it was he, sitting at Stimson's left, who brought up the subject by asking the Secretary whether a nonmilitary demonstration was feasible and that "the Secretary opened this question for general discussion by those at the table."

If such an open test (over Japanese territory) were made first and failed to bring surrender, the chance would be gone to give the shock of surprise that proved so effective. On the contrary, it would make the Japanese ready to interfere with an atomic attack if they could."

The outcome of the discussion, as Compton saw it, was final: "No one could suggest a way in which [a demonstration] could be made so convincing that it would be likely to stop the war."

Lawrence remembered two additional aspects: nobody at the luncheon table considered that the character of the bomb differed from that of conventional weaponry; and it was Oppenheimer who dominated the negative evaluation of the demonstration option and carried the conversational ball that rolled over the idea and killed it. As he described the conversation to a historian friend just after the war: "(a) the number of people that would be killed by the bomb would not be greater in order of magnitude than the number already killed in fire raids and (b) Oppenheimer could think of no demonstration that would be sufficiently spectacular to convince the Japs that further resistance was useless. Oppenheimer felt, and that feeling was shared by Groves and others, that the only way to put on a demonstration would be to attack a real target of built-up structures."

Byrnes administered a last chilling squelch that stopped the abortive table talk: "If the Japanese were told that the bomb would be used on a given locality, they might bring our boys who were prisoners of war to that area."

As if the luncheon thoughts had blown away a blanket of fog, accidentally baring immediate problems for the first time, Stimson ordered a new turn in his agenda when the group returned to his office at 2:15 for another formal session. The surprise drop of the bomb having been all but formally assured, he wanted the committee's views on its probable effects upon the Japanese and their will to fight.

Again someone pointed out that the destructive impact "would not be much different from the effect caused by any Air Corps strike of present dimensions." However, Oppenheimer predicted that the visual effect would be "tremendous" and that the "brilliant luminescence" would rise 10,000 to 20,000 feet. And for the first time the unprecedented use of radiation was mentioned. Oppenheimer said that its effects "would be dangerous to life for a radius of at least two-thirds of a mile." The legitimacy of radiation as a weapon and the possibility of lingering illness from radiation were not mentioned.

Oppenheimer's observations caused no stir because he and the committee grossly underestimated the strength of their nuclear muscle. Indeed, they proceeded to consider the "desirability" of attacking several targets at once. Oppenheimer, emerging as the most enthusiastic hawk among these hawks, liked the idea. It was Groves, of all people, who cautioned against it for three reasons. Successive bombings would yield valuable additional knowledge from the study of each drop; further attempts to rush the assembling of bombs might lead to errors; and several simultaneous bombings might not set the weapon sufficiently apart from the running program of conventional air strikes.

After the group weighed some of the desirable types of targets, Stimson concluded—and all agreed—that the Japanese would be bombed without warning; that the drop should "not concentrate on a civilian area"; but that it should produce "a profound psychological impression on as many of the inhabitants as possible." The Secretary also agreed with Conant's suggestion that the most desirable target would be "a vital war plant employing a large number of workers and closely surrounded by workers' houses."

How could a drop "not concentrate on a civilian area" and at the same time be targeted to destroy a maximum number of workers' homes? The contradiction was not remarked upon. Neither was the impossibility of going easy on a "civilian area" with a weapon carrying a radiation kill radius of nearly a mile.

Deliberations continued until 4:15, but Stimson departed at 3:30 to nap for an hour at Woodley, his Washington home, and then to relax on his porch. Lieutenant Arneson was sitting nearest the office door when the Secretary took his leave, his gait uneven. Arneson opened the door for him, thinking that the boss looked "very feeble."

George Harrison, taking over as chairman, asked the science advisers to draft, "as speedily as possible," a report on "just what sort of organization should be established to direct and control this field."*

---

* Compton recollected in his memoirs that at this point "we were asked to prepare a report as to whether we could devise any kind of demonstration that would seem likely to bring the war to an end without using the bomb against

Compton, all too aware of the searching interrogation he would face back in Chicago from Szilard, Franck, and their fellow worriers, asked what he and the other laboratory leaders who attended the meeting could tell their staffs about the Interim Committee.

The response suggested something less than full trust in the men who made the bomb possible. Compton, Oppenheimer, Lawrence, and Fermi were instructed to say that the committee was dealing with long-range issues, "specifically with the problems of control, organization, legislation, and publicity." Stimson could be identified as chairman, but names of committee members must not be divulged. Nothing was said about short-term problems, but the science advisers were told to convey back home that they were enjoying "complete freedom to present their views on any phase of the subject."

Byrnes thought the meeting so important that he reported to the President at the White House as soon as the sessions ended. His presentation was that of a skillful advocate addressing an appeals judge. First he reminded the President of the scheduled invasion of Japan and the projected casualties of 500,000 or more men. Then he announced that the Interim Committee wanted the bomb dropped without warning. Truman assented. As Byrnes remembered, "With reluctance he had to agree that he could think of no alternative."

Five days later, Stimson reported on the Interim Committee's deliberations to the President in more detail and raised some new questions. While the committee had decided that nothing should be said to the Russians about the bomb until after its successful drop on Japan, what if the President wanted to mention the project at the forthcoming conference of the Big Three in Potsdam?

Truman said he had just postponed the start of that summit meeting until July 15 to give Oppenheimer more time to test the first bomb. Stimson was only somewhat relieved. The timing remained uncomfortably tight. If Oppenheimer's test at Alamogordo were to be delayed much beyond July 15, the unruly Russians might become even harder to handle.

---

a live target." This seems to be wishful thinking. It is not supported by Arneson's minutes or other official accounts. Harrison did ask for such a report, but not until June 16; by that time the early ruminative interest in a demonstration had turned into a clamor, at least among the scientists in Compton's own Metlab (see page 167).

Stimson also shared with the President his two concerns about the rain of destruction already hitting the Japanese from American Air Force bombers. The Secretary "did not want to have the United States get the reputation of outdoing Hitler in atrocities." The ferocity of the conventional raids was such that the atomic bomb might soon not seem much worse. There was a risk that it might lose its shock value.

Truman said he understood, and he laughed. Stimson was not disposed to laugh. Loss of life troubled him deeply, no matter how unavoidable it might be. But outright dissent about the use of the bomb would be up to lesser voices.

Fifteen

The Dissenters:
Buried in the S-1 File

Leo Szilard listened with disdain as Arthur Compton delivered his report to the scientists at the University of Chicago on the afternoon of Saturday, June 2, immediately after the Metlab director's return from the Interim Committee's sessions. Szilard's respect for Washington decision makers had hit another low since his fiasco with Byrnes in Spartanburg. Moreover, he lacked confidence in Stimson's four science advisers—and Szilard's analysis of the individual weaknesses of the three he knew was nearly psychic.

Oppenheimer, he judged, would not resist using the bomb after working so hard to give it life; Oppie had acquired a stake in displaying his weapon's terrible potency on a Japanese city. Fermi, whose personal quirks Szilard knew so well, would state his views privately, whatever they might turn out to be, but would not insist on getting them transmitted further, and he would not speak up again. Compton, the only adviser under pressure from his constituents, might well want to go along with them and oppose using the bomb but would not risk incurring the displeasure of his bosses, the Washington power elite. Of Lawrence's views the Chicagoans knew little.

Feeling honor-bound by the secrecy rule that the Interim Committee had imposed on its four science advisers, Compton did not disclose that the decision to drop the bomb—and without warning—had already been made. Instead, he told his restless flock that the science advisers would meet again in mid-June in Los Alamos. He would be willing to convey any proposals to the group there.

Mindful of his long-ago promise to James Franck that he would bring Franck's view to top-level attention, Compton appointed the beloved Nobel laureate to head a new Committee of Social and Political Implications. Szilard was named a member. Unaware that they would be hammering on locked doors, the committeemen hurried to work on Monday, June 4, to fill their private vacuum with their private anguish.

Although their final report likened nuclear warfare to the use of poison gas—it was the first recognition of radiation as a unique weapon—their focus was not on the morality of the bomb but on the urgency of agreement for international control. "Clear that if no agreement, are sunk," said the handwritten notes of the Franck committee's first meeting in informal shorthand. And the proposed first step toward agreement was summarized in another conclusion drawn from the same session: "The manner in which the new weapon is introduced to the world will determine in large part the future course of events."

Since "Pa" Franck still had difficulty with English, he turned over the drafting of the report to his assistant, Eugene Rabinowitch, who wondered at first whether any secret report could accomplish anything in such a desperate situation. "I remember sleepless nights," he said later. "I asked myself whether perhaps we should break through the walls of secrecy and get to the American people the feeling of what has to be done." But such a plunge beyond official channels would have been illegal.

Buckling down to writing the Franck report, Rabinowitch relied principally on his close and "deep-thinking" friend Szilard. It was Leo who zeroed in on the benefits of not dropping the bomb on Japan. Hour after hour the two scientists walked up and down the tree-lined Midway that dissected the Chicago campus, immersed in wording their lonely campaign to avoid the destruction of civilization.

A surprise attack against Japan was "inadvisable," warned the report. It would be a virtual veto of international control. "This kind of introduction of atomic weapons to the world may easily destroy all our chances of success. Russia and . . . even neutral countries

166

may be deeply shocked. It may be very difficult to persuade the world that a nation which was capable of secretly preparing and suddenly releasing a weapon as indiscriminate as the [Nazi] rocket bomb and a million times more destructive, is to be trusted in its proclaimed desire of having such weapons abolished by international agreement."

Instead, "a demonstration of the new weapon might best be made before the eyes of representatives of all the United Nations on the desert or a barren island. . . . This may sound fantastic, but in nuclear weapons we have something entirely new in order of magnitude of destructive power, and if we want to capitalize fully on the advantage their possession gives us, we must use new and imaginative methods."

Like Stimson and his policy makers, the Szilard-Franck group wanted to capitalize on the shock value of the bomb. The scientists hoped to shock the entire world into disarmament. Stimson and his men wanted primarily to shock Tokyo into surrender. If, coincidentally, they could also shock Moscow into international cooperation, that would be a welcome dividend. The scientists took the long view; the statesmen soldiers concentrated on instant gains.

The Franck report was ready on Monday, June 11, but how could the scientists make certain that it would reach Stimson's desk?

"We were surrounded by a kind of soundproof wall," remembered Rabinowitch, "so that you could write to Washington or go to Washington and talk to somebody but you never got any reaction back." Remembering his last useless foray to the capital to see Henry Wallace with his earlier memorandum—the one that vanished in Bush's files—Franck volunteered to deliver his report in person. Only an upper berth was available on the night train, and the elderly "Pa" climbed into it. This time he would try even harder to reach the one ear in Washington that, next to that of the President himself, was worth reaching.

Compton was already in the capital, preparing to travel to Los Alamos for the science advisers' meeting during the weekend of June 15-16. With Franck in tow he went to the Pentagon, asked to see Stimson, and was told by an aide that the Secretary was out of the city.* The Chicagoans then asked to see George Harrison. Told that

* This was not true. According to Stimson's diary, the Secretary conferred that day with Frankfurter, who had called on him to intercede on behalf of Niels

he was not available, they left the report with Lieutenant Arneson, along with a covering note from Compton that was in effect a dissent. It pointed out:

"While [the report] called attention to difficulties that might result from the use of the bomb, [it] did not mention the probable net saving of many lives,* nor that if the bomb were not used in the present war the world would have no adequate warning as to what was to be expected if war should break out again."

Arneson was not interested in burdening the frail Secretary with the stirrings of the Chicago scientists. He knew their pleas would be pointless. "The mind-set was to use the bomb," he recalled many years later. So, following the rut of normal channels, he eventually transmitted the report to Harrison, whom he knew to be easygoing and disinclined to look for needless trouble.

"Well," Harrison told him, "this report really ought to be examined and commented upon by the Scientific Panel before the Interim Committee is asked to express its views." By that time Compton was in Los Alamos. Harrison phoned him on June 16 and said he wanted to know what the four science advisers thought about it. Stimson evidently never saw the Franck report. Whatever his motive, Harrison had defeated the purpose of Franck and his colleagues in producing it. "We waited for some reaction," said Rabinowitch, "and we waited and waited and we had the feeling we could as well have dropped this report into Lake Michigan."

Szilard, also waiting behind the scientists' "soundproof wall," had every reason to suspect that they had once more been prevented from reaching an influential ear in the government. He began to consider still a different way to make his views heard. He wanted contact with President Truman personally.

Like the science advisers' fateful deliberations with the Interim Committee on May 31, their two-day meeting at Los Alamos con-

---

Bohr, the "fine old fellow" who was still trying to advance his ideas for international control of the bomb.
* This was also not true. The Franck report stated: "The saving of American lives achieved by the sudden use of atomic bombs against Japan may be outweighed by the ensuing loss of confidence and by a wave of horror and repulsion sweeping over the rest of the world . . ."

vened in great secrecy but with a nebulous initial agenda.* On Friday, June 15, Oppenheimer, Compton, Fermi, and Lawrence drafted two reports. One recommended that the Interim Committee encourage postwar atomic research with a $1-billion-a-year program. The other urged that spending for future-oriented research begin at once at the rate of $20 million a year. Harrison's unexpected call to Compton on Saturday, asking the panel to reconsider the use of the bomb against Japan in the light of the Franck report, introduced the realities of the war into the proceedings and transformed the placid atmosphere.

The final top-secret "recommendations on the immediate use of nuclear weapons," signed by Oppenheimer for the panel, offered not a hint, however, of the debate that developed within Oppie's soundproofing.

In its opening passages the 400-word memorandum affirmed the wish of the panelists to reconcile "a satisfactory adjustment of our international relations" with the obligation "to help save American lives."

They recommended, first, that Russia, France, and China "be advised that we have made considerable progress in our work on atomic weapons, that these may be ready to use during the present war, and that we would welcome suggestions as to how we can cooperate in making this development contribute to improved international relations."

The second recommendation did honor to Oppenheimer's reputation for language skills and for maneuvering a disputatious group into a consensus. It was artfully hedged. It conceded that "the opinions of our scientific colleagues on the initial use of these weapons are not unanimous." Some, unnamed, wanted a "purely technical" demonstration. Unnamed others favored immediate military use to save American lives and to prevent all future wars—presumably by sheer fright—rather than focusing on eliminating a specific weapon.

As Oppenheimer phrased it, the science advisers found themselves

---

* No minutes were kept. No secretary was present. Not even Oppenheimer's best friends knew that the meetings were being held. No mention of the sessions exists in the Los Alamos records. Oppenheimer had extended Washington's "soundproof wall" and obscured his own domain.

"closer to these latter views" because they dismissed any alternative to military use as academic: "We can propose no technical demonstration likely to bring an end to the war; we see no acceptable alternative to direct military use." Having thus pronounced death sentences on two Japanese cities, the panelists entered an adroit qualifier. They possessed "no claim to special competence in solving the political, social and military problems . . ."

In later years, only a dim outline emerged of how Oppenheimer engineered the panelists' agreement. Certainly they were operating with little information. The possible fizzling of a demonstration bomb worried them, especially since the forthcoming Alamogordo test would test components, not a fully assembled bomb. They were offered only Compton's verbal briefing on the Franck report; "we had nothing in writing," Oppenheimer recalled later. And they could not judge whether the bomb was really essential for ending the war.

"We didn't know beans about the military situation in Japan," he said in 1954. They did know where their superiors stood, as Oppenheimer remembered well: "In the back of our minds was the notion that the invasion was inevitable because we had been told that."

Wartime logic, distorted by manipulation, deadlines, obsessive secrecy, the President's ignorance, and poor communications, was ensuring a final decision to use the Japanese as live guinea pigs for Oppenheimer's bomb. He could blame the decision makers for representing its military use as inevitable and as a lifesaver. The decision makers could blame the scientists for their inability to conjure up the capability to stage a peaceful demonstration.

But these were afterthoughts. On June 16, so Compton recalled in his memoirs, "our hearts were heavy" as the panelists scotched the demonstration option. "Ernest Lawrence was the last one of our group to give up hope for finding such a solution," he wrote; others also remembered Lawrence's "obvious distress that weekend though they did not know the cause."

Only in 1983 did evidence emerge that the four scientific principals behind the bomb had engaged in more than wistful rummaging through their technical tools. Anne Wilson Marks, Oppenheimer's principal secretary and one of his confidantes, recalled a conversation with Oppie after the secret weekend. It had been the normally taciturn Fermi, so Oppenheimer reported to her, who had resisted him most stubbornly. He wanted the panel to hold out not for a demonstration but for no drop at all. Men will always fight wars, Enrico had argued. One could not responsibly place nuclear weapons into circulation. Their existence had to remain concealed as long as possible.

It took the others until after 5 a.m. on Sunday, June 17, to "talk him down," recalled Oppenheimer, the engineer of consensus.*

The record did show a consensus. The facts were otherwise. Oppenheimer's official summary of the weekend sessions omitted any reference to another debate among the science advisers during the same weekend. As Compton noted in a subsequent memorandum of his own: "There was not sufficient agreement among the members of the panel to unite upon a statement as to how or under what conditions such [military] use was to be made." Oppenheimer covered up this deadlock by not mentioning the matter.

Moves toward another shaky consensus were under way that same Sunday at Woodley, where the ailing Secretary was contemplating tactics with the Assistant Secretary of War, John J. McCloy, for a crucial decision session the next day with the President and the Joint Chiefs of Staff on ways to end the war in the Far East.

"We should have our heads examined if we don't consider a political solution," said "Jack" McCloy, a New York lawyer with international experience. He thought the President should send the Japanese a personal message offering them honorable surrender, including retention of the Emperor as a constitutional monarch, but this gesture should be coupled with the threat that failure to comply would bring on the use of the new atomic bomb. Such an ultimatum might con-

---

* It is unlikely that Oppenheimer was shocked by the peaceable orientation of his hero Fermi. In the 1960s Oppie offered an interviewer a recollection that set Enrico apart from the self-confessed scientist-slaves at Los Alamos. "After he had sat in on one of his first conferences here," recalled Oppenheimer, "he turned to me and said, 'I believe your people actually *want* to make a bomb.' I remember his voice sounded surprised." How strongly Lawrence and Compton might have argued for a bomb demonstration during that long 1945 weekend in Los Alamos is not known. But in 1983, Edward Teller, who had not been informed of the conference during the war, or of Anne Wilson Marks's memories later, speculated about the roles that were played out within Oppie's soundproof walls. "From God's point of view, it may have been three to one," Teller said.

clude the war without more casualties. If it failed, the United States would be in a better moral position to drop the bomb.

Stimson agreed to advocate this strategy at the Monday meeting, but on Sunday evening he phoned McCloy to say he was suffering from one of his chronic migraine headaches: "Jack, I'm not up to going to that meeting tomorrow. I'll arrange with the White House to have you take my place." By the following afternoon, however, he had changed his mind again. Worried, he dragged himself from his bed to the White House conference room at 3:30, looking exhausted and in pain.

At Truman's invitation, Marshall opened the meeting by justifying Operation Olympic, scheduled for November 1, although this initial landing of 766,000 troops on the southern Japanese island of Honshu might cost 31,000 casualties in the first month alone. A second landing would be required on the Tokyo plain in the spring of 1946. The war would drag on into the late fall of that year, but air power alone would not force the Japanese to capitulate.

The Air Force and Navy representatives agreed. So did Stimson. The Secretary spoke vaguely of possible victory "through other means," but to McCloy's boundless surprise said nothing about specific political options or the atomic bomb. Truman agreed to the invasion plans without enthusiasm. The 48,000 recent casualties on Okinawa were fresh in his mind and he still hoped to avoid "an Okinawa from one end of Japan to the other." He did not mention the bomb either.

As the conferees picked up their papers, ready to leave, Truman said, "McCloy, you didn't express yourself and nobody gets out of this room without standing up and being counted. Do you think I have any reasonable alternative to the decision which has just been made?"

McCloy looked at Stimson. "Say what you feel about it," encouraged the Secretary.

"Well, I do think you've got an alternative," McCloy began, "and I think it's an alternative that ought to be explored and that, really, we ought to have our heads examined if we don't explore some other method by which we can terminate this war than just by another conventional attack and landing."

He outlined the idea of offering honorable surrender terms to the Japanese and suggested some arguments for a negotiated peace.

"Well, that's what I've been thinking about," said Truman. "I wonder if you can put that down and give it to the Secretary of State and see what we can do from that." He did not explain why he had not ordered an investigation of political solutions if the concept had occurred to him.

"I'm very glad the subject was brought up," said Stimson, as if he had meant to mention it but had simply forgotten.

Then McCloy asked whether "we oughtn't to tell them that we had the bomb and that we would drop the bomb."

Something like a shudder seemed to go through the room at the first use of the word "bomb." All those present knew about it, but McCloy felt as if he were back at Yale and had mentioned the unmentionable secret society, Skull and Bones. Suddenly the bomb was no longer a "project." It was a weapon and had somehow to be reckoned with. But how?

Sensing the resistance of his audience, McCloy ventured on: "I think that our moral position would be better if we gave them specific warning of the bomb."

This brought protests. What if the bomb didn't go off? What would happen to American prestige?

McCloy countered, "I think that the moral position that we would have would transcend the temporary disadvantage that might occur from our taking the risk of a dud."

This brought out further negative comments. Only the President's personal military adviser, Admiral William Leahy, liked a political settlement.* McCloy retreated slightly: "If you don't mention the bomb, at least mention in general terms what its capacity is, something in the nature that with one blow we would wipe out a city. They'll know what we're talking about."

The President told McCloy to give "further thought" to an ulti-

---

* Astuteness did not lead Leahy to this position. He thought that the bomb was nonsense, a "professor's dream." Some months ago he had assured Groves that he knew it would fail because the Navy had taught him all there was to know about explosives, and besides, no weapon developed during a war had ever been worth much in the same conflict. To Truman the admiral had said flatly: "The bomb will never go off."

matum but to forget any mention of the bomb "at this stage." Groves and Byrnes had done their work well. Secrecy, stealth, surprise . . . these advantages could not be surrendered. In effect, the decision to drop the bomb without warning had been confirmed by the President and the military.*

On June 21, the Interim Committee, living up to the tentativeness of its name, met for the last time. Stimson was trying to regain some strength by taking a five-day rest in the comforts of his Long Island estate. George Harrison, the routine-minded insurance executive, presided. The committee rubber-stamped the June 16 recommendations of its science advisers without ever having seen the text of the Franck report; again it recommended dropping the bomb without warning. Prodded by Bush and Conant, it did reverse itself to the extent of recommending that "the President advise the Russians that we were working on this weapon . . . and that we expected to use it against Japan."

No study of the Franck report was ever made. No careful explorations of the demonstration and the warning options were ever ordered.

Navy Under Secretary Bard had meanwhile been sitting through the smooth proceedings of the Interim Committee and growing increasingly uncomfortable. Like Arthur Compton, he had sensed that the use of the bomb was a foregone conclusion, and so he had been saying little. Bard, a massively built, gray-haired Chicago financier, was anything but squeamish. He was "not opposed to dropping" nuclear weapons. But between May and July he had become convinced that "the Japanese war was really won," that Japan could be starved into surrendering, and that it wasn't "necessary for us to disclose our nuclear position and stimulate the Russians to develop the same

---

* During his distinguished career after the war—he became president of the World Bank, U.S. High Commissioner in Germany, and a leading Wall Street lawyer—McCloy's indignation over the 1945 decision-making machinery grew. In interviews during the 1960s he charged that each of the military services was too eager to employ its own forces to conclude the war. In 1983 he told the author that the decision makers interpreted political solutions as a sign of weakness. "Groves and Harry Truman were exactly the right guys to open this [nuclear] Pandora's box," he said. "They didn't step back to get the whole picture, they didn't look ahead."

thing much more rapidly than they would have if we had not dropped the bomb."

Though he never saw Szilard's identical argument in the Franck report, Bard had come to believe that the bomb should certainly not be dropped without warning. He knew he was not alone. Word had reached him that "many of the scientists" shared this view. He had heard of McCloy's attempts to lobby for a political solution and of Admiral Strauss's idea of demonstrating the bomb in the woods of Japan. Bard was also concerned about the nation's moral position if the United States were to cast itself in the role of a surprise nuclear aggressor.

Several worried phone calls to the equable Harrison got him nowhere, so on June 27 he submitted a top-secret memorandum dissenting from the Interim Committee and resigned his Navy post as of July 1.

"The stakes are so tremendous," warned his protest note, "that Japan should have some preliminary warning for say two or three days in advance of use . . . [in keeping with] the position of the United States as a great humanitarian nation and the fair play attitude of our people." He conceded that a warning might be ineffective, but what if it was? "I don't see that we have anything in particular to lose . . ."

To make his protest count as much as possible, Bard managed to wangle an appointment with Truman. He wanted to explain his reasoning in person.

"For God's sake," he told the President, "don't organize an army to go into Japan. Kill a million people? It's ridiculous." Bard thought that interservice rivalry was behind the momentum to visit further large-scale violence upon the Japanese: "The Navy knew the Japanese were licked. The Army wanted to be in on the kill."

Truman, in a rush to leave for the Big Three conference at Potsdam, listened politely and assured Bard that the questions of invading Japan and a possible warning to the Japanese had received most careful attention. It was a perfunctory brushoff.

As a recently naturalized American citizen, Szilard had been studying the Constitution, and its First Amendment guarantee of the people's right "to petition the Government for a redress of grievances" struck him as an attractive device for bringing the despair of the antibomb scientists before the court of last resort, the President, even though their petition, paradoxically, had to remain classified "secret."

Dropping the idea of a demonstration, he drew up a formal "Petition to the President of the United States" and, early in July, circulated it among his colleagues at the Chicago Metlab. Groves was furious but did not dare suppress this poignant plea for morality: "The United States shall not resort to the use of atomic bombs in this war unless the terms which will be imposed upon the Japanese have been made public in detail and Japan, knowing these terms, has refused to surrender."

Only a minority of the Chicago scientists—sixty-seven, including all leading physicists and most leading biologists—signed this document. The chemists refused to go along. They told Szilard that they simply felt more lives would be saved by using the bomb than by continuing the war without it. Szilard tried unsuccessfully to shame them by responding that this was "a utilitarian argument with which I was very familiar through my previous experiences in Germany."

Still others felt that morality in fact dictated the bomb's use. "Are we to go on shedding American blood when we have available the means to speedy victory?" one note demanded of the embattled Arthur Compton. "No! If we can save even a handful of American lives, then let us use this weapon—now!"

To spread his protest to the Oak Ridge laboratory, Szilard enlisted his old friend Eugene Wigner; work on reactor design had made Wigner one of the heroes of the Metlab project and it frequently took him to Oak Ridge. Himself an enthusiastic signer of the petition, Wigner was given an extra copy by Szilard for circulation within the Tennessee installation. It had attracted eighty-eight signatures from physicists and chemists and many more were ready to sign when military authorities stepped in. They prohibited further circulation and a colonel "bawled out" Wigner. The document supposedly violated security by hinting that the bomb was approaching readiness.

Szilard knew that the imminence of the Alamogordo test—and Oppenheimer's hawkish views—would make it difficult to enlist Los Alamos colleagues in his latest conspiracy. The date of the New Mexico test was not disclosed to the Metlab staff, but Szilard guessed that it was near when Los Alamos was all but sealed off. The men in Chicago were no longer allowed to telephone Site Y and almost nobody was permitted to travel there. Dr. Ralph E. Lapp, a cheerful, hyperenergetic young physicist, was an exception because he was designing a last-minute bomb part made of tungsten, so Szilard gave him a sealed envelope with eight sets of the petition to hand to a friend of both at Los Alamos, Ed Creutz.

"Please give one set to Oppenheimer for his information and give the other sets to such men as are willing to circulate them," Szilard asked in a covering letter. He made clear that he realized the petition would not enjoy great popularity. "Of course you will find only a few people on your project who are willing to sign such a petition," he told Creutz. Gratuitously he added his low opinion of the Los Alamos bomb enthusiasts: "I am sure you will find many boys confused as to what kind of a thing a moral issue is."

Oppenheimer never gave the petition a chance, although, in a separate letter, Szilard tried cleverly to defer to him as a responsible, moral scientist/statesman. "I hardly need to emphasize that such a petition does not represent the most effective action that can be taken," he began in a veiled reproof of Oppie's manipulating of the Interim Committee. "But I have no doubt that from a point of view of the standing of the scientists in the eyes of the general public one or two years from now it is a good thing that a minority of scientists should have gone on record in favor of giving greater weight to moral arguments."

It was another confrontation Szilard could not win. Oppenheimer ruled that the petition must not be allowed to circulate, and when Edward Teller came to see him about it he managed to justify himself as he always did: convincingly.

Szilard had sent a petition directly to his old chum Teller, who later said that he wanted to sign and circulate it but felt he should seek Oppenheimer's approval. Not only was Oppie the constituted authority at Los Alamos, "he was more," Teller explained. "His brilliant mind, his quick intellect, his penetrating interest in everyone in the laboratory made him our natural leader as well. He seemed to be the obvious man to turn to with a formidable problem, particularly political." And still another personal element endowed Robert Oppenheimer with extraordinary power over Los Alamos. As Teller phrased it, "Disappointing him somehow carried with it a sense of wrongdoing."

Oppenheimer was scathing in his opposition to the petition. He opened up his meeting with Teller by volunteering "uncomplimentary comments" about the petitioners, Szilard in particular, and said in a "convincing way" that scientists had no right to use their prestige as a platform for political pronouncements.* Besides, their fulminations were superfluous. Teller recalled how Oppenheimer won him over: "He conveyed to me in glowing terms the deep concern, thoroughness and wisdom with which these questions were being handled in Washington. Our fate was in the hands of the best, the most conscientious, men of our nation. And they had information which we did not possess."

Teller accepted Oppenheimer's authority with relief† and composed an elaborately reasoned letter to Szilard which he submitted to Oppenheimer for approval and for forwarding to Post Office Box 5207 in Chicago, Szilard's official address at the Metlab, explaining why he had decided not to support the petition.

"I have no hope of clearing my conscience," Teller professed. "The things we are working on are so terrible that no amount of protesting or fiddling with politics will save our souls . . . Our only hope is getting the facts of our results before the people. This might help to convince everybody that the next war would be fatal. For this purpose, actual combat-use might even be the best thing. . . . The ac-

---

* Oppenheimer's stance that day was one of the triggers in the blood feud between him and Teller that broke into the open after the war and still smoulders. In a 1983 article in the journal *Los Alamos Science,* Teller complained bitterly: "Years later I learned that shortly before this interview [about the Szilard petition] Oppenheimer not only had used his scientific stature to give political advice in favor of immediate bombing, but also put his point of view forward so effectively that he gained the reluctant concurrence of his colleagues. Yet he denied Szilard, a scientist of lesser influence, all justification for expressing his opinion."

† It is unclear whether Teller experienced "relief" chiefly because the delicate controversy had been taken out of his hands or for other reasons. Some historians have found it noteworthy that Teller's letter to Szilard failed to mention either his talk with Oppenheimer or Oppenheimer's veto of the petition, and that Teller's covering note to "Dear Oppie" suggests that he may never have disagreed with Oppenheimer in the first place. "I should feel better if I could explain to [Szilard] *my point of view* [emphasis added]," Teller wrote Oppenheimer. "This I am doing in the enclosed letter. What I say is, I believe, in agreement with your views." Yet in 1983 Teller wrote: "I have long regretted the fact that I allowed myself to be so easily persuaded."

cident that we worked out this dreadful thing should not give us a responsibility of having a voice in how it is to be used . . . I should like to have the advice of all of you whether you think it is a crime to continue to work. But I feel that I should do the wrong thing if I tried to say how to tie the little toe of the ghost to the bottle from which we just helped it escape."

Oppenheimer had kept the lid on the scattered social consciences at Los Alamos. The little toe of the atomic ghost was free to float from its bottle.

Faced with the by now familiar dilemma of attracting the attention of the President, Szilard wanted to send his signed petitions directly to the White House. Several of his colleagues, including Pa Franck, objected. Groves had ordered Compton to conduct an official opinion poll of the Chicago scientists, and Szilard's colleagues did not wish to antagonize the general unnecessarily. They refused to sign unless Szilard agreed to transmit the signatures through official channels. With utmost reluctance, Szilard turned over his package of petitions to Compton on July 19—two days after the Alamogordo test. Truman was already at Potsdam, where the Big Three conference had just gotten under way. Compton did not forward the package and the results of his poll* until July 24. His covering note pointed out that his shipment was of "immediate concern," yet Groves carefully routed it through a circuitous obstacle course to be sure the President would be out of the country when it arrived in Washington. The general

---

* The results of the poll were inconclusive. Many of the 150 respondents faced its five complicated questions for the first time and had only a few minutes to ponder an answer. Only 15 percent wanted the bomb used "in the manner that is from the military point of view most effective"; 26 percent wanted an "experimental demonstration in this country with representatives of Japan present"; 11 percent wanted no military use but a "public experimental demonstration"; 3 percent wanted secrecy and no use in the war. A problem of interpretation arose when 46 percent, by far the largest segment, voted for "a military demonstration in Japan to be followed by a renewed opportunity for surrender before full use of the weapon is employed." What this "military demonstration" would consist of was left unclear, although it could be inferred that it meant less than "full use," possibly a drop on an unpopulated Japanese target. Compton, no statistician, somehow concluded that "87 percent voted for military use," and when Groves pressed him for his personal vote he ducked the issue with a fence-straddling memo so murky that it could have meant anything at all: "My vote is with the majority. It seems to me that as the war stands the bomb should be used, but no more drastically than needed to bring surrender."

ordered Compton to forward the package to his assistant, Colonel Nichols, at Oak Ridge. Nichols sent it to Groves, who retained it until August 1, when it was delivered to Stimson's office by messenger only to be placed in the S-1 file by George Harrison.* The petitions were never seen by Truman, who was returning from Potsdam and was still at sea when the bomb was dropped on Hiroshima on August 6.

* Lieutenant R. Gordon Arneson, the secretary of the Interim Committee, confirmed the fate of the petitions in a memorandum of May 24, 1946: "Since the question of the bomb's use 'had already been fully considered and settled by the proper authorities,' . . . it was decided that 'no useful purpose would be served by transmitting either the petitions or any of the attached documents to the White House, particularly since the President was not then in the country.' "

Part 5
Rush to Decision

Sixteen

The War:
The Final Days Begin

As the war in the Pacific entered its climactic phase, General Curtis LeMay briefed his B-29 crews at the Guam headquarters of the 20th Air Force on March 9, 1945, for a daring new kind of raid on Tokyo. The chunky, cigar-smoking chief of the 21st Bomber Command had designed its radical tactics himself, without consulting Washington. If they worked, the Air Force could claim another innovation, a fresh standard of destruction for an urban target.

The bombers would strike at night, flying at 5000 to 8000 feet, LeMay ordered, instead of the 30,000-foot altitude customary for daytime sorties with high explosives. To increase their payloads for the 3000-mile round trip—this time the raiders would carry M47 incendiary bombs—all armaments except tail cannons would be removed.

Protests from his audience were audible. The mission, code-named Meetinghouse, seemed suicidal, but LeMay concluded on a cheerful note: "You're going to deliver the biggest firecracker the Japanese have ever seen!"

It was mostly bravado. Intelligence had informed the general that Tokyo was defended by 105 twin-engine interceptors, 322 single-engine fighters, and 331 heavy-caliber guns. LeMay could only hope that the Japanese pilots had still not developed night-fighting capabilities and that the antiaircraft artillery, manually operated and reportedly lacking radar control, would react too slowly to interfere with a low-level assault.

The general had grown impatient with the impotence of his high-altitude daylight raids. Two-thirds of all Japanese industry had been dispersed among homes and tiny factories employing thirty or fewer workers. Their productivity had been little affected so far. Thousands of such flimsy wooden home factories operated within the scope of Meetinghouse, a three-by-four-mile downtown area populated by 750,000 low-income workers. It was time to take these industries out of the war.

At 5:36 p.m. the first of 333 B-29s took off from Guam's North Field and headed north, followed at fifty-second intervals by eleven more. These were pathfinders. They would demarcate the target area and light it up with a gigantic "X" by dropping canisters of magnesium and phosphorous as well as jellied gasoline, the dreaded napalm.

Undiscovered on their low sweep over southeast Tokyo, the pathfinders began to discharge their fiery markings at 12:08 a.m. The new moon was dim. A chill 28-mile-an-hour wind swept the sky clear. Air-raid alarm sirens did not wake the population until 12:15. Antiaircraft fire was scattered and ineffective. No fighters intercepted. When the main force of three wings started to arrive at 12:30 and dropped two-foot-long napalm sticks at altitudes ranging from 4900 to 9200 feet, it was plain that LeMay had won his gamble.

Under a stiffening wind, flames fanned out rapidly. Within minutes huge balls of fire torched structure after structure and fueled an incandescent tidal wave carrying temperatures exceeding 1800 degrees Fahrenheit. "It's spreading like a prairie fire," General Thomas Power, LeMay's chief of staff, radioed to his boss from an observation plane circling at 15,000 feet. "The blaze must be out of control . . . ground fire sporadic . . . no fighter opposition."

The turbulence of the firestorm tossed the bombers hundreds of feet into the air, then pulled them downward. Many fliers vomited, first from airsickness, again when the sickly-sweet stench of burning bodies hit them from the ground. Some crews put on oxygen masks. As the last B-29 escaped to the south at 3:30 a.m.—only 14 planes were lost—General Power radioed LeMay: "Target completely alight. Flames spreading well beyond Meetinghouse. All Tokyo visible in the glare. Total success."

Rush to Decision

On the ground, Koyo Ishikawa, a cameraman for the police department, was photographing LeMay's handiwork. "The very streets were rivers of fire," he said later. "Everywhere one could see flaming pieces of furniture exploding in the heat, while the people themselves blazed like matchsticks." Many were incinerated in their wooden shelters. Masao Nomura, a reporter for the newspaper *Asahi,* described the scene after the raid: "Long lines of ragged, ash-covered people straggled along, dazed and silent, like columns of ants. They had no idea where they were going."

Mrs. Yohie Sekimura, trying to make her way back to her home with her baby on her back, found the bridge across the Sumida River clogged with bodies, the river choked with swollen corpses. Mechanically she walked past bodies of neighbors and could shed no tears. The pool of emergency water at her neighborhood hospital was filled with layers of sprawling bodies. Survivors were scrawling charcoal messages for their missing loved ones on the sidewalk. Her home was in ashes, along with 267,170 others; 15.8 square miles were burned out; 72,489 people died, 130,000 were injured.

In Washington, Secretary Stimson told Oppenheimer that he "thought it was appalling that there should be no protest" in the United States over such wholesale slaughter. Vannevar Bush could not sleep.* On Guam, General LeMay, vindicated, planned to run 7000 more sorties by September. Convinced that he could burn Japan into surrender, he began by ordering further "firecrackers" delivered upon Osaka, Kobe, Nagoya, and other targets, including areas of Tokyo that had been largely spared so far.

On Friday, April 13, the alert sounded at 10:40 p.m., and thirty-four minutes later 160 of LeMay's B-29s again swooped onto the capital. This time 640,000 lost their homes, including Yoshio Nishina and his family. The little nuclear physicist was still laboring to build an atomic bomb, but the fire raid also left his Riken Institute in the Koishiwa district all but homeless. Several buildings burned to the ground, though not No. 49, the wooden laboratory that housed his

---

* "For years after the war Van Bush would wake screaming in the night because he burned Tokyo," remembered his friend, the physicist Merle Tuve. "Even the atomic bomb didn't bother him as much as jellied gasoline. Oh yes, we all suffer scars."

team's prized achievement: a uranium separator patched together by Masashi Takeuchi, the ingenuous lover of cosmic rays.

Working frantically through the night, firemen assisted by some of Takeuchi's colleagues succeeded in quenching the sea of flames that surrounded No. 49. But as they were resting at dawn a strong wind blew up and, probably triggered by sparks from debris smoldering in the vicinity, flames erupted in Takeuchi's building. It burned down rapidly as the scientists could only watch. Takeuchi did not have to witness the catastrophe. The trains were not running and he was marooned at home in a distant seaside suburb, as helpless as he had been all along.

Some weeks before, after his uranium-purifying device had repeatedly failed and been repeatedly redesigned, he had produced a tiny sample of a mysterious substance and run it through the cyclotron for analysis. He knew only that his machine had separated it from some uranium hexafluoride which a colleague had taken more than a year to produce. The cyclotron yielded a painful answer: Takeuchi's separator had not separated anything useful, certainly no precious U-235.

No matter. Nishina and his team—it consisted of only fifteen full-time workers, all very young and none a recognized nuclear expert—had never begun to develop a reactor and possessed no remotely worthwhile quantities of uranium to purify. The supposedly promising "wrinkles" in the Burmese earth turned out to be just wrinkles. Black sand from Malaya and Korea contained less than one-tenth of one percent uranium. Pitchblende that the Germans promised to deliver by submarine had failed to arrive.

Takeuchi hoped that the great fire would be the last indignity he would have to suffer in the war, but the worst came later that month when Nishina summoned him into the director's office on the second floor of Building No. 37. The director did not appear angry, and if he was upset at having to live with his family and some of his staff in the cramped emergency dormitory next door he gave no sign of it. He simply told Takeuchi that since his uranium separation efforts had been unsuccessful he was responsible for the Riken Institute's failure to create a bomb. He should act accordingly.

Takeuchi said, "Ha!" and left. He was stunned. He had been reporting constant failures to his boss for more than two years. Nishina had kept pacifying him. "Well, don't worry," he had said. "Just keep on with it." Takeuchi understood that the collapse of the bomb project had been brought on by many technical and economic inadequacies. And surely he could not be held responsible for the destruction of the laboratory. But he grasped what was happening to him. The army was powerful and had to be offered a scapegoat. So be it. Takeuchi felt he was a soldier, he said years later, and a soldier was supposed to keep his mouth shut.

This is what he did. He also resigned, as Nishina clearly expected, and transferred to the Navy. He was supposed to improve radio communications between planes. It was uninspiring work, but at least his atomic war was over.

So was that of the Germans, but in Washington General Groves was not yet willing to admit it. In mid-April 1945 he appeared in Secretary Stimson's office to brief the Secretary and General Marshall on the importance of having the advancing American troops take the Black Forest village of Hechingen. Groves was now reasonably certain that the Germans were not making a nuclear bomb, but he wanted physical evidence of their failure. Their principal laboratories and scientists were clearly in the Hechingen area that had been previously pinpointed. This would place them in the line of advance of French troops, which worried Groves. The French might reach Hechingen first, and Groves considered them untrustworthy.

Embarrassingly, he could not find Hechingen on the huge map that covered one wall of Stimson's office. Neither could Stimson or Marshall. All three dignitaries were almost on their hands and knees—Groves reflected that the scene would have made a memorable photograph—and still the tiny target eluded them. One of Stimson's assistants was called and located the town near the floor end of the map, whereupon the strategists set about planning its capture as if it were Berlin.

Colonel Pash of the Alsos mission had drawn up plans for a parachute assault to blow up the laboratories and kidnap the scientists. Groves preferred more muscle. He wanted an entire U.S. army corps to cut diagonally across the French front and withdraw after accomplishing the mission. He called it Operation Harborage. Stimson and Marshall approved, but by late April the French were advancing so rapidly that Pash and a few Alsos scientists headed a mere battalion, the 1279th Combat Engineers.

Pash and his band stormed into the town on April 23. In a textile factory that had been taken over by the Kaiser Wilhelm Institute, they seized an experimental isotope-separation apparatus that had never yet been tested. In the same building, Pash found Heisenberg's office and a photograph of the professor saying farewell to Sam Goudsmit, Alsos' chief scientist, at dockside in New York in 1939—but Heisenberg had escaped by bicycle two days earlier. Fanning out to nearby villages, the investigators found a primitive nuclear pile—it was not self-sustaining—in a cave; secret records in a canister hidden in the cesspool of a scientist's home; some heavy water and uranium in the cellar of an old mill; and a ton and a half of metallic uranium cubes buried under a plowed field. All told, this evidence of the Nazi nuclear effort was even more pitiful than the relieved Americans had anticipated.

In an old school at Tailfingen they captured a chemistry laboratory and its chief, Otto Hahn, whose fission experiment in Berlin had started all the bomb efforts in 1938. "It was just like a business call on a customer," said the two Alsos chemical engineers who arrested him; the Americans were on leave from the DuPont Company. Hahn looked ill and emaciated—the war diet had taken thirty pounds off him—but unlike his colleagues, he did not claim that his records had been destroyed. "I have them here," he said.

By May 3 Colonel Pash had advanced to Heisenberg's home town, Urfeld, near Munich. Groves had been urging the colonel on, fearful that the professor might fall into Russian hands. Heisenberg was waiting with his bag packed. "I have been expecting you," he told Pash. The professor was placed between two armed guards in an armored car which lumbered down the main street behind a tank and was followed by another tank and several jeeps. Townspeople remarked that not even Stalin could have been given more careful handling.

When Heisenberg arrived at Alsos headquarters in Heidelberg, Goudsmit greeted him cordially and they chatted.

Rush to Decision

"Would you want to come to America now and work with us?" the American asked. "If American colleagues wish to learn about the uranium problem," Heisenberg replied archly, "I shall be glad to show them the results of our research if they come to my laboratory."

Seventeen

The Target: Picking the Death City

While Heisenberg sought refuge in arrogance, the Americans were progressing from the experiment of making a bomb to the realities of delivering it—a very different phase that required the kind of specialist who was working his way slowly down the assembly line of the Martin bomber plant on the south side of Omaha, Nebraska.

Clambering up and down one scaffolding after another, Colonel Paul W. Tibbets was checking out all the B-29 Superfortresses under construction in search of the most carefully assembled aircraft. The stocky, medium-sized Air Force pilot was living up to his reputation as a perfectionist.

It was May 9, two days after the end of the war in Europe, time to select the plane that would drop the A-bomb. Tibbets the perfectionist had been picked to fly it. Finally the senior plant foreman who guided him shouted over the din of the riveting, "This is the one for you." Tibbets agreed and gave the plane his mother's first and middle names, Enola Gay.

His mother had wanted Paul to go into medicine. Paul wanted to fly, a career that his father, a prosperous businessman in Quincy, Illinois, and a rigid disciplinarian, did not consider entirely respectable. Already cool and detached, Paul ignored family opposition and enlisted in the Army Air Corps in 1937. After acquiring a superior war record in Europe and Africa as a combat pilot and operations officer, Tibbets headed the flight testing of the new B-29 when it was still dangerous to fly, and thus came to the attention of the Air Force commander, General Henry H. Arnold.

"The best damned pilot in the Air Force," said Hap Arnold—precisely the man General Groves wanted for the most momentous flying job of the war.

Accustomed to command, Tibbets was also qualified to handle the administrative part of his job: organizing and training the new elite outfit that Groves was assembling to back him up: an autonomous Air Force unit known as the 509th Composite Group. Tibbets told its 1767 men at their first formation that theirs was a "very special mission"—but not a word about the bomb. "You are here to take part in an effort that could end the war," was as far as he went.

Tibbets himself was accorded more congenial treatment. "You had better know everything," Oppenheimer told him when the colonel, who had been a physics major in college, reported to the director's office in Los Alamos. For security reasons Tibbets had exchanged the Air Force insignia on his uniform to the Corps of Engineers emblem commonly seen around the laboratory.

Oppenheimer delivered a briefing on the nuclear explosion of uranium and then took Tibbets to another building marked "Positively No Admittance"—the home of the supersecret Delivery Group. Oppenheimer introduced Tibbets to its chief, Deke Parsons, the Navy captain, and said that Parsons would probably be aboard for the first bomb drop.

"Good," said Tibbets crisply. "Then if anything goes wrong, Captain, I can blame you."

"If anything goes wrong, Colonel, neither of us will be around to be blamed," said Parsons.

The captain's ensuing lecture on the gun-type bomb educated Tibbets about a variety of hair-raising things that could go wrong with it. And as the colonel prepared to leave Los Alamos, Oppenheimer took him aside and made clear that the risks would not cease with the dropping of the weapon. "Your biggest problem may be after the bomb has left your aircraft," Oppie said. "The shock waves from the detonation could crush your plane. I am afraid that I can give you no guarantee that you will survive."

Tibbets' troops, meanwhile, were trying to come to terms with their new desert base, Wendover Field, Utah, in the salt flats 125 miles west of Salt Lake City, almost on the Nevada line. Again Groves got what he wanted: isolation. "The end of the world, perfect," Tibbets said when he first saw the place. "Leftover Field" cracked Bob Hope, who once came to entertain. There were rats, the drinking water tasted bad, sand permeated food, clothes, everything.

During a two-month interlude the air crews operated out of Batista Field in Cuba, simulating the prospective mission of the *Enola Gay*. They practiced long over-water runs, flying singly to perfect their skills at navigating independently. Returning to Wendover, they bombed the Salton Sea with dummy bombs for ballistic testing. The "engineers" who kept visiting from Los Alamos had to know exactly how these test "pumpkins" behaved when they were released from various altitudes and in different wind conditions. The "pumpkins" were about 120 inches long and weighed 9000 pounds. These were the specifications for the "Little Boy," but only the visiting "engineers" and Tibbets knew it. Still nobody told the men of the 509th what was so "very special" about their mission.

As his troops grew increasingly stir-crazy, Tibbets spent more and more time with them, and his already troubled marriage underwent great strain. Lucie, his Georgia-born wife, was warm, pretty, eager for company and conversation. Paul never seemed to have time to talk any more, not even to their two small sons. When he did come home he talked only about work. Lucie complained. Tibbets told her he was a loner. Lucie was not appeased. She thought Paul was becoming more distant and too preoccupied with his strange new command. Her insight did not help her, but it was accurate.

The 509th reached its breaking point during the weekend of April 21. As usual, the men took off for their fling in Salt Lake City. This time Wendover Field received not only an account of a redhead running naked down a corridor in the Hotel Utah with several pilots in pursuit, but a flood of police complaints reporting drunken assaults and property damage.

Tibbets the perfectionist had had enough of Wendover. The forward base of the 509th was ready on Tinian Island in the Marianas. Tibbets' ground troops were ordered to leave Seattle on May 6 by ship. The air crews would fly out later. Tibbets stayed behind to finish his business with the newly appointed Target Committee in

Washington. It was trying to decide on which city the death sentence of his bomb would fall. It was a delicate negotiation.

Groves considered the target selection his personal responsibility and he liked Kyoto best. When he first discussed alternatives with Tibbets in a tentative way in his Washington office as early as December 28, 1944, the general had toyed with the idea of placing the bomb on Tokyo. He wanted to administer the most horrifying possible psychological blow to shock the Japanese into surrendering and that meant he needed maximum casualties. The huge capital seemed the most promising prospect, but only briefly.

Groves hoped for a drop between June 15 and July 15. However, "rain could be expected rather frequently" over the capital until August 15, which made Tokyo undesirable. Poor weather would affect the weaponeer's accuracy. Two other inconveniences were recorded in the notes of Groves's discussion with Tibbets. "To enable us to assess accurately the effects of the bomb, the targets should not have been previously damaged by air attacks," which disqualified the capital; the Air Force could not be expected to exempt Tokyo from heavy bombardment in the coming months. Also, a smaller target would yield more precise information: it was "desirable that the first target be of such size that the damage would be confined within it, so that we could more definitely determine the power of the bomb."

Kyoto qualified as a target on all critical counts, Groves pointed out. It was especially valuable psychologically. It was Japan's most treasured city, its ancient capital, and dated back to the eighth century. The 3000 temples and shrines scattered throughout its spectacular mid-city gardens made it a "historical city and one that was of great religious significance to the Japanese." With an estimated population of a million, Groves thought it was "large enough to ensure that the damage from the bomb would run out within the city." He also reasoned that "like any city of that size" it was bound to be a legitimate military objective because it "must be involved in a tremendous amount of war work."

The Target Committee gathered for its initial formal meeting in the anonymity of a Pentagon conference room at 8:40 a.m. on April 27, and complexities crowded in quickly. William G. Penney, a veteran of many such gatherings, was impressed by the air of unusual seriousness.* He was one of only two scientists summoned from Los Alamos; the other, Johnny von Neumann, the mathematical wizard, would be responsible for the many computations pinpointing every step of Colonel Tibbets' unprecedented mission. Penney noted that the normally ebullient Johnny was subdued in the prevailing military atmosphere. The other eight target planners in the room were officers and scientists attached to the 20th Air Force.

Groves opened up by demanding "the highest degree of secrecy," a needless injunction for such a select group. Next the general issued a pointed reminder for the Air Force strategists present. He had become disturbed by their casual attitude toward the bomb. They seemed to think that they would be in charge of dropping it. Not so. He wanted advice only on how best to employ his weapon. The decision on its actual use, he emphasized, would be made by "higher authority." Whereupon he departed, leaving only the technical questions to the technicians.

Bill Penney felt uneasy. How could scientists advise on a maximum shock for the Japanese when they still had no idea of the bomb's potency? He felt "fairly sure" that the Little Boy, the gun-type bomb that would be ready first, would yield the equivalent of at least one to five kilotons of TNT. Fat Man, the plutonium bomb, represented guesswork of a much greater order. There was an "unknown chance" that it might produce only one-tenth of a kiloton.†

The Target Committee zeroed in on a more elemental worry. To insure accuracy, Groves was insisting on visual rather than radar bombing. An efficient drop therefore required clear weather. The Air Force officers in the room thought that clouds were not significant obstacles. This attitude agitated their principal scientist, Dr. D. M. Dennison from the University of Michigan. Bill Penney was surprised to see him display so much exasperation and anxiety.

---

* Penney, a British authority on explosives, had been imported for the expertise on bombing effects that he had acquired in the European war. He discoursed so genially on this subject that physicist Viki Weisskopf nicknamed him "the smiling killer." After the war Penney was knighted and became chairman of the British Atomic Energy authority.
† All the scientists' advance estimates proved that they did not realize the scope of the power they were unleashing. The gun-type bomb dropped on Hiroshima eventually yielded 13.5 kilotons. The plutonium bomb yielded 20 kilotons at its Trinity test in Alamogordo.

Rush to Decision

The summer months regularly produced the year's worst weather in Japan, Dennison lectured. In July they could expect no more than seven "good days" with less than three-tenths overcast. In August there would be six days at most, and probably only three. The good days could never be predicted more than forty-eight hours in advance. Tokyo was particularly chancy. Only once in five years had the city seen more than two successive summer days adequate for visual bombing.

Brigadier General Thomas F. Farrell calmed Dennison down. Farrell, a former New York State Commissioner of Canals and Waterways, accustomed to dealing with politicians and other civilians in Albany, was Groves's deputy and something of a diplomat. He said that the best available meteorologists would go to work on charting the weather problem. As for Tokyo, it was no longer anything more than "a possibility" as a target; the recent night bombings had made the capital useless, "practically rubble." Nearby Yokohama with its naval installations was a better bet. So was the steel industry in Yawata. Hiroshima seemed most suitable of all. No details about the city were offered. It was simply a place that the Air Force had not yet got around to bombing—"the largest untouched target on the 21st Bomber Command priority list."

When the meeting adjourned at 4 p.m., the group had settled on little more than an approximate notion of the first target's dimensions: an urban area measuring not less than three miles in diameter in its most populated areas. The list of candidates was sizable. Seventeen cities were recommended "for study," including Yokohama, Hiroshima, Nagasaki, and Kyoto.

Security precautions were extraordinary when thirteen insiders gathered in Los Alamos at 9 a.m. on May 11 for further deliberations of the Target Committee. Maps of the Far East were spread across the table of Oppenheimer's conference room for the first time. Oppie, Bill Penney, and Johnny von Neumann were joined by only two additional scientists of the laboratory staff: Captain Deke Parsons, the head of the Delivery Group, and his deputy, Norman Ramsey. Others were summoned and quickly dismissed as the sessions ran on for two days. Hans Bethe, head of the Theoretical Division, was questioned about desirable heights for detonating the bomb without even being

195

informed of the group's function. Contrary to Los Alamos custom, an officer of Groves's staff kept notes on the contingencies discussed.

What if bad weather or enemy defenses were to make a bomb drop impossible and Colonel Tibbets' *Enola Gay* returned to its base too damaged to make a normal landing? The scientists warned that such an emergency would be "complicated." A nuclear explosion would be set off if water leaked into the bomb. The gunpowder would have to be removed from its gun before the bomb could be jettisoned prior to a crash landing near friendly territory.

The committee narrowed the list of targets to five cities which the Air Force had agreed to exempt from conventional raids and "reserve" for a nuclear weapon. Conforming to Groves's personal preference, Kyoto headed this priority list. The minutes explained, "From the psychological point of view there is the advantage that Kyoto is an intellectual center for Japan and the people there are more apt to appreciate the significance of such a weapon."

Kyoto had been classified as an "AA" target, an honor it shared with only one other city: Hiroshima, by now identified as an army depot and industrial area of "such a size that a large part of the city could be extensively damaged"; its adjacent hills were "likely to produce a focusing effect which would considerably increase the blast damage."

Two additional targets were also to be "reserved" by the Air Force: Yokohama and Kokura Arsenal. These were "A" targets. The fifth, Niigata, labeled "B," was reprieved; the planners dropped it from the list. Groves's choice, Kyoto, received a further boost when the committee discussed the world-wide impact of the bomb. Its initial use had to be "sufficiently spectacular for the importance of the weapon to be internationally recognized when publicity on it is released." It was felt that the people of Kyoto would be helpful in maximizing the international impact because they were "more highly intelligent." Presumably the protests of its survivors would be unusually articulate.

Good progress was reported at the final Target Committee meeting, on May 28 in Conference Room 4E200 at the Pentagon. Colonel Tibbets said that his 21 flight crews had been whittled down to the best 15. Each bombardier had practiced at least 50 bomb releases;

some had flown between 80 and 100 practice runs. Most drops landed within 500 feet of the target.

Five bomb-detonation heights, ranging from 700 to 2100 feet, were announced. Adequate weather reporting was arranged. Trials of the B-29's banking and turning capabilities had been completed to ensure the getaway after the bomb drop. The possibility of stationing a submarine three miles off the Japanese coast to help with navigation would be further investigated despite the negative opinion expressed by Tibbets' radar man. "It's bullshit," the officer had assured the startled conferees; tides would pull the sub off track.

Bending over their files of maps, reconnaissance photographs, and data sheets, the conferees learned new details about Kyoto, still the prime target. Lacquer factories had been converted to explosives, rayon plants were making cellulose nitrate. Some 26,446,000 square feet of industrial plant area had been identified from photographs and prisoner-of-war reports. Four plants were within 5000 feet north and west of the probable aiming point, the roundhouse of the Umekoji freight yards. Two miles west of the station a new factory was turning out 400 aircraft engines a month.

There were not many unbombed cities of appropriate size remaining, but the other priority target, Hiroshima, also qualified. Its dimensions were perfect: four miles from north to south, three miles from east to west. Various military headquarters, supply depots and a garrison of at least 25,000 troops made it "an army city." Artillery, aircraft parts, and machine tools were produced in home factories. The only disappointing note was sounded by Johnny von Neumann. He had calculated that the surrounding mountains were not close enough to heighten the bomb's effects appreciably.

Reporting on his overall progress to Secretary of War Stimson on June 12, Groves learned that the selection of the first atomic target was too important to be left to generals, including Groves. Stimson asked whether his report on the targets was ready. Groves replied that he planned to show it to General Marshall in the morning.

"Well, your report is all finished, isn't it?" asked Stimson.

"I haven't gone over it yet. I want to be sure that I've got it just right."

"Well, I would like to see it," Stimson insisted.

"Well, it's [at the office] across the [Potomac] River and it would take time to get it."

"I have all day. Here's a phone on this desk. You pick it up and call your office and have them bring the report over."

While they waited, Groves explained that he had not wanted to go over the head of General Marshall, the chief of staff.

"This is a question I am settling myself," Stimson said. "Marshall is not making that decision." What *were* the targets?

"The primary is Kyoto," Groves said.

"I will not approve that city!" snapped the Secretary. He pointed out the great religious significance of Kyoto to the Japanese and said that he had been "very much impressed by its ancient culture" when he visited there during his tenure as Governor General of the Philippines.* He said that its bombing would damage America's postwar stature. When Groves's report arrived, Stimson walked to the door separating his office from Marshall's and asked the four-star general to come in.

"Marshall," he said, "Groves has just brought me his report on the proposed targets. I don't like it. I don't like the use of Kyoto."

Groves was doubly annoyed. He had been made to look as if he had approached Stimson over Marshall's head, and he had been maneuvered out of his favorite target by a sentimental old civilian. He protested further but soon bowed to higher authority. He would nominate Kyoto for destruction again later. For the moment, Hiroshima was due to die by default.

"The various waterways give [us] ideal conditions," said Colonel Tibbets. He was meeting in the Pentagon office of the Air Force's

---

* In 1975, investigations by Professor Otis Carey of Amherst College and Kyoto's Doshisha University (where Carey's grandfather had taught in the 1890s) revealed that Stimson's affinity for Kyoto was not casual. He visited the city three times in the 1920s. On October 2, 1926, shortly before President Coolidge dispatched him to the Philippines, Stimson stayed with his wife in Room 18 of the Hotel Miyako. The couple enjoyed the city's cultural attractions so much that they returned October 30 for a five-day visit at the Miyako. In 1929, after he had been nominated Secretary of State by President Hoover, Stimson again stopped overnight in Kyoto en route to Tokyo and the United States.

commanding general, Hap Arnold, on June 23 with Arnold, General Groves, and General LeMay, who had flown in specially from Guam. The planners were studying freshly snapped aerial photographs of Hiroshima. The prints, 30 inches square, showed how the broad Ota River, heading for the Inland Sea and breaking into tributaries at the city's northern outskirts, provided an unusually distinctive landmark.

Groves asked Tibbets the best way to approach Hiroshima. Tibbets thought that the juncture of the Ota's tributaries might make a convenient aiming point. He suggested approaching it sideways. If he flew down the river, the bombardier would be concentrating on water for some time and might find it unnecessarily difficult to tell when he was approaching the aiming point (AP), the planned point of impact.

"Colonel," said Groves, "I think by the time your bombardier gets over the target, he'll be able to spot it blindfolded."

The war came late to Hiroshima. Long after Tokyo and other cities had learned to endure nights of wailing air-raid sirens and mass death, Japan's seventh-largest city seemed to bask securely in a charmed life. By spring of 1945 more and more B-29s could be spotted overhead. Susumu Desaki and his playmates shouted "B-san! (Mr. B!)" at the specks shimmering high up in the sun, but the bombers were too far away to seem real and disappeared quickly without doing harm.

For Susumu, a ten-year-old fourth-grader, the war was happening on the East Drill Ground. He lived on the eastern edge of this grassy military reservation. Half a mile wide and almost a quarter of a mile deep, this perfect playground behind Hiroshima Station became even more interesting because of the war. Soldiers drilled there with their horses. They were fun to watch and Susumu wanted to help them win the war. As he practiced charging with his bamboo spear during daily defense drills in school, he imagined sticking his weapon into the bodies of enemies, the Americans. The teachers had said they were "real devils."

By April the war had moved closer to the East Drill Ground. Anticipating an invasion of Japan, the Army divided the country into two commands. The first was in Tokyo; the newly created Second General Army covered southern Japan from Hiroshima's harbor vantage point on the Inland Sea and opened its headquarters in the former school buildings on the western edge of Susumu's great playing field.

Stepped-up invasion preparations left Susumu with little time for fun. With his parents and neighbors he had to dig an earth-covered air-raid shelter about 1½ meters deep and large enough for twenty people. Similar dugouts began to dot the entire drill ground and its earth also provided food. People in town were planting vegetables on rooftops and many were reduced to eating river reeds, pumpkin stalks, and roasted worms and beetles; that spring the sweet potatoes planted by Susumu and his neighbors were delicacies beyond price.

Susumu spent many hours each day taking care of his four-year-old brother. His father, an official for the post office, traveled much on business. His mother, bearing Susumu's nine-month-old sister on her back, had to report to her new municipal job by 7 a.m. The work was hard and depressing but was considered vital for the survival of the city.

Built on a delta surrounded on three sides by mountains and dissected by seven rivers, Hiroshima was a city of water. People loved to breathe their tangy sea air and looked to the profusion of rivers for fire safety.* But well before the peach trees blossomed that spring the authorities had decided that more defenses were needed against the inevitably coming air raids, and so Susumu's mother and crews of housewives all over town were tearing down houses to clear space for belts of vacant fire lanes.

The loss of so many homes, which would have been catastrophic in normal times, became just another bizarre statistic of Hiroshima in that bewildering springtime. The officials could no longer keep track of the seesawing exodus and influx of people. Almost 3000 homes were sacrificed before count was lost, but more than 50,000 people were evacuated to the countryside for safety, about half of them children. Tens of thousands of men went off into military service, but more than 40,000 soldiers in khaki flooded into town from elsewhere. By summer the pre-1945 population of about 400,000 had

---

* *Hiro* means "wide" in Japanese; *shima* means "island." But water was infinitely more than an amenity and protection for the residents or a pathfinder for the attackers from the air. According to ancient Japanese tradition, water can restore life in the dying; water *is* life.

shrunk to some 350,000, civilian and military, and the distinction between the two groups became increasingly blurred.

When the docks of nearby Ujina no longer embarked troops for fresh conquests, Hiroshima had ceased to be a significant military target. Its factories manufactured mostly canned meat and alcoholic drinks. But as invasion threatened in that troubled spring of 1945, civilian men dressed in the same drab khaki work clothes that looked like the uniforms of the soldiers and the women wore dark *mompei,* work pants with the bottoms tied around the ankles. Parts for bombs and shells and kamikaze planes were manufactured in many homes; children were shown how to make and hurl gasoline bombs; patients confined to beds and wheelchairs assembled booby traps to hold off the Americans at the beaches.

At Hiroshima Station, little Susumi Desaki spotted a straw figure caricaturing President Truman. A spear stood next to the scary image with its horns and devil's visage. Passersby were supposed to stab this enemy, but Susumu did not take advantage of the opportunity and saw very few who did. Perhaps the Americans really were devils whose bombs would yet fall on the city, but there were reasons why Hiroshima might remain spared. Its relationship with America was special and personal. Large waves of immigrants had left the city for the United States beginning in 1899 and thousands of families had relatives there.* A rumor circulated that President Truman had an aunt in Hiroshima. The closeness of Japanese family ties made it difficult to believe that the Americans would bomb their own relatives.

Such fantasies of immunity failed to impress realists like Dr. Kaoru Shima, the owner of the small private Shima Hospital, centrally located near Hiroshima's two most recognizable landmarks. So many surrounding houses, stores, tea rooms, and bars had been leveled for fire lanes that the doctor could look out on the concrete four-story Industry Promotion Hall with its soaring copper dome, 530 feet to the northwest. Beyond, 270 feet further in the same direction, stretched

---

* Hard times first triggered massive eastward migrations in 1894, when 11,065 Hiroshima residents—one-third of all immigrants who left Japan that year— moved to Hawaii. About 5000 a year left the city for the islands thereafter. With the turn of the century still more went directly to America.

the uniquely T-shaped Aioi Bridge, the longest of Hiroshima's forty-nine lines of life, the river crossings.*

The debris around him depressed Dr. Shima and reinforced his conviction that air raids had to be impending. Listening to the radio as a skeptical clinician, he knew that the fighting was drawing closer. When Japanese announcers spoke of "strategic withdrawals" on Iwo Jima he made the correct prognosis that the island would fall. Although the penalty for listening to enemy broadcasts was death, the doctor heard on American shortwave transmissions that Tokyo was being destroyed, that only surrender could keep all Japan from being razed.

Dr. Shima realized that he and the doctors in the city's twenty-two other hospitals could do little for massive casualties of major bombings. Medications and bandages were already scarce. Even keeping staff and patients clean was impossible; the available soap, made of rice bran and caustic soda, caused rashes. So many of his colleagues were in the military that Dr. Shima often had to go on his bicycle to perform surgery in outlying hospitals. Though the debris of the fire lanes forced him into long detours that depressed him further, the doctor maintained a façade of fatalism. "Be glad you are alive," he told anyone who complained.

At 6:55 a.m. on April 30, Dr. Shima was awakened by the first of ten 500-pound bombs that began to explode two blocks from his clinic, killing ten people. He phoned friends at army headquarters who assured him that the bombing must have been a fluke. One B-29 had probably become detached from its squadron, missed its designated target, and jettisoned its bomb load on the city because it was the nearest large settlement.

Sitting cross-legged on the floor of his hospital and calmly sipping tea, Dr. Shima mentioned this as casually as possible at his daily staff meeting. It explained that morning's break in Hiroshima's charmed existence but offered no reassurance for the future. That was taking shape in a place called Trinity.

---

* The Aioi Bridge, whose 400-foot main link spanned the Honkawa and Motoyasu rivers, would become the aiming point for the *Enola Gay*. The central portion of the Industry Promotion Hall and its "A-bomb dome" would survive as the best-known symbol of the attack.

Eighteen

The Trinity Test:
"There Could Be a Catastrophe"

Tension was palpable when General Groves drove into the heavily guarded desert base camp of the Trinity test site toward 7 p.m. on Sunday, July 15, accompanied by Vannevar Bush and James Conant.* Oppenheimer was to brief them on preparations for the test of the Fat Man plutonium bomb, scheduled for 4 a.m. Monday. President Truman was anxiously awaiting word from them in Potsdam, where he had just arrived for the Big Three meeting. The shot had had to be postponed twice before. Would it be delayed again? Everybody in the base camp was eying the sky for the answer.

It had begun to drizzle. Lightning flashed through the gloomy overcast. Rain could knock out electrical connections of the "gadget." The test site at the Alamogordo Air Base 210 miles south of Los Alamos had been chosen for its bleak isolation. The region was called Jornada del Muerto (journey of death) because many early-day travelers had succumbed to thirst there, but nuclear disasters were not likely to be confined to such a small area. In the event of strong winds, radioactive fallout would be scattered over hundreds of square miles.

Groves lacked patience for such proliferating consequences. Secrecy was more important to him than the safety of civilians. "What

* The "Trinity" code name was picked by Oppenheimer in an allusion to a John Donne sonnet containing the line "Batter my heart, three-person'd God . . ."

are you, Hearst propagandists?" he had snapped at two physicians of Oppenheimer's staff who had presented him with large-scale evacuation plans. Annoyed at the possibility of disaster headlines in the sensationalist Hearst newspapers, the general had agreed to have trucks stand by to remove the 1500 people of the nearest town, Carrizozo, if necessary; it was 30 miles east of the test site. Residents of Albuquerque and Amarillo, 125 and 300 miles distant respectively, would have to rely for guidance on a series of the general's hold-for-release press announcements offering spurious reasons for contingencies ranging from relatively manageable disasters to vast cataclysms causing the "strange deaths of many famous scientists."

Groves was infinitely more concerned about Oppenheimer's state. Oppie was emaciated, coughing and obviously exhausted. In his head Groves had already determined a new chain of command in case of his collapse. He flew in Isidor Rabi, whose mere appearance with Homburg and umbrella was a steadying influence. But Groves did not grasp the extent of Oppenheimer's psychic decline. While the general badgered the meteorologists for more weather data, Robert opened up the turmoil of his mind—only momentarily and in his obscurantist manner—to the thoughtful Vannevar Bush. Oppie did this by reciting a poem he had translated from the Sanskrit:

> In battle, in the forest, at the precipice of the mountains
> On the dark great sea, in the midst of javelins and arrows,
> In sleep, in confusion, in the depths of shame,
> The good deeds a man has done before defend him.

Was Oppenheimer bidding farewell to his era of good deeds? Was something transporting him into the depths of shame? Fear of failure at Trinity? Or fear of success? In any event, the test was a watershed for him.

Back at Los Alamos, as Oppenheimer knew, verse with a less ethereal theme was making the rounds:

> From this crude lab that spawned a dud
> Their necks to Truman's ax uncurled
> Lo, the embattled savants stood
> And fired a flop heard round the world.

A flop. Considering the extreme time pressures and the unnerving variety of unexpected crises failure was more than a threat. Some of Oppenheimer's colleagues believed it was probable, and when he disclosed the first in the series of most recent emergencies to Groves in a phone call to Washington on July 2, Oppie had told him the situation was "frantic."

Enough plutonium had finally arrived from Hanford.* Nobody had ever seen this temperamental substance. Almost none of its properties were known—not even its density—except that its toxicity was deadly. Arriving as a syrupy nitrate, it had to be purified and transformed into metal. To form the core of the bomb, 13½ pounds of the metal had to be shaped into two identical, absolutely smooth spheres and protected against corrosion by nickel plating.

Because of imperfect electroplating, blisters had suddenly formed in the worst possible places: along the matching surfaces of the hemispheres. The flaws were being abraded with dental instruments by a team of scientists, so Oppenheimer informed Groves, but some uneven spots would remain. Cyril Smith, the chief metallurgist, proposed to compensate for the imperfections by inserting a layer of gold foil between the halves at the last minute. Nobody could be certain that this improvisation would work.

The next crisis blew up before sunrise on Friday the 13th. When George Kistiakowsky arrived at Trinity base camp with a convoy carrying the explosives assembly—he had left Los Alamos just after midnight because he thought the date would bring good luck—he found headquarters in an "absolute uproar." The "X Unit" containing the firing device had failed. Oppenheimer, frantic throughout the night, came down on Kisty "like a ton of bricks." Kistiakowsky took the unit apart; it had merely overheated from too much testing.

The spheres of the plutonium core had already been driven to the

* Both the Hanford works and the uranium plant at Oak Ridge underwent near-fatal crises. At 3 a.m. on September 27, 1944, the chain reaction in the first operational Hanford reactor started to die off, poisoned by xenon 135 gas. It took Enrico Fermi until Christmas to fix it. Oak Ridge risked blowing itself up altogether. In keeping with General Groves's policy of compartmentalization, the scientists at Los Alamos were not allowed to tell the Oak Ridge officials anything about the characteristics of the uranium they were purifying. As a result, so much uranium was being piled up in one place that in time an explosion was inevitable. Richard Feynman was eventually sent to Tennessee to save the plant.

camp in the sedan owned by Robert Bacher, head of the Gadget Division. A car filled with security men was in the lead, another with more armed men brought up the rear. Tucked into two carrying cases, the plutonium, flanked by Oppie's former student, physicist Philip Morrison, and an expert in radiation monitoring, rode on the back seat to the McDonald ranch where the final assembly of the bomb began at 9 a.m.

The McDonald family would have been startled by the happenings in the home they had vacated. The rooms were vacuum-clean. Black tape sealed the windows against sand. Under Bacher's direction eight scientists in white surgical coats manipulated the plutonium spheres on a table. One wrong move would have brought slow radiation death to all. Slowly, with intense concentration, physicist Louis Slotin pushed the pieces toward each other until they almost "went critical."*

Like an expectant father Oppenheimer paced in and out of the silence of the house until Bacher quietly asked him to leave. His presence was adding too much to the tension.

Around noon, Cyril Smith, the metallurgist, gently positioned a sheet of gold foil on the flat surface of one hemisphere and adjusted the other on top for a smooth fit. The metal was warm; he would never forget its feel.

At 3:18 Kistiakowsky called from the 100-foot steel test tower at ground zero. He and his team were ready to insert the core into their explosives assembly. Slotin slipped the cylinder with the initiator between the plutonium hemispheres. The 80-pound core was carried on a litter to Bacher's car. Very slowly, Bacher drove it to Kisty's tent below the tower.

It was cool and dark under the canvas as the core was raised by manual hoist and very, very slowly lowered into the opening of the

---

* Using a screwdriver as a lever, Slotin, a cheerful, bronzed Canadian of thirty-four, also performed this operation routinely in experiments to determine the point of criticality for various reacting masses. This was known as "tickling the dragon's tail." At 3:20 p.m. on May 21, 1946, in Omega Canyon, Slotin's luck ran out. His screwdriver slipped. He hurled himself onto the mass and tore it apart with his bare hands to protect the others in the room. His treatment was limited to penicillin, eleven pints of blood, and ice packs for high fever. He died an agonizing death nine days later. According to Dr. Louis Hempelmann, the Los Alamos radiation authority, the "dragon" experiment was by this time "unauthorized."

explosives unit. Never had so much active material come so close to high explosives. A jar could have set off a chain reaction. Bacher followed the oscillations of the Geiger counter, its ticking rising rapidly. One of his assistants leaned his head into the bomb to guide the hoist by hand. Oppenheimer, immobile, watched in silence. Wind gusts made the tent flap.

Suddenly, just before the core was to click into place, it inexplicably got stuck. Cursing was heard.

Bacher was distressed. The operation had worked perfectly when he rehearsed it with dummy parts. Had heat expanded the plutonium? He counseled with Oppenheimer and Kistiakowsky and they decided simply to wait. Oppenheimer paced in front of the tent with his pipe clenched between his teeth. Within a few minutes they tried lowering the core again. The temperature of the bomb assembly had cooled it down. The pieces fit, but Oppenheimer's relief was short-lived.

The next crisis hit the following morning, Saturday, and nearly overwhelmed him. The assembled weapon was already dangling en route to the top of the tower, with the hoist grinding upward at a foot per minute, when he was told by phone from Los Alamos that his bomb would never go off. A dummy model of the explosives assembly had just been tested; it had produced a ragged shock wave instead of the required perfect symmetry.

With unrestrained fury Oppenheimer ripped into Kistiakowsky, accusing his top explosives man of having miserably failed not only him but also General Groves, the hierarchy above Groves—indeed, the entire project. Clearly desperate, Oppenheimer paced up and down trying to decide how to face final ignominy. Bacher analyzed the Los Alamos findings and also told Kisty he believed the bomb would fizzle.

"Look, Oppie," Kisty said in exasperation, "I'll bet one month of my salary against $10 that this bomb will work!" Unappeased, Oppenheimer took the bet. He asked Hans Bethe, who was still at Los Alamos, to recheck every step of the unsuccessful test and continued his worrying. At least the bomb had made it to the top of the tower. Twenty feet of mattresses had been piled up to cushion a possible fall. The bomb swayed dangerously in the strong wind, but even the derailment of a skate carrying one of the hoisting cables caused no damage.

Day One

In his cubicle that Saturday night Oppenheimer tossed through fits of coughing and slept little. Too much was new and unknown about the operation. The intensity of the chain reaction. Harnessing so much unpredictable plutonium. Neddermeyer's revolutionary implosion idea. The possibility of a fallout disaster. The unsettled weather that the meteorologists were predicting for the next two days. Any or all of this or any number of unforeseeable technical hitches could bring a fizzle, a dud, a flop—and embarrassment to the President needing support to face off Stalin at Potsdam.

The doubts of Oppenheimer's colleagues had never lessened since, earlier in Los Alamos, 103 of them had tossed dollar bills into Robert's famous pork-pie hat for their betting pool on the bomb's power. It had been designed to yield an explosive force equivalent to 20,000 tons of TNT. Only the exuberant Edward Teller had bet more: 45,000 tons. Rabi bet 18,000, Bethe 8000, Kistiakowsky 1400, Oppenheimer 300, Louis Slotin 200. In contrast with his military demeanor, Norman Ramsey, the head of the bomb Delivery Group, bet zero.

Sunday, July 15, began auspiciously for Oppenheimer. The weather was clear. Bethe phoned to report that the test on the dummy version of the explosives assembly meant nothing. He had spent all night analyzing it. It could not have measured the implosion, only its aftereffects. But in midafternoon gloom returned. Thunder became audible at the base camp, ten miles from ground zero, and by the time of Groves's arrival the weather was the focus of fierce anxiety.

Concerned about the impact of the growing tension on his people, Groves managed to add to their misery. He growled at the meteorologists who could draw no firm reassurance from the readings of the weather balloons they had floated overhead. Then the general became furious with Fermi, who was offering to bet the test would wipe out all the world's human life, with special odds on the mere destruction of New Mexico. Rumors that the bomb would set the atmosphere on fire were sweeping through the camp. Ken Bainbridge, the test director, much alarmed by the drop in morale, said his teams were overtired and at the brink of cracking up. Postponement of the test would be devastating.

Deciding at last that nothing further could be accomplished before midnight, Groves turned in and slept soundly. Bush and Conant tossed sleeplessly on cots until their tent collapsed in the wind-swept rain. Oppenheimer smoked and coughed.

About midnight Groves and Oppenheimer met again. Was postponement unavoidable? The rain continued. Mist enveloped the test tower. Storms were said to be moving in its direction. The meteorologists, having held out some hope earlier that conditions might clear after all, were "completely upset." Groves dismissed them. "After that," he claimed later, "it was necessary for me to make my own weather predictions—a field in which I had no special competence."

Suddenly the general decided that security was lax at the test tower. Saboteurs might have designs on the bomb. The Japanese might launch a parachute assault. Kistiakowsky, the old Tsarist soldier, was dispatched at the head of a force to guard their secret.* Cursing, Kisty spent the rest of the night perched on the tower. Below, soldiers with flashlights and a submachine gun patrolled ground zero with Bainbridge.

In the mess hall, Oppenheimer gulped coffee, rolled cigarette after cigarette, and endured conflicting advice. Isidor Rabi had somewhat calmed him down when Fermi rushed in to urge postponement. His usual cool was not in evidence. A wind shift followed by a radioactive rain shower would threaten everybody in the test area. The evacuation routes—few and rough even under optimal conditions— might become impassable. "There could be a catastrophe," he told Oppie. Several colleagues urged postponement for at least twenty-four hours.

Groves paced the mess hall like a trapped lion. His deputy, General Farrell the politician, tried gallows humor. "We've all had a long joyful life," he cracked. "Why not leave it in a blaze of glory?" Unamused, Groves decided to maneuver Oppenheimer away from the center of agitation. Toward 2 a.m., over the protests of the other scientists, the general drove Robert more than four miles to S-10,000, the control dugout 10,000 yards south of ground zero, where they resumed waiting, worrying, trying to outguess the weather.

* Kistiakowsky could also point to more recent military experience. For the Office of Strategic Services (OSS) he had invented an explosive that could be smuggled easily into enemy countries. It was nicknamed "Aunt Jemima" because it looked and tasted like pancake mix. Kisty demonstrated it at a high-level War Department meeting by eating some cookies baked with it.

The rain was driven by thirty-mile-an-hour winds. The lightning was moving closer to the tower. Every five to ten minutes Groves and Oppenheimer went outside to stride about, dodging pools of water, assuring each other that one or two visible stars were turning brighter. At times Groves draped a fatherly arm around Oppie's sloping shoulders. They decided that they would not fire after 5:30 a.m. Past that time too much light would nullify the essential photographic measurements.

Dr. Louis H. Hempelmann, the radiation safety officer, was the forgotten man at S-10,000. In his medical judgment a shot in rainy weather was "very risky." He kept saying so. Nobody listened. He found an army typewriter and poured out his fear in a memorandum. Nobody paid attention.

The gentle Dr. Hempelmann was accustomed to being ignored. He did not even know much about the ordinary hazards that had surrounded them every day in Los Alamos. The dangers were new, unprecedented. He had to have a hair-raising laboratory spillage of plutonium cleaned up because nobody realized that radiation weakened the glass vessels used in experiments. Even more distressing than ignorance was the cavalier attitude of the scientists toward all radiation hazards. Dr. Hempelmann diagnosed it as "lack of respect."

By 2:15 a.m. a 4 a.m. deadline for the shot had been scrapped, but the meteorologists predicted a lull in the storm sometime between five and six o'clock. At first the weather appeared not to be listening to their optimism. At 2:30 the storm hit ground zero and plunged the tower into darkness by knocking out the principal searchlight. Groves kept taking Oppenheimer into the drizzle outside to shield him from the mounting excitement of the technicians in the dugout. "If we postpone, I'll never get my people up to pitch again," Oppie said.

Shortly after three o'clock the rain stopped. About 4 a.m. the cloud cover broke and the wind died down somewhat. At 4:45 the meteorologists, who had been sending balloons aloft every fifteen minutes, handed Oppenheimer the report of his reprieve:

"Wind aloft very light, variable to forty thousand, surface calm

. . . conditions holding for next two hours." Groves no longer trusted his weathermen, but he agreed with Oppie: they would fire at 5:30.

As the general retreated alone twenty miles northwest to Compania Hill to watch the test with Bush, Conant, and high-ranking scientists from Los Alamos, the arming party under Kistiakowsky at the tower checked the bomb's electrical connections, threw the final switches, and hurried back in their jeeps to the control bunker at S-10,000. It was getting so crowded there that Dr. Hempelmann crawled under a table and read a detective novel until Sam Allison, facing two microphones, started the countdown:

"It is now zero minus twenty minutes!"

Allison, a physicist from the University of Chicago, was one of the Manhattan Project's steadiest hands. Increasingly he had inherited the management of day-to-day operations at the Chicago Metlab from Arthur "Hollywood" Compton. Allison would never panic. Intercoms, public-address systems, and FM radios all over the area began to spill out his announcements, first at five-minute intervals; then in minutes. For the last half-minute, the calls would be in seconds. Oppenheimer, his face white and lifeless, came in from the desert and watched from the doorway of the control shelter.

On Compania Hill, every observer was handed a plate of welder's glass through which to watch the explosion effects. Edward Teller smeared suntan lotion on his face as protection against ultraviolet rays. Groves stretched out on the ground between Bush and Conant, facing away, as instructed, from the direction of the tower. Only Dick Feynman, the independent spirit, ignored the rules and watched from behind the windshield of a truck. He had to *see* the result of his handiwork. At twenty miles, he said to himself, nothing could hurt his eyes.

"It is now minus five minutes," intoned Allison.

To break the tension in S-10,000, a young scientist, standing at the knife switch that could still stop the shot if anything went wrong, tried some humor. He turned toward Oppenheimer and said, "What's likely to happen, Oppie, is that at minus five seconds I'll panic and say, 'Gentlemen, this can't go on!' and then pull the switch." Oppenheimer glowered at him. "Are you all right?" he asked. He moved away to lean against a wooden pillar as if to support himself against

211

whatever shock the explosion might bring. He almost seemed to have stopped breathing. Later he would remember having said to himself, "I must remain conscious!"

In the background of the countdown, a radio station that used the same frequency could be heard, eerily, playing Tchaikovsky's *Nutcracker Suite.* But Allison's voice was clear as he parceled out the seconds: "Five . . . four . . . three . . . two . . ." It occurred to him suddenly that the detonation might work like lightning. Could the microphone electrocute him? At minus one second he dropped it and yelled at the top of his voice: *"Zero!"* It was 5:29 a.m.

Nothing. At 5:29:45, suddenly, noiselessly, the sky ignited. A yellow-reddish fireball infinitely brighter than the sun, its temperature 10,000 times greater, began an eight-mile ascent, warming the faces of the men at Trinity, turning night into day for more than a hundred miles.

William L. Laurence of the *New York Times,* prone on his belly, thought of the Lord's command, "Let there be light!"* Isidor Rabi feared the boiling brightness would glare "forever." Behind the windshield of his truck, Dick Feynman, temporarily blinded, turned away in pain. General Farrell exclaimed, "The long-hairs have let it get away from them!"

Oppenheimer remembered a line from the Bhagavad Gita: "I am become death, the shatterer of worlds!" Kistiakowsky, exuberant, slapped him on the back and shouted, "Oppie, I won the bet!" Oppenheimer, trembling, pulled out his wallet, couldn't find ten dollars, and muttered, "George, I don't have it."†

Bainbridge grasped Oppenheimer's hand. He was smiling, greatly relieved because he had just avoided the worst job of all. He would not have to climb the test tower alone to find out why the bomb had fizzled—and perhaps inadvertently set it off after all. Yet his mood was dark. He thought of the bomb damage he had seen in England

---

* Laurence, the *Times*'s science writer, had been picked by General Groves as the only reporter to record the Trinity test as well as the ensuing final secret phases of the Manhattan project. Laurence became a valuable government propagandist. His warmly admiring dispatches were embargoed and published shortly after the war ended. They displayed no reservations about anything he saw or heard. Indeed, Laurence's admiration of atomic bombs approached the worshipful. Of the Nagasaki weapon he wrote, "It is a thing of beauty to behold."

† Oppenheimer paid off the bet on VJ-Day and also gave Kistiakowsky a kiss.

and as he shook his friend Robert's hand he sounded the first public note of regret: "Oppie, now we're all sons of bitches!"

On Compania Hill, Enrico Fermi, the irrepressible experimenter, waited almost forty seconds after the fireball erupted to start his instant test of the bomb's power. Holding up his right hand to a height of about six feet, he released some paper scraps he had been clutching. The wind had died down, yet as the bomb's blast wave hit—at a distance of twenty miles it felt like little more than a caress—the scraps floated for about two and a half meters, causing Fermi to estimate that the blast had been as potent as 10,000 tons of TNT.*

Sitting on the ground, Conant and then Bush reached out to shake hands with Groves. Bush said that the blast had seemed brighter than a star. Groves, hoping for promotion to the three-star rank of lieutenant general, pointed at his major general's two stars and cracked, "Brighter than two stars!" Rising, they joined the euphoria swirling around them. As Laurence would record, scientists were "shaking hands, slapping each other on the back, laughing like happy children." Some broke into a jig, "like primitive man dancing at one of his fire festivals at the coming of spring."

Not Rabi. "At first I was thrilled," he remembered later. "It was a vision. Then, a few minutes afterward, I had gooseflesh all over me when I realized what this meant for the future of humanity." His gooseflesh recurred as dawn broke and Rabi watched Oppenheimer get out of the car that brought him back from S-10,000. Oppie's bearing was easy, confident, and Rabi would never forget his walk. It was the strut of a man who shattered worlds, not the walk of an ordinary mortal.

At 5:55 Groves phoned Mrs. O'Leary, who had been waiting in his Washington office for almost two hours. Using a private code they had prearranged, the general told his assistant the good news. She rushed to the Pentagon to see Stimson's man George Harrison. Together they composed a message to the Secretary of War at Potsdam: "Operated on this morning. Diagnosis not yet complete but results seem satisfactory and already exceed expectations. Local press release necessary as interest extends a great distance. Dr. Groves pleased . . ."

---

* The correct figure turned out to be 20,000 tons. Rabi's guess of 18,000 tons was the closest and won the scientists' pool.

Newspapers, wire services, and sheriffs within a radius of 300 miles were flooded by inquiries and eyewitness accounts—including one from a blind woman who had seen the light. To quiet the alarm, Groves ordered the Alamogordo Air Base to release one of his prepared press handouts: "A remotely located ammunition magazine containing a considerable amount of high explosives and pyrotechnics exploded. There was no loss of life or injury . . ." At the last minute Groves added a new sentence: "Weather conditions affecting the content of gas shells exploded by the blast may make it desirable for the Army to evacuate temporarily a few civilians from their homes."

The "gas" that Groves had excellent reason to fear was in fact a radioactive cloud, and it was being chased by jeeps loaded with fallout monitors in white coveralls and gas masks. One of them, Dr. Joseph O. Hirschfelder, encountered a totally paralyzed mule 25 miles from ground zero. Victor Weisskopf, driving about in his own battered jeep, saw what was facing the radiation detectives and grew increasingly embarrassed at the nickname his Los Alamos associates had bestowed upon him.

Ever since he had been placed in charge of predicting the bomb's effects, they had called him "the oracle." He knew that his calculations were no more than "imaginative guesswork." The outer layers of the bomb would expand under pressure a thousand times greater than anything investigated before. Nevertheless, he had considered it safe to predict that radiation should drop to harmless levels about three miles from ground zero. Clearly this was not happening.

By 4:20 p.m., a Geiger counter in Carrizozo jumped off its scale. Before dusk, sections of the radioactive cloud were dropping fallout on Vaughn, a town 112 miles north, well beyond the area the monitors had been assigned to investigate. By nightfall, measurements were dropping and the danger was thought to be over. Not until the war was over in mid-August did ranchers on the Chupadera Mesa west of Carrizozo report that cattle were losing their hair and suffering severe skin blisters.

In the car headed back to Los Alamos, Oppenheimer was all but robbed of speech. He had wanted to drive himself, but Norman

Ramsey thought he looked too jittery and volunteered to chauffeur Oppie and Rabi. Oppenheimer's nervous exhaustion reminded Ramsey of the letdown he had often seen in his physics students after an exam. Nobody in the car spoke of anything except, occasionally, the scenery.

At Los Alamos, euphoria had taken a noisy turn. A snake dance was winding its way through the streets. The dancers were shouting, hugging each other, and passing liquor bottles up and down the line. The observers trickling back from Trinity were mobbed. Some, dead tired, dropped straight into bed. Others, still too tense to relax, burbled like enthralled tourists recalling an exotic fireworks display: "It was fabulous! You should have seen it!"

One scientist sat on the radiator of a jeep playing an accordion. Others banged the lids of garbage cans as if they were cymbals. The joyous party at Oppenheimer's house that night went on long into the night. One physicist leaned over the stair railing, threatening to dive off and detonate just above the floor. Another pretended he was Groves guarding the shot tower.

Not everyone was caught up in the hilarity, however. In a hallway of the Tech Area, Dick Feynman, who had been sitting on a jeep firing up the celebration by beating on a set of Indian drums, ran into Robert Wilson. Wilson, who had recruited Feynman for Los Alamos and brought him west with his Princeton team, looked morose.

"What are you moping about?" Feynman asked.

"It's a terrible thing that we made!" Wilson said.

"You're crazy! What's the matter with you? You, of all people! You're the guy that got me into it."

Feynman could not understand—not yet, that is—how the light that turned the Alamogordo night into noon had just as radically transformed Wilson's Magic Mountain Fever into fear and disgust at what he and his friends had perpetrated.* "I was a different person from then on," Wilson said years later.

The ebullient Kistiakowsky was caught in the ambivalence of sec-

---

* Feynman's euphoria turned into depression after Hiroshima. Sitting in a restaurant on New York's 59th Street he reflected that a bomb would pulverize all buildings as far as 34th Street. Such thoughts persisted. He wrote: "I would see people building a bridge and I thought they're crazy, they just don't understand. Why are they making new things? It's so useless."

ond thoughts. When Bill Laurence of the *Times* cornered him in the cafeteria and asked what he thought of the Trinity results, the Russian explosives expert said, "I am sure that at the end of the world, in the last millisecond of the earth's existence, the last human will see what we saw."

At least two men who had been invited to witness the test were happy that they had decided not to see it. Dr. David Hawkins, a philosophy professor Oppenheimer had assigned to write the project's history, had felt that, his official position notwithstanding, he could not quite face the destructive event. Seth Neddermeyer, the father of implosion, was already dreading the power of his creation. "I'd hoped the damned thing wouldn't work," he recalled long afterward.

Dr. Charles L. Critchfield was surprised at the depth of his reaction to the test. The sight had hit him so strongly that he flinched reflexively for weeks whenever he saw lightning flash during one of the thunderstorms that blew up almost every afternoon over Los Alamos.

Gangling and laconic, Critchfield was one of the precocious old-timers of nuclear physics. In the mid-1930s he had been one of Edward Teller's first graduate students at the "G Street High School" in Washington and had been friends with Oppenheimer since that innocent time. Like Oppie, he had to brush up his German to be accepted as an equal in the shoptalk of Teller, Szilard, and the other noisy pace setters of the new science.

In Los Alamos, the systematic, unemotional Critchfield had been proud to lead the group that perfected the troublesome initiator of the implosion bomb ("It was my device that made the thing go!"). The delight in his achievement would never leave him, yet the visual impact of the Trinity gadget triggered reservations he had not felt before. He could share them only in private and with no one but Oppenheimer.

"It's stupid to use this as a weapon, Robert," he told the director. "Let's do something imaginative!"

Some nonmilitary demonstration of the bomb was what Critchfield had in mind. It seemed a new notion to him. He had not heard it discussed by anybody and could think of no scheme to bring it off. Surely a brilliant thinker like Oppenheimer could devise a way.

Oppenheimer, listening patiently, offered no hint that he had ever discussed the subject before. He looked exhausted and responded non-committally in a hoarse, barely audible whisper. Critchfield assumed that the voice loss was an emotional reaction to the Trinity test. It did not surprise him that the spectacle should literally have taken his tempestuous boss's voice away.

Disappointed, he left Oppenheimer's office only to reappear a few days later to renew his proposal—with the same results. When Critchfield brought the subject up in yet a third private interview, he was becoming angry. There absolutely *had* to be some way to show off this weapon without dumping it like any ordinary bomb. Oppenheimer's unenterprising attitude struck Critchfield as unreasonable and he said so.

Oppenheimer, his voice improved, said that the military experts did not like the demonstration idea because the trial bomb might be a dud. Critchfield shrugged. There would be more bombs. In response, Oppenheimer praised the judgment of America's top military men. Not wishing to challenge that judgment, Critchfield waited to hear more justification for rejecting the demonstration idea.

Whereupon Oppenheimer said, "George is an angel," and terminated the discussion.

Critchfield inferred correctly that Robert was talking about Chief of Staff George C. Marshall, and Oppie's strange phrasing did not trouble him. Robert was emotional and did not talk like other people. He often spoke in riddles and was addicted to dark sayings. Critchfield thought he liked to make a point of sounding mysterious. It seemed a harmless eccentricity. He thought Robert could be relied upon to "do what was right."

Critchfield did not learn for years that he had not been the lone champion of the demonstration idea; that his baby had been strangled weeks before he thought he had given birth to it; and that Oppie had pulled the noose.

He told Oppenheimer that he would not mention the subject again but that he was disappointed. Oppie said nothing. Inscrutability suited him.

Klaus Fuchs, the Russian spy and the one scientist at Los Alamos leading an inner life more lonely than Oppenheimer's, had watched the Trinity blast, typically, inscrutably, alone. He had stationed himself on a saddle linking two hillocks at Compania Hill and remained standing. The official calculations on the power of the blast and on its curves as a function of distance had convinced him that it was unnecessary to lie down. Fuchs had confidence in the figures because he was largely responsible for working them out.

Good things had been happening to the German Communist émigré since his admittance to the mesa via Great Britain and New York. His sallow complexion was ruddier. His five-foot-nine frame had filled out to about 150 pounds. He enjoyed mountain climbing, skiing, and touring the countryside in his battered blue Buick convertible—although it lacked a speedometer and the tires needed constant patching.

Having rapidly advanced to stardom in Hans Bethe's Theoretical Division, he seemed more assured and basked in popularity and success. Working once again with Rudolph Peierls and Otto Frisch, his first mentors back in Birmingham, Fuchs was in the vanguard of the pioneering on implosion and became Peierls's deputy. His precision and imagination elicited admiration from his superiors, men not easy to please. Bethe liked Fuchs's willingness to volunteer for ever more work. Edward Teller considered him "kind" and "helpful." Bob Bacher admired his versatility and the brilliant mind hungry for involvement.

Involved—that was the word for Fuchs. He was the first at work in the morning. Chain smoking, peering owlishly through tortoise shell spectacles, he poured out computations of such quality in his 10-by-12 cubicle that he was the logical man to be appointed liaison between the theoretical and the explosives divisions. It made him one of the best-informed hands at the 4 p.m. Friday meetings of the Coordinating Council, the top leadership. His overview of the most advanced work on the mesa was superb, probably second only to those of Oppenheimer and the division chiefs.

Not ill at ease or shy in the conventional sense, Fuchs was obsessively reticent and eager not to be noticed. He hated to have his picture taken and did not walk down the middle of hallways; he hugged the walls as if seeking cover. He did not mention politics or his family or indeed much of anything except work. Mrs. Peierls called him

"Penny-in-the-slot Fuchs" because words came out of Klaus only after words were inserted into him.

Women looked protectively upon Fuchs, the gentle bachelor. An Italian scientist's wife called him *"poverino"* (pitiful one). At parties Klaus was an enthusiastic dancer, but his palms were wet and his repertoire was limited to a waltzing three-step. Children loved him and he was a favorite baby-sitter, usually available, ever reliable. Romantic attachments were so obviously lacking in his life, however, that the fun-loving Dick Feynman took him to task about his monastic existence as they sat on Fuchs's G.I. bed in the austere Bachelor Dormitory No. 102, drinking orange juice.

Fuchs frowned at Feynman's frivolousness and turned, as always, toward work. "Don't you think the Russians should be told what we're doing?" he asked. Feynman nodded vaguely. It was not an unusual suggestion in those war days of close collaboration with the Soviets. "Then why don't we send them information?" Fuchs insisted. Feynman said that such a decision was hardly up to them and he soon forgot what sounded like an abstract—but for Fuchs probably unique—outburst.

By the time of the Trinity test, Fuchs had fed the Russians atomic information seven times, always through Harry Gold, the pudgy biochemist courier who reported to Anatoli Yakovlev, the Russian vice consul in New York. The Russians had become increasingly excited as the progress achieved by Oppenheimer and his men produced information of growing importance. Fuchs reported on the successful production of plutonium. He revealed details of the plutonium bomb and the implosion lens that would set it off. These and other secrets Fuchs handed to Gold in sheaves of meticulous notes.

Their seventh meeting began a few minutes after 4 p.m. on Saturday, June 2, under the noses of General Groves's counterintelligence agents. Previously the spies had scheduled their meetings during Fuchs's holiday trips to the East Coast. This time, by prearrangement, they met on the Castillo Bridge in Santa Fe. Since it was Gold's first visit to the Southwest, he had purchased a map so he would not have to ask for directions.

He got into Klaus's Buick and they drove about, chatting, for half an hour. Progress on the mesa had been dramatic, Fuchs remarked.

Day One

It was a gratuitous comment because the Russians could see Oppenheimer's successes in technical detail in the new package of notes Fuchs turned over to Gold in the car.* If these two men had not actually fired the first silent shots of the Cold War, they had certainly fed it the intelligence information that made its escalation inevitable, and escalation was the name of the game already in progress around the conference table at Potsdam.

* Unknown to Fuchs, Gold moved on by bus to the Hilton Hotel in Albuquerque, and the next day dropped in at the apartment of a draftsman from the Los Alamos workshops: David Greenglass, a member of the Young Communist League who had been recruited for spy duty by his brother-in-law, Julius Rosenberg. Gold's recognition signal, "I come from Julius," was one of the recollections made famous in the trial of Rosenberg and his wife, Ethel, which culminated in their executions as Communist spies. Greenglass drew a sketch of the implosion lens for Gold. The Russians had urgently asked for such a drawing and the judge in the Rosenberg trial elevated it to the status of pricelessness. Subsequently sworn expert opinion called the sketch "amateurish" and "bungling." It was not, however, an accurate reflection of Greenglass's knowledge, for the Atomic Energy Commission, nervous about the risk of still more leaks, would not let him testify to all he knew. The point remained: Greenglass's grasp of the secret material within his purview was laughable compared to Fuchs's extraordinary expertise and access. At his final meeting with Gold on September 19 near a church on a road leading out of Santa Fe, Fuchs gave away the rest of Oppenheimer's store. The package he handed Gold contained notes on the precise size of the plutonium bomb, the dimensions of its parts, and how it was constructed and detonated.

Nineteen

The Big Three at Potsdam: "Release When Ready"

President Truman was much in need of good news from Trinity.

"How I hate this trip!" he had written in his diary on the way to Europe. Jaunty in a double-breasted plaid suit and a cloth visor cap, he put in a smiling appearance on the deck of the U.S.S. *Augusta* to watch the practice firing of the cruiser's eight-inch and five-inch and forty-millimeter guns, but his cheer was false.

"I'd still rather fire a battery than run a country," the former artillery captain confided to his diary. His nervousness at having to face his formidable allies, Stalin and Churchill—he thought of them as "Mr. Russia and Mr. Great Britain"—was only slightly tempered by the poker-playing shipboard presence of Jimmy Byrnes, "my able and conniving Secretary of State."*

Their arrival late on July 15 in the Potsdam suburb of Babelsberg outside Berlin, once the elegant seat of the German movie colony and now occupied by the Russians, did not lift the President's spirits. His three-story stucco villa at No. 2 Kaiserstrasse—renamed the "Little White House" by his staff although it was yellow—had been looted by Soviet troops. American officers made it barely livable with a scattering of makeshift furniture. "Nothing matches," Truman recorded. "Basement used as outdoor toilets."

By contrast, the conference headquarters, the 176-room Cecilien-

---

* The diary pages dealing with the President's Potsdam trip were misfiled and not unearthed until 1979.

hof, was outfitted with exquisite furnishings specially imported from Moscow. Stalin's staff had carpeted the courtyard of this palace, originally built for the last crown prince of the Hohenzollerns, with a brilliant 24-foot red star of geraniums, pink roses, and hydrangeas.

Secretary of War Stimson, who had not been invited to the conference but invited himself, had arrived ahead of the President and gone to work on long-pending policy questions that kept his mind in anguish. While Truman and Byrnes toured the nearby ruins of Hitler's bombed-out Berlin ("retribution to the nth degree" the President self-righteously called the sight), Stimson drafted a memorandum urging that the proposed American surrender ultimatum to Japan be proclaimed immediately.

"Now is the psychological moment," he wrote. He hoped that Truman and Byrnes would take him literally; the time was clearly ripe to give the Japanese a diplomatic shove. They were receptive to peace negotiations. Only three days earlier the United States had decoded secret cables from the Japanese Foreign Minister asking his Ambassador in Moscow to push the Russians to act as mediators. Stimson knew the Japanese mentality: the Emperor would be the key to ending the war. Truman's ultimatum would be more effective if it assured the enemy that the Emperor might be acceptable as a constitutional monarch, and so the Secretary recommended.*

At 7:30 p.m. on Monday, July 16, Stimson received the news he hoped for. He had just sent copies of his memorandum on Japan to Truman and Byrnes, who shared quarters in the Little White House, when the first flash from George Harrison and Mrs. O'Leary arrived, reporting success at Trinity ("Operated on this morning. Diagnosis not yet complete . . ."). Elated, Stimson replied: "I send my warmest congratulations to the doctor and his consultant." Then he rushed to show the message from Washington to Truman and Byrnes. They were pleased but, in the absence of details, not excited.

The following morning Byrnes received Stimson alone and rejected his advice about an ultimatum to Japan. Any warning to Japan should be delayed, Byrnes said. In any event, it should be silent

---

* The chaos of conflicting advice among the Americans at Potsdam was such that within the next few days Stimson twice changed his mind about Hirohito. First he withdrew his support of the Emperor. Then he reverted to his original advice in favor of the Emperor's retention. No matter. Stimson was no longer an influential adviser.

about the Emperor, the despised symbol of the sneak attack on Pearl Harbor. Roosevelt's Secretary of State, the aged and ailing "Judge" Cordell Hull, had cautioned Byrnes that any ultimatum would sound "too much like appeasement." And if it failed, "terrible political repercussions" would follow in Congress and in the press. Byrnes had agreed and so had Truman. The President wanted to deal sternly with the enemy who had treated American prisoners of war abominably. "The Japs are savages," he wrote in his diary.

A second cable arrived from Harrison that night: "Doctor has just returned most enthusiastic and confident that the little boy is as husky as his big brother. The light in his eyes discernible from here to Highhold and I could have heard his screams from here to my farm." The decoding officers were delighted; they thought Stimson had become a father at the age of seventy-eight and that the conference might take a day off to celebrate. Stimson explained the cable's private code to Truman, who was less impressed.* He wanted more solid details about the effectiveness of the new weapon.

At his office in Foggy Bottom, General Groves was working at top speed to do justice to that very subject. He had asked that the courier plane to "Terminal," the code name for Potsdam, scheduled to depart at 2 a.m., be held up while he polished his report on Trinity for the President.

"The test was successful beyond the most optimistic expectations of anyone," the account began. Not only had the test tower "evaporated." Half a mile from Ground Zero another steel tower, 70 feet high, had been ripped apart although "none of us had expected it to be damaged." Windows were broken 125 miles away. Unsuspecting citizens reacted in alarm within a radius of 200 miles. "One of these was a blind woman who saw the light."

Groves's deputy, General Farrell, appending his personal impressions to the report, wrote that the blast had made him think of doomsday. He felt "that we puny things were blasphemous to dare tamper with the forces heretofore reserved for the Almighty." Putting piety aside, he reminded the negotiators at Potsdam that the

---

* Highhold, Stimson's hundred-acre estate near Huntington, Long Island, was 250 miles from Washington. Harrison's farm at Upperville, Virginia, was 50 miles from the capital.

United States now had "the means to insure [the war's] speedy conclusion and save thousands of American lives."

The courier plane took off with the report shortly after 2 a.m., and at 3:30 p.m. (European time) on Saturday, July 21, Stimson read it aloud to Truman and Byrnes in the second-floor sun room of the Little White House. Stimson's normally careful speech became blurred with excitement, and since the villa lacked window screens the three statesmen had to keep swatting mosquitoes. But this time Groves had sold his bomb convincingly.

"The President was tremendously pepped up," Stimson recorded in his diary. "He said it gave him an entirely new feeling of confidence." In his own diary the President called Groves's news "startling—to put it mildly." Cataclysms from the Old Testament came to his mind: "It may be the fire destruction prophesied in the Euphrates Valley Era after Noah and his fabulous Ark."

Churchill, too, resorted to biblical terms when Stimson handed him Groves's report on Sunday morning. The Prime Minister brimmed over with exuberance: "Stimson, what was gunpowder? Trivial. What was electricity? Meaningless. This atomic bomb is the second coming in wrath." The bomb also explained the dramatic transformation Churchill had witnessed in President Truman at Saturday's formal conference session with the Soviets.

"Now I know what happened to Truman yesterday," he told Stimson. "I couldn't understand it. When he got to the meeting after having read this report he was a changed man. He told the Russians just where they got on and off and generally bossed the whole meeting." Suddenly the President was no longer "hating" his first venture into world politics.

Much more than the level of Truman's confidence was changed by Groves's vivid reporting. The general's evocation of Trinity made the bomb a reality to the decision makers. At that instant, nuclear weaponry assumed a towering influence that it would never lose. It was, as Stimson reflected, "a final arbiter of force." And the United States held it in exclusive control.

The Russians were first to feel the effects of Truman's nuclear muscle because they were becoming increasingly aggressive at the conference table. In addition to pushing for maximum influence in

Austria and Eastern Europe, Stalin was demanding bases in Turkey and showing interest in Italy's Mediterranean colonies. With the bomb in his pocket, Truman found it easy to dismiss these new moves as bluff. At the same time, his new nuclear asset promoted radical changes in long-standing American policy positions.

Stimson, recognizing this, wrote in his diary, "The program for S-1 is tying in what we are doing in all fields."

Truman had come to Potsdam eager to persuade the Soviets to enter the war against Japan at the earliest moment. After receiving the news from Groves, the President no longer felt a need for Russian military support and stopped pressing for it. Until Potsdam, international control of atomic energy had remained a live issue. Now it was dead. Before Potsdam, Truman had planned to tell Stalin the secret of the bomb's existence. Instead, when he brought up the subject at the end of the formal conference session, at about 7:30 p.m. on July 24, he managed even to avoid calling the weapon by its name. Why compromise such an overwhelming secret?

The President's effort to achieve the desired staging for his revelation was extraordinary. Although he had previously rehearsed the scene with Stimson, Byrnes, and Churchill, he acted it out with a light touch. To make his approach to Stalin look offhand, he instructed his interpreter to stay behind. Alone, he walked around the circular conference table in the dark-paneled room, sidled up to Stalin and the Russian interpreter, and "casually mentioned" that the United States "had a new weapon of unusual destructive force."

In his memoirs Truman recorded: "The Russian Premier showed no special interest. All he said was that he was glad to hear it and hoped we would 'make good use of it against the Japanese.'"

Churchill recalled that Stalin's "face remained gay and genial." The British Prime Minister's memory of the bizarre encounter was vivid: "I was perhaps five yards away, and I watched with the closest attention the momentous talk. I knew what the President was going to do. What was vital was to measure its effect on Stalin. I can see it all as if it were yesterday. He seemed to be delighted. A new bomb! Of extraordinary power! Probably decisive on the whole Japanese war! What a bit of luck!"

Waiting for their cars outside the Cecilienhof Palace, Churchill asked Truman, "How did it go?"

"He never asked a question," the President replied.

Both men were convinced that they had fooled Stalin, that the Russian had not realized the import of what he was told. They would have been greatly shaken had they heard Stalin, shortly afterward, telling Molotov about his conversation with Truman. The Russians knew perfectly well that the President's thickly veiled reference had been to an *atomic* bomb. Molotov confirmed their understanding by telling Stalin: "We'll have to talk it over with Kurchatov and get him to speed things up."*

Shortly after his return to Moscow, Stalin summoned Kurchatov and his colleagues. "A single demand on you, comrades," he said. "Provide us with atomic weapons in the shortest possible time. You know that Hiroshima has shaken the whole world. The balance has been destroyed. Provide the bomb—it will remove a great danger to us." And from then on, to the envy of other scientists, Kurchatov was a regular caller at the Kremlin.

The Cold War was going into a new round of escalation just as the hot war moved into its climactic phase.

Truman decided to fire the opening salvo at 7 p.m. on July 26 by making the Japanese taste his freshly found authority. Without bothering to inform the Russians, he released the long-discussed surrender ultimatum for Tokyo. Its details were largely the handiwork of Jimmy Byrnes and the wording could hardly have been harsher—or less helpful to Japanese politicians interested in negotiating peace—but the enemy needed to be shaken up.

"Following are our terms," it began peremptorily. "We will not deviate from them. There are no alternatives. We shall brook no delay." The text demanded "unconditional surrender" and held out no hope for the retention of the Emperor. It ignored this godly figure. Nor did the document contain the warning, discussed earlier in Washington, that a *nuclear* holocaust lay in wait for Japanese cities. It did not mention any new weapon. It simply promised the Japanese

---

* At this point the Russian leadership and their principal nuclear research chief, Kurchatov, "The Beard," had been informed of western progress with the bomb for more than two years by their spy Klaus Fuchs. It is possible but unlikely that by July 24 the Russians had somehow already received word of the previous week's successful test at Trinity. The net effect of Truman's attempt to deceive the Russians was to intensify their paranoia and accelerate their efforts to acquire a bomb of their own.

"prompt and utter destruction" and kept the atomic ace hidden in Truman's sleeve.

In a lonely rear-guard action, Stimson did manage to get his reprieve of Kyoto reaffirmed. In keeping with the new martial spirit of the decision makers, Groves reopened the controversy about the usefulness of dooming the holy city. Still wanting to impress the Japanese with his might by making the old capital a prime target, the general persuaded George Harrison to cable Stimson: "All your local military advisers engaged in preparations definitely favor your pet city and would like to feel free to use it as first choice if those on the ride select it out of possible four spots in the light of local conditions at the time."

Stimson's reply bounced back within hours: "Aware of no factors to change my decision. On the contrary new factors tend to confirm it."

When Stimson informed Truman of this exchange the following day he was relieved to find the President in agreement. "The target will be a purely military one," Truman wrote in his diary. Stimson spelled out in his own record the new considerations for sparing Kyoto: "The bitterness which would be caused by such a wanton act might make it impossible during the long postwar period to reconcile the Japanese to us in that area rather than to the Russians."

While he disclaimed "wanton" acts against the Japanese, Truman never questioned whether the bomb should be dropped at all. He was carried along on the momentum generated by Groves, Oppenheimer, Byrnes, and, somewhat more cautiously, Stimson. The saturation bombings of Europe and Tokyo had inured the President to mass killing, and he was hardly qualified to understand the unique biological consequences of the bomb that were unclear even to the scientists. Pearl Harbor and the whole course of the war made retribution attractive. The prospect of long casualty lists from Japanese invasion beaches was chilling. As a dividend, his handy atomic club might induce some tractability in the Russians, who in the long run promised to be more trouble than the Japanese "savages." No wonder Churchill recalled that the use of the bomb "was never even an issue."*

---

* Ironically, key military leaders who were at Potsdam did express reservations about the bomb. Admiral Leahy had developed moral compunctions.

In the absence of policy complications, Groves's scenario began to unfold smoothly, with George Harrison, as always, the middleman.

On July 21, Harrison cabled Stimson: "Patient progressing rapidly and will be ready for final operation first good break in August."

This was earlier than Stimson had expected. He checked with Truman and responded, "We are greatly pleased with apparent improvement of patient's progress." Remembering Groves's relentlessness, Stimson still did not trust the general to leave Kyoto unscathed. The Secretary asked again for confirmation of the target cities, "always excluding the particular place against which I have decided. My decision has been confirmed by highest authority."

On July 23, Harrison cabled Stimson: "Operation may be possible any time from August 1 depending on state of preparation of patient and condition of atmosphere. From point of view of patient only some chance August 1 to 3, good chance August 4 to 5 and barring unexpected relapse almost certain before August 10."

On July 24, at an all-day meeting in the Pentagon, Nagasaki, a seaport with industrial establishments, was added to the target list. And there was one note of slight uneasiness about dropping such an "unusual" weapon. The responsible field commander, crusty General Carl ("Tooey") Spaatz, commander of the United States Strategic Air Force, said he preferred more than verbal orders. He wanted "a piece of paper."

Groves had prudently drawn up such a directive in May. He now revised it slightly and at 6:35 p.m. on July 25 it was cabled to Potsdam for approval: "1. The 509th Composite Group, Twentieth Air Force, will deliver its first special bomb as soon as weather will permit visual bombing after about 3 August 1945 on one of the targets: Hiroshima, Kokura, Niigata and Nagasaki . . . 2. Additional bombs will be delivered on the above targets as soon as made ready by the project staff . . ."

Air Force chief General Arnold, prompted by General LeMay of his bomber command, thought conventional bombing would suffice to force Japan's surrender. General Eisenhower, briefed on the bomb by Stimson, "expressed the hope that we would never have to use such a thing against an enemy because I disliked seeing the United States take the lead in introducing into war something as horrible and destructive . . ." The doubts aired earlier by Assistant Secretary of War McCloy, Under Secretary of the Navy Bard, and Rear Admiral Strauss were forgotten.

Groves's assembly line, then, was geared to drop atomic weapons indefinitely beyond the first hit on Hiroshima, and the decision makers at Potsdam knew it. Oppenheimer would have his lone gun-type uranium bomb ready about August 1. The first plutonium bomb, as tested at Trinity, would be assembled—so Stimson had been informed by another cable from Harrison—about August 6. Oppie would have his second plutonium bomb finished by August 24. Beginning in September, the production schedule called for an estimated three plutonium bombs a month. Starting in December, seven or more per month could be expected.

Earlier, Groves had talked casually to Bush and Conant of dropping only one or two bombs, but the approved plan was open-ended. Since the July 25 order called for "additional bombs" to be delivered on targets "as soon as made ready," Groves's path was clear. He was to keep on dropping bombs, one after another, unless he received an order to stop.

It was Chief of Staff General Marshall who within six hours cabled back approval of the July 25 order, but nobody doubted that presidential authority stood behind it. "With this order the wheels were set in motion for the first use of an atomic weapon against a military target," Truman wrote in his memoirs. "I had made the decision. I also instructed Stimson that the order would stand unless I notified him that the Japanese reply to our ultimatum was acceptable."

Having returned to Washington by air, ahead of the presidential party, Stimson was in his Pentagon office when the *New York Times* headlined on July 30: JAPAN OFFICIALLY TURNS DOWN ALLIED SURRENDER ULTIMATUM.

It was another long day for the ailing Secretary. In the morning he worked with Bundy, Harrison, and Groves on the draft of the presidential press release that would announce the first bomb drop. Truman was likely to be on his way home by sea when the bomb fell on Hiroshima, so Stimson wanted stand-by authority from the President to release the statement in Washington.

"We made some changes in it which were induced by the difference in psychology which now exists since the successful test," he wrote in his diary. The "difference" was the same lift that Truman had experienced when he heard Groves's first report about Trinity read to him at Potsdam only nine days before. Stimson wanted to be sure to inject a triumphant note into the Truman statement: "We put some more pep into the paper and made it a little more dramatic . . ."

With almost no time left before the first bomb drop, Stimson cabled Truman: "The time schedule on Groves' project is progressing so rapidly that it is now essential that statement for release by you be available not later than Wednesday, August 1." He then sent Lieutenant Gordon Arneson, secretary of the defunct Interim Committee, to Berlin by late-night courier plane with two copies of the presidential statement.

On Tuesday, July 31, Truman routinely passed up another chance to alter Groves's scenario. Having read the statement drafted by Stimson and his men, the President wrote his reply in longhand and gave it to Lieutenant George M. Elsey, his assistant naval aide, to be transmitted via the traveling White House cryptographic equipment: "Suggestions approved. Release when ready but not sooner than August 2. HST."

Elsey knew the significance of the August 2 date. It was the day Truman would leave Potsdam. If the bomb were to fall before then, the President might be cross-examined about it by Stalin after all, and that might spoil what had turned into a great trip.

Just as Stimson had surmised, the Emperor was indeed pivotal in any Japanese moves toward surrender. And he was more. Unknown to the West, Hirohito had injected himself into the turbulent Tokyo political scene and seized the initiative by devising maneuvers startlingly out of keeping with imperial custom.

The idea of asking the Japanese Ambassador in Moscow to enlist the Soviets as active peace mediators had been his. Vague Japanese diplomatic talks in Moscow had been dragging on fruitlessly. The week before the Potsdam Conference was to begin, the Emperor summoned Prime Minister Kantaro Suzuki and questioned him with uncharacteristic impatience. Why was nothing happening in Moscow? Suzuki, a retired admiral of seventy-seven, quite deaf, made embarrassed excuses. Curtly the Emperor said he wanted to dispatch a personal envoy to the Kremlin. Moscow should be so informed. Precious moments were being wasted.

Rush to Decision

Long unhappy to be at war,* Hirohito had decided it was most urgent for him to use his unique influence to stop it. While his generals agitated for a last-ditch defense of the homeland, the Emperor's conviction that this was folly received final confirmation on June 12 when he received his private investigator, Admiral Kioshi Hasegawa, the former governor general of Formosa, behind the wide moats separating the Imperial Palace grounds from the rest of Central Tokyo.

They met in emergency quarters surrounded by calamitous evidence of war. Three weeks earlier one of General LeMay's fire raids had destroyed the palace and twenty-six of its satellite buildings. Forty fire engines and almost 10,000 firemen and soldiers could not save the imperial compound which had previously seemed immune. The Emperor had survived in a bomb shelter beneath his temporary war residence, a concrete structure known as the *Obunko*.

Commissioned by Hirohito to conduct a personal investigation of Japanese bases and arsenals, Admiral Hasegawa stood stiffly before him and read his report aloud. Its findings were devastating. The generals who argued for more war were clearly living a fantasy. There was no way to continue. Steel production had dropped to less than one-fifth of prewar output. Only the manufacture of bamboo spears had increased. The Emperor asked the admiral to sit down, questioned him intently, and then took to his bed for two days, depressed and suffering from a painful stomach disorder.

His position was as delicate as his deviation from his historic role was drastic. He was revered as human deity on a scale unfathomable to westerners. At public mention of the word "Emperor" all audiences sat stiffly at attention. Children were taught that they would be struck blind if they looked at the face of this exalted yet benevolent father of all. Even his picture was sacred. In government councils he was expected to sit rigidly, look impassive, and speak cryptically, if at all.

His newly adopted activism also did not mesh with Hirohito's per-

---

* The popular American image of Hirohito as a treacherous warlord was grossly wrong. Although tradition dictated that he remain silent, the Emperor made his views clear unexpectedly at a crucial Imperial Conference before Pearl Harbor. Gently but unmistakably he damned the decision to attack by reading a poem: "When I regard all the world / As my own brothers / Why is it that its tranquillity / Should be so thoughtlessly disturbed?"

sonal modesty. At forty-four he was one of the world's richest men. His tax-exempt annual salary was $1.6 million and his household staff numbered 5000. Yet he wore pencils down to stubs and his underwear was said to be patched. Round-shouldered, he shuffled about his grounds in baggy, frayed pants, peering through thick round spectacles, preoccupied with research in marine microbiology that had gained him international respect. Trips abroad had left him with an interest in golf, whiskey, and the British constitutional monarchy, but the war had plunged him into worry and insomnia, reducing his weight from 140 to 123 pounds.

Given his fragile condition and his despair over the fate of his nation, Hirohito was somewhat relieved by a visit from Suzuki's foreign minister, Shigenori Togo, on the evening of July 27. The tough American-British surrender ultimatum, released by Truman and Byrnes at Potsdam, had been recorded by Japanese radio monitors at six o'clock that morning. Togo brought the Emperor the English text, a Japanese translation, and the analysis of his ministers. To them the word from Potsdam seemed to add up to mildly encouraging news, for in dissecting the text and debating its meaning all day the cabinet had talked itself into remarkable misinterpretations.

The lack of any reference to the Emperor worried the ministers most, but perhaps the omission meant that his status could remain unchanged. Surrender was distasteful to contemplate, but the Potsdam Declaration called for "unconditional surrender of all Japanese armed forces" and not, as the Cairo Declaration of 1943 had specified, of Japan itself. Most encouraging, the document was not signed by the Soviets. To the Tokyo politicians this meant that the Russians remained neutral and could yet be mobilized to help negotiate for slightly easier terms.

The prowar military faction and the antiwar civilian faction of Hirohito's government had decided on a compromise. They would "ignore" the ultimatum pending a Soviet reply to the Emperor's request for mediation. The Emperor consented although the Soviets had obviously been stalling. On July 18 the Japanese Ambassador in Moscow had been told that they were "unable to give any definite reply" and that the Emperor's proposal to send a personal emissary was "not clear." But with Molotov due to return from Potsdam, surely a response was imminent. Or so the Emperor's cabinet hoped.

No one suspected that the Russians were only waiting for the last possible moment to join the war and stab the Japanese in the back.

Hirohito agreed there was time to wait a little longer for Soviet help.

The next morning—it was Saturday, July 28, another hazy, muggy day in Tokyo—the newspaper headlines caused the Foreign Ministry much discomfort. Foreign Minister Togo suspected that the army had secretly inspired the slant of the stories. *Mainichi* labeled the Potsdam proclamation "laughable." *Asahi Shimbun* called it "of no great moment" and thought it would reinforce the government's resolve to carry on the war.

At 4 p.m., a Japanese reporter asked at a press conference: "Recently the enemy powers have been making various kinds of propaganda about terminating the war. What is your opinion about this?"

"The government does not see much value in it," Suzuki said. "All we have to do is *mokusatsu** it."

While Truman and General Groves dealt with this apparent rejection of the Potsdam ultimatum as they had planned all along, the Emperor sought solace in routine duties. On July 30, he presided at a formal ceremony to celebrate the completion of his new personal air-raid shelter on the palace grounds, an occasion that was ended abruptly by an air raid. The next day he summoned his Privy Seal to discuss the fate of Japan's most hallowed "Three Sacred Treasures"—a certain mirror, a sword, and some jewels. The Emperor wanted the treasures moved from the Atsuta Shrine to the palace grounds so he might protect them with his person in case of enemy attack.

On August 2, his government was still unable to face the fact of

---

* Although the use of the word had been carefully planned by the cabinet, its ambiguity produced an unplanned surprise and was perhaps directly responsible for the continuation of the war and, thereby, the dropping of the bomb. *Mokusatsu* could mean anything from "to ignore" to "to treat with silent contempt." In the West, the latter interpretation was adopted and the Potsdam ultimatum was consequently considered to have been "rejected." Japanese cabinet officials later said they had really meant to convey a bland "no comment" reaction. Such a bizarre misunderstanding is plausible because problems with precision of language are common in Japanese. The word *hai*, for example, can mean anything from an unqualified "yes" to the vaguest form of acknowledgment, or sometimes nothing more than a friendly noise, no more significant than static.

surrender, still immobilized by wishful thinking about the benign influence of Soviet mediation—but a desperate tone crept into yet another cable from Togo to his negotiator in Moscow: "Since the loss of one day relative to this present matter may result in a thousand years of regret, it is requested that you immediately have a talk with Molotov . . ."

Not until August 5 could the Ambassador get an appointment with the Soviet Foreign Minister. It was fixed for August 8 at 8 p.m., two days after the bomb drop on Hiroshima, one day before the second drop on Nagasaki. The Ambassador tried to start the meeting with talk of mediation. Molotov cut him short and read a brief note ending ". . . from tomorrow, that is from August 9, the Soviet Union will consider herself in a state of war against Japan"—by which time even General Groves had relaxed somewhat and slowed the pace he had set to get ready for the bombings.

Twenty

Hiroshima I: "My God, What Have We Done?"

Realizing all too well how much high-precision planning and plain luck would be required to make reality of the bomb deliveries that he kept promising Stimson and Truman, Groves lavished his personal attention on the details.

"You're going to take a package to Tinian," the general informed his roving trouble-shooter, Major Robert R. Furman, in the Manhattan Project's Washington office. The package was a "Bronx" shipment, code for "irreplaceable." It was the U-235 core for the Hiroshima bomb. The uranium had just been delivered. There was no more. If anything happened to this shipment, the drop of a uranium bomb would be delayed indefinitely.

Since Oppenheimer's ordnance chief, Navy Captain Deke Parsons, did not trust airplanes, Furman was to take his package on its 6000-mile ride across the Pacific aboard the U.S.S. *Indianapolis,* a heavy cruiser. Nobody had informed Groves that the creaky old *Indie* lacked underwater sound equipment and lifeboats and that its center of gravity was so high that one torpedo hit could sink her quickly.

At Los Alamos, Furman, a low-keyed Princeton engineering graduate, picked up his package and a fellow traveler. The uranium was encased in a lead cylinder only eighteen inches in diameter, less than two feet high and deceptively heavy. It was carried by a metal handle but one man could not lift it. It weighed 300 pounds, 200 of them being lead insulation. Furman's companion was a merry Irishman,

Day One

Captain James F. Nolan, whom Groves called a "radiologist." In fact he was the chief physician of the Los Alamos hospital, a gynecologist who had taken some courses in X-ray therapy for gynecologic cancer.

Parsons had told Groves that the Navy would be reassured by the presence of such a "scientist." Nolan equipped himself with a Geiger counter and, like Furman, camouflaged himself with Field Artillery insignia. Wearing these emblems upside down, the two emissaries presented themselves before Oppenheimer, who impressed on them the irreplaceability of their cargo and ordered the release of their convoy: a black truck containing the bomb core and seven cars of security men armed with shotguns and rifles.

A mile out of Los Alamos the car carrying Furman and Nolan had a flat tire and nearly careened off a mountain precipice, but by July 16—the day of Trinity—they had made it to the *Indianapolis* at Hunter's Point Navy Yard in San Francisco. Two sailors followed them aboard over the rear gangplank, the precious lead container swaying from a crowbar across their shoulders. In their portside cabin, Nolan and Furman watched as the cylinder was welded to the deck with metal straps.

Deke Parsons briefed the ship's captain: "You will sail at high speed to Tinian where your cargo will be taken off by others. You will not be told what the cargo is, but it is to be guarded even after the life of your vessel. If she goes down, save the cargo at all costs." Parsons' farewell shook the captain thoroughly: "Every day you save on your voyage will cut the length of the war by just that much."

Shortly before weighing anchor, the mystified skipper sent for Nolan, who, as instructed, revealed that he was a medical officer but said the sensitive cargo "contained nothing dangerous to the ship or crew." The captain was unconvinced. "I didn't think we were going to use bacteriological weapons in this war," he said. Nolan said nothing and left as soon as possible, so he and Furman could start taking turns running the Geiger counter across their "package."

When it dropped anchor a thousand yards off Tinian Harbor on July 26—the day after Truman approved Groves's operational order for the bomb drop—the *Indie* was surrounded by numerous small craft. High-ranking brass climbed aboard to observe the unloading of Groves's cylinder, an operation that succeeded only on the second try. The first cable that lowered the top-secret cargo to an LCT (Landing Craft Tank) proved six feet short, and the sailors operating the winch were jeered by their sizable audience.*

Ashore, the soldierly Norman Ramsey, Parsons' deputy and the chief scientist on Tinian, signed a receipt for the uranium. He calculated its approximate value, and then wished he hadn't. "The government would have to spend a long time taking half a billion dollars out of my salary," he reflected.

The 509th Composite Group, the Air Force bomb-delivery team that the scientists were joining, felt far from comfortably settled on Tinian. Smaller than Manhattan but shaped somewhat like it, Tinian Island had become the world's largest air base. Sometimes nearly a thousand B-29s took off in fifteen-second intervals from six ten-lane runways to bomb targets in Japan. Crashes were common and combat casualties heavy, but in their Quonset huts at "Eighth Avenue" and "125th Street" the 509th mostly waited for action in its secret enclosure, safely sequestered behind machine guns and barbed wire.

Other outfits ridiculed Groves's men because the 509th dropped only occasional single practice bombs. Jeers and catcalls accompanied their takeoffs from North Field and a ditty made the rounds:

> Into the air the secret rose
> Where they're going nobody knows . . .
> Don't ask us about results or such
> Unless you want to get in Dutch.
> But take it from one who is sure of the score,
> The 509th is winning the war . . .

At night rocks pelted the roofs of the 509th and the men felt like lepers. They still had not been told about the bomb or the complex operations for its drop, code-named "Centerboard."

In Washington on July 30, General Groves faced a delicate eleventh-hour complication. An urgent cable from cautious General

---

* Less than four days later the *Indianapolis* was torpedoed by a Japanese submarine. It sank in twelve minutes. Of her 1196-man crew, only 315 were rescued.

"Tooey" Spaatz on Guam said, "Reports, prisoner of war sources, not verified by photos, give location of allied prisoner of war camp one mile north of center of city of Nagasaki. Does this influence the choice of this target for initial Centerboard operation? Request immediate reply."

Obviously Stimson would have to be the final arbiter, but Groves wanted to influence the response in the light of his earlier problems concerning Kyoto. Determined not to lose another target from his list, the general drafted a cable instructing Spaatz to retain Nagasaki as a target. However, the exact aiming point for the bomb (which was local Air Force responsibility anyway) could be moved so as to decrease the risk of hitting a POW camp. Taking the cable to Stimson, Groves said he would send it on his own responsibility; he was showing it to the Secretary only for his information. The strategy worked. Stimson acquiesced in Groves's decision, merely thanking the general for his courtesy. The old man did not have to condemn prisoners of war to death.

Another cable had meanwhile arrived from Spaatz: "Hiroshima according to prisoner of war reports is the only one of four target cities for Centerboard that does not have allied prisoner of war camps. Advise."

Groves replied: "If you consider your information reliable, Hiroshima should be given first priority."

Only poor weather could now reprieve that city, yet the shooting phase of Groves's scenario still could not begin. Production schedules at Los Alamos, Oak Ridge, and Hanford had been so tight that all the critical "Bronx" parts of the general's Centerboard jigsaw puzzle did not fall into place until August 2.

At 2:30 that morning the last of five C-54 transports and three B-29 bombers from Kirtland Field in Albuquerque landed safely on "Papacy," the code name for Tinian. Over a period of six days this fleet had delivered "active material"—a plutonium sphere and a final chunk of uranium; the target assembly for the uranium Little Boy weapon; the initiator and preassemblies for the implosion Fat Man; and three complete sets of tools for every imaginable step of assembling the bombs.

Groves had worried over every one of the planes like a mother hen. "I want to reiterate the absolute necessity of flying the airplanes only in good weather," he admonished the commanding general of the Air Transport Command in a top-secret memorandum. Once all was in place, Groves queried Tinian: "Is there anything left undone either here or there . . . ?" His deputy, General Farrell, responded with a one-word cable: "No." Groves's scenario was out of his hands. It was up to Deke Parsons and the general's other handpicked specialists on Tinian to make the bomb operational, especially Colonel Paul Tibbets of the 509th, the pilot of the *Enola Gay*.

Tibbets reported to General LeMay's 20th Air Force headquarters on Guam early in the afternoon of August 2 and brought along Major Thomas Ferebee, the bombardier who would make the drop.

"Paul, the primary is Hiroshima," LeMay confirmed.

The chunky general led his visitors to his map table, bent over the latest reconnaissance photos of the city, and asked Ferebee for his proposed aiming point. Ferebee, an unemotional professional with a reputation as a champion poker player, put his index finger on the unmistakable T-shape of the Aioi Bridge near the city's center, slightly southwest of the Japanese Second Army headquarters and the East Drill Field. LeMay agreed.

"It's the most perfect AP I've seen in this whole damned war," said Tibbets.

By 3 p.m. mimeograph machines were grinding out the top-secret field orders for the unprecedented operation, Special Bombing Mission No. 13. History's first atomic attack was set for August 6. The Hiroshima "urban industrial area" was reconfirmed as the primary target. The principal alternate was Kokura and its arsenal. The second alternate was Nagasaki. Niigata had been eliminated from the target list the previous day as too small and too distant. The order called for "only visual bombing"—not radar—which meant that visibility had to be good. Bombing altitude: 28,000 to 30,000 feet.

Seven B-29s would participate. One would stand by on Iwo Jima in case the *Enola Gay* developed mechanical trouble. Two would escort Tibbets to the vicinity of the target. One would take photographs. The other was a flying laboratory. It would drop three parachutes carrying cylinders that looked like fire extinguishers and would radio back measurement records of the explosion. Also, three planes would precede the *Enola Gay* to each of the targets and radio back weather observations.

At 3 p.m. on Saturday, August 4, Tibbets, wearing freshly pressed khakis, mounted the dais in the briefing hut of the 509th on Tinian and faced the seven crews of Special Bombing Mission No. 13. Military Police had sealed and surrounded the narrow building. "The moment has arrived," Tibbets said. After two officers removed cloths shrouding two blackboards that displayed reconnaissance photos of Hiroshima and the alternate targets, Tibbets introduced Deke Parsons, who would fly on the mission as the weaponeer.

"The bomb you are going to drop is something new in the history of warfare," Deke announced, perspiring profusely. "It is the most destructive weapon ever produced. We think it will knock out almost everything within a three-mile radius."

A gasp came from the audience. Parsons briefed the group about the Manhattan Project and then motioned a technician to start the projector for a film he had brought along showing the Trinity test. Something went wrong with the machinery and it began shredding the film. Parsons then calmly proceeded to describe the explosion from his vivid memory. The men were stunned. Even Tibbets, who knew the story, was "overwhelmed."

"No one knows exactly what will happen when the bomb is dropped from the air," Parsons went on. Even if it exploded at the planned altitude of 1850 feet it might crack the earth's crust. The explosion's flash of light would be "much brighter" than the sun and could cause blindness. Tinted welder's goggles were distributed and Parsons demonstrated how they could be adjusted to produce maximum darkness above the target.

Even before this inside group Parsons still refrained from using the telltale words "atomic" and "nuclear." He did warn the pilots that under no circumstances were they to fly through the mushroom cloud. It would contain radioactivity. Some of the airmen whispered to each other about the danger of sterility. At least they now knew why they had been practicing steep, breakaway turns during their training missions.

. . .

Rush to Decision

At 3:30 p.m. on Sunday, August 5, in the air-conditioned bomb assembly hut of the 509th, the five-ton Little Boy bomb swung from its chain hoist and was gently lowered onto a trailer. The weather report was in: OK for takeoff after midnight. A good-sized group had gathered for the weapon's last trip on the ground: physicists, security agents, ordnance specialists, and the brass led by the "Tinian Joint Chiefs," Deke Parsons and Groves's deputy, General Farrell. Messages were scribbled onto the bomb in crayon—ribald words wishing bad luck to Japan and Hirohito, gung-ho encouragement for Tibbets and his raiders.

Hidden under a tarpaulin, the bomb was pulled slowly into the tropical heat and glaring sunlight by a tractor. A Military Police captain and seven of his men stood along both sides of the trailer like Secret Service agents guarding the President. In solemn procession a convoy of jeeps and other vehicles escorted the bomb from the Tech Area to the hardstand half a mile distant. Somebody remarked that it looked like a funeral cortège.

At North Field the Little Boy was lowered into the bomb pit. The *Enola Gay*—formally aircraft No. 82—was towed over it. A sign on the fuselage warned, "No smoking within 100 feet." A hoist winched the weapon into the forward bomb bay. Special shackles clamped it in place. The fifteen-foot bomb-bay door clanged shut, but the Little Boy was still not fully armed.

As the spectators dispersed, Parsons took Farrell aside. Months ago he had wanted to insert the conventional explosive and its detonator into the uranium gun in the rear of the bomb himself, after the plane was in flight. Groves had vetoed the idea. He thought it was an unnecessary precaution, and it would be far too easy for something, anything, to go wrong in the darkness and cramped space of the bomb bay.

On the eve of the mission—takeoff was about ten hours away—Parsons had further thoughts about his private plan and how to sell it. He told Farrell that the night before he had seen four B-29s roll off the runway on takeoff and burn up. One of the bombers had sprayed machine-gun bullets that killed rescue workers as they ran to extricate the trapped crew.

"If that happens on takeoff tomorrow morning," Parsons said, "we could get a nuclear explosion and blow up half the island."

"I know it," Farrell replied, "but what can we do about it?"

"If I put off the final assembly until after takeoff, the island wouldn't be in any danger in case we crash."

Farrell looked doubtful. "You've never done such a job. Do you know how?"

"No, but I've got all day and night to learn."

With Farrell's blessing, Parsons climbed into the stifling bomb bay, squeezed himself into a squat behind the bomb, and practiced into the evening under a flashlight. Stopping by to check on his progress, Farrell found that Parsons' hands were black from graphite lubricant and bleeding from sharp-edged parts and tools.

"For God's sakes, man," Farrell exploded, "let me loan you a pair of pigskin gloves. They're thin ones."

"I wouldn't dare," Parsons said. "I've got to feel the touch." He joked that he would have to bomb Japan "with dirty hands." But he knew how.

At 7:17 p.m. Farrell cabled Washington: "Judge [Parsons' code name] to load bomb after takeoff . . ." Groves received the message too late to object. The mission was now beyond even his control.

The night of August 5-6 was hot and muggy. Colonel Tibbets ate several portions of pineapple fritters with bombardier Tom Ferebee and Theodore ("Dutch") Van Kirk, the navigator. Then the colonel tried to nap, but there were too many interruptions. Van Kirk took two sleeping pills but found he could not relax and stayed up playing poker with Ferebee, the local champion, and two other officers.

In the new assembly hall, at about midnight, Tibbets addressed the crew who would fly with him. Even now he called their bomb merely "very powerful," not "nuclear" or "atomic." He told the men to be sure to wear their goggles and announced their new radio call sign: "Dimples."

At 12:15 Tibbets motioned to the Lutheran chaplain, who asked the crews to bow their heads as he sought heavenly assistance for their mission: "We pray Thee to be with those who brave the heights of Thy heaven . . . armed with Thy strength may they bring this war to a rapid end . . ."

Filing into the mess hall for the traditional preflight supper, the men found a menu annotated with G.I. humor: "Look! Real eggs! How do ya want them? . . . Sausage (we think it's pork) . . ."

At 1:37 a.m. the three weather scouts took off from North Field, departing simultaneously but from separate runways. The plane that headed for Hiroshima was the *Straight Flush,* commanded by Major Claude Eatherly. At 2 a.m. the crews of the *Enola Gay* and its two escort planes arrived in trucks at the flight line and blinked their eyes in amazement. Tibbets' plane was surrounded by floodlights, klieg stands, movie cameras, film crews, generators, and a band of milling still photographers. Groves still had not released his grip on his men.

The general had sent a message to Tibbets that he wanted the departure recorded for history, but the pilot was taken aback as he faced the incongruous Hollywood première atmosphere. "I expected to see MGM's lion walk into the field," he remembered. "It was crazy." One of the photographers jostled the dignified Deke Parsons against the *Enola Gay* and instructed, "You're gonna be famous, so smile!" A civilian scientist grumbled that the scene looked like a drugstore opening.

After the last group photograph was taken at 2:20 a.m.—everyone managed to smile and appear relaxed—Tibbets said, "OK, let's go to work." Awkwardly, one by one, the twelve-man crew climbed up the ladder and squeezed through the hatch behind the nose wheel. They were encased in flight coveralls with layers of equipment underneath: survival vest with emergency rations and fishhooks; a parachute harness with clips for a life raft; an armorlike flak suit to protect against flak fragments. Tibbets and several others wore baseball caps.

Deke Parsons was the only one who had forgotten to draw a pistol and holster. "Where's your gun?" General Farrell asked at the last minute. Parsons borrowed one from a nearby MP, buckled it around his waist, and clambered aboard.

In the cockpit Tibbets leaned out of a side window where the cameramen had congregated. "OK, fellows," he shouted. "Cut those lights! We've gotta be going!"

At 2:27 he ordered the engines started and called the tower: "Dimples Eight-Two to North Tinian Tower. Taxi-out and take-off instructions." The tower came back: "Dimples Eight-Two from North Tinian Tower. Take off to the east on Runway A for Able."

At 2:45 Tibbets turned to his copilot, Captain Robert Lewis. "Let's go," he said, thrusting all throttles forward and concentrating on a more urgent worry than his atomic bomb.*

The *Enola Gay* began rolling down the oiled coral runway uncomfortably overweight at 150 tons, which included 7000 gallons of fuel. Tibbets had quietly made the risky decision to keep it on the ground until the ultimate moment to build up speed for liftoff. With more than two-thirds of the runway gone, he was still too slow. Crew members glanced nervously at each other.

"She's too heavy!" shouted the copilot. "Pull her off—now!"

Tibbets said nothing. He held the bomber on the runway until his speed exceeded 180 miles per hour, then he eased his wheel back and lifted the nose off just as the ground seemed to fade and make way for the void of the sea.

"I never saw a plane use that much runway," said General Farrell in the North Field control tower, severely shaken. "I thought Tibbets was never going to pull it off."

In his cockpit, Tibbets stretched, drank some coffee, and considered telling his crew precisely what kind of weapon lay cradled in their bomb bay. One final secret he would not mention: the little metal box in his coverall pocket. It contained twelve cyanide capsules. Only in the event of disaster over Japan—so Tibbets had been instructed—was he to tell his men that they could choose from two ways of avoiding torture and giving away crucial military details of the atomic secret: suicide by gun or by poison.

At 2:52 a.m., with the *Enola Gay* cruising at 4,000 feet, Parsons knocked out his cold pipe, tapped Tibbets on the shoulder, and said, "We're starting."

Squatting in the bomb bay as his assistant, Lieutenant Norris R. Jeppson, held a flashlight, Deke removed an eleven-point check list from his coveralls. Jeppson handed him tools one by one. The scene might have been in a surgery except that Parsons' labors again turned his hands black and bloody. Repeatedly he assured Tibbets on the intercom that the operation was going well.

At 3:10 Parsons started to insert gunpowder in the Little Boy and connected the detonator. In total silence he reinstalled the armor

* It was 1:45 a.m., August 6, in Japan and 11:45 a.m., August 5, in Washington.

plate and the rear plate. "OK," he told Jeppson. "That'll do it." But still the bomb could not explode. One critical electrical circuit had been carefully left unconnected.

Tibbets turned over the controls to the copilot, crawled through the padded thirty-foot tunnel to the crew compartment in the rear, and tried to nap. He had been up for twenty-four hours, but he could not sleep. After fifteen minutes he headed back into the eighteen-inch-wide tunnel. Bob Caron, the tail gunner, tugged at his shirt.

"Say, Colonel, are we splitting atoms today?"

"You're pretty close, Bob," said Tibbets.

At 4:55 Japanese time, the laboratory and photo planes joined the *Enola Gay* and Tibbets became the point of a V formation flying on top of an undercast into dazzling sunlight. Some of the men felt their stomachs tightening, but still nobody knew which of the three cities on the target list they would bomb.

Shortly after 6:30, Jeppson returned to the frigid bomb bay, unscrewed three green plugs from the bomb—each about three inches long and half an inch in diameter—and replaced them with three plugs almost identical but red. The final electrical connection was in place. The bomb was fully armed. Jeppson informed Parsons, who told Tibbets, who announced into the intercom: "We are carrying the world's first atomic bomb."

Several crewmen gasped. The copilot gave a low whistle. Most were hearing the chilling word "atomic" for the first time.

Tibbets told his men that once they were near the target their words would be recorded. "This recording is being made for history. Watch your language . . ."

At 7:25—the *Enola Gay* was at 26,000 feet and climbing to 31,600—the vital message arrived on 7310 kilocycles from Major Eatherly's *Straight Flush*. Cruising over Hiroshima with no fighter opposition and very little flak, he radioed: "Cloud cover less than three-tenths at all altitudes. Advice: bomb primary."*

---

* In 1957 Eatherly became a *cause célèbre*. After several stays in Veterans Administration mental hospitals and a forgery conviction, the hard-drinking Texan received front-page attention because of several post-office burglaries and became the martyr/hero of some early-day "ban the bomb" groups. It was falsely claimed that this "American Dreyfus" had commanded the Hiroshima raid; had flown through the bomb clouds; and was being punished because he professed guilt for his part in the bombing.

"It's Hiroshima," Tibbets said into the intercom.

At 8:05, the two escort planes having fallen a few miles behind, Dutch Van Kirk, the navigator, called, "Ten minutes to AP."

At 8:09, Parsons came to the cockpit and stood behind Tibbets. In a large opening of the clouds, a city appeared outlined below.

"Do you agree that's the target?" Tibbets demanded.

"Yes," said Parsons and nodded.

"We are about to start the bomb run," Tibbets announced into the intercom. "Put on your goggles."

In his little bombardier's chair Tom Ferebee bent forward, brushed his mustache against the Norden bombsight, fastened his left eye to the instrument, and gave Tibbets a small heading adjustment.

"Roger," said Tibbets.

At 8:13½, the pilot told Ferebee, "It's yours."

The bombardier assumed control of the aircraft, flying west at a ground speed of 285 miles per hour. Ferebee had studied every inch of the target photographs so many times that the landscape looked totally familiar to him. The seven fingers branching off the Ota River stretched out below like the lines inside a familiar open hand. The T of the Aioi Bridge moved toward the cross hairs of the bombsight.

"I've got it," he said.

Seventeen seconds after 8:15 the bomb-bay doors swung open automatically. Through his legs and the looking glass below Ferebee watched the bomb tumble down, first broadside, then with its nose pointed to the target.

"Bomb away," shouted Ferebee.

Lightened by nearly 10,000 pounds, the plane lurched up. Tibbets rammed it into a simultaneous 60-degree dive and 158-degree right turn. The bomb was set to detonate at 43 seconds. At 35 he pulled his goggles over his eyes but couldn't see through them and threw them to the floor.

"See anything yet, Bob?" he asked Caron, the tailgunner, on the intercom.

"No, sir."

Jeppson had started his own count. He reached 43 and stopped. "It's a dud," he thought.

At that moment a bright light filled the plane and Caron saw a huge, circular mass of air shooting up and outward, as if a "ring around some distant planet had detached itself and was coming up toward us."

He yelled a warning. A noisy shock wave jarred the aircraft upward. To Tibbets it sounded like a German 88-millimeter shell.

"Flak!" he yelled.

A roar of alarmed voices hit the intercom, but nobody could see smoke puffs.

"There's another one coming," yelled Caron.

Another strong bounce upward. Again it passed quickly. Again no sign of damage.

"OK," Tibbets announced. "That was the reflected shock wave. There won't be any more. Stay calm."

As Hiroshima receded, Caron dictated his account into a recorder: "A column of smoke is rising fast. It has a fiery red core . . . Fires are springing up everywhere . . . there are too many to count . . . Here it comes, the mushroom shape that Captain Parsons spoke about . . ."

Lewis, the copilot, pounded Tibbets' shoulder and kept saying, "Look at that! Look at that!" Ferebee, the bombardier, wondered aloud whether the radioactivity would make them all sterile after all. Tibbets told the recorder he was "shocked" by "destruction bigger than I had really imagined."

Then the pilot radioed General Farrell on Tinian a message in the clear: "Target visually bombed with good results."

When Parsons heard the wording he bristled: "Good? Hell, what did he expect?" In code he wired Farrell: "Results clear-cut. Successful in all respects. Visible effects greater than Alamogordo. Conditions normal in airplane following delivery. Proceeding to base."

In the copilot's seat, working on his own record of Mission No. 13, Lewis wrote: "My God, what have we done?"

THE A-BOMB STORY

Theory Becomes Reality

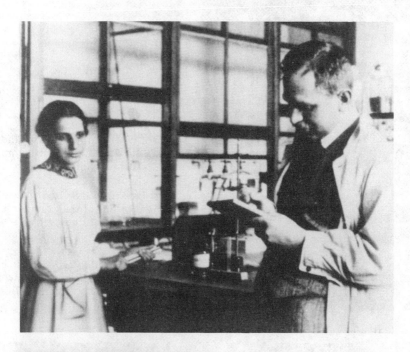

BERLIN, 1938: Otto Hahn (*above, at right*) discovers a phenomenon he can't explain. Lise Meitner tells him he split the atom.

Leo Szilard was first to think that an A-bomb was possible.

Theory Becomes Reality

Ernest Rutherford (*left*), godfather of the world's physicists, considered atomic energy "moonshine."

Albert Einstein and Szilard (*below*) re-enact the writing of their famous letter warning President Roosevelt of a Nazi A-bomb.

Roosevelt listened to his scientific high command (*right*): Ernest O. Lawrence, Arthur H. Compton, Vannevar Bush, James B. Conant.

Theory Becomes Reality

Mark Oliphant came from Britain
to urge greater speed.

General Leslie R. Groves got the
job to build the bomb.

The Race Begins

The army turned a boys' school at Los Alamos, New Mexico, into a secret city (*above*).

The nation's brightest nuclear physicists moved into teachers' homes on "Bathtub Row" (*right*).

April 1943: In the administration barracks (*below*), director J. Robert Oppenheimer ventured into the unknown.

The Man Behind the Bomb

At the University of California in Berkeley, Oppie was an admired professor (*above*).

Complex and charismatic, Oppenheimer had been a child prodigy (*right*).

The Man Behind the Bomb

At Los Alamos, Oppenheimer developed into an administrative genius (*top, right*).

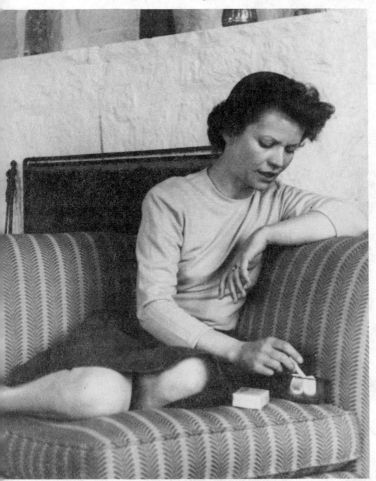

His wife, Kitty, was difficult and controversial.

Eventually Oppie would die a broken man.

Los Alamos: The Oppenheimer Team

Robert Serber briefed the scientists on their task.

Isidor I. Rabi was Oppie's most senior adviser.

Robert F. Bacher became the boss's deputy.

Los Alamos: The Oppenheimer Team

Hans Bethe (*right*) was principal theoretician.

Enrico Fermi (*below, right*) was chief experimentalist.

George ("Kisty") Kistiakowsky (*below, left*) knew explosives.

Los Alamos: The Oppenheimer Team

John ("Johnny") von Neumann calculated the mathematics.

Victor ("Viki") F. Weisskopf tried to assess the radiation.

Edward Teller campaigned for bigger bombs.

Robert R. Wilson (with wife, Jane) wanted a peaceful demonstration.

Los Alamos: The Oppenheimer Team

Richard P. Feynman (*above, left*) supplied ingenious comic relief.

Seth Neddermeyer (*above, right*) invented the revolutionary implosion.

James F. Nolan, M.D., delivered the wives' babies.

Los Alamos: The Oppenheimer Team

There was time to enjoy the mountain scenery for Bethe, Fermi, and their children.

Everybody worshiped Oppenheimer (here at a party with Weisskopf).

The Enemy Camp

The Americans believed that the Germans, headed by Werner
Heisenberg (*above, left*), would make the bomb first.

Samuel Goudsmit (*above, right*) headed the front-line U.S. team
that captured German atomic installations.

Dismantling a Nazi "uranium machine," the Americans finally
learned how dismally their German competitors had failed (*opposite
page, top*).

Arrested by U.S. occupation troops, Otto Hahn (*opposite page,
bottom*, with cap) could not believe that the Germans had lost
the race.

The Enemy Camp

The Enemy Camp

In Tokyo, Yoshio Nishina, Japan's leading atomic scientist (*right*), was also ordered to build an A-bomb.

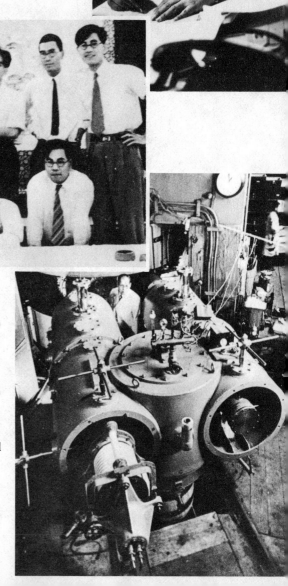

Nishina's team, led by Masashi Takeuchi (standing at extreme right), got nowhere.

After Hiroshima, General Groves ordered the destruction of Nishina's beloved cyclotron (*right*).

The Enemy Camp

Igor ("The Beard") Kurchatov made good progress building the first Russian A-bomb.

The Soviets enjoyed crucial support from spy Klaus Fuchs (*above, right*). This is the identification photo that gave him access to every secret at Los Alamos.

Leo Szilard (*right*) and his colleagues were stunned when the Soviets had a bomb by 1949.

Alamogordo, N.M.: The Trinity Test

July 1945: The desert site of the world's first atomic explosion was picked for its isolation. Kenneth Bainbridge (*left*) was the physicist in charge.

The plutonium bomb core leaves for its test tower (*opposite page, top*).

Test device is hoisted into position (*opposite page, bottom*).

Alamogordo, N.M.: The Trinity Test

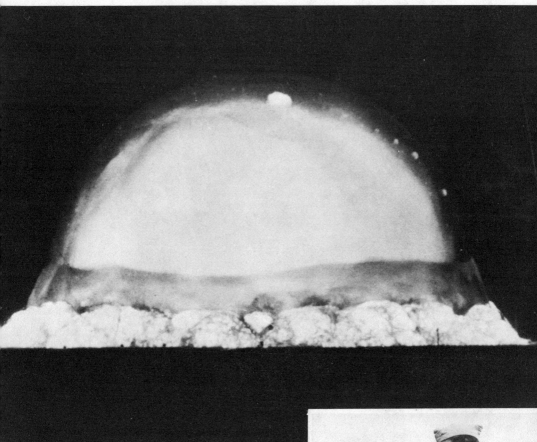

0.034 SEC.
N

100 METERS

It worked: fireball ascending .034
seconds after blast.

The oddest couple: Oppenheimer and
Groves after the test.

Decision at Potsdam

July 1945: New in office, President Truman leaves reluctantly for Big Three conference with Secretary of State James F. Byrnes (bareheaded, at rear).

Truman (flanked by Churchill and Stalin) grew confident and aggressive when word came that the A-bomb worked.

Three Tormented Advisers

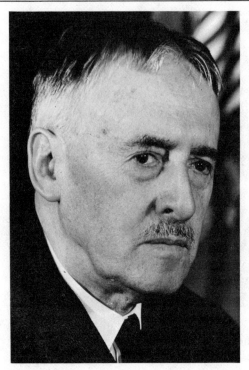

Secretary of War Henry L. Stimson, seventy-eight and frail (*above, left*), dreaded the bomb but went along with it. Niels Bohr, elder statesman of science (*above, right*), lobbied unsuccessfully for world control. James ("Pa") Franck (*right*) wanted a peaceful demonstration but was kept away from Truman.

Tinian: The Bomb Goes Operational

Senior scientist Norman F. Ramsey (shown here in 1945 and 1980) became appalled by the sudden, unexpected risks of the bomb's use in combat.

Ordnance chief "Deke" Parsons (*right*) decided to arm the weapon in flight to Hiroshima.

Tinian: The Bomb Goes Operational

Colonel Paul W. Tibbets piloted the first bomb mission.

Tibbets' plane, the B-29 *Enola Gay* (*below*), was named for his mother.

Tinian: The Bomb Goes Operational

The crew wasn't told until the last moment that its weapon was atomic.

The uranium bomb dropped on Hiroshima was nicknamed "Little Boy" (*above*). The plutonium bomb dropped on Nagasaki three days later was called "Fat Man" (*right*).

The Death City

August 6, 1945, 8:16 a.m.: Hiroshima dies. The above photo was taken from the burning roof of the Fukuya department store.

Shielded by reinforced concrete walls, teacher Katsuko Horibe survived on the ground floor of the Honkawa school (*right*), 650 feet from the blast.

The Death City

The Death City

The bomb missed its aiming point, the T-shaped Aioi Bridge, by 800 feet.

Sakae Ito (*below*) was helping to wreck houses for fire lanes. As a town councillor and peace worker, she was received by the Pope.

The Death City

Policeman Motoji Maeoka (shown in 1945 and 1983) offered water to the dying and cremated the dead.

Now a TV executive, Susumu Desaki was a tenth-grader in 1945 (*left*) when he saved his mother.

Michiko Yamaoka became one of the "Hiroshima Maidens" whose disfigured faces were reconstructed in the U.S.

The Death City

Dr. Michihiko Hachiya (*left*), director of the Communications Hospital, did not know for weeks that his patients were dying of radiation.

Shinzo Hamai (*below, left*) scrounged food for his city and was acclaimed a hero.

Drs. Stafford Warren (*below, at left*), and Masao Tsuzuki (*seated, center*) headed the medical investigators.

The Death City

Colonel Seiichi Niizuma (*left*) was dispatched from Tokyo to advise the government whether the bomb really was atomic.

Emperor Hirohito maneuvered his ministers into surrender.

The Death City

Lt. John D. Montgomery (*above, left,* in front of "A-bomb Dome"),
a military government officer, advised city planners.

Shinzo Hamai (*below,* with family) became mayor and spent twenty
years rebuilding the city.

Today: Not Everyone Remembers

In Hiroshima, a prosperous new city (*above*, with Aioi T-Bridge toward left center), newcomers find the memory of the bombing depressing. Old-timers flock to the annual anniversary memorials (*below*) and want the "error" of 1945 to remain vivid as a warning.

Today: Not Everyone Remembers

Los Alamos, another gleaming new community (30 square miles, 20,000 population), is producing more nuclear weapons (*above*). The town's peace advocates (*below*) remember Hiroshima, but their group is small.

Book Two
After the Bomb

Part 6
The Death City

Twenty-One

Hiroshima II:
"This Is Hell on Earth!"

Facing the T-shape of the Aioi Bridge, the teachers' room of the Honkawa Elementary School was suddenly bathed in blinding bluish light. It was eight seconds past 8:16 a.m. in downtown Hiroshima. Teacher Katsuko Horibe heard nothing. The window near her exploded. Glass bombarded her scalp, forehead, and left arm, but she felt nothing. She flung herself under a desk but did not bother to protect her head as everybody had been taught in air-raid drills: hands shielding the eyes, thumbs plugged into the ears. Whatever was happening was evidently already over. It was silent and dark as night.

A teachers' meeting had been scheduled for 8:30, but since commuting schedules had become unreliable Miss Horibe had taken an early street car and been the first to arrive. All ten of her colleagues died on their way to work.

Innumerable other accidents of time and place spared and took lives in Hiroshima on that hot and muggy morning, beginning with the accidental course of the *Enola Gay*'s bomb itself. It had missed the Aioi Bridge by 800 feet and exploded instead 1850 feet above Dr. Shima's hospital, just 650 feet southeast of Miss Horibe's school. The Shima hospital and all its patients were vaporized, but its owner, the fatalistic Dr. Shima, kept pedaling unscathed on his bicycle. He was between house calls in the suburbs.

The "hypocenter" was in the courtyard of his hospital. It was ground zero, the hub of the nuclear death wheel, the point on the

253

ground directly underneath the explosion, the focus of Hiroshima's new universe. Eighty-eight percent of the people within a radius of 1500 feet died instantly or later on that day. Most others within the circle perished in the following weeks or months. All who were in Hiroshima on August 6 would come to know precisely how far fate had placed them from the hypocenter at 8:15.* And everyone would learn at least one new English word: "hypocenter," the place from which all life and death was measured.

The handful of survivors who, like Miss Horibe, escaped almost automatic death near the hypocenter owed their lives to luck and to the sturdiness of the very few structures not made of wood.† The stone railings of the Aioi Bridge tumbled like bowling pins into the river and segments of its concrete pavement were curled like ocean waves, but somehow the 400-foot bridge survived. So did the shell of Miss Horibe's long, three-story Honkawa School; it was built of reinforced concrete and surrounded by a thick brick wall. Its interior was gutted, along with all of central Hiroshima for 1.2 miles and, in many sections, far beyond. In less than half a second, heat rays with

---

* That was the time of the attack as recorded in the official records. Groves had achieved total surprise. Nobody had sought shelter. Major Eatherly's weather reconnaissance had triggered the short siren blasts of an alert at 7:09, but the long uninterrupted all-clear signal had sounded at 7:31. The Japanese air defense officials did not think they faced attack from a mere three planes, the *Enola Gay* and its escorts. Nevertheless, the old school bell at NHK, the Hiroshima radio station, rang a few seconds before 8:15, indicating that a precautionary alert was being phoned in from military headquarters. Unworried because there had been many false alarms, the announcer on duty, Masanobu Furuta, trotted down the hall to the studio and picked up the usual printed form that already had the details of his routine announcement penciled in. He flicked the black buzzer interrupting the normal program; pushed the button of the stop watch that he used to make a record of his working time on the air; and began to read: "Chugoku District Army announcement: three large enemy planes proceeding . . ." The station went dead. The building tilted. The announcer's body hurtled through the air, but he survived because it was a reinforced concrete structure. At the city's outskirts a group of soldiers had broken into applause when the planes of Tibbets' group approached. The men thought one of the planes was being shot down because parachutes emerged from it. But these were the parachutes carrying the cylinders with the instruments to measure the explosion that was only seconds away.
† The man who survived perhaps closest of all to the hypocenter owed his life to both factors. He was Eizo Nomura, a clerk of the Fuel Distribution and Control Cooperative, housed in a concrete building more than a hundred yards downstream along the Motoyasu River from the Aioi T-Bridge. At the time of the bombing he had just descended into the deep concrete basement to retrieve a document that his chief had forgotten to bring upstairs.

temperatures of more than 3000 degrees Celsius caused primary burn injuries within two miles of the hypocenter. About 130,000 of Hiroshima's 350,000 people would die.

Dashing out of the school into clouds of thick, swirling dark dust, Miss Horibe spotted seven moaning children lying and sitting on the playground where they had been playing hide-and-seek. They were bleeding and blackened by burns. Their school uniforms were in shreds. Patches of skin dangled from their bodies. Miss Horibe saw them but her eyes were hunting for an escape route from the area. The Aioi Bridge would have been perfect, but it was blocked by flames leaping out of nearby buildings.

"To the river," she shouted to the children. "It's the only way out!"

Water. The sacred water of the city's many rivers was on her mind as it was on the mind of everyone that morning. Water would stem the all-consuming fires, and the broad Motoyas River was only a few yards from the Honkawa school. The children understood and dragged themselves slowly across the rubble-filled ground with Miss Horibe's help. They were crying and shouting how much they hurt, how they hated war and the Americans.

The trek to the river seemed to take forever, and when Miss Horibe reached the steps at the top of the neat, steep, seven-foot seawall she found herself pulled along in a wave of bodies shoving to reach the water. She lost contact with the children from her school and never saw them again. Having reached the river early, she could still squeeze onto the rocky four-foot-wide riverfront, but the water offered no escape. It was a barrier.

The churning Motoyas itself seemed on fire. Flaming debris from burning homes and floating wood from the nearby lumberyards blocked any swimmers. Most of the many bodies floating past Miss Horibe seemed lifeless. She saw people diving from the seawall into this caldron—she could not tell whether they leaped or were pushed—but most were huddling skin-to-skin along the riverfront, trapped.

"Mother! Mother!" and "This is hell on earth!" were shouts that Miss Horibe could distinguish from some of the survivors pressing against her. Most faces and bodies were grotesquely bloated by burns. Many were obviously dying. Some were clearly dead and Miss Horibe felt that her own life, too, was inevitably over at the age of 18.* Her shock was wearing off and she began to feel great pain. Her face, her purple shirt, and her dark blue *mompei* were spattered with blood. She kept vomiting a strange yellow liquid. Immobilized between watery fires in front of her and fires whipped by westerly sea breezes advancing from the buildings at her back, she was convinced that her world, all Japan, was going under.

Only the Aioi Bridge seemed as immune as all Hiroshima had been until this morning. She could see it through the smoke. There was no life on it, but it stood.

So did the Tsurumi Bridge, much to the surprise of Mrs. Sakae Ito, who glanced in its direction toward 9 a.m. Looking from the foot of suburban Hijiyama Hill toward the city and the hypocenter, one mile to the west, she could see nothing else standing. But now a mass of blackened, bleeding people surged across the bridge—the lifeline. Their hair, frizzled from burns, was standing on end. Most were nearly naked. Some screamed or whimpered. Many held their hands and arms and extended in front of them, with elbows out.† Others held on to each other and stumbled because they could not see. When the people reached Mrs. Ito's elevated spot they stopped, turned toward Hiroshima, and began to cry.

Mrs. Ito was even more bewildered than shocked. Like most Hiroshima citizens, she had at first concluded that she had escaped a nearby hit of a conventional bomb. A tiny, thirty-four-year-old housewife with sparkling dark eyes and a quick smile, Mrs. Ito was one of 10,000 "volunteers" assigned to tear down houses to clear fire lanes that morning. She was the deputy leader of a group of some forty of her neighbors and proud of her job. She was doing something for the war, just like the men.

By 8:15 her team had lined up before a row of wooden homes they were supposed to wreck. Their thick cotton air-raid hoods dangled down their backs. A handful of the oldest workers had been designated to stay behind and watch the lunches. "We envy you!"

---

* Miss Horibe had been given one year's training for her teaching job, and eighteen-year-old teachers—as well as eighteen-year-old policemen—were not uncommon. Some Hiroshima telephone operators were only twelve.
† People all over town were thus trying to ease the pain of their burns. They had quickly discovered that by elevating hands and arms they could reduce the friction and pain of raw surfaces rubbing together.

Mrs. Ito called out to them, and everybody laughed. "Let's go!" commanded the group leader, a stockbroker, and suddenly Mrs. Ito's right shoulder was on fire. She slapped the flames with her work gloves. The gloves caught on fire. And then it was dark, her fires extinguished, and Mrs. Ito was frantically clawing out from under the debris of the house she was supposed to wreck.

Her fellow workers were screaming "Help! Help!" from under other houses, and Mrs. Ito, a large patch of skin dangling from her burned shoulder, began pulling out one after another. Their faces were so hugely swollen from burns that they thought they were blind. Their leader was among those who could not see, so Mrs. Ito called the roll. Only about a third of the original group responded.

Rain fell. It was black, gritty, and left big greasy spots on their clothes, but Mrs. Ito and her fellow survivors were so dazed they barely noticed this eerie phenomenon.* When the smoke lifted and revealed the rubble that had been Hiroshima, one of the men said: "Strange to see the whole city bombed all at once. This must be a new kind of bomb!"

The arrival of more people fleeing across the Tsurumi Bridge stirred Mrs. Ito's leadership instincts. A naked father cradling a baby tried to give it water from a tap that still worked, not realizing that his child was dead, and the desperate crowd from town kept growing. The people had to keep moving up Hijiyama Hill, where no fires were burning and where somehow, sooner or later, someone might at least soothe the pain of their burns. Mrs. Ito found a few soldiers and policemen who had been stationed nearby. She told them to lead the refugees up the hill and returned to what she considered her principal responsibility: digging out more of her teammates who were moaning for help from underneath the houses they would no longer have to tear down.

Just below Mrs. Ito, the chaos around the Tsurumi Bridge was growing. When Miyoko Matsubara, a twelve-year-old schoolgirl, reached the bridge from some nearby homes where she had been sal-

---

* Because of worldwide ignorance about radiation problems, the harmfulness of the black rain was greatly exaggerated in the ensuing years, its high visibility having frightened many. Researchers eventually concluded that the rain carried minimal amounts of fallout and could not have been very harmful. It was black because dirt was blown into it by the blast.

vaging roof tiles with a wrecking crew of youngsters from her school, she found hundreds of people who could no longer flee across the bridge. They had to stop to deal with the pain of their burns. Some were standing skin-to-skin in the water of the little emergency fire tanks that families had built near their homes and that had become refuges for burn victims all over town. Most had jumped into the river, and even there they still kept holding their arms up in the air as if ready to surrender to an unseen enemy.

Most were schoolchildren. They cried, "Mother! Mother!" and "Help me!" and looked up beseechingly at Miyoko. One child called, "Aren't you Matsubara?" The face in the water was so blackened that Miyoko could not recognize it. "I'm Hiroko!" said the face, but Miyoko barely heard. Her own burned arms and legs hurt so much that she too forgot about crossing the bridge and jumped fifteen feet into the river.

When Fumiko Morishita reached the Tsurumi Bridge toward 10 a.m., trotting hand-in-hand with her brother-in-law, her niece, and one of her neighbors, they were the subjects of envious looks from crowds of people huddled at the roadside too exhausted, too injured to go on. Fumiko and her people seemed so strong. None had been burned. Fumiko's sister could not walk and had to be carried piggy-back by her husband; she had sustained a back injury when the second floor of their home 900 yards from the hypocenter collapsed. But remarkably, Fumiko and the others did not seem hurt at all.

The people at the bridge were no longer jumping into the river. It was full of floating corpses, a reminder that the soothing water could quickly become a grave to a weakened body. Fumiko had wanted to wade in the river to cool off, but she turned away nauseated and ran on with the others. "Look at us," said several of the people by the road. "We are not so lucky."

Fumiko, who was twenty-five and had been working as an inspector in an artillery-shell factory, did indeed feel lucky. She was alive and so was her sweetheart, who had left for the army three and a half years ago but was still writing her faithfully. She was determined to marry him and return to work in her brother-in-law's fish restaurant with its Kabuki dancers.

Even now her luck was holding, for at the Tamonin Temple near the foot of Hijiyama Hill she encountered a policeman of her acquaintance who presented her with two plump tomatoes on which she feasted with her little band of fellow survivors. And around her waist she carried a money belt with 5000 yen. Citizens had been urged to make such belts for themselves as a precaution against air raids. Not many wore them so early in the morning. Fumiko, the lucky one, was relatively rich. She could not guess that she would hover for months near death while her companions on the road up Hijiyama Hill would all be dead within seven weeks. Having been lucky enough to live through the bomb's blast damage and its fires, they would become victims of its lingering radiation.

Taeko Teramae had had the Tsurumi Bridge and Hijiyama Hill on her mind from the moment she jumped out of the second-floor window of the telephone exchange 600 yards from the hypocenter. Taeko, fifteen, had just returned from her 8 a.m. tea break and was waiting in line to resume her 8:15 shift along with some of the 120 teenage students rotating as switchboard operators in the concrete building. She had put her earphones and speaker around her head when she saw a blue flash. Boxes of telephone equipment tumbled on her. She crawled to the stairs. They were blocked by the bodies of other operators. A few cried, "Mother!" Most were dead.

From the window facing City Hall, Taeko saw that the entire city was being engulfed by flames. Only the Hijiyama Hill area to the east seemed unaffected. If the Tsurumi Bridge was standing she could reach the hill and save herself. She climbed on the window sill, jumped without hesitating into the street, scampered across some burning telephone poles, and ran toward the Bridge. She became aware that she was barefoot, that blood was streaming from her right arm and face, and that she could not see out of her left eye. But she felt no pain.

No one else seemed to be running. The street was packed with charred, swollen bodies, shuffling slowly, silently, sometimes vomiting, away from the flames, away from the city, arms and hands aloft, patches of skin flapping in the rising wind. Taeko ran past two school friends, neither she nor they giving any sign of recognition. Out of breath, she stopped and saw a boy of about ten bending over a much smaller girl. "Mako! Mako! please don't die!" cried the boy. The little girl remained silent. "Mako, are you dead?" The boy cradled his sister's body in his arms.

Nobody paid attention. The fires were closing in. Taeko resumed running. All her life she would feel that she should have given help to less fortunate survivors that morning; she blamed herself for having shown no kindness, no ordinary humanity.

When Taeko reached the Tsurumi Bridge toward 11 a.m., it was packed solidly with people, some lifeless, some sitting, some crawling toward Hijiyama Hill. No one was pushing them along because fires were blocking the bridge entrance.

At the seawall Taeko found one of the two female teachers who supervised the student operators in the telephone exchange. The teacher, who had stayed behind to help any of her charges who might yet reach the bridge, showed shock at Taeko's left eye and her face wounds, and tried to stanch them with the only material at hand: cigarette tobacco. Still Taeko felt no pain.

Since the heat of the spreading fires was constantly rising, the teacher decided to help Taeko swim across the river. Taeko was an excellent swimmer and they were able to dodge the bodies and debris floating in the water. But soon Taeko was exhausted and called out that she felt herself sinking. "Take courage, child!" her teacher said. "You can't die here!" With the teacher pulling at one arm she was able to continue. On the Hijiyama side of the river the teacher told Taeko, "Be strong!" Then she plunged into the water and swam back toward the fires in search of other students. Taeko never saw her again.

Trudging up Hijiyama Hill sometime after noon, Taeko still felt no pain. The asphalt was very hot and soft under her feet. Bodies of people, living and dead, lined the roadside, but the first sign of civilization was in evidence. Bodies no longer littered the road where the fleeing masses would step on them. Fewer people were on the move now and they were advancing very slowly, quietly, like sleepwalkers, occasionally urged on by a policeman.

Halfway up the Hill, Taeko, her face now so swollen that she could only peek through a tiny slit of her right eyelid, found a long line of injured people sitting in front of an emergency aid station under a suspension bridge. They were shouting, *"Mizu! Mizu!* Water! Water! Give me water!" and "Hot! Hot! I'm hot!" Several kept screaming, "Kill me! Please kill me!" The nurses and soldiers who ran the aid post were bent over the wounded and paid no attention to the waiting line.

Taeko sat down with the others. Her face was beginning to be painful. She could no longer see anything, but she heard people call weakly, "Go back! Go back!" Evidently some of the people in line were trying to cut in ahead of their turn. The line seemed hardly to move at all. When Taeko's turn finally came, the soldiers stitched her cuts without giving her a painkiller and bandaged her head so only her nose and mouth remained uncovered. When she winced one of the men said, "You should be stronger, otherwise we cannot win!"

One of the policemen helping refugees across the Tsurumi Bridge and up Hijiyama Hill road was Motoji Maeoka, eighteen years old and only a month on the force. At 8:15 he had been resting on his light green blanket at the provisional police post in the Tamonin Temple near the foot of the hill when he felt himself lifted up and swept, still on his blanket, about seven feet toward a flight of stairs. He tumbled down the steps holding on to his blanket. The roof was collapsing. His right leg bleeding, he limped outside, wrapping the blanket around his head to protect it from roof tiles hurtling through the air. He would always believe that his green blanket saved his life.

Since no one seemed in charge, the baby-faced officer decided on his own to encourage the nearly naked people fleeing up the Hijiyama road. Many were so badly burned that he could not distinguish men from women. He stationed himself in the middle of the road, motioned toward this traffic of the desperate, and shouted, "Climb! Climb! You'll be all right on top."

By early afternoon the sorry condition of the refugees told Maeoka that no amount of encouragement would enable many of them to make it to the top. For one thing, their thirst was obviously excruciating. Maeoka filled a large teakettle with water and walked uphill. All along the road people begged him for water. Many were dying and he had to place the nozzle of his kettle between their lips. Maeoka had been instructed in police training that water, although believed capable of restoring life, was severely harmful for burn victims.* Almost all the people along the road were burned, but he could not bear to see them suffer and he gave water to all.

Food for the survivors had been Shinzo Hamai's preoccupation ever since he left his family and his badly damaged house in the suburbs a few minutes after the bombing to head for his office in the City Hall downtown. He was chief of the Municipal Distribution Section in charge of rationing food and other supplies. Food having been very scarce even while the town was still undamaged, Hamai knew that hunger would spread rapidly unless he was on the job.

Pushing his bicycle because it was impossible to ride it across the debris, he found his normal route blocked by fires. Trying one detour after another, he eventually encountered the city treasurer, who told him that City Hall was in flames. While they debated what to do, the deputy mayor and the city auditor happened by. The mayor, Hamai learned, had died at his official residence. So had almost all other city officials, 280 by later count. No one had seen any firemen, so the fire department and its equipment obviously were not functioning. Society had broken down.

Driven by his sense of being personally responsible for feeding his city, Hamai took charge of the little group of officials on the street, the remnant of all civil authority. Huddling amid the fires, his colleagues witnessed a personality change in Hamai that people who had known him would remark upon for years. At thirty-eight he was a genteel middle-rank civil servant, a graduate of Tokyo University, reserved and rather bookish. His ambition had been to teach sociology some day. The immensity of the emergency turned him, on the spot, into a tough organizer, an authority figure, a bulldozer of obstacles.

He told the other officials to set up emergency headquarters as close as possible to City Hall. He would scout for food and bring it to them somehow.

Heading south through masses of survivors still fleeing the city,

* Innumerable burn victims were made to suffer needlessly because police and fire personnel had been taught that this myth was fact. The deputy director of the Red Cross Hospital posted a signed notice at the East Drill Ground declaring water to be harmless for burn cases, but few believed him. Officer Maeoka still believed in 1982 that he had hastened many deaths because he could not refuse water to anyone.

he walked toward the port of Ujina and its Armored Car Training Center. He needed trucks and he was authorized to use the center's vehicles in an emergency. But when he arrived there about noon, the officers in charge told him in their usual placid, bureaucratic way that he could have no vehicles. There were no drivers. Besides, they were closing down and going home themselves.

Hamai was incensed. Slight of build and normally meek, he lost his temper. He shouted at the officials that their selfishness was inexcusable. Didn't they realize that the survivors in Hiroshima faced starvation?

"What good is armored-car training?" he yelled.

Two college students who worked as helpers at the center had been watching the confrontation. They approached Hamai and said, "We heard you. Let's go!"

Toward 3 p.m. Hamai arrived at the square in front of City Hall with two trucks loaded with bags of *kanpan* (dried bread). The fires in the three-story concrete City Hall were dying down. Yet the trucks had to be unloaded hurriedly and leave; heat and sparks remained so intense that the vehicles were in danger of blowing up.

The deputy mayor and his few surviving colleagues had set up shop in the City Hall square. There was ample space because surrounding homes had lately been torn down to prevent the spreading of fires. A large crowd of hungry, injured people milled about in this center of authority, begging for medical attention and food.

For the rest of the day and most of that night Hamai scurried about, handing out food and negotiating future deliveries. Up and down side streets he carried sacks of bread on his back. He arranged for daily supplies of rice balls to be prepared by volunteers of women's organizations in three surrounding counties. And he energized the dazed officialdom, shouting at the deputy mayor and other superiors.

"I did not know I was doing this," he recalled later. "I was working like a man in a dream."

Surrounding him in front of City Hall were many reminders that the dream was real. A girl of about twelve stopped Hamai. Her face, legs, and hands were severely burned and she pleaded for help. Hamai found her a chair and told her to sit quietly. He promised to return shortly and take her to a hospital. The girl smiled and sat down. When Hamai returned a few minutes later she was still sitting erect in the chair. Hamai tried to lift her. She was dead.

It reminded him of the request that his wife had shouted to him just as he left home that morning. She wanted him to be sure to find out what had happened to her parents, who lived not far from the hypocenter. Hamai had been too busy to attend to this family responsibility and he felt terrible about it.

Responsibility had driven five employees of the government Communications Bureau to a locked door on the fourth floor of their concrete building adjoining the military headquarters compound, about seven-eighths of a mile northeast of the hypocenter. The bureau's official portrait of the Emperor was kept behind that door. Nobody had a key, so the men broke the door open with an ax. One of them lifted the sacred picture on his back, the others ran interference through the panicked crowd surging toward the relative safety of the Ota River.

"The Emperor's picture! The Emperor's picture!" shouted the men, and the crowds gave way. Soldiers stopped to salute, citizens bowed, the disabled by the roadside clasped their hands in prayer. A boat was found, the rescue party propped up the Emperor's portrait for the crossing, and all along the riverbank half-naked and naked people paused to stand at attention.

When the fires spreading from the hypocenter caught up with the crowd a few minutes later, a young woman clerk from the Communications Bureau shouted for everybody to swim across the river. She jumped and was followed by many others, even though the river was more than 300 feet wide and the current swift.

Among the swimmers who made it across was Mr. Mizoguchi, administrator of the Communications Hospital.* But by the time he reached the opposite bank, flying embers were setting houses on fire. He lay down in shallow water, splashed water over his head, and hoped there would be air for him to breathe. The main thing was to remain calm, not to panic like the hundreds who had escaped to the

---

* The Communications Hospital, next to the office building of the Communications Bureau, was normally reserved for employees of the postal, telegraph, and telephone services.

nearby park but had been forced by fires to the high riverbank above him.

They wanted to jump into the water, but across the river, near the spot from which Mizoguchi had escaped, a bare-chested officer brandished a sword. "Don't cross the river!" he shouted. "If anyone tries, I shall kill him with this sword!" Mizoguchi concluded that the officer wanted to keep people from swimming toward certain death. The river had become a trap between fires on both banks.

Above Mizoguchi's hiding place in the river, the pine trees of the park were going up in flames. Shouting, crying, hundreds of people overhead jumped or were pushed until they "toppled like dominoes" into the river. Mizoguchi watched as most of them drowned. When the heat around him became intolerable he still managed to stay calm. He crept through the water to a bridge, waited until afternoon for the fires to abate, and decided that it was his responsibility to return to his hospital. If any of his staff were left, they would need help.

The urgent necessity for large-scale help to Hiroshima from elsewhere in Japan had been clear to Satoshi Nakamura since earlier that morning. He was a reporter for Domei, the official government news agency, and at the time of the bombing he had been starting to eat breakfast at the home of a friend eight miles to the west. Suddenly the windows facing east were shattered. Nakamura was thrown to the floor. Running outside, he saw an enormous mushroom-shaped cloud of black smoke rising over Hiroshima. It turned into a ball of flame. It looked to him like the instant blossoming of a fantastic flower.

Nakamura pedaled to Hiroshima on his bicycle, absorbed the dying city's staggering sights and sounds along his way, and found one telephone line that functioned from the local NHK broadcasting station as far as its sister station in the nearest large city, Okayama, eight miles east toward Tokyo. It was 11:20 a.m. "Please relay the message I will now give you to Domei's Okayama office at once," he said to the man at the other end of the line.

Then he dictated his incredible flash: "At about 8:16 a.m., August 6, one or two enemy planes flew over Hiroshima and dropped one or two special bombs—they may have been atomic—completely destroying the city. Casualties are estimated at one hundred seventy thousand dead."*

Later Nakamura got through directly to the chief of his Okayama office. A Domei man took down their conversation in shorthand. The bureau chief was displeased with Nakamura's original bulletin. He wanted a second, more reasonable story correcting the previous exaggerations. The Army authorities in Tokyo were releasing much less distressing information.

"You tell those bastards in the Army that they are the world's biggest fools!" Nakamura yelled into the telephone. He proceeded to dictate detail after detail of what he had seen since his first call, unaware that tears were pouring down his cheeks and onto his notebook. How could Hiroshima be helped if the authorities in Tokyo were blinding themselves to the facts?

The heat near the hypocenter had grown so intense that Katsuko Horibe, the teacher in the Honkawa School at the Aioi T-Bridge, buried her most valuable possession, her commuter ticket, under some stones, left the group of the dying on the bank of the Motoyas, and immersed herself up to the neck in the river. From time to time she swallowed a little river water and took bites from an apple that had, by some miracle, come floating toward her.

By midday the interior of her school had been burned out, the heat was subsiding, and she heard a familiar voice: "Any teachers or children here from the Honkawa School?" It was Watoji Miaji, one of her teaching colleagues. He had been in charge of a student group tearing down houses. Having conducted them to safety he had returned to the school to look for survivors. His face was badly blackened and swollen.

Miss Horibe was the only one who answered his call. As she held on to Miaji's arm, he walked ahead, and they inched across smoldering rubble past the Aioi Bridge, in the direction of the farm of Miss Horibe's parents in the countryside. Some people were standing on the Aioi Bridge. Miss Horibe wondered why they were not leaving.

* Although Nakamura's guess about the number of fatalities was twice as high as the first official postwar estimates, his figure later proved to be more accurate than any of the various others proposed during all of 1945.

The Death City

. . .

With the worst of the fires beginning to subside, some of the sturdier survivors started to drift back into the city, and the Aioi Bridge was one of their principal destinations; it was a gateway to the worst destruction around the thickly populated hypocenter where the remains of their loved ones were waiting to be cremated*—and, just possibly, some family members might still be alive.

Among these pilgrims was Tsuneo Okimoto, a thirty-four-year-old bookkeeper, who arrived at the Aioi Bridge at 5 p.m. A well-organized man, he would remember the time because he wore a watch and, unlike many watches and clocks in Hiroshima, it had not stopped at 8:15.

Okimoto, who lived only 500 feet from the hypocenter, had survived because one of his bicycle tires went flat overnight and he had to leave extra early for his job in a distant suburb. The bomb caught up with him at Hiroshima Station, a mile from the hypocenter. He had just boarded the 8:15 train. Several people were hurled on top of him. When he extricated himself, his back was full of blood—theirs, not his. His fellow commuters had insulated him from injury.

He walked all day, first north out of the city to get away from the fires, then, thinking methodically as always, southwest to see whether he might succeed in circling back to his home and his wife. His clothes and money belt were intact, but his hopes kept dwindling. Fleeing in the morning, he had been surrounded by so many fellow citizens. Returning in the afternoon, he was almost alone.

Crossing the Tsurumi Bridge shortly after 3 p.m., he saw no one alive except for an occasional passerby. The eastern river bank was covered solidly with bodies. Most were obviously youngsters who had been working on house-wrecking crews. They wore shredded remnants of school uniforms. A few still moved occasionally.

Okimoto did not stop. Frightened because his home was another mile further east toward the fires of the inner city, he hurried on as fast as he could, sometimes trotting. Blackened bodies filled the sides of the streets. When the heat of the fires in the inner city became too intense and he could no longer head directly for his house, he de-

* In Japanese culture, prompt and respectful cremation is essential if the soul of the departed is to return to the soil to rest in peace.

toured past the NHK radio station and saw a streetcar jammed with passengers. All were standing, all were dead.

Heading for the Aioi T-Bridge, Okimoto almost stumbled across a teenage girl lying near an air-raid shelter, grasping her stomach in pain. He recognized her as the daughter of a friend, a barber. He carried her to the bridge, placed her on its pavement, and sat down beside her, determined to wait for the fires on the other side to die down so he could search for his wife.

The bridge was littered with bodies, living, dying, dead. Many survivors moaned for water. Okimoto led a group to the burned-out shell of Miss Horibe's Honkawa School, where they found a working pump and all drank. But since there was no glass or other container to be found, they could not take back any water to those who could not walk.

Darkness brought a chill to the bridge. Some of the survivors, like Okimoto, were fit enough to leave, but they were waiting to enter the fire zone at the earliest possible moment to look for kinfolk. They collected enough wood from nearby ruins to build several small warming fires along the bridge. Okimoto huddled close to one of the bonfires, consulting his watch and thinking of his wife. Chances for her survival seemed to fade as he observed the great fires throughout the city—red flames toward the east and the hypocenter, blue gasoline fires to the west, where piles of the dead were being burned in mass cremations.

Soldiers arrived with cold rice balls for the survivors on the bridge. Okimoto tried to feed a rice ball to the barber's daughter. She could not keep it down and soon she died in his arms. Toward 10 p.m. other soldiers brought sacks of *kanpan*. Okimoto walked up and down the bridge helping to distribute it. The heads of many burn victims were so swollen that the people could barely whisper, "Thank you." There was enough to give two slices to everyone, but some mumbled, "One is enough for me," and indicated that it hurt them too much to chew.

Then there was only silence and occasional groaning on the bridge. Okimoto did not sleep all night. He kept consulting his watch, waiting for dawn and thinking of his wife in the redness of the fires.

Shortly before 10 a.m. on August 7, he stood at the site of his home. He had found only ashes, infinitely small pieces of debris, and his wife's blackened head. He wanted to cremate it promptly, but there were no pieces of wood large enough for a fire. Dry-eyed, methodical as ever, he placed his wife's head in his air-raid hood, walked two hours to his mother's house in the northern suburbs, and cremated it there.

Having narrowly escaped its designated fate as the target of the *Enola Gay,* the Aioi Bridge became the scene of vengeance against the Americans. When Isoko Tamada, eighteen, walked across the bridge in search of her sixteen-year-old sister, an appalling sight stopped her at the eastern end. Tied to a stone post was the body of a tall man in American uniform. A semicircle of ten or more Japanese civilians was in motion around him, yelling and throwing rocks. Shocked, she hurried away, unable to tell whether the man was dying or dead.

The soldier on the bridge represented another miscalculation of General Groves and the American military. There had been twenty-three U.S. prisoners of war in Hiroshima when the bomb was dropped.

Twenty-Two

Hiroshima III: "Water! Water!"

On August 7, the second day after the bombing, thousands who had managed to escape from Hiroshima returned, hoping to find something left of their lives. Among them was Susumu Desaki, the ten-year-old fourth-grader who lived near the East Drill Ground and used to watch the soldiers' horses prance about its expansive grassland. Susumu was searching for his mother and someone had told him that the East Drill Ground was where he should look for her. His playground had become the city's principal evacuation center.

Susumu remembered little of the bombing. His father had been away on a business trip. His mother had left at 7 a.m. to report for work with a house-wrecking crew and had carried his year-old sister on her back, as usual. Waiting to go to school and having heard or seen nothing unusual, Susumu suddenly found himself pinned down under the fragments of his home.

When he clawed his way to the sunlight, the remaining houses looked eerie; they were skeletons and he could see through them as though he had "X-ray eyes." Within minutes, long lines of nearly naked people hurried past, their hair so disheveled that they reminded Susumu of a bogeyman he had seen in a picture book. The pigtails of some girls were burned to a crisp and stood stiff like horns. Many people were "crying and running like pigs being chased." Some ambled slowly and moaned for help. Nobody seemed to hear them.

Susumu had been instructed by his parents that it was improper to show emotion, so he did not cry when he saw the burned people or when a neighbor woman took him away to the country.

Back on his own on the morning of August 7, badly frightened and lonely for his mother, he found his home in ashes. Not even a chunk of roof beam was left. Digging through the dust, Susumu found blackened remnants of his tricycle and his skates. They were bent as if a giant had twisted them out of shape. Still dry-eyed, he ran to the East Drill Ground, and when he first looked across the field he was so stunned that he became dizzy and could barely stay on his feet.

Corpses were piled high in many places. Three fires were blazing to cremate bodies and soldiers were digging holes to bury the remains. Injured people covered the ground as far as Susumu could see. They were packed so close together that he could hardly move without stepping on someone. Many groaned and cried out, "Water! Water!" No one helped. Some kept trying to rise only to fall again, calling out the names of loved ones. After a while they no longer got up.

Near the center of the field, the remnants of the Hiroshima military garrison were gathering. Some soldiers were putting up a tent, but most of the men in uniform sat about, injured and listless. No officers seemed to be in charge. Carcasses of the Army horses that Susumu used to admire lay scattered about. The stench was dreadful.

Slowly Susumu walked up and down among the dead and injured trying to find his mother. The bodies were so disfigured that he had to bend way down to their faces, but often it was impossible to see their features. Suddenly, from a considerable distance, he spotted a woman who looked like his mother. She was sitting, cradling a baby in her arms. Crying at last, Susumu dashed to her side. She was in rags. Her face was so swollen from burns that she could not speak. Torn between shock and happiness, Susumu could not say a word either.

When he saw that his baby sister, whom he adored, was so badly burned that she was barely living, Susumu collapsed next to his mother, sobbing uncontrollably.

But only momentarily. Aware that he had to act as the head of his family, Susumu ran to a friend's house, borrowed a hand cart, and returned there with his mother and sister. The baby was beyond help and died. With his friend Susumu sawed boards from some broken doors, hammered a coffin for her, and carried it to an emergency open-air crematory in the neighborhood. Many people with coffins were waiting there. The boys placed their small coffin next to a stack of others. The next day Susumu returned to pick up the remains and took them to relatives for burial in the family graveyard.

An uncle gave Susumu a 1.8-liter bottle of coconut oil and the boy gently rubbed this precious liquid on the burns that covered his mother's body.* Daily he washed her bandages. They were strips he had torn from gaily colored kimonos. Despite his efforts, maggots crawled across her wounds. When all his mother's hair fell out, he thought she might die at any moment. All over the neighborhood people were dying after their hair fell out. Susumu did not know what was wrong with them or with his mother and there was no doctor or nurse within reach.

Susumu kept on rubbing oil over his mother's body and washing her bandages day after day. They ate rotten sweet potatoes which he stole from the East Drill Ground. When he could find no more, they ate the leaves of potato plants. But they survived.

Having had no word from her husband, the head of the city's emergency food distribution system, Mrs. Shinzo Hamai decided to follow him to City Hall on the afternoon of August 7. Holding her daughters, aged six and eight, by their hands and carrying her three-month-old baby on her back, Mrs. Hamai kept her head down so she would not have to see too many of the bodies lying along the sides of the deserted streets. Festering red burns made the dead and dying look like "demons" to her. Her children would not stop crying.

On the square in front of the burned-out City Hall she found her husband helping to load a truck with shallow wooden crates containing rice balls cooked by women volunteers in the countryside. He had just received a note from his sister-in-law, he said, reporting that his mother-in-law was missing; his father-in-law was dying and

---

* For most burn patients oil was the only treatment available. Cooking oil, castor oil, rapeseed oil, and, not infrequently, machine oil were prized as remedies.

kept calling for him. Mrs. Hamai understood. The two men were unusually close. Should they not all go to her family's side?

Her husband said that he had sent the relatives a note promising to come as soon as his duties would permit. The truck he was loading was destined for the east side, where his in-laws lived, but the food for the hungry had to be distributed first. With his wife and children assisting, Hamai rode through the streets giving out the rice. When they were done and reached the house of his in-laws toward 8 p.m., his father-in-law was dead.

"Where is Mother? Look for Mother," he had kept calling before he died. The mother-in-law was never found, and Hamai never overcame the heartbreak of the conflict between his official and his family duties that kept him from his father-in-law's deathbed.

"I still feel miserable about it," he said a generation later.

The wish of the able-bodied to be reunited with their kin, living or dead, was as strong an obsession as the frantic desire of the helpless to be found by the searchers.

In the 400-bed Red Cross Hospital, Hiroshima's largest and most modern, patients advertised their presence by finger painting their names on the walls of the lobby with their blood.

Along the rivers, small boats cruised up and down bearing white pennants on which the names of missing relatives were scrawled in large letters.

Many searchers wandered about the city, relentlessly scrutinizing corpses that floated in emergency fire tanks or at the river banks. They turned over bodies in the streets and peered at unrecognizable faces on the floor mats of the hospitals, asking patient after patient, "Who are you?" Eventually Kanji Kuramoto, a nineteen-year-old student, gave up hope of finding a body that looked anything like his father. Instead he searched bodies for the big old-fashioned pocket watch that the elderly man wore on a chain in his vest. The two-week effort was futile.

So was the quest of survivors who came to the Nido Needle Company, where the tin roof collapsed and forty-eight workers were incinerated by fire. The company president, Masato Tamura, cremated the remains himself and placed all ashes in a large box. Whenever a survivor called on him to look for kin, he apologized that he had been unable to perform individual cremations and invited the relative to take along a handful of ashes. In the end, many ashes were left, along with the only remaining possessions of his employees: watches, belt buckles, and parts of neckties that he had laid out for relatives along the stone foundation of the factory gate, which was all that was left intact of his family's 104-year-old firm.

Florence Garnett, thirteen, one of the 3200 second-generation Japanese-Americans in Hiroshima, was looking for the grandparents with whom she had been living. Her father, a produce dealer in Los Angeles, had wanted her to get a Japanese education, but she hated it in Japan. Florence was homesick; she dreamed of hamburgers and hot dogs and was repeatedly reprimanded for talking to boys, which nice girls were not supposed to do. She had managed to get excused from wielding her bamboo spear in defense drill, but now the Americans, her own people, had bombed her.

Vomiting, weakened by diarrhea, spotted with the grit of black rain, she finally found the bones of her grandparents. She had piled them on some newspapers and wood when a soldier stopped and offered to complete the cremation for her.*

For Motoji Maeoka, the baby-faced eighteen-year-old policeman who had helped so many survivors along the Tsurumi Bridge and up Hijiyama Hill, there was no escape from the remains of the bombed. For three days, wearing no gloves, he helped firemen stack bodies near the bridge. When the piles were about seven feet high, he poured gasoline on them and watched them burn.

The police felt that somehow a record should be kept of the cremations. Since almost all bodies lacked identification, an officer from the East Police Station came to compile lists of their actual or estimated clothing sizes. Nobody questioned the uselessness of this gesture of respect toward the dead.

Occasionally people wandered by the bridge who hoped to find the remains of relatives, but none approached the bodies. The living merely watched the scene silently and drifted away.

* In 1983, Garnett worked as a registered nurse in a Los Angeles hospital and supported a vigorous but apparently hopeless campaign for congressional appropriations to pay for bomb-connected medical expenses of some 1000 *hibakusha* living in the United States as American citizens.

The Death City

. . .

The groans and stench of survivors assaulted Dr. Michihiko Hachiya as he awoke lying in blood-soaked bandages in a ground-floor ward of the Communications Hospital. Surgical instruments, window frames, fragments of walls and furniture, mounds of shattered glass littered the floor. Smoke curled from the second story. Looking around in amazement, Dr. Hachiya began to remember how he had dragged himself some 200 yards from his home on the previous morning, August 6, and collapsed in the garden of the hospital. The hospital was the place for him to be, but not as a patient. He was its director and should have been at work to help his staff cope with whatever disaster had befallen their city.

Two of his doctors, their own injuries bandaged, hurried to him to discourage his small efforts to stand up. One of them, the chief surgeon, told Dr. Hachiya that he had stitched forty wounds in his body the night before. Dr. Hachiya and his colleagues did not know it, but only 28 of Hiroshima's 300 physicians were still able to function, and as 2500 ill and injured citizens stormed the 125-bed Communications hospital within twenty-four hours, Dr. Hachiya and his staff faced conditions that he found, as he later wrote in his diary, "inconceivable."

Patients were squeezed into every available inch of space, his associates told him: the ward floors, corridors, toilets, stairways, the outside grounds. Dr. Hachiya had been enormously lucky, they said. He did not suffer from the most prevalent symptoms: raw, festering burns, vomiting, and a suspicious type of diarrhea.

Some patients reported up to fifty bloody stools in one night. There were no bedpans. Patients urinated and defecated wherever they lay. There were almost no personnel to help the dying; certainly no one could be spared for any efforts to clean up. No one could avoid stepping in filth. Dr. Hachiya concluded that he and his staff were dealing with an epidemic of infectious bacillary dysentery and ordered the construction of a shack to make at least the semblance of an effort at creating an isolation ward.

Two doctor friends from nearby towns who arrived to check on Dr. Hachiya's safety told of witnessing appalling scenes on their way through Hiroshima. "The sight of the [fleeing] soldiers was more dreadful than the dead people floating down the river," one of the visitors reported. "They had no faces! Their eyes, noses and mouths had been burned away, and it looked like their ears had melted off. It was hard to tell front from back."*

Another doctor told Dr. Hachiya, "I saw fire reservoirs filled to the brim with dead people who looked as though they had been boiled alive . . . I saw a man . . . drinking the blood-stained water . . . there were so many dead people there wasn't enough room for them to fall over . . . One pool wasn't big enough to accommodate everybody who tried to get in . . . I don't know how many were caught by death with their heads hanging over the edge . . ."

The same visiting doctor told Dr. Hachiya he had heard that a "special new bomb" had been responsible for the devastation. For Dr. Hachiya, relieved to discover that he was well enough for his accustomed scientific curiosity to be reviving, this speculation only added to his puzzlement. How could a single bomb inflict such overwhelming damage? It had to have been a very "special" weapon indeed. Few people had heard the noise of an explosion. Nobody had found the slightest sign of any crater. Dr. Hachiya thought of the dysentery infesting his hospital. Had the bomb dropped poison gas or germs? Medical detective work had always challenged him. How could he solve the mystery so he might devise some treatment for his patients?

As evening came on August 7, conditions in his wards were still worsening. More dead were sandwiched in between the ill and injured. Relatives of missing people greatly upset the patients by roaming about and peering at every face. One woman wandered through the wards shouting her child's name. Another kept mournfully calling out a name from outside the front entrance.†

With the onset of night, a profound sense of isolation settled upon

* Another observant survivor, Father Wilhelm Kleinsorge, a Jesuit missionary from Germany, later told the American writer John Hersey that he saw twenty soldiers with similar "nightmarish" injuries. In his classic account, *Hiroshima,* Hersey described these men: "Their faces were wholly burned, their eyesockets were hollow, the fluid from their melted eyes had run down their cheeks. (They must have had their faces upturned when the bomb went off.)" In later years, medical investigators reported that the number of severe eye injuries had indeed been large but that they had generally been caused by burns and by glass splinters sent flying by the bomb's blast.
† Similar scenes were reported from all the emergency first-aid posts being set up in outlying districts, usually on the grounds of schools.

Dr. Hachiya. His wife was in an adjoining bed, not too severely injured, but the sobs and groans of his helpless patients and their calls of "Mother!" and *"Eraiyo!"* ("The pain is unbearable!") were dreadful to hear. The darkness and his detachment from the rest of the world were total. There was no candle, no radio, no information. The doctor was further depressed by the thought that the war was lost. Later he wrote in his diary that he was certain the Americans would soon land and there would be fighting in the streets.

His thoughts were interrupted by a patient shuffling toward his bed in the dark. In the moonlight the doctor could discern that the man's face had been melted away. He was blind and lost. Terror-stricken, Dr. Hachiya yelled at him, "You are in the wrong room!" Immediately he felt ashamed, "more awake than ever, every nerve taut." Sleep would not come. The question would not leave him: What had happened in Hiroshima?

In the next two days, August 8 and 9, Dr. Hachiya's staff was cheered to see the doctor gaining strength. Small and of slight build, he was a warm and popular boss, round-faced, nearly always smiling, seemingly never hurried. He was modest—hardly a universal trait among chief doctors in Japan or elsewhere—and he had personally tended his little patch in the hospital garden where staff personnel grew sweet potatoes. When his doctors and nurses saw that Dr. Hachiya's appetite was returning, everyone felt encouraged, especially since loss of appetite was a worrisome problem with many of the hospitalized bomb victims, along with other developing symptoms.

Bloody diarrhea was increasing among those who had previously reported ordinary diarrhea. Others reported sore gums and petechiae, small purple spots on their bodies. The spots were subcutaneous hemorrhages and Dr. Hachiya considered them "bizarre"; they appeared to have been caused by injury, yet the patients reported no injuries that seemed connected with their purple spots. In his diary the doctor recorded "an insult heretofore unknown" and theorized that it might be due to a sudden change in atmospheric pressure caused by the bomb's great blast force and heat.

The aftereffects of the explosion were still crowding in on the doctor. The interiors of concrete buildings, still afire, threw huge silhouettes against the skies at night. The odors from the funeral pyres nauseated him. In his diary he noted: "These glowing ruins and the blazing funeral pyres set me to wondering if Pompeii had not looked like this during its last days. But I think there were not so many dead in Pompeii."

Infectious dysentery still worried him the most. Visiting doctors told him that all the area's hospitals and aid stations were filled with patients suffering from this condition. When Dr. Hachiya was informed that an emergency isolation ward for such cases had been installed in the basement of the Fukuya department store, he wanted to see the medical work being done there. Able to move about once again with the help of a cane, he limped to the store. At the entrance a sign said, "Contagious—Stay out!" The doctor could not bring himself to face the horror of the ward's sounds and smells: "One peep into the basement was enough."*

Not until a week after the bombing did Dr. Hachiya receive the first meaningful word about the weapon that had obliterated his surroundings. An old friend, a Navy captain from Okayama, came to check on him and said, "It is a miracle you survived. After all, the explosion of an atom bomb is a terrible thing."

"An atom bomb!" the doctor yelled, stunned. He had heard rumors of such a bomb earlier in the war. It was supposed to be able to blow up islands as large as Saipan with "ten grams of hydrogen." He did not, however, connect such a bomb with radiation or with his patients' symptoms. Even when the visiting captain said that one of the

---

* The Fukuya department store, an eight-story landmark of reinforced concrete and brick veneer, 650 yards from the hypocenter, became a microcosm of Hiroshima before and after the *pikadon* ("flash-boom"), as the bombing was known. Founded in 1929, the store offered the high style that New Yorkers associate with Bloomingdale's. During the war, mercantile operations were suspended and the building buzzed with official activity: offices and storage for the Army, the postal savings system and other departments. A canteen in the basement served watery rice soup. On the top floor classes met for high-school students being trained to become government clerks. Most occupants escaped from the sturdy Fukuya after the bombing (more than 500 came down with radiation sickness). Since it was the largest structure standing, Mitsugi Kishida, a portrait photographer, climbed up the outside emergency staircase while the interior was still smoldering and took the best existing panoramic views of the city's smoking and deserted ruins from the roof with his F-50 Contax. He had been too pained until then to shoot any pictures. Though he finally decided to make a pictorial record, he secreted his film until 1970. Noting that similar photographs in the city's Peace Museum were not as revealing as his own, he donated his haunting work to that institution, where it is on conspicuous display. The versatile Fukuya store is once again an oasis of elegance.

area's naval hospitals had found that its Hiroshima patients were suffering from a low white-blood-cell count, Dr. Hachiya did not become suspicious. His friend not being a doctor, he had no doubt garbled whatever scientific information he had picked up.

In Dr. Hachiya's wards the medical mystery was deepening still further. He was examining severely injured patients who were improving, as he was himself. But others who seemed relatively well, including one of his nurses, collapsed and died within two days, with bloody sputum and vomitus and purple skin hemorrhages. Bloody stools and diarrhea, on the other hand, were decreasing, and so he had to abandon his earliest theory of a germ bomb spreading infectious dysentery.

"The more I thought, the more confused I became," he wrote in his diary.

Calling on his superior in the medical department of the Prefectural Office to beg for hospital supplies, Dr. Hachiya found that this doctor was not confused at all. "You've no doubt heard that an atom bomb was dropped on Hiroshima," he said in considerable agitation. "Well, I've learned that no one will be able to live in Hiroshima for the next seventy-five years."*

The prefectural chief doctor seemed to believe the report and so did a great many others. Dr. Hachiya did not. He was feeling stronger daily. So did some of his patients. How, then, could the entire area be uninhabitable? There had to be a more explicit reason why certain people, including so many who seemed to feel all right, were still dying daily.

The most incredulous people in Hiroshima those first two weeks—and among the most terrified—were not local or even Japanese. They were ten American prisoners of war, the crew of a B-29 that ditched off Japan on August 8. They had spent a week on life rafts in the water before being picked up by a Japanese fishing boat. On the

---

* A report to this effect, widely broadcast and printed on August 8, probably reached Hiroshima by word of mouth from listeners to shortwave broadcasts in neighboring cities. The first version of this myth originated in New York with one Harold Jacobson, a chemist who had worked on the Manhattan Project in a minor capacity and claimed that dangerous secondary radiation would linger in Hiroshima for "seventy" years. Although Oppenheimer issued an official denial, the story made headlines in the Tokyo newspapers and all over the world.

17th they were in Hiroshima, though they didn't know it. Blind-folded, their hands and feet tightly bound by rope, they lay silently on the East Drill Ground. Whenever one of them tried to talk, he was kicked on the head by someone from the crowd that was assembling around them and making threatening noises.

The airmen were protected only by a kindly guardian angel, a Japanese Military Police captain named Nobuichi Fukui who had been assigned to them as an interpreter. His superiors did not know that Fukui had had a liking for Americans since his student days at Dartmouth in 1928, or that he had happened to come upon the fliers shortly after the fishermen who had picked them up had decided to behead them and had already set up a chopping block for the purpose.

Responding to the ugliness of the throng milling around the East Drill Ground, Fukui intervened again and ordered the prisoners loaded onto a truck to take them to the port of Ujina. "I am responsible!" he shouted at the mob, and they let him leave. He was too much a patriot, however, to pass up the opportunity of lecturing his charges on the inhumanity of the atomic bomb.

In front of Hiroshima Station Fukui ordered the truck stopped and the prisoners' blindfolds removed. "Look what you have done," he shouted. "One bomb! One bomb!" The Americans sat dumbfounded in their truck as it drove through the city. "It was a spooky ride," remembered Martin L. Zapf, the crew's radio man. No house was standing. Nothing moved, not even a dog. There was a strange smell of singed hair, but no sound except Fukui yelling in fury, "One bomb! One bomb!"

On the edge of town the truck stopped and two more American POWs were loaded aboard: a Navy aviator named Norman Roland Brisset, from Lowell, Massachusetts, and an Air Force sergeant, Ralph J. Neal, from Corbin, Kentucky. They were in appalling condition and suffering from much pain and nausea. "I'll never forget this horrible green stuff that came out of their mouths and ears," remembered Stanley Levine, the B-29 crew's radar officer.

The two ailing men were able to relate that they had been among several groups of American fliers held in Hiroshima on August 6. They remembered an explosion, fires, total hysteria and confusion among the Japanese, and how they had saved themselves by diving into a cesspool.* They had never heard of an atomic bomb and no one on the truck knew that Brisset's and Neal's symptoms signified that they were fatally ill of radiation poisoning.

That night, confined in the cells of a Japanese military camp, the two dying men were screaming in pain. The men of the B-29 crew were given a first-aid kit in which they found morphine, which they administered.

When this did not help, a Japanese doctor appeared and the men asked him, "How about doing something for these guys?"

"Do something?" asked the doctor. "You tell me what to do! You caused this. I don't know what to do."

The agony of the dying men continued through the night.

"They were begging us to please shoot them and end it all," Levine recalled. "And finally they died before daylight."

Although the deaths of Americans at Hiroshima soon became known to General Groves and the War Department, the United States Government never informed the families of these men that the cause of their death had been an American A-bomb.

* They were the only known immediate survivors among twenty-three American aviators held prisoner at three locations in downtown Hiroshima at the time of the bombing.

Part 7
False Dawn

Twenty-Three

Washington: "The Greatest Day in History"

Washington being fourteen hours behind Tinian time, General Groves had expected to hear by 1 p.m. on Sunday, August 5, that the *Enola Gay* and its two escort planes had taken off. Having arrived in his office early that morning and finished some paper work, he waited fretfully until well past the deadline hour.

At about 3 p.m. the general decided to work off his anxiety by playing some tennis. He told the duty officer where he could be reached and took along another officer to sit by a telephone at the courts. The officer called headquarters every fifteen minutes. No word.

Shortly before 5 p.m., back at his office, Groves was informed that General Marshall had phoned from his Leesburg, Virginia, weekend home to inquire about the mission but asked that Groves not be summoned to the telephone. "He has enough to think about without being bothered by me," Marshall said. "I hope he will have news soon."

At about 6 p.m., accompanied by his wife and daughter, Groves met for a previously arranged dinner with Stimson's aide George Harrison at the Army-Navy Club. "Still no news," Groves whispered to Harrison as they sat down at table. General Thomas T. Handy, Marshall's deputy, dining at another table, came over to ask Groves what he had heard. "Nothing," said Groves, sighing.

At 6:45 p.m. Groves was called to the telephone. "As I went, I noticed both Harrison and Handy had stopped eating and I could feel their eyes boring in my back," Groves wrote later. The duty officer told him that the *Enola Gay* mission had left on schedule but no further word had come. Groves whispered the progress report to Harrison and Handy, but by this time he had expected to have news of the raid's results. Not for some days did he learn that routing mixups across the Pacific were responsible for still further communications delays.

As he resumed waiting in his office, staff people gathered quietly in the outer rooms. Tension mounted steadily. Picking up his paper work, Groves rolled up his sleeves, took off his tie, and opened his collar. This was unprecedented. The general was hoping to create "a more informal, relaxed atmosphere." It didn't work; "the hours went by more slowly than I ever imagined hours would go by."

At 11:15, the secretary of the General Staff called seeking word for General Marshall. By now Groves was greatly distressed. A communications breakdown seemed to him unlikely; urgent messages had never been so long delayed. The possibility of failure seemed real.

At 11:30 the strike message from Captain Parsons arrived. Groves decoded it personally: "Results clear-cut. Successful in all respects." Relief, excitement, and congratulatory shouts swept the office. Marshall was notified; "thank you very much for calling me" was all he said. Groves went to sleep on a cot in his office, but his closest aides, too excited to rest, started a poker game.

Jean O'Leary, Groves's executive assistant, had accumulated a stack of change and dollar bills by 4:30 a.m. when a long cable arrived from Tinian with some hoped-for details of the strike. The Pentagon decoding officer had addressed it to "Major O'Leary." Over a pot of coffee Groves read to his colleagues about the "purple clouds and flames boiling and swirling upward" into a mushroom at least 40,000 feet high. Parsons reported that he believed "this strike was tremendous and awesome even in comparison with New Mexico test." However, no photographs were yet available and the message relayed nothing about damage to Hiroshima except these words: "It looked as though whole town was being torn apart."

Freshly shaved and looking crisp in a clean uniform, Groves was waiting with a two-page report on the latest good tidings when General Marshall arrived in his Pentagon office at 6:58 a.m. His sense of triumph was complete. "It was a bolt out of heaven," he wrote later. "There has never been a surprise to equal it since the Trojan horse."*

General "Hap" Arnold, the Air Force chief of staff, and George Harrison hurried in within a minute or two. The question before them was how to manage the atomic news so that its enormity would yield maximum impact on the Japanese and perhaps move them toward surrender. Their answer was to hit the enemy fast. Subject to Secretary of War Stimson's approval, the presidential statement on the bomb drop, prewritten and honed for effect by Groves, should be released immediately.

At 7:45, Marshall reached Stimson over the secure scrambler phone at Highhold, where Stimson was resting after his exertions at the Potsdam Conference. The Secretary agreed to break the five-year blackout on the atom. He urged that President Truman be promptly notified—the President was coming home aboard the U.S.S. *Augusta*—and he made a point of extending his "very warm congratulations" to Groves.

Marshall invited Groves to work out of the Secretary's empty office that morning, and in those imposing surroundings, pleased and proud, Groves held court as the Secretary's staff counseled him on the final wording of the presidential message. Earlier that morning Marshall had cautioned against crowing with "too much gratification" in light of the undoubtedly large Japanese casualties. This injunction had annoyed Groves, and in his moment of personal triumph he had not hesitated to tell Marshall that revenge, not civility, was on his mind.

"I replied that I was not thinking so much about those [Japanese] casualties as I was about the men who had made the Bataan death march,"† the general remembered in his memoirs.

Nevertheless, Groves recognized that it would be imprudent to risk making claims that the Japanese might refute. It was only his "guess"

---

* Groves enjoyed placing himself in a historical context. Eventually he would liken the leanness of his staff to that of General Sherman. His mastery of atomic complexities he compared to the pluck of Christopher Columbus.
† Beginning on May 7, 1942, at least 7000 (possibly as many as 10,000) American and Philippine soldiers died of starvation, disease, beatings, and executions as their Japanese captors marched them to Bataan after the surrendor of Corregidor.

that the city had been destroyed. He had no hard evidence. His frantic efforts to extract more data out of Tinian had yielded nothing new; it succeeded only in routing Deke Parsons from bed to the teletype just after he had taken several sleeping pills.

After listening to numerous conflicting suggestions, Groves decided to follow the advice of Robert A. Lovett, Assistant Secretary of War for Air. Lovett counseled caution. He reminded Groves that the Air Force had more than once claimed the destruction of Berlin. "It becomes rather embarrassing after about the third time," Lovett said.

After last-minute editing by Groves, the presidential announcement made no claim of any destruction on the ground. It relied for shock value on the destructive force of the bomb itself. "Sixteen hours ago an American airplane dropped one bomb on Hiroshima, an important Japanese Army base," the release began. "The bomb had more power than 20,000 tons of TNT." That figure too was a guess—and a wrong one at that—but at least the Japanese were not likely to marshal scientific evidence to quibble over it.*

It certainly hooked the White House press corps. As the words "20,000 tons of TNT" came out of the mouth of Truman's press secretary at 10:45 a.m., the reporters stampeded to the table near the exit for stacks of the release. Its text continued: "It is an atomic bomb. It is a harnessing of the basic power of the universe." The President called again on the Japanese to surrender or face "a rain of ruin from the air, the like of which has never been seen on this earth."

At the same time—the clock at sea called it an hour later—President Truman had just begun lunch with six enlisted men in the after mess hall of the *Augusta*. He never finished the meal. The Army captain in charge of the traveling White House "map room" hurried in and handed him a map of Japan and a just-decoded 26-word flash. The

---

* The figure was based on the experience of the Trinity test. No figure on the Hiroshima drop was available to Groves at the time of the presidential announcement. On Tinian, the scientists analyzing the measurements taken by the instruments that were dropped over the target by parachute concluded initially that the blast had been equal to about 8000 tons of TNT. Later they found an error in their calculations and fixed the force at 17,000 tons. Eventually the final figures showed a power equivalent of 13.5 thousand tons. Oppenheimer and his men literally did not know their own strength.

message began: "Big bomb dropped on Hiroshima." On the map the officer had circled Hiroshima with a red pencil.

The President took a deep breath, grasped the captain's hand, and exclaimed, "This is the greatest day in history!" He did not explain himself until, some ten minutes later, another officer handed him a more detailed confirmatory message and told him that the radio in the map room had just carried a news bulletin on Groves's release from Washington.

Barely able to contain his excitement, Truman clanged a fork on the side of a water glass, asked the crewmen for silence, and told them of the "atomic bomb." While the men broke into cheering the President dashed out the door clutching the messages and headed, smiling proudly, to the officers' mess. He burst through the wardroom door, waved the amazed officers into their seats when they began to rise, and repeated his sensational announcement.

"It was an overwhelming success," he exulted. "We won the gamble!" And as he spread the word about the ship he said he had never been happier about any announcement he had ever made.*

At Los Alamos, Oppenheimer got the word by phone from Groves, who assured him that the bomb had gone off "with a very big bang indeed." Looking relieved and proud, Oppie dictated a terse announcement to his principal secretary, Anne Wilson, disclosing no more than that a "successful combat drop" of one of the laboratory's "units" had taken place. On the run, Wilson took the note to the WAC soldier who operated the public address system. Not knowing what the "unit" was, the soldier read the news as mechanically as a lost-and-found notice.

"The place went up like we'd won the Army–Navy game," Wilson remembered, and not long after the whooping subsided in the laboratories, Oppenheimer addressed his assembled troops in the theater that had been the scene of his colloquia and many of the crises that

---

* Truman never entertained second thoughts about dropping the bomb and always claimed the decision was a very easy one for him to make. As the years went by, he said so, vehemently, again and again. In 1958 he even wrote a letter to the Hiroshima City Council confirming a statement he had made on television that he would order the bomb used again, given similar circumstances. "We'll send it airmail," he instructed his secretary. "Be sure enough stamps are on it!"

had nearly overwhelmed them all. It was a showman's climactic moment and Oppie made the most of it.

For the colloquia he usually arrived more or less on time and slipped casually onstage from a wing. This day he entered very late and strode down the aisle from the rear of the auditorium, making no effort to calm the clapping, foot-stomping, yelling scientists. They broke into their demonstration as Oppie entered and continued for a long time after their leader clasped his hands together overhead in the classic boxer's salute and mounted the podium. Hiroshima was their sweet victory.

That evening, another victory party in one of the men's dormitories got off to a sluggish start. At 8 p.m. only a handful of the approximately fifty celebrants were dancing. Others were talking and drinking quietly, as if they could not decide whether the day's joy had been appropriate. In a corner Oppenheimer was showing Bob Bacher a telex that had arrived from Washington relaying damage reports from Hiroshima. Bacher was shaking his head. Both became increasingly depressed as they went over the details, and they soon left the party. Outside, Oppenheimer spotted a scientist vomiting in the bushes and said to himself, "The reaction has begun." In the dormitory, the celebration was already breaking up. It was 9 p.m.

At 7:15 p.m. European time, there was a knock on the door of the room occupied by Otto Hahn at Farm Hall, a large country estate not far from Cambridge, England, where the chemist from Berlin who had first split the atom was interned along with Germany's principal nuclear scientists. Holding a bottle of gin in one hand, the British major in charge of the group told Hahn of the bomb drop on Hiroshima.

"I didn't want to believe it," Hahn wrote in his diary, "but the major said that this was the official word from the President of the United States." Hahn was "incredibly shocked and depressed." The death of so many "innocent women and children was almost intolerable." After bracing himself with some gin Hahn went downstairs to dinner, where the British major announced the news to the other scientists. The ensuing excited discussion revolved principally around another internee in this elite group, Werner Heisenberg, the leader of the inglorious German effort to develop an A-bomb.

. . .

HAHN: . . . If the Americans have a uranium bomb then you're all second-raters. Poor old Heisenberg!

HEISENBERG: Did they use the word "uranium" in connection with this atomic bomb?

HAHN: No.

HEISENBERG: Then it's got nothing to do with atoms . . .

For hours the researchers bickered about the bomb's morality and feasibility. Some who believed that it was real called it "dreadful" and "madness." But the group could not agree on how the Americans might have hit on the technical solutions that had eluded their own team, and the Germans retired for the night on a note of wishful thinking.

HAHN: Well, I think we'll bet on Heisenberg's suggestion that it is bluff.

Hahn was not really convinced of this, and he remained so upset that Heisenberg and the others thought he might commit suicide. They kept looking in on his room until 2 a.m., when they saw that he was asleep.

Groves took special delight in the Germans' reactions. He chuckled as he followed their arguments word for word in the transcripts sent to him in Washington. It was he who had ordered their conversations bugged. Two comments pleased him particularly. One, from Hahn, complimented the efforts of Groves and his intelligence operatives in keeping the lid on all progress with the bomb. "If they have really got it," said Hahn, "they have been very clever in keeping it secret." The other remark, from Heisenberg, constituted ultimate praise for Oppenheimer and his scientists.

Heisenberg said: "I find it is a disgrace that we, the professors who worked on it, cannot at least work out how they did it."

At Groves's bomber base on Tinian, his team was ordered to go on three shifts a day to do it again—and more rapidly than scheduled. Truman's radio announcement had buoyed the spirits of the general's men, but when Norman Ramsey, the chief scientist, tuned the short-wave radio in the air-conditioned bomb hut to the Tokyo frequency, the cheerful voice of Tokyo Rose merely said that three planes had staged a minor raid on Hiroshima. About an hour later Tokyo announced that train service to the city had been temporarily suspended. No details about the raid came through. If the Japanese leaders were shaken by history's first atomic bomb drop, they gave no sign of it.

Groves had originally estimated that he would not have enough plutonium in existence to drop the Fat Man bomb before August 20. As July ended he advanced the strike date to August 11. Immediately after Hiroshima he began to push for a drop on the tenth, because of "the importance of having the second blow follow the first one quickly, so that the Japanese would not have time to recover their balance."

The weather was uncooperative, however. It would be adequate on August 9 but unsuitable for the following five days. Whereupon Groves started to push for a drop on the 9th. Ramsey and his men demurred. Such a headlong rush might introduce technical slipups. Groves was not dissuaded. "I decided," he wrote later, "that we should take the chance." He kept peppering his deputy on Tinian, General Farrell, with "inquiries as to how we were coming on" and requests to let him "know as soon as possible when we were ready."

Throughout, Groves tactfully kept in touch with Generals Spaatz, LeMay, and the other Air Force commanders on Guam, but President Truman and the civilian authorities in Washington were no longer included in the decision-making circuit. No one ever considered the options of delaying a second bomb drop and reviewing the decision to continue atomic assaults. Once the President had decided on July 25 that future bombs were to be dropped "as soon as made ready," no further civilian involvement was contemplated or necessary. The bombs were to be kept coming automatically.

Working at top speed on the Fat Man in his bomb hut, Norman Ramsey managed also to continue listening to Tokyo Rose, and when she began to speak of radiation injuries and deaths in Hiroshima he became "puzzled" and "upset." Any irradiated victims were supposed to have been killed by "a brick first." The bomb was planned as a blast—not a radiation—weapon. But, lacking scientific confirmation, Ramsey initially suspected that Tokyo Rose's scoop might be propaganda fakery and he did nothing about it. He was plagued by a far more pressing concern anyway. "All of us were expecting that maybe fifty of these bombs would be required to finish the war," and so he composed a long letter to Oppenheimer asking for immediate design changes to make future bombs safe for the launching base and crews.

The Fat Man was too complex to be assembled in the air, and since Ramsey felt that an eventual crash on takeoff was "inevitable" because of conditions on Tinian, the safety issue was his priority. The local Air Force command had gotten wind of the danger that their island might be blown up and demanded that he and Captain Parsons sign a statement guaranteeing that the bomb was safe on takeoff. They signed though they were far from fully convinced.

Ramsey was growing fatalistic. When *Bock's Car,* the B-29 carrying the plutonium bomb, took off at 3:49 a.m. on August 9, he stationed himself at the end of the runway to watch the liftoff. The aircraft made it; if it had not, Ramsey thought, his personal problems would have been settled without further headaches: "We would have been blown up, too, and we wouldn't have to do any explaining."

Bock's Car was less lucky than the *Enola Gay,* at least for a while. Just before takeoff, General Farrell had received word that the weather would worsen. Mindful of Groves's urgings, Farrell decided not to delay the drop.

"Young man, do you know how much that bomb cost?" the principal naval officer present asked the pilot, Major Charles W. Sweeney, shortly before takeoff.

"About $25 million."

"See that we get our money's worth!"

They almost didn't. After making three runs and wasting 45 minutes over the primary target, Kokura and its arsenal, Sweeney decided that visual bombing was not possible although the weather plane had radioed that it would be. Diverting to the secondary target, the port and shipbuilding center of Nagasaki, Sweeney computed that he had enough gas for only one bomb run.

Encountering a thick overcast at Nagasaki, the pilot and the weaponeer decided to violate their specific orders and made almost the entire approach by radar. Only at the very last moment did a sudden break in the clouds permit visual bombing.

Day One

The bomb exploded one and a half miles from the aiming point, but it destroyed 44 percent of the town. According to official American estimates, 35,000 people were killed. Actually the death would number 60,000, possibly 70,000.* Sweeney made it back to his alternate landing field on Okinawa with not enough gas to taxi off the runway.

Forebodings about the debut of atomic power were voiced by a few. "The world is not yet ready for it," Einstein told a *New York Times* reporter who called at the professor's Princeton home. In Rome, the Pope protested the lack of immunity for civilian populations. In Chicago, Leo Szilard asked the pastor of the Rockefeller Memorial Chapel at the University of Chicago for a "special prayer to be said for the dead of Hiroshima and Nagasaki." And in Washington, President Truman received a telegram from the general secretary of the Federal Council of Churches of Christ in America opposing further use of the weapon.

Truman's reply was in keeping with preponderant sentiment in the Western nations: "Nobody is more disturbed over the use of the atomic bomb than I am, but I was greatly disturbed over the unwarranted attack by the Japanese on Pearl Harbor and their murder of our prisoners of war. The only language they seem to understand is the one we have been using to bombard them. When you have to deal with a beast you have to treat him as a beast . . ."

General Groves's factories were still producing plutonium and uranium, and in Los Alamos Oppenheimer was still assembling more bombs, but shortly after the Nagasaki bomb drop, Groves and General Marshall decided to hold up further shipments to Tinian. Reports from Tokyo were beginning to suggest that the Japanese were considering surrender. But unless they gave up by August 13, the deliveries were to resume.

In Los Alamos, the departure of the core for the third bomb was

---

* Perhaps the most unlikely of miraculous experiences were the escapes of nine men found by Robert Trumbull of the *New York Times*. Most of them worked for the Mitsubishi Shipbuilding Company and had been sent from its Nagasaki plant to work temporarily at its Hiroshima shipyards. All nine survived the August 6 raid, returned home to Nagasaki, and survived the second bomb there.

intercepted at the last moment. An Army captain was signing for it and was about to hand the receipt to Bob Bacher when Oppenheimer arrived on the run and announced, "We've got a hold order!"

On August 13 in Washington, Groves discovered that he was unable to obtain any decision on whether to resume shipments. He could not even manage to see Stimson or Marshall. They were too busy trying to decipher the intentions of the Japanese.

Twenty-Four

Tokyo: The Emperor Speaks

Among the key officials in Tokyo, it quickly became apparent on the morning of August 6 that something catastrophic had occurred in Hiroshima, but nobody could determine what it was. Shortly after 8:16 a.m. the control operator of NHK, the Japan Broadcasting Corporation, noticed that his telephone line to the Hiroshima radio station was dead. Minutes later, the Tokyo railway signal center found that its telegraph line had been cut near Hiroshima. Before 10 a.m., Central Command Headquarters in Osaka reported that military communications to the city had failed.

By 1 p.m. the government suspected that Hiroshima was a dead city, but the precise cause remained obscure. In addition to the eyewitness dispatch dictated over the one functioning regional phone line by the Domei correspondent who had bicycled into the flames, a message had been relayed from an Army depot near the city's waterfront: "Hiroshima has been annihilated by one bomb and fires are spreading." Nothing was said about the nature of this fantastically powerful bomb.

Marquis Koichi Kido, the Keeper of the Privy Seal, hurried to the *obunko* emergency annex of the Imperial Palace to notify the Emperor. Hirohito could not mask his distress over this mysterious new calamity. "No matter what happens to me, we must put an end to this war as soon as possible," he said gravely. "This tragedy must not be repeated." But the two men agreed that it was not yet time for the

Emperor to act. He would have to wait for the crisis to reach its acute stage.

It was a wise decision, because in Japan's controlled society the Army possessed machinery to keep even the atomic bomb substantially secret—and the population unalarmed. In midafternoon the managing editors of Domei and of Tokyo's five large newspapers were summoned to the Information and Intelligence Agency, where an Army press officer told them:

"We believe that the bomb dropped on Hiroshima is different from an ordinary one. However, we have inadequate information now." When "proper information" was available an appropriate announcement would be made. Meanwhile, the docile editors were to treat the story "no different from one reporting on an ordinary air raid."

Accordingly, the 6 p.m. NHK newscast could hardly have been less revealing: "Hiroshima was attacked by B-29s this morning at 8:20. The planes have turned back after dropping incendiary bombs. Damage is now being investigated."

At about 1 a.m. on August 7, the chief of Domei's elaborate radio-monitoring station outside Tokyo was awakened and told that the Americans were broadcasting a statement by President Truman claiming that "an atomic bomb" had been dropped on Hiroshima. The chief monitor phoned Domei's foreign-news editor, who called the chief secretary of the cabinet, who called Prime Minister Suzuki, but the cabinet wasted the day with fruitless bickering.

Foreign Minister Togo argued that the bomb "drastically alters the whole military situation and offers the military ample grounds for ending the war."

"Such a move is uncalled for," responded War Minister Korechika Anami. "We do not yet know if the bomb was atomic."

Even some of the more reasonable ministers were reluctant to believe what they feared had happened, and the government was in no hurry to address itself to the plight of Hiroshima. The mood of the officials generally was to minimize the enormity of the event not only to the populace but to themselves, and to dismiss the Truman announcement as propaganda. The War, Navy, and Home ministries organized an "Atomic Bomb Countermeasures Committee" whose members denied that the United States had the know-how to transport an "unstable" nuclear device across the Pacific, and so the

Army merely decided to dispatch Dr. Nishina, as the nation's leading nuclear authority, to investigate on the scene the scientific novelty of the city's fate.

Meanwhile, an announcement by Japanese Imperial Headquarters at 3:30 p.m. went little further than the communiqué of the previous day: "Yesterday Hiroshima was considerably damaged by the attack of B-29s. Our enemies have apparently used a new type of bomb. Investigation of the effects is under way."

An MC transport plane had indeed taken off for Hiroshima at 1:30 p.m., carrying Nishina and a military delegation headed by Lieutenant Colonel Seiichi Niizuma, a physics graduate of Tokyo University. But near Mount Fuji one engine failed. The plane returned to Tokorozawa airfield and a replacement was said to be unavailable until the following day.

At his Riken Institute office that night, Nishina, greatly depressed, wrote a letter to his closest associate, Hidehiko Tamaki, who was out of the city that day:

"If the Truman statement tells the true story, I think it is time that we, the responsible staff of the NI [Nishina] Project, should commit harakiri. The time for the suicide will be discussed upon my return from Hiroshima. You will wait for me in Tokyo. I feel Truman told the truth [and that] the researchers of the USA and England won a big victory over the Japanese and the scientists of Riken Laboratory No. 49. . . . Their character exceeded the level of our character."

Nishina handed the letter to his secretary, Sumi Yokoyama, who had served as his closest personal assistant since before Pearl Harbor. She read the letter and cried but said nothing. She sealed it in a brown envelope and handed it to Tamaki when he arrived at Riken the next day. Tamaki read it aloud to four staff members. All were stunned.

By then Nishina was back at the airfield, but the promised MC transport failed to arrive. The government was not pushing the mission for speed; it behaved like a patient who did not want to hear the doctor's diagnosis of terminal illness. In the afternoon Colonel Niizuma finally persuaded the pilot of a DC-3 to fly his delegation to Hiroshima.

The plane was delivering ammunition to a nearby city and lacked passenger seats. Perched on their parachutes, Nishina and Niizuma discussed what they were fairly certain they would find. If Nishina was still depressed, he hid it well. To Niizuma he acted like any scientist bent on pursuing a technical problem about which he was thoroughly knowledgeable.

Since there was reportedly no electricity in Hiroshima, Nishina had not bothered to take along a Geiger counter. He told Niizuma he would need no instruments. He handed the colonel a 510-page book on radiation effects and said that the injuries and damage would be sufficiently revealing. There would be characteristic burns. Iron rail tracks might have melted. And white-blood-cell counts were telltale evidence; anyone with a count under 2000 would require total rest and very great luck to recover.

At 6:30 p.m. the DC-3 circled over the scorched desert that was Hiroshima. Nishina and Niizuma felt their fears confirmed before they ever landed. When the bandaged soldiers at Kichijima airfield described how they had been burned at the instant the bomb flashed, there was no longer any doubt. From the Navy base at the port of Ujina later that evening, Niizuma telegraphed the mission's preliminary findings to his Army superiors in Tokyo. Nishina's detailed investigation would not begin until the next day.

In the capital, August 8 had been another day lost in dithering. A report arrived from Field Marshal Shunroku Hata, commander of the Western District Army headquarters in Hiroshima, and it was designed to please the fanatical Army leaders in Tokyo who wanted to continue the war. If the bomb turned out to be real—and persuasive U.S. shortwave broadcasts and leaflets in Japanese were beginning to reach some of the population at large—then its destructiveness had to be minimized.

So Hata emphasized that defensive measures against the bomb were possible. Burns sustained by survivors wearing light clothing had been relatively light. Most important, Hata mistakenly concluded, the fires and burns had been so intense because the bomb exploded at a time when many people were using fires to prepare breakfast.*

* This was not nearly as preposterous as the conclusions reached by several military investigators before Nishina's arrival. At a meeting of Navy officers on

Day One

Following an air-raid alarm in Tokyo that afternoon, Foreign Minister Togo briefed the Emperor in the imperial bomb shelter on Truman's threat to wipe out Japan in a "rain of ruin." Togo advised that it was imperative to end the war. Hirohito agreed and urged Togo to step up his peace efforts in the light of the new bomb. "Since the nation can no longer continue the struggle with this weapon opposing it," said the Emperor, "Japan should not miss the chance for peace by vain efforts to secure better terms."

Some of the leaders being unavailable that day, it was not until 11 a.m. on August 9 that the Supreme War Council convened in emergency session in the bomb shelter of the Premier's office building. More bad news had hit them during the night. At dawn the radio room of the Foreign Ministry had monitored an announcement from Moscow that the Soviets had declared war and invaded Manchuria. The dream of using the Russians as peace mediators had evaporated.

"Under the present circumstances, I have concluded that our only alternative is to accept the Potsdam Proclamation and terminate the war," began Prime Minister Suzuki. "I would like to hear your opinions on this."

Nobody responded.

"Why are you all so silent?" demanded Admiral Mitsumasa Yonai, the Navy Minister, who agreed with Suzuki. "We won't accomplish anything unless we speak frankly."

An officer arrived to bring word that the Fat Man bomb had fallen on Nagasaki two minutes before the present meeting had begun. It was as though the militarists in the room had not heard. They had been shaken by the news of the Soviet invasion—more so than by news of either atomic bomb—yet they fiercely resisted any idea of surrender and continued to talk a good fight.

"With luck we will be able to repulse the invaders before they land," insisted General Yoshijiro Umezu, chief of the Army General Staff. "I can say with confidence that we will be able to destroy the major part of an invading force."

That afternoon a cabinet meeting also ground into deadlock. "We must fight to the end no matter how great the odds against us," ex-

---

the morning of August 8 at the East Drill Ground, a Navy surgeon announced that the American weapon had been an "electron incendiary bomb." An Army weapons specialist had decided it was a "sulphuric acid bomb."

horted War Minister Anami. The argument continued until nearly 11 p.m., when the Premier arranged for an immediate Imperial Conference in the air-raid shelter of Hirohito's *obunko*.

The shelter was poorly ventilated and sweltering even before the momentous session began. It was a starkly austere room, eighteen by thirty feet, its ceiling supported by exposed steel beams. Twelve men wearing either morning clothes or formal uniforms with swords faced each other across two long, cloth-covered parallel tables and kept their white handkerchiefs fluttering in vain attempts to fight perspiration and make the oppressive air more bearable.

The Emperor entered at ten minutes to midnight, looking tired and worried, and took his seat at a small brocade-covered table on a dais in front of a six-paneled screen near the door. In accordance with protocol, everyone bowed and avoided looking at him. Rising to stand at his left, the aged Prime Minister Suzuki asked the chief cabinet secretary to read the Potsdam Proclamation.

Foreign Minister Togo opened the discussion by quietly counseling that the proclamation be accepted, subject only to maintenance of the "national essence"—the status of the Emperor. Navy Minister Yonai rose to agree. Their sentiments drove War Minister Anami into a frenzy. His cheeks wet with tears, his voice growing increasingly shrill, he insisted that the Army would not surrender unless Japan not only was guaranteed the integrity of the Imperial structure but could also conduct her own war-crimes trials, disarm her own soldiers, and limit the occupation forces.

"If not," Anami cried, "we must continue fighting with courage and find life in death!"

The war minister was supported by General Umezu of the General Staff, who assured the meeting that better antiaircraft defense measures could control future atomic attacks.

The old arguments of the deadlocked previous conferences were repeated for over two hours, often verbatim, but the Emperor was prepared to break the stalemate. Just before the conference he had received Suzuki and Togo in audience. They had briefed Hirohito on what to expect and had made obvious what they expected him to do. The crisis had reached the boiling point.

Under normal conditions the cabinet would have resigned, but the leaders realized they could no longer dally. A third atomic bomb might fall at any moment; a rumor was spreading that Tokyo would be A-bombed on the 12th. Tradition—that great rule of Japanese conduct—was strongly against Imperial intervention. True, tradition had already been broken when the leaders presented diverse views to the Emperor. Only unanimous recommendations were supposed to be brought before him, and he was expected to sanction these regardless of his own opinions. Most of the conferees were amazed to hear Premier Suzuki say:

"With the greatest reverence I must now ask the Emperor to express his wishes."

As the heads around the tables bowed, the Emperor rose. His normally neutral voice was strained.

"I cannot bear to see my innocent people suffer any longer," he said. "Ending the war is the only way to restore world peace and to relieve the nation from the terrible distress with which it is burdened." He paused and paid tribute to those who had fallen "in far-off battles" and "in the air raids at home." His voice was all but stilled by emotion. His white-gloved hands wiped tears from his cheeks. The conferees had thrown themselves upon the tables and were sobbing without restraint or embarrassment.

"The time has come when we must bear the unbearable," said the Emperor.

The conferees stood. Slowly, heavily, Hirohito left the shelter.

Suzuki announced: "His Majesty's decision should now be made the unanimous decision of this conference."

The leaders responded to the Imperial command by signing the minutes of the meeting approving acceptance of the Potsdam Proclamation with the understanding that "the supreme power of the Emperor" remain recognized. The last signature was affixed at 2:30 a.m. The war was over, and yet it was not.

In Hiroshima, Professor Nishina pursued his scientific investigations as if the city were a laboratory and time were standing still. With Colonel Niizuma at his side, he spent all of August 9 collecting evidence. By questioning the officers of an antiaircraft battery, the professor pinpointed the epicenter of the bomb at a point 22 yards east of the gate to the Shima Hospital. By car he and Niizuma proceeded to its ruins at what had once been No. 19 Saikucho and, within a radius of 500 yards, collected numerous specimens of soil, rocks, and pieces of wire and wood for shipment to Tokyo and analysis at the Riken Laboratory. Widening their search to a radius of 2000 yards, they plodded on, pouring samples of well water into three beer bottles, collecting exposed X-ray film from the Red Cross Hospital and from the remnants of a photographer's shop.

Nishina was immersed in his labors. His work uniform was crisp, his mood good. More and more soil specimens went into the envelopes that he carried in a box under his arm. The dead fish with their burned white backs that he found floating in the rivers had clearly been irradiated, but Nishina thought the well water was harmless. Whenever he became thirsty in the steaming heat he drank some of it from one of the beer bottles.

Not until 10 a.m. on August 10, more than seven hours after the Emperor had persuaded the government to surrender, did the professor take his seat at a rectangular conference table in an Army supply shack near Hijiyama Hill, along with some twenty Army and Navy officers. The ceiling and pillars had been slanted by the bomb at a precarious angle. Colonel Niizuma chaired the meeting, which lasted nearly all day.

Spread across the table lay a bizarre selection of small wreckage, including pieces of glass from neon signs and the tube of a trench mortar. Local citizens believed that these souvenirs might be fragments of the bomb and could therefore be helpful to the investigators. Niizuma laughed at the display and instructed some soldiers to remove it. Nishina briefed the group on his findings, stressing that some survivors without visible injuries had died a day or two after the blast and that the exposure of X-ray films and the low white counts of many patients were also unmistakable radiation effects.

The group spent much time debating the value of light-colored clothing and other "countermeasures" which they were eager to recommend in the report that Colonel Niizuma dispatched to Tokyo that evening. Somehow the conferees had convinced themselves that the Americans had ten or more atomic bombs ready to drop but that Japan would be able to withstand them. Nishina left for Nagasaki to see whether the ruins there held additional lessons. The citizens of Hiroshima were left to help themselves as best they could.

· · ·

Day One

In Tokyo that sultry day, the government suddenly began to speak in three very different voices. The Army, hoping for a snag in the surrender proceedings, issued a belligerent statement: "We are determined to fight resolutely, although we may have to chew grass, eat dirt and sleep in the fields." The cabinet enigmatically called on "the people to rise to the occasion" without hinting what occasion was being faced. Foreign Minister Togo, anxious to forestall a third atomic attack, ordered Domei to broadcast, in English and in Morse code, the midnight surrender decision of the Imperial Conference.

He hoped that Truman, Byrnes, and their advisers would accept the Morse communiqué as the official Japanese position. They did and their reply on August 11 noted only one significant reservation: "The authority of the Emperor and the Japanese Government shall be subject to the Supreme Commander of the Allied powers."

While the militant among Hirohito's ministers quibbled about semantics concerning the Emperor's status, a score of staff officers gathered secretly at the War Ministry to plan a coup. They wanted to isolate the Emperor by surrounding the Palace grounds with local troops, occupy crucial government buildings, control press and radio, and cut communications. The rebels lobbied without success for support among senior officials, but for three days the machinery of government was paralyzed.

Spurred by American leaflets dropped by a lone B-29 at dawn on August 14, which disclosed the texts of the surrender messages to the Japanese citizenry for the first time, the Emperor decided he must assert himself again; he summoned another Imperial Conference for 10:50 that morning. Again the militant cabinet members said they wanted to fight on. Brushing tears from his face, his voice breaking, the Emperor again elicited sobs from his ministers by insisting on surrender.

"I wish to save the people at the risk of my own life," he said. "I am ready to do anything. If it is for the good of the people, I am willing to make a broadcast."

The cabinet agreed with one reservation. His Majesty, whose voice had never been heard in public, must not be asked to stoop to the indignity of having to address his people directly. His rescript (decree) would be issued through a recording, and at 11:30 p.m. the Emperor was escorted to a microphone that had been set up by NHK engineers on the second floor of the Household Ministry, just east of the Emperor's *obunko*.

"How loudly shall I speak?" asked Hirohito.

Although he was advised that his ordinary voice would serve well, the Emperor unconsciously lowered it and stuttered several times as he informed "our good and loyal subjects" that the government had already notified the Allied powers of its surrender.

"The enemy has begun to employ a new and most cruel bomb," he said, "the power of which to do damage is indeed incalculable, taking the toll of many innocent lives. Should we continue to fight, it would not only result in an ultimate collapse and obliteration of the Japanese nation, but also it would lead to the total extinction of human civilization . . ."

His will having finally become fact, the Emperor turned and asked, "Was it all right?"

An embarrassed engineer said he was sorry but some words were unclear. Reading his script again, the Emperor pitched his voice too high. He offered to do a third reading, but the broadcasters wanted to spare him such an "ordeal." The second of the two ten-inch disks was declared the official version; the first would be an emergency spare. Each was tucked into an eighteen-inch-square khaki-colored cotton bag normally used to hold air-defense uniforms. And with rumors afoot about an Army coup, it was decided to hide the records in the ministry until morning.

A chamberlain found a small safe in a room used by the retinue of the Empress. After locking up the records he camouflaged the safe with piles of papers.

It was the night's wisest move, for the interception of the recordings had become the priority objective of rebels infiltrating the palace grounds. At 1:45 a.m. on August 15, the commanding general of the Konoye Division, which was in charge of guarding the Emperor, fell dead of a fellow officer's pistol bullet. More than a thousand men shut off the grounds. The huge palace gates thundered closed, and a succession of comic-opera interrogations ensued.

"Did you give the records to this chamberlain?" a soldier asked a handcuffed NHK official.

"No," lied the broadcasting man, "it was a much taller man with a big nose."

Exasperated, the soldiers kicked through sliding doors with their boots and scattered the contents of drawers across the floors, but they never located the records.

Before dawn, high-ranking officers had persuaded the rebels by telephone to withdraw the troops. The coup would get no outside help. Its cause was lost. One company of *putschists,* determined to keep the Emperor's recording from being broadcast, stormed into NHK and locked up sixty night-duty employees in Studio 1. But this effort, too, collapsed when the ranking rebel officer was firmly ordered to desist by a telephone command from Eastern District Army headquarters. In essence, the conspirators, now dying in a wave of suicides, had been paralyzed by their ambivalence between obedience to the Emperor and their warrior tradition of no surrender.

At 7:21 a.m. NHK announced: "At noon today the Emperor will broadcast his rescript. Let us all respectfully listen to the voice of the Emperor."

While organized resistance against the surrender had collapsed, the Emperor's staff still feared for the safety of the recordings. One of them was placed in a lacquer box with the Imperial insignia and paraded conspicuously through the corridors of the Household Ministry. The other, stamped "original," was spirited out of the building by a chamberlain in the lunch bag that he hung from his shoulder. It was taken to NHK in a police car.

These too were sensible precautions, for plenty of prowar fanatics remained in sensitive places. When the Emperor's recorded voice was heard outside Studio 8 at 11:20, a military police lieutenant who had been waiting there drew his sword and shouted, "If this is a surrender broadcast, I will kill every one of you!" Not realizing that he was listening to a test playback, he was seized and taken away by guards.

Precisely at noon, the Emperor's obstacle course ended in peace at last. An announcer said, "This will be a broadcast of the gravest importance. Will all listeners please rise . . ."

At Dr. Nishina's Riken Institute not far away, many staff members who had worked with the little physicist on a Japanese atomic bomb had gathered around the bulky upright radio in his office to hear the Emperor speak. They heard the voice, unknown and godly, and, as throughout Japan, many of the men and almost all the women wept.

False Dawn

At the Riken Institute, incongruously, the occasion also turned into one of joy. The Emperor's broadcast had barely faded when Dr. Nishina walked in unannounced, back from his mission to Hiroshima and Nagasaki. Delighted to welcome their leader, his people were also relieved to see him cheerful. His failure to produce an A-bomb was unmentioned, apparently forgotten. Instead of contemplating suicide, he asked about his beloved cyclotron and expressed delight when he was told it was safe. It was time to return to work. If his American colleagues had overcome the problems of the bomb, so be it. There was plenty of other science left to conquer. In Tokyo, the Emperor's message did not sound like the end of the world, as it did where the bomb had fallen.

Twenty-Five

Hiroshima IV: Death Without End

In the burned-out City Hall of Hiroshima, Shinzo Hamai, the suddenly energized provider of emergency food supplies, stood by a radio with other surviving municipal officials. Hamai had been sleeping every night on a desk in one of the two still usable first-floor rooms of the building and he was exhausted.

His successes at scrounging food were becoming part of Hiroshima legend, and none too soon. People were scooping dead fish from the rivers and eating them although they had turned white—and deadly—from radiation. Hamai made deals for healthier fare. Learning that the refrigerator of an army warehouse had broken down and a large store of beef was beginning to rot, he negotiated its release without charge and had the meat distributed. Borrowing a pump from the East Fire Station, he dispatched it to the Ujina docks and emptied a tanker of cooking oil; there was enough to distribute 1.8 liter to every functioning household. But what was happening in the outside world?

Hamai had been informed that the Emperor would speak on August 15, but the radio signal was so weak that he and his colleagues could not make out the words. As rumors spread through the town, they guessed that the war was over. Hamai did not want to believe it until he read the speech in a newspaper the next day. It made him collapse and cry. "I felt as if all of my strength fell out of my body with a loud crash," he wrote later.

False Dawn

While Hamai fell into depression, Mitsuo Tomasawa, a fifteen-year-old student, felt deep sorrow for the Emperor. Surrounded by his neighbors, Tomasawa listened to the barely audible speech on a radio that had been set up on a table among the ruins of his street. He cried, not for Hiroshima but over the indignity to which the Emperor was being subjected. Why did he have to undergo such an ordeal?

Michiko Yamaoka, a twelve-year-old telephone operator, listened to the broadcast with thirty other injured survivors in a suburban military hospital. Burns along her eyes, the left side of her mouth, and across her throat made her look, as her friends later said, like "a living ghost." Her gums were bleeding. Her bowels were bloody. All her hair had fallen out. Purple spots covered her legs. Burns had contracted her finger muscles so that her right hand resembled a claw. For seven years she would not be able to close her left eye.*

As Michiko absorbed the Emperor's words she grew furious with him, and so did most of the other bomb victims in her ward. Even as they broke into tears, they muttered that their present misery was the Emperor's fault. He should have ended the war sooner, then Hiroshima would have survived unbombed. When the radio was turned off, some of the patients angrily heaved pillows across the ward. Michiko clenched a fist with her good left hand and pounded it on the window sill near her bed.

At the Communications Hospital, the Emperor's address derailed the medical detective work of its director, Dr. Hachiya. The doctor had listened to the message with officials of the Communications Bureau, and had caught few words amid the static except, "suffer the insufferable," but the chief of the bureau had stood close to the radio and confirmed: "He has just said that we've lost the war."

Dr. Hachiya had anticipated nothing like this. "I had been prepared for the broadcast to tell us to dig in and fight to the end, but this unexpected message left me stunned," he recorded in his diary. "My psychic apparatus stopped working and my tear glands stopped, too. Like others in the room, I had come to attention at the Emperor's voice, and for a while we all remained silent and at atten-

---

* Beginning in 1955, she would undergo thirty-seven operations in New York as one of Norman Cousins' "Hiroshima Maidens" (see page 340).

309

tion. Darkness clouded my eyes, my teeth chattered, and I felt cold sweat running down my back."

Limping back to his hospital, he crawled into bed and listened sympathetically as the patients around him clamored for revenge and for continuing the war. "Only a coward would back out now!" someone shouted. "I would rather die than be defeated!" yelled another bomb survivor. The second sentiment was echoed by other patients and reflected Dr. Hachiya's own feelings. What good were his investigations into his patients' symptoms if the nation was dying?

During the week after the Emperor's surrender, the extent of the medical catastrophe facing the doctor—but still not its nature—became clearer and the symptoms took on more distinct patterns. One out of five patients had developed the purple skin hemorrhages. The closer the patients had been to the hypocenter at the time of the bombing, the more likely they were to develop them, so there had to be some connection between the bomb and the spots. They did not itch or hurt, but they defied diagnosis, and Dr. Hachiya felt reprieved nightly when he pored over every inch of his body and found his skin clear.

Starting the third week after the bombing, patients with the skin hemorrhages began to die, and the death rate increased daily. Outpatients were beginning to show up with the same mysterious spots. Patients with these petechiae were more likely to die than others who suffered from symptoms that appeared much more life-threatening. Fearfully patients began to search each other's bodies for the dreaded skin spots. Some were also inexplicably losing their hair.

All the hospital's laboratory equipment had been destroyed, but on August 20, at last, a new microscope arrived from Tokyo. Dr. Hachiya quickly had blood specimens taken from fifty patients. The findings were alarming. Many samples showed white blood-cell counts of 500 to 600 (3000 being the danger point, 5000 to 6000 being normal), but Dr. Hachiya and his staff could not determine why. In his diary the doctor recorded: "Some toxic substance must be responsible."

From August 21 on, patients lost hair by the handful. The doctor tugged at some of his own hair; not much came out, but it was enough to make him feel nauseated with apprehension. That night all the members of the hospital staff tested their hair by pulling at it. This time none of the doctor's came out. Again he felt reprieved.

Starting August 23, without explanation, a hopeful trend set in. Some patients were definitely better. Their skin spots were fading. Even some patients with total hair loss seemed otherwise well. ("Epilation could no longer be called the halo of death," Dr. Hachiya told his diary.) His own white count was up from 3000 to 4000. Every inpatient now had petechiae and epilation, but only those who also had sore mouths (stomatitis), rising temperatures, and low white counts were getting worse. Dr. Hachiya decided that this combination of symptoms had to be feared the most.

As the fourth week after the bombing began, the doctor received the results of the first autopsy of one of his hospitalized bomb victims. It revealed that the purple skin spots had been minor surface indications of terrible internal injuries. Death was caused by multiple internal hemorrhages—petechiae in the stomach, intestines, liver, the lining of the abdominal cavity. This clue was conclusive for Dr. Hachiya. The mysterious malady he had been battling, without the slightest outside assistance or information, had a name, although no treatment was known to him.

"Notice Regarding Radiation Sickness" was the title of the message to patients that he ordered posted throughout his hospital. It contained but one bit of treatment advice: "Persons whose white blood counts are low must take care to avoid injury or exertion because their body resistance is low."

At last he knew why so many seemingly well patients had died without explanation and why, all over the city, many survivors who felt vigorous and were trying to tackle life after the bombing were living on borrowed time. Without knowing it, they were vulnerable to sudden death. How could they guess that they suffered from invisible internal radiation "insults"? No one told them that it was dangerous to lead a normal life, that many might be spared if only they knew they had to rest.

Mrs. Sakae Ito had been lucky. Since the work crew which she had helped to command had been assigned to tear down houses a full mile west of the blast, just across the Tsurumi Bridge, and she had sustained only a minor shoulder burn, she was able to fulfill her duties as the director of the All-Japan Women's Organization in her suburb of Yano. Her children's school, directly across the eight-foot-wide street from her home, was turned into an emergency hospital for bomb survivors, its fifteen rooms jammed with groaning people. There were no doctors, nurses, or medications, only a handful of volunteers from Mrs. Ito's organization. As for leadership, she was it.

Mrs. Ito felt very weak and anorexic. Her suppurating shoulder wound was painful and she had only a small amount of cooking oil to rub on it. Then she used machine oil (she had a supply because her parents owned a machine factory). She also took machine oil to the hospital and gave it to burn victims. She felt lucky because she could see; many could not. She would cheer the blinded and the feverish by walking through the building shouting "All clear!"—the words everyone had welcomed whenever they were heard during the war.

Within a few days she felt too weak to drag herself to the hospital. She was dizzy and suffered from bleeding gums, diarrhea, and bloody stool. She thought she would die like so many people she had nursed in the hospital, although most of those people had also lost all their hair. Whenever they combed it they looked angrily at the hair that came out and seemed to want to curse it. Mrs. Ito carefully watched her comb whenever she fixed her own hair; it did not fall out, and her husband was well enough to look after her.

For weeks he wheeled her in a baby carriage to the hospital in the next village. Doctors gave her injections. When she waited her turn in a dark room filled with wounded people, one of her neighbors said, "Mrs. Ito, do you remember that lady who said her hair was falling out? She died today. Look, my hair is falling out now."

Soon the neighbor was also dead. Mrs. Ito would never forget the sight of women combing their hair, dreading to find loose hair in the comb.

Katsuko Horibe, the eighteen-year-old teacher who had been trapped near her Honkawa School and the Aioi T-Bridge, was less fortunate than Mrs. Ito. Mr. Miaji, the colleague who took her home to her family's farm, died three days later, quickly and without warning, and so, later, did his two sons and Katsuko's sister. Katsuko developed a very high fever, diarrhea, and a few purple spots; nearly all her hair fell out, but her gums did not bleed. No medical attention was available, but there was plenty of food. The family owned a wheat field, potatoes, and white radishes. After six months of complete bed rest—she felt too exhausted to get up—her health gradually improved.

Taeko Teramae, the telephone operator whose teacher had helped her swim across the river when the Tsurumi Bridge was blocked, also recuperated at home. She suffered from all the radiation symptoms, including bleeding gums. Her mother treated her condition with a dried weed, a home remedy that had to be burned on the back of Taeko's neck. Her family had hidden all mirrors in the house, but when her bandages were removed and she saw her deformed face reflected in a plateful of soup, Taeko learned that she had lost her left eye. She did not cry. Her hatred for Americans did not abate for many years, but Taeko too slowly recovered reasonably good health.

At the City Hall, Shinzo Hamai, the municipal food provider, had turned his attention to tracking down emergency clothing for the survivors. Most people owned only the rags on their bodies. Hamai talked the Army out of 10,000 complete sets of men's military clothing, including underwear, caps, and shoes. The Navy surrendered a hoard of cotton which he had cut into women's skirts, blouses, and dresses.

While handing out uniforms one morning he noticed that some blisters on his feet were infected. He could no longer tolerate shoes. He limped barefoot on his errands but eventually consulted Dr. Shima, the doctor whose hospital had been incinerated at the very hypocenter. Shima was now operating an aid station at an elementary school.

"No, no, you can't cure this externally," said Dr. Shima after one quick look at the blisters. "Please have a blood examination."

Hamai's white count was taken at the Mitsubishi Hospital on the city's outskirts and turned out to be 3200, about half of normal and just above the danger level, clearly the result of radiation. The Mitsubishi doctor told Hamai he required total rest and urged him to take leave from his work. Though Hamai was "terrified," he followed orders—in his own style. He "rested," but he did so in his office, managing to get all his work done from there.

Most physicians were still not as well informed as Dr. Shima or Hamai's doctor at the Mitsubishi Hospital or Dr. Hachiya at the Communications Hospital. Dr. Goro Ouchi, having watched his private hospital burn down with only one inpatient escaping* from the second-floor ward, had set up a new practice in a suburban home where he had stored some medical supplies in anticipation of an emergency.

Immediately he was overrun by patients suffering from hair loss. Unlike other surviving Hiroshima doctors, Dr. Ouchi at once surmised that epilation was an effect of radiation, and he arrived at this diagnosis by a curious route. He had often treated scabies with X-rays. Epilation followed frequently, but it was temporary and never seemed to become a serious side effect.

Hair loss following the bombing therefore did not trouble him, especially since neither he nor anyone else knew much about the spectrum of radiation dosages and their varying effects. Unable to differentiate between the aftereffects of scabies treatments and of A-bombs, Dr. Ouchi sent epilation patients on their way, unaware that without total rest many of them would die.

As August ended, Dr. Hachiya at the filthy and malodorous Communications Hospital took time for his first sponge bath since the bombing, which made him feel vastly better although there was no soap. Some of his doctors were still sleeping on desks and in chairs. There was still no electricity. Camphor wood was set out to smolder in smudge pots around the hospital to fight clouds of mosquitoes. A university pathologist arrived carrying a rucksack with autopsy equipment. He said that the authorities were trying to prohibit autopsies; they revealed too much information that was unwelcome to the government. He had told the officials they were fools. Dr. Hachiya, unwaveringly respectful of authority in the past, agreed.

* Dr. Ouchi was amazed to see this patient move normally while hurrying to the street after the bomb fell. The doctor was even more surprised to run into the man three months later in evident good health. This nimble patient had been admitted to the Ouchi Hospital for acute appendicitis and had been scheduled for surgery the morning of August 6.

False Dawn

The list of his critically ill patients was still lengthening. More died daily of massive internal hemorrhages. The new pathologist found changes in every organ of every case he autopsied. Moreover, even seven hours after death the blood had not coagulated. Greatly distressed, Dr. Hachiya ordered new blood examinations and found that the hemorrhages and the failure of the blood to coagulate had an unsuspected, devastating cause: a lack of blood platelets.

Not until September 3, nearly a month after the bombing, did Dr. Hachiya's professional isolation cease. He and all other surviving doctors in Hiroshima were invited to attend a presentation on radiation illness by Dr. Masao Tsuzuki, an eminent sixty-five-year-old professor of surgery from Tokyo Imperial University, who had come to study the atomic disaster.

Walking into the conference room on the second floor in the scorched ruins of the Geibi Bank, Dr. Hachiya found attendance sparse. He greeted the handful of other physicians ("We congratulated each other on being alive") and looked out of the window across the desolation. Almost all buildings having vanished, the view was spectacular. Able to see as far as the waterfront, more than two miles south, the doctor mourned that Hiroshima looked "like a small fishing village rather than the once proud city."

To Dr. Hachiya, Professor Tsuzuki's qualifications were as impressive as his personality. The professor was probably the foremost Japanese authority on radiation. He had performed total body radiation of rabbits in the early 1920s when he was a graduate student at the University of Pennsylvania and had achieved distinction by publishing details of the lingering, deadly effects in the *American Journal of Roentgenology and Radium Therapy* in 1926. During the war he had served as an admiral. He faced the sad little Hiroshima group erect, immaculate in khaki uniform and leggings, speaking loudly in short, sharp blasts.

Dr. Hachiya learned little of practical value that he had not already clarified for himself step by step while watching his patients die over the weeks. Only their symptoms were treatable, not the cause; rest, so the professor confirmed, was the most important therapeutic measure. It was also the only readily available palliative. Blood transfusions, also recommended by the professor, would not become feasible until hygienic conditions and the medical-supply situation improved. The recommended calcium and liver injections were even more academic. And next to rest, the professor's most valuable therapy suggestion—plenty of "fresh food of high nutritional value"—was a fantastic prescription in a city still near starvation, about as unreal as what was taking place in Washington.

Twenty-Six

An Unexpected Turn

The taste of triumph that General Groves had savored when his bomb produced peace threatened to turn sour for him toward the end of August.

The protests of religious leaders against the immorality of atomic warfare were getting on the nerves of his superiors. In the *New York Times,* Hanson W. Baldwin, the military editor, an Annapolis graduate, pointed to the "unknowable effects" of The Bomb and warned: "We have sowed the whirlwind." In the *Saturday Review of Literature,* Norman Cousins, the thirty-year-old editor, published a remarkably prescient editorial, "Modern Man Is Obsolete." He warned that "human self-destruction-extinction" had become possible with the new push-button warfare: "The first button might lead to universal catastrophe as all the other nations rush to their switchboards of annihilation."

Most of all, Groves disliked the frightening disclosures about radiation problems. The published speculation that Hiroshima would be uninhabitable for seventy or seventy-five years was stirring up headlines and protests around the world. The Tokyo radio broadcasts about radiation illness in Hiroshima did not subside.

Groves found the Japanese bid for international sympathy particularly annoying. He was certain that the radiation accounts were "hoax or propaganda." And yet: what if some small kernel of truth was buried in the Japanese stories? What if The Bomb was even more potent than they had all believed? After all, he knew very well that they had not had even a "basic concept of the damage that it would do." If radioactivity was contaminating Hiroshima, might it yet harm American occupation troops once they reached the city?

Notwithstanding all his meticulous planning, Groves was not prepared for what was already, at the very least, a public relations headache. Fortunately, his deputy on Tinian, General Tom Farrell, the former New York State waterways commissioner, was a polished PR man. Groves ordered Farrell to pull together an impromptu investigative mission of physicists and medical people on Tinian and to proceed immediately to Hiroshima. It was time to find out what was really happening there.

The same sense of urgency was moving Dr. Marcel Junod, although his motivation was very different. Dr. Junod, a Swiss surgeon, had just arrived in Tokyo to direct relief efforts in Japan for the International Red Cross. For eleven years he had performed the same function in the Ethiopian War and the Spanish Civil War, in China and other bloody trouble spots, but the rumors that "thousands were dying every day of strange new and inexplicable symptoms" made Hiroshima uniquely troubling.

On September 2 a telegram finally arrived from the Red Cross representative whom Dr. Junod had dispatched to the disaster scene.

"Situation horrifying," the message read. "Conditions indescribable . . . Bomb effects mysterious . . . Deaths still occurring in great numbers . . . Appeal [to] High Command asking supplies be parachuted immediately into center of town . . . Immediate action necessary."

Since General Douglas MacArthur and his troops had not yet occupied the capital, Dr. Junod rushed to the temporary American headquarters at the Yokohama Chamber of Commerce and showed his report to a general and three colonels of MacArthur's staff. The general read the telegram twice and turned to Dr. Junod: "What do you want us to do?" The doctor was taken aback by the question. The answer was obvious: perhaps 100,000 wounded people needed bandages, blood plasma, antibiotics. A rescue operation had to be launched at once.

False Dawn

The general turned to Colonel Howard Sams, an Army physician in charge of civilian health problems, and said, "That's your department, I think." Whereupon the officers put their heads together and announced they would take up Dr. Junod's request with MacArthur.

To Colonel Sams, the Swiss physician's humanitarian zeal was secondary; the proposed relief mission would be a convenient "cover for us to get in there" and have General Groves's physicists determine whether Hiroshima was safe for the occupation troops. Sams knew Groves's men. They had arrived in Japan on the same ship with him. Their chief, General Farrell, was being pounded by impatient telegrams from Groves in Washington to rush without delay to Hiroshima. Farrell was buttonholing MacArthur's staff for permission, but Colonel Sams and his superiors were in no hurry to respond.

They were pursuing other priorities, especially the release and care of malnourished, maltreated Americans from Japanese prisoner-of-war camps. American newspaper readers were preoccupied with the dramatic reappearance of heroes like General Jonathan M. Wainwright. Gaunt as a moving skeleton, the defender of Corregidor and leader of the Bataan Death March burst into tears as MacArthur embraced him when the two old warriors were reunited in a Yokohama hotel. Dr. Junod, Colonel Sams, General Farrell, and the needy of Hiroshima would have to wait their turn.

William H. Lawrence of the *New York Times* was more aggressive and made faster headway. A tough, beefy correspondent who had covered the bloody campaigns of the Pacific islands with distinction, Lawrence scented a dramatic story.* Almost a month after the atomic drop there was still no reliable account from the target area. By Monday, September 3, a chilly, drizzly day, Lawrence and a few other American reporters had persuaded MacArthur's press officers to send them to Hiroshima for a few hours aboard a B-29 called *The Headliner*. Lawrence's 2300-word eyewitnesser on this visit began

---

* This Bill Lawrence, a *Times* war reporter and later political correspondent, was not to be confused with Bill Laurence, the *Times* science writer then serving as Groves's personal historian. At the *Times* they were thereafter known, respectively, as "Atomic Bill" and "Non-Atomic Bill."

319

at the top of the *Times*'s front page and made arresting reading for the uninitiated, but luckily for Groves it contained little to aggravate his public relations problems.

Lawrence did not catch up with such knowledgeable physicians as Dr. Hachiya of the Communications Hospital or Professor Tsuzuki, the Tokyo expert who had briefed the Hiroshima doctors on radiation illness and was still working in the area. So while the *Times*'s report said that "the atomic bomb is still killing Japanese at a rate of 100 daily" it was possible for readers to infer that most of these victims were slowly succumbing to burn injuries. Lawrence listed the principal radiation symptoms but did not feature them. He pinned the continuing deaths vaguely on the "lingering effects" of the weapon and never specifically mentioned radiation or radiation illness, surely the biggest news since the bombing. Instead, his account focused on the physical destruction. "Visit to Hiroshima Proves It World's Most-Damaged City," said the headline.

"A visit to Hiroshima is an experience to leave one shaken by the terrible, incredible sights," wrote Lawrence, a correspondent as unaccustomed to adjectives as he was to the unburied corpses still scattered in the ruins. "It was enough to take your breath away."

Not entirely. At an extraordinary press conference in the Prefectural Office, three Japanese reporters asked the American correspondents about the future of the bomb. In his dispatch for the *Times,* Lawrence related: "We told them it was our purpose as one of the United Nations to make certain that peace is maintained throughout the world." The Japanese reported that Lawrence was much less diplomatic. They said that he "extolled the obvious superiority of the bomb's potential" and that "its victims interested him only as proof of that might."

Not only was it unusual for a *Times* interviewer to turn himself into an interviewee; the *Times*'s editors, in a rare lapse, permitted him to polemicize in his news article by coming out as an early advocate of deterrence. Lawrence evidently thought the bomb would be a desirable big stick for the United States to wield in the postwar era. "It should be the last evidence needed to convince any doubter of the need to retain and perfect our air offense and defense," he wrote, "lest the fate of Hiroshima be repeated in Indianapolis or Washington or Detroit or New York."

Which happened to coincide precisely with General Groves's appraisal.

The day after Lawrence's account appeared in New York, another reporter with a different orientation observed the same scenes but published quite another conclusion in London. Wilfred Burchett of the *Daily Express,* an Australian journalist with strong Communist sympathies, reached Hiroshima on September 4 aboard a train jammed with demobilized (and hostile-looking) Japanese soldiers. He too reported that people were "still dying mysteriously," but he was not at a loss for a name of their disease. He simply made it up. He attributed the deaths to "an unknown something which I can only describe as atomic plague."

Burchett's dispatch fueled Groves's world-wide public relations firestorm to a new heat level, and the editors of the *Express* helped by adding headlines that could hardly have been more inflammatory. "THE ATOMIC PLAGUE," screamed the top line. Then followed an anguished quotation from the author's text: "I write this as a warning to the world."

Lawrence of the *Times* interpreted Hiroshima as a signal to America to arm and be strong. Burchett saw the bomb as a disease that must spread no further. The same battle lines would stay drawn for decades.

Both writers had raised—and left unanswered—the question of whether Groves's target city had been rendered uninhabitable because of radioactivity, possibly for many years. Not until September 8 was an official delegation permitted to leave Tokyo's Atsugui airfield for Hiroshima to deliver fifteen tons of American medical supplies and to investigate the radiation situation.

The key man was General Farrell, and his assignment was unequivocal. He was to put out Washington's public relations fire and he was to squelch it fast, regardless of any complications.

The visitors' first concern, that armed Japanese at their still unoccupied destination might be hostile, disappeared the moment the investigators landed at an airfield twenty miles north of Hiroshima. A deferential Japanese colonel greeted them at the head of an honor guard of soldiers and naval cadets and invited them to refresh themselves from bottles of beer and pots of tea that had been laid out on a long table covered with a white cloth.

But there was no time for amenities. Almost immediately Farrell learned that he was running a losing race. An airport functionary told him that Bill Lawrence and his group of correspondents had already departed from the same field headed back to Tokyo. Fearful of the propaganda fallout that their stories might have on Groves's problems, Farrell brusquely declined the beer and tea and herded his team onto a bus ordered by the Red Cross.

In addition to Dr. Junod of the Red Cross and Colonel Sams of MacArthur's staff, Farrell's investigators included formidable home talent: physicist Phil Morrison, the Oppenheimer student who had transported the core of the plutonium bomb from Los Alamos to Trinity; and wispy Bob Serber, the Oppenheimer disciple who had given the basic briefing lectures when Los Alamos opened up. They would have little time for investigating, however; all were due to return to Tokyo with their findings within twenty-four hours. Other doctors, led by Lieutenant Colonel Stafford Warren, the Manhattan Project's senior military physician, and including Jim Nolan, the gynecologist who had escorted the uranium bomb core aboard the *Indianapolis* to Tinian, were to stay behind and examine medical conditions in greater detail.

Eventually the investigators' bus stopped at a sideless shed that had been erected amid the rubble of Hiroshima and they were briefed by Professor Tsuzuki, the radiation expert from Tokyo. The westerners were less impressed by him than the local doctors whom Tsuzuki had addressed some days earlier. Dr. Junod found the professor "highly emotional" and too eager to dwell in elaborate detail on the rabbits he had irradiated in his famous experiments during the 1920s. Though Tsuzuki's English was adequate, his vehement staccato delivery and his self-advertising seemed odd.

"Hiroshima—terrible," he pronounced. "I saw it coming over twenty years ago."

Phil Morrison had already been startled by Tsuzuki in Tokyo, where the professor had presented him with a copy of his 1926 paper about his unfortunate rabbits. Morrison remembered: "When I handed the thesis back to him, he slapped me on the knee and said,

'Ah, but the *Americans*—they are wonderful. It has remained for them to conduct the *human* experiment!' "

Speaking to General Farrell's group in the airy shed at Hiroshima, Tsuzuki sounded neither admiring nor authoritative, just worried. The casualties had been so huge, he suggested, that many had perhaps been due not only to blast, burns, and radiation but to "unknown factors." Might perhaps poison gases have been released as well? Farrell, alarmed that his PR problems might escalate still further, authorized one of the scientists to explain the workings of the bomb sufficiently for Tsuzuki to see that gas could not have been involved.

As the session was about to end, Tsuzuki came to his main point: Was Hiroshima safe to live in? The Americans replied that they could not be certain until they had made their rounds, but if they had thought the city was unsafe they would not have risked being there. Tsuzuki looked relieved. He bowed and sat down.

Urged by Farrell to hurry up, the scientists took their Geiger counters and Lauritzen electroscopes and split up, walking and thumbing rides to various parts of town. Primarily they were interested in evidence that their bomb had behaved as they had planned. The local people took no interest in the scientists' work. The instruments picked up no clicks of unusual radioactivity, but in a school one and a half miles from the hypocenter Bob Serber was pleased to locate a char mark in a section of wallboard that indicated the bomb had released the correct amount of flash.* On the canvas back of a chair in the Red Cross Hospital, Phil Morrison discovered a crisscross pattern from a nearby window sash; it convinced him that the bomb had detonated at the altitude planned in Los Alamos. If it had exploded closer to the ground, radioactivity would have made the ground unsafe at Hiroshima for a long time.

When Morrison passed the wreckage of the castle that had been a Japanese army headquarters, his guide said that the water lilies in

* Prior to the Hiroshima mission, Serber had called on Professor Nishina at the Riken Institute in Tokyo to obtain definitive proof for Groves that the Japanese efforts to build an atomic bomb had been abortive. Serber had found the visit depressing. He considered Nishina's laboratory "pathetic" and was touched by the group's efforts to grow vegetables in their back yard. "They were just trying to live," he said later.

the moat had turned black in the blast but were growing again. Morrison stopped to be sure the water lilies were indeed coming back. They were and he was pleased. They would not have been growing if radioactive elements had been present in the soil.

Professor Tsuzuki led some of the visiting physicians on a tour of hospitals. Dr. Junod was appalled to hear him talk of the patients, in their presence, as impersonally as he had earlier discussed the town's ruins. "White corpuscles almost entirely destroyed," he snapped, pointing at one woman. "Gamma rays. Nothing to be done about it. She'll be dead this evening or tomorrow. That's what an atomic bomb does." In another ward he waved an arm across the patients and said loudly, "All these people here are lost. In many cases it is impossible to administer blood transfusions; the vessels burst."

In a laboratory he turned to Dr. Junod, holding a dissected brain congested and suffused with blood.

"Yesterday it was rabbits," he said; "today it's Japanese."

Did the visiting westerners disbelieve the strange Professor Tsuzuki? Were they too unlettered in the field of radiation to accept what should have been obvious—that the absence of contamination in the air and on the ground did not preclude rays lingering in human bodies? Did the American military men, in particular, not *want* to hear what Tsuzuki was saying?

"It was just a case of a town burned down," diagnosed Colonel Sams, the Army doctor, and back in Tokyo on September 12 General Farrell summoned a press conference at the Imperial Hotel to announce much the same conclusion. There would be no further deaths as a result of the bombing, Farrell said. According to "Non-Atomic" Bill Lawrence, reporting for the *Times,* the general "denied categorically that the bomb produced a dangerous, lingering radioactivity." He conceded that "some persons" were dying from lack of white blood corpuscles, but brushed off this phenomenon as if it had been a medical side effect too rare to affect the value of medication successfully administered.

In effect, Farrell confirmed that the medication dropped on Hiroshima was—as Oppenheimer and Groves had been maintaining all along—little more than a conventional explosive with an unconventionally big bang.

False Dawn

The press conference was nearing its end when Wilfred Burchett arrived, unshaven, grimy and disheveled. Delayed in his return from Hiroshima, he had just run into a colleague who told him that Farrell's briefing was in progress.

When Burchett rose to relate that he had seen innumerable people suffering and dying from radiation illness, and then asked for explanations, Farrell continued giving reassurances. According to Burchett, Farrell said that the patients whom the man from the *Daily Express* had seen were "victims of blast and burn, normal after any big explosion. Apparently the Japanese doctors were incompetent to handle them or lacked the right medications."

Burchett persisted and offered more first-hand details. The general shut him off. "I'm afraid you've fallen victim to Japanese propaganda," he said, and sat down. Someone shouted the customary, "Thank you!" which ended the conference—and also Groves's most immediate public relations problems.

As the general began preparing for his next line of defense in Washington—justifying his nuclear stewardship before Congress—he received a boost from his senior medical officer, Colonel Warren, whose secret report, cabled to Washington on September 10, was usefully vague: "Number dead or injured by radiation unknown, but preliminary survey indicates that there are only a small percent of injured survivors." By November, Warren told Congress that 7 to 8 percent of deaths had been caused by radiation, but the following year a thorough investigation by a large team from the United States Strategic Bombing Survey called his figures grossly wrong:

"Most medical investigators who spent some time in the areas feel that this estimate is far too low; it is generally felt that no less than 15 to 20 percent of the deaths were from radiation. In addition, there were an equal number who were [radiation] casualties but survived." Most significantly, the bomb survey accepted the judgment of Dr. Robert S. Stone of the University of California at Berkeley, the Manhattan Project's foremost civilian authority on radiation, who told the investigators: "The fundamental mechanism of the action of radiation on living tissues has not been understood."*

* According to Stuart C. Finch, M.D., former director of research at the Radiation Effects Research Foundation in Hiroshima, at least 20,000 people died of

(In a 1965 medical book, Warren was lamenting "problems of a medical nature not hitherto encountered" and "the then unknown effects of ionizing radiation.")

In Tokyo, General MacArthur found it convenient to treat all aftereffects of the bomb as if they did not exist. After warning the Japanese press against publishing "inflammable" headlines and "needling" articles, he temporarily suspended two leading dailies, *Asahi* and *Nippon Times,* and on September 19 imposed a prior censorship on all media. As part of a new press code, the publication or broadcasting of all reports on A-bomb damage, including those on medical treatment, were unconditionally prohibited.

Colonel Sams, MacArthur's health man, was especially gratified. The new rule would simplify a delicate part of his job. Russian medical officers had appeared in Tokyo. They were being inquisitive about the effects of the bomb, and Sams had orders to stonewall their inquiries.

American politics, not merely possible leaks of scientific intelligence, was influencing MacArthur and the advisers freshly assigned to him from the State Department. A Gallup poll showed that a remarkable 85 percent of Americans approved the dropping of the bomb. Nevertheless, too much graphic detail about the suffering of burned and irradiated victims might yet sway fickle public opinion and inhibit the production and testing of the "much-improved" weapons under development.

The persuasive power of film was particularly feared and resisted

---

radiation in the Hiroshima bombing. Another 20,000 sustained radiation injuries. These are very conservative estimates; the actual numbers will never be known and may have been twice as high. Nevertheless, distinguished American scientists who held key positions in atomic work before and after Hiroshima still prefer to believe that only a handful of survivors experienced radiation problems. "At Hiroshima *and* Nagasaki [emphasis added], I do not believe that there were more than one or two thousand people who were left with radiation burns (but not killed)," Dr. Joseph O. Hirschfelder said at an academic meeting in 1980. "The biological effects were quite accurately assessed." Along with Victor Weisskopf, Dr. Hirschfelder was responsible at Los Alamos for predicting the effects of the bomb. At the Crossroads atomic tests of 1946 he served as "chief phenomenologist." Later he was director of the Theoretical Chemistry Institute at the University of Wisconsin and received the National Medal of Science from President Ford. Yet there is room to disagree with him. No accurate assessment was made forty years ago or later. Indeed, the controversy about what constitutes realistic radiation tolerances still rages today.

for decades. First to feel the blackout was Akira Iwasaki, a producer commissioned by the Japanese Ministry of Education to film a documentary in Hiroshima and Nagasaki. His advance party left Tokyo on September 7 and began operations on September 25, but not for long.

"In the middle of the shooting, one of my cameramen was arrested in Nagasaki by American Military Police," Iwasaki recalled. "I was summoned to GHQ [MacArthur's General Headquarters] and told to discontinue shooting." Again not for long. By December, the U.S. Strategic Bombing Survey team had arrived. It liked Iwasaki's footage and wanted more for its own use. "Now they allowed—or, better—ordered me to continue," Iwasaki said. When Iwasaki delivered a 15,000-foot film and 30,000 feet of negatives to the bomb survey officials, all his work was confiscated, classified "secret," and shipped to Washington, where it disappeared from view for nearly twenty-five years.*

Fear was also the force behind a personal campaign by General Groves to punish his Japanese enemies by crippling their nuclear research. Professor Nishina at the Riken Institute in Tokyo was astounded to learn of this decision at 8:30 a.m. on November 23, when officers of the U.S. Army's Eighth Engineer and Ordnance Battalion arrived and told him that the destruction of his cherished cyclotron would begin at 10 a.m.

Incensed because he had previously received American assurances that he was welcome to continue nuclear research for peaceful purposes, Nishina rushed to MacArthur's headquarters to have the order reversed. He got nowhere. The instructions had come from Washington. News correspondents had already filed dispatches based on an advance press release: "The move was another step in the Allied policy of destroying Japan's war-making potential."

* The distinguished film historian Erik Barnouw, who brought Iwasaki's film to American attention, commented in 1982: "If it hadn't been suppressed, and if the public had seen it and Congress had seen it in the 1950s, it would have been a lot harder to appropriate money to build more bombs." Also in 1982, a U.S. Air Force archivist confirmed that 95,000 feet of color film shot by an Air Force film crew in Hiroshima and Nagasaki had been classified "top secret." The archivist, Daniel McGovern, said the government wanted the footage "buried" because of the "medical aspects, the horror, the devastation it showed." He blamed the Atomic Energy Commission. "At a time when they were working on upcoming atomic tests they didn't want the public to know what the weapon had already done."

Which was ridiculous, as every scientist knew. Smashing the Tokyo cyclotron—and others in Osaka and Kyoto—was like destroying the microscopes in the design laboratories of Detroit to stop the manufacture of automobiles. Cyclotrons were only general research tools.

Devastated, Nishina returned to his institute and watched American soldiers wield cutting torches, sledges, and crowbars so that the pieces of his cyclotron could be loaded on barges and dumped at sea. His staff had seen Nishina near tears only once before: when his mother died. When his cyclotron died, he looked worse.

In the ensuing furor—Groves's own scientists were among the many who denounced the action—MacArthur pointed out that he had had unequivocal orders from the War Department. The directive had, in fact, come from General Groves in the name of the new Secretary of War, Robert P. Patterson, who had replaced Stimson on his retirement. Groves, the hands-on executive who took pride in personally following through relentlessly on his orders, claimed that the message had been prepared by a subordinate who had misunderstood the general's verbal instructions.

Patterson issued a statement calling the destruction "a mistake" and added: "I regret the hasty action on the part of the War Department."

In 1982, Gordon Arneson, the Secretary of War's aide who had kept the records of the fateful deliberations by the Interim Committee, disclosed why the dismantling of the cyclotrons had not been stopped.

Groves's order arrived in the Secretary of War's office on a Friday at about 5 p.m. The Secretary having departed, Arneson took the order to his immediate supervisor, George Harrison, the easygoing insurance executive who had been the Interim Committee's deputy chief and, more recently, the link between Washington and the presidential party at Potsdam while the decision was shaped to drop the bomb.

"George, this looks very unlikely to me," said Arneson.

"Oh, if that's what Groves wants to do, I don't see any objection," said Harrison. "I approve. I'm going home."

His work was done. For the victims, the long climb back to life was just beginning.

Twenty – Seven

Hiroshima V:
The End Is the Beginning

Hunger stalked them next. Shinzo Hamai, the provider of rations at Hiroshima City Hall, had performed so ingeniously at scrounging food for the survivors that he was persuaded to take on the job of deputy mayor. His reservations toward this responsibility were profound. He did not feel up to it. Besides, it was a doubtful honor in this Job of cities. He accepted only after an elderly retired mayor insisted that Hamai's own survival constituted something of a civic obligation.

"Heaven gave you life to help Hiroshima," the ex-mayor said.

Yet throughout the fall and winter after the Bomb there was never remotely enough of anything. Survivors subsisted mostly on dumplings of tall horseweed grass mixed with flour ground from acorns. Even Hiroshima's unspoiled consumers gagged. "Hey, you!" said a citizen accosting Hamai. "These dumplings aren't only covered by hair; they're full of hairs on the inside, too!"

The hunger placed a mask of listlessness on the townspeople. Mark O. Hatfield, a twenty-three-year-old lieutenant (j.g.) from Dallas, Oregon, was shaken by the emaciated faces as he and some other Navy officers stepped off their LCVP (landing craft vehicle and personnel). Equipped with sandwich lunches, the Americans had taken the day off from their mother ship and floated up the Ota River to tour the A-bomb ruins.

They absorbed the smell, the silence, the bodies in the rubble, the people-shaped shadows left behind by incinerated victims and charred forever into the concrete of the Aioi Bridge. The hunger pangs of the teenagers who stared at the well-fed officers of the occupation were almost visible. Hatfield took out a sandwich and offered it to one of the boys. The boy shook his head. Hatfield took a bite out of the sandwich to encourage him. More head shakings. After further urging the boy eventually smiled, bowed, stepped forward to accept the sandwich, and gulped it greedily. For Hatfield the memories of that day were beyond forgetting.

"I began then to question whether there could be any virtue in war," he wrote later.*

Thirst, the great scourge that followed the bombing, plagued the survivors for seven months. Like food, water was sold at outrageous prices by black-market dealers operating from illegal stalls near Hiroshima Station. But for citizens without financial resources, the only alternative was to tap the underground water pipes.

The reservoirs were full again,† but the bombings—and then the thirst of the survivors—had caused so many leaks to be torn in the pipes that water pressure could never rise sufficiently to supply household faucets. Month after month more new holes were illegally punched into the lines than the city repair gangs could patch. Finally Hamai found an aggressive young civil engineer, just discharged from the Army, whom he authorized to recruit rugged fresh crews of his own. Within a month they won the race against the porous water mains by sealing some 70,000 breaks.

At City Hall, Hamai and his colleagues labored through the winter wearing hats and coats. Snow blew through holes that had once been windows. When the officials tried to burn waste materials to generate heat, black smoke billowed through the offices. The City Council convened with its members sitting on the canvas-covered floor.

---

* On March 10, 1982, Hatfield, a United States Senator and Chairman of the Senate Appropriations Committee, sponsored, with Senator Edward Kennedy, the congressional resolution for a mutually verifiable nuclear weapons freeze.
† On August 17, a typhoon had turned Hiroshima into an enormous lake. Among the many who drowned were entire teams of physicians and research physicists who had come from Kyoto and other cities to help.

False Dawn

The outside world acted as if nothing special had occurred in Hiroshima. A delegation from City Hall traveled to Tokyo in search of credits for reconstruction projects and was told that the government had 120 bombed-out cities to worry about. Next the city fathers approached the American occupation authorities. They shrewdly asked only for "advice," hoping that money would follow. Again the outcome was disappointing.

The Americans did dispatch an adviser, Lieutenant John H. Montgomery, a twenty-two-year-old six-footer with a master's degree in municipal administration from his home-town college in Kalamazoo, Michigan. Hamai and his people liked Montgomery. He was low-keyed, imaginative, and had acquired remarkably proficient Japanese language skills in the Army. And he was sensitive to Hiroshima's suffering.

Unfortunately, although he lobbied diligently at MacArthur's headquarters in Tokyo, Montgomery was unable to arouse sympathy among the occupation bosses and could do little more for his charges than encourage them by cheering them on. He advised them to think lofty. In a formal address he told the City Council about the beauty of Washington, D.C., and attributed it to its reconstruction after the capital was torched by the British in the War of 1812.

The analogy sank in. Hamai, especially, was thrilled. He was fond of quoting a Japanese folk saying that urged those who were out of luck to "turn calamity into good fortune." Already he was talking about a new "city of brightness" with a Peace Boulevard 100 meters wide. To him such dreams were not crazy. When skeptical members of the reconstruction planning committee suggested that the remnants of Hiroshima be abandoned for a brand-new site, he pointed out that the citizens had already "voted" to stay by erecting shacks on the rubble fields.

With the greening of springtime came hope for the end of hunger. Food seemed to sprout from every inch of open space. Wheat was growing across the street from City Hall. Around the ruin of the A-bomb dome—the former Industrial Promotion Hall—tomatoes, cabbages, and potatoes were thriving.

The turning point along the road to rebirth arrived when Hamai looked out his office window one morning in April 1946. Just about all surviving trees had been burned as firewood in the course of the winter, but the city administration had sentimentally preserved a cluster of scrawny, smoke-blackened cherry trees on the south side of the municipal building. Now Hamai thought he saw something he had not dared to hope for. He ran down the steps, up to the trees— and yes, the first white traces of cherry blossoms were in evidence. The trees created a great stir throughout the city; hundreds came to view the wonder that confirmed the reality of survival.

That same month an American writer arrived in town who would, for the first time, open eyes around the world to the travail of Hamai's constituents. At thirty-one, John Hersey was experienced at reporting human misery. He had helped to carry wounded Marines from Guadalcanal as a war correspondent for *Time*. He had witnessed death in the Warsaw Ghetto and the Nazi extermination camps. When William Shawn, the gentle, shy managing editor of *The New Yorker* magazine, took him to lunch, Hersey, also gentle and shy, agreed that the image of Hiroshima was still murky. A story remained to be told, and Hersey knew how to tell a story. The previous year his novel *A Bell for Adano,* on the American occupation of Italy, had won the Pulitzer Prize.

In the library of an American destroyer crossing the Pacific, Hersey chanced upon Thornton Wilder's *The Bridge of San Luis Rey,* a disaster novel that suggested the narrative pattern he was searching for. To bring the awesome scope of the Hiroshima bombing to human scale, he hoped to unreel its horrors through the eyes and ears of half a dozen survivors—ordinary people but eyewitnesses blessed with reliable and almost photographic recall.

Interviewing in Hiroshima for three weeks, Hersey found himself "terrified the whole time." The grisly visual details were only a part of the burden imparted by the victims; Hersey also had to deal with the impact of his interviewees on himself. "I identified with them," he recalled almost forty years afterward, "to get the reader to identify, so the reader would be there."

Writing at the home of his wife's family in Blowing Rock, North Carolina, Hersey unfolded the Hiroshima story step by step in very simple language and in four parts, managing to sound cool, almost detached. After Shawn had finished editing the first part, he told Hersey that *The New Yorker* would combine all four pieces and run them as one 26,000-word article on August 31, 1946. For the first time the magazine would devote an entire issue to one subject. For a moment Hersey thought his editor was joking. Actually Shawn had engineered a coup of editorial genius, an overnight sensation.

The intensity of the reader reaction "astonished" Hersey. It should not have. Before he traveled there, Hiroshima had been dead debris. Hersey recognized it as much more: the home of some 100,000 atomic survivors struggling with their lot. Like Job.

More than Hersey's artistry was responsible for the shock that moved his readers. The sum of his report was news, even a year late, because American censorship had kept many details of the bombing's results bottled up. MacArthur's men acted as if the suppression of these macabre reminders of Groves's and Oppenheimer's work would make the facts go away.

Japanese medical findings could be circulated among local scientists only through private underground channels. At a conference in the Japanese Education Ministry in Tokyo, Dr. Nishina, still mourning the destruction of his cyclotron, pointed out to MacArthur's representatives that scientific investigations of the bombing effects could not possibly be used in making a weapon. And Professor Tsuzuki, the radiation authority, was furious. Blunt as ever, he said that it was "unforgivable" to muzzle scientific publications when people in Hiroshima were "at this moment when I speak, dying of a new disease, 'A-Bomb Sickness.' "*

No matter. Over the years the censorship of science would be relaxed, but in 1946 the Americans applied their press code literally: nothing could see print that "might, directly or indirectly, disturb the public tranquility."

While readers of *The New Yorker* consequently found out more about the "A-bomb disease" syndrome than was known to the citizens of Hiroshima,† nobody anywhere had any inkling of the bombing's gravest and most frightening aftereffects. These were yet to appear. Hersey could describe only a vague—and usually no longer

* Eventually Tsuzuki's vehemence and candor became too much for the occupation authorities. He was placed on a "purge list" and barred from public life, including all academic posts.
† The Hersey article appeared in book form in November 1946, but the Japanese translation was delayed until 1949.

fatal—malaise among the survivors, mostly a lack of energy. The harsh specifics—leukemia, cancer, and the rest—lay dormant and did not materialize on a significant scale until 1949.

In the intervening years Shinzo Hamai—he was first elected mayor in 1947 at the age of thirty-seven and remained the city's dominant personality for a generation—confronted another unique phenomenon: he had to nurture two populations. His new constituents—returnees from the countryside and from the military, along with new settlers scenting economic opportunity—wanted to get on with their lives. They quickly outnumbered the *hibakusha,** the bomb survivors who could never stop struggling to come to terms with their memories.

Each August 6 the memories were rekindled at anniversary ceremonies. Hamai opened them at 8:15 a.m. near the Aioi Bridge, but the emotional climax came after sundown at the banks of the Ota River. Tens of thousands gathered there to place small paper lanterns in the water, the symbol of life. Each carried a candle within. On the outside a survivor had written the name of a loved one who perished in the bombing. As the lights floated flickering toward the Inland Sea, the survivors prayed for the water to bring tranquillity to the souls of the departed.

Guilt never left many of the living. They felt shame over their behavior after the bombing, the friend they left behind, the plea for water they ignored in their panic. Worse, they felt guilty for being alive.

For some guilt became an energizer. One of these lucky ones was Mrs. Sakae Ito, the little deputy leader of the crew that was tearing down houses at the Tsurumi Bridge on August 6, 1945. Feeling guilty because she had not spoken out against war before or after the Japanese surrender, she vowed to work for peace to expiate her "sin." She got herself elected to the town council in her suburb of Yano. She lobbied in Tokyo on behalf of health benefits for A-bomb survivors. As the director of the Hiroshima Council of the Organizations of Atomic Bomb Victims—many of these organizations sprang up in the city—she journeyed all over the world to march in ban-the-bomb demonstrations. The Hiroshima delegations stood out in

---

* Pronounced *hi-bak'-sha.* This word was newly coined after the bombing. It means "explosion affected person(s)" or "the people who received the bomb."

these marches because they displayed that most bizarre of civic slogans, "No More Hiroshimas!"

As for many other survivors, the bomb had become Mrs. Ito's personal enemy. She was unusual, however, because her energy remained undimmed and she was blessed with a strong ego. Many *hibakusha* felt they had been set apart by the bomb. They felt alienated, too damaged to live whole lives. Among these was Fumiko Morishita, the young waitress whose seeming well-being had been the envy of the injured when she fled with her relatives across the Tsurumi Bridge on August 6. Her determination to live so that she could marry her fiancé, the soldier who had been away so long, had been rewarded.

Her sweetheart returned while she was in the hospital recovering from radiation illness. He visited her daily and still wanted to marry her. She felt she had to refuse him. All over the city women who had been pregnant and close to the hypocenter at the time of the bombing were giving birth to mentally retarded babies with abnormally small head circumferences. So Fumiko agonized about "the third person," the child they would probably have.

Her sweetheart wanted to marry anyway and became very angry at Fumiko's refusal. They walked in the hospital garden—Fumiko was still feeling dizzy but he supported her—and argued often and long. Though he was a gentle person, he shook her so hard that she fell to the ground. She remained adamant. She loved him "too much to marry" and perhaps to perpetuate "A-Bomb disease" into another generation. He eventually found someone else. She never married.

The loyalty of Fumiko's fiancé was an exception; generally the *hibakusha* were treated as outcasts, especially if they bore visible marks of the bombing—disfigured faces, fleshy keloid scars,* fingers splayed and contracted by burns so the hands looked like claws. Resentment against physical disfigurement runs strong in Japanese culture; the branded ones were rejected as marriage partners, barred from some bathhouses, avoided because they were a depressing sight,

---

* Keloids were considered the most repulsive stigmata of the *hibakusha* and the principal symbol of their leperlike identity. This whitish-yellow overgrown scar tissue can be caused by burns of any kind and can severely disfigure faces and hands, especially when complicated by infection and debilitation.

an inconvenience. They were reminders of a past that outsiders wanted to forget.

Whenever they could, the survivors hid by wearing long-sleeved clothing; by never speaking of their bombing experiences, not even to their children; and sometimes by not registering for official *hibakusha* benefits as these were doled out slowly, grudgingly, over the years.* Some of the maimed, particularly women, simply stayed secluded at home so they would not be stared at. *Hibakusha* who ventured into the business world were often turned down for jobs because they tired easily and were afraid of hard physical work. Any symptom, meaningful or not, sent them to the doctors—who at last knew enough to tell them not to overdo.

Shinzo Hamai, known among his people as "The A-Bomb Mayor," understood that the survivors' psychological bind would be unending. "They know there is no effective treatment," he said. "They feel doomed. I do not know how long this mental suffering will continue." His political opponents accused Hamai of "selling the bomb." Eventually he had to leave his party and run for reelection as an independent, but his loyalty to his fellow survivors never faltered. Since he was one of the lucky *hibakusha* not visibly stigmatized by the bomb, he could face the past as well as the future.

Hamai was pleased, therefore, when a young American medical officer called on him in 1947 and announced that the United States Government would start a clinic to determine the health consequences of the bombing with scientific precision. The mayor offered a site conveniently near downtown. The Americans objected; the area might be subject to flooding. They wanted their Atomic Bomb Casualty Commission atop Hijiyama Hill, where it would tower 500 feet over the city. Hamai advised against this choice and offered another hill site. He pointed out that a military cemetery and a memorial to an ancient emperor made Hijiyama sacred ground. The citizens would resent having an American institution desecrate this choice spot. The occupiers were adamant. So was Hamai. Eventually

* The Tokyo government's first formal Survivors Medical Assistance Law was not adopted until 1957. The Hiroshima A-Bomb Hospital, a special treatment center for *hibakusha,* opened with 120 beds in 1956 and was enlarged later to 170 beds.

he was summoned to the welfare ministry in Tokyo and surrendered after being threatened with "disagreeable" consequences.

The anticipated resistance against the ABCC developed at once. Since it offered only annual examinations and no treatment, the *hibakusha* felt they were being exploited as guinea pigs.* Nor did it help that the research was financed by the hated U.S. Atomic Energy Commission, which was building more and bigger bombs, and that the ABCC findings were not published in Japanese. Inevitably the Japanese felt that while some of the forty American doctors were discreetly sympathetic, the group had a stake in minimizing the bombing effects; the Americans thought the Japanese had an emotional need to exaggerate the horrors. And the scientific detachment of the physicians was interpreted by their frightened and reluctant clients—not always inaccurately—as a lack of sympathy.

"No air of atonement is suggested in any way by the Commission," diagnosed a 1952 internal report by a Japanese-American sociologist on the ABCC staff.

To encourage Japanese cooperation, especially in obtaining more permissions to perform "worthwhile" autopsies, the American researchers polished their public relations.† Cars picked up clients for appointments. On Hijiyama Hill the research subjects were greeted by pleasant young Japanese women. Japanese magazines appeared

---

* The Americans justified their "no treatment" policy by suggesting that Japanese physicians would have resented such competition on economic grounds (there was reason to believe this was true); also, the U.S. doctors held no Japanese licenses for practicing medicine (a lack for which there might have been bureaucratic remedies that were never even considered). As a practical matter, a commitment to undertake treatment of survivors would have required sizable long-term appropriations which Congress would no doubt not have approved.
† A *modus vivendi* was finally reached in April 1975, when the ABCC became the RERF (Radiation Effects Research Foundation), with all staffing, policy making and financing split equally between the Japanese and the Americans. In 1984 the RERF was still costing American taxpayers $8 million a year and remained destined to operate another twenty years or more, and for a newly emerging, totally unexpected reason. While "chromosomal aberrations" have been observed in survivors, the development of genetic changes in coming generations, while possible, is regarded as unlikely. However, recently discovered increases in cancers suggest to researchers that children who were under ten when they were exposed in Hiroshima are only beginning to move into an endangered category. As one expert says: "They are now less than fifty years old and most of their cancers have yet to appear."

in the waiting rooms. Research results began to be published bilingually. But the ABCC gained respectability mostly because the pragmatic Japanese recognized that the ABCC's examinations were better than those available from local doctors; in addition, the scientific findings were considered sound and perhaps helpful to the future of humanity.

In the early and mid-1950s the medical news grew to especially harrowing proportions. The incidence of leukemia in survivors who were irradiated within 1100 yards of the hypocenter at one point climbed as high as fifty times the normal rate. Other cancers—notably malignancies of the thyroid, lung, and breast—multiplied three to six times. These forms of "invisible contamination"* were even more mysterious and therefore more dreaded than external scarring. And once the censorship terminated at the end of the American occupation in 1952, newspapers fanned the fears of a permanently lingering death taint by a drumbeat of headlines such as "Life Claimed by A-Bomb Disease," "Fear Caused by Secondary Radiation Drives Young Man to Death," "Leukemia Continues to Increase," and stories of suicide pacts between afflicted young lovers.

Early in 1955, as the curve of leukemia cases peaked, the disease took the life of twelve-year-old Sadako Sasaki. She had been left apparently unharmed by the bomb at a distance of one mile, but she had been made aware of the event's significance because each August 6, with her parents, she placed into the Ota River a lantern she had marked with the name of her grandmother, one of the six relatives who died that day when Sadako was two years old.

Sadako had just been picked for her school relay team—she was the fastest runner in her class—when she fainted in the schoolyard and was admitted to the Red Cross Hospital. According to Japanese folk belief, the crane lives for a thousand years, and the folding of a thousand paper cranes is said to cure any illness. Sadako fought to maintain her life by folding cranes.

When she died, thirty-six cranes short of her goal, her classmates made up the difference. They placed the full one thousand cranes into her coffin—and all Japan wept. The children founded the Folded

---

* The term was applied by the American psychiatrist Robert Jay Lifton, M.D., in his monumental psychological study of the survivors, *Death in Life,* published in 1967.

Crane Club and continued to fold cranes to commemorate more young radiation deaths. The club also raised money for a monument to Sadako, keeping alive the memory of a girl as inspiring as the Anne Frank of another holocaust.

On the whole, however, Mayor Hamai's relentless campaigning to mobilize material aid for ailing and needy *hibakusha* encountered heartbreaking indifference. He lobbied for funds in Tokyo; the government kept turning him down. He hired a Madison Avenue public relations firm to organize fund raising in the United States; the PR men had to give up because American sponsors backed away.

One of Hamai's most tenacious allies was the Reverend Dr. Kioshi Tanimoto, the aggressive little pastor of the Nagarekawa United Church of Christ. John Hersey had made Tanimoto famous.* In his memorable account Hersey described how the minister had operated a one-man rescue squad on the day of the *pikadon* (flash-boom): carrying a basin of water among the thirsty lying on the East Drill Ground; rowing a boat back and forth across the Ota River to ferry escapees from the fires of the Asano Park.

In the ensuing sad years Tanimoto made his church a haven for some sixty "Hiroshima Maidens," young women so disfigured by the bomb that most of them had become reclusive shut-ins. His friend Hamai had to reject Tanimoto's pleas for city funds to help them. Whereupon Tanimoto turned to another of Hamai's friends, Norman Cousins.

Cousins, the boyish-looking editor who had tried to awaken the American public to the radical long-term impact of a nuclear arms race right after the bomb was dropped, had adopted Hiroshima as a cause for himself and his *Saturday Review*. When Hamai guided him through the city's hospitals in 1949, the year the Soviet Union exploded its first nuclear bomb, Cousins' big, piercing dark-brown eyes absorbed sights that other westerners wanted to avoid: "You saw beds held together with slabs of wood; nowhere did you see sheets or pillows; you saw dirty bandages and littered floors and rooms not

---

* Like Hamai, Tanimoto had to demonstrate his selflessness again and again for many years before the chronically suspicious Japanese would accept the notion that he was not primarily motivated by greed for personal profit or publicity. Like the mayor, Tanimoto, who had studied theology at Emory University in Atlanta, was accused of "selling the bomb."

much larger than closets with four or five patients huddled together. You looked in on an operating room that seemed little better than a crude abattoir . . ."

The day before Cousins left Hiroshima* he asked Hamai whether there was anything he wanted to say to people in the United States. The mayor wrote out a message that was eventually signed by 75,000 of his fellow citizens. It warned of "a war which would see thousands of Hiroshimas" and concluded with a touching proposal: "The people of Hiroshima ask nothing of the world except that we be allowed to offer ourselves as an exhibit for peace."

Cousins could never persuade a great many Americans to act on the lesson of Hiroshima, but he did help the *hibakusha* on a meaningful scale. In the *Saturday Review* he promoted a "Moral Adoptions" project that cared for about 400 of the more than 4000 children orphaned by the bomb; eventually the scheme sent most of its charges to college or vocational schools. And in August 1953 Tanimoto greeted him at the Hiroshima railroad station so that, together with Hamai, they could plan for Hiroshima Maidens to receive plastic surgery in the United States.

The project required four years of campaigning against strong resistance. One American foundation after another turned down Cousins' request for financing. Help came from two religious minorities accustomed to supporting unpopular causes: the Jews and the Quakers. At the request of Cousins' personal physician, Dr. William M. Hitzig, Mount Sinai Hospital in New York volunteered to supply free surgical facilities and hospital beds for twenty-five women, each requiring up to six months of care for repeated operations. Two plastic surgeons, Drs. Arthur J. Barsky and Bernard Simon, operated without charge. The American Friends Service Committee recruited families who opened their homes to the women between hospital stays.

In the first six months the visitors underwent 129 operations, and on August 6, 1955, the tenth anniversary of the bombing, Cousins was greatly moved when they gathered to talk by phone to their families back home and one girl began to weep. "It is not only be-

---

* Cousins traveled to Hiroshima five times in fifteen years. After the usual suspicions of his motives waned, he became revered as something of a local saint.

cause of my happiness that I cry," she explained to her people. "I cry because I am holding the telephone with my own hand and you cannot see it. I can move my elbow—like this—and I can move my fingers . . ."

The women returned to Hiroshima and to marriage, to teaching, to business enterprises. They had come away with more than improved physical appearances. Michiko Yamaoka, who had been a schoolgirl that day in the hospital when she hammered her fist on the window sill in protest against her Emperor's surrender broadcast, was now teaching advanced classes in design and dressmaking. She told Cousins of returning home with an unexpected gift: "I came back with a new heart. It is more important than anything physical. And it has made for me an entirely new life."

Dr. Robert Jay Lifton, a psychiatrist from Yale University, found impressive new life in Hiroshima when he arrived with his family in 1962 for six months of psychological research. Rebuilt factories poured out Mazda cars and heavy machinery. Unemployment was low. A glistening new skyline of glass-and-steel office buildings had sprung up. The Peace Boulevard cut through the city's center and actually was 100 meters wide. A Peace Park covered 122,100 square meters of the once devastated area near the hypocenter. Thousands of tourists shuffled daily through the park's focal point, the Peace Museum, a rectangular concrete box on stilts; it displayed artifacts of the bombing, most of them very small.

Hamai had spread his "city of brightness" everywhere except in the minds of the *hibakusha*. Lifton interviewed seventy-five of them and uncovered a battlefield of lasting carnage. He found the survivors haunted by a continuous "death imprint." The bombing was merely its onset. The "invisible contamination" of radiation, followed by the unending threat of "A-bomb disease" in its many guises, had, along with widespread guilt feelings, produced a "psychic closing off." Next came a massive mental paralysis that Lifton called "psychic numbing." It expressed itself in a form of hypochondria which the psychiatrist sympathetically described as "psychosomatic entrapment."

The less severely handicapped *hibakusha,* such as Hamai, talked with Lifton about the *ayamachi,* "the mistake." Hiroshima was preoccupied with the term because of a public furor concerning the inscription on the Cenotaph, the central A-Bomb monument in the Peace Park. "Rest in peace," it said, "the mistake shall not be repeated." Some citizens interpreted this as an accusation against the Japanese for having started the war. Hamai and most others felt that the mistake was of American making. The mayor told Lifton that it was "the use of the fruits of science for killing, maiming, and destroying."

People were no longer suggesting, as they had to John Hersey, that the men responsible for dropping the bomb be hanged. But the absence of American regrets rankled. "I think the atomic bomb was an inhuman weapon and should never have been used," Hamai told Lifton.* "But the bomb was dropped during wartime, and of course such things can happen in war, so I can understand how America came to use it. But what I cannot understand—and what we in Hiroshima greatly resent—is Truman's claim that he did the right thing in dropping the bomb and that he has no regrets."

The schism between the two Hiroshimas, the *hibakusha* minority who had to remember and the newcomers who hoped to forget, found a symbol in the controversy over the future of the A-Bomb Dome, the old Industrial Exhibition Hall at the Aioi Bridge—the monument left behind by the bomb.

Most old-timers and their peace groups wanted it preserved as a reminder of human vulnerability, especially for American visitors to see. The new generation of local pragmatists wanted it torn down because it took up prime real estate and was depressing. Hamai's administration favored an Asian-style compromise: action through inaction. They proposed to let the dome crumble slowly without human intervention and to cart away the remains once they became a safety hazard.

---

* Only a few American scientists eventually came to concede that the bombing had been an error, among them Albert Einstein. "I made one great mistake in my life—when I signed the letter to President Roosevelt recommending that an atomic bomb be made," Einstein told fellow Nobelist Linus Pauling not long before his death. Even fewer physicists had refused to work on the bomb in the first place. One of these early resisters was Einstein's friend Max Born, former head of the physics department at Göttingen and also a Nobel winner. Born, who worked in Edinburgh during the war, said: "I was opposed to taking part in war work of this character which seemed so horrible."

Hamai told Lifton that he felt ambivalent about the dome. He liked to retain it as "evidence." He also wished it gone because it was painful to many *hibakusha* who wanted no reminding. "My wife lost her parents and her uncle and many other relatives," he told the psychiatrist, "and she simply cannot tolerate seeing the Dome—or even relics of the experience—she just can't look at these things."

Emotions were driven to a head beginning in 1965 by the erection of an office building immediately next to the dome. The sleek nine-story structure dominated and belittled the deteriorating relic. Where-upon the City Council—"as if in contrition," Lifton wrote—finally voted to preserve the ruin. The campaign to raise the required $110,000 did poorly at the outset. Hamai energized it. He turned it into a national act for peace and created a sensation by personally collecting money on the streets of Tokyo and in the capital's Sukiya-bashi Park. On March 14, 1967, he announced that reinforcing work on the dome was about to start for its "eternal preservation."

At the August 6 anniversary celebrations, emotions never ceased overflowing. By the time of Dr. Lifton's attendance, merchants were exploiting the occasion and turning it into a carnival. Stores were advertising "peace sales." Before the lantern ceremony at the Ota River citizens shopped at booths for food and knickknacks. The utensils of mourning, paper lanterns and incense sticks, were huckstered alongside of candy. Spectacular fireworks were ignited at the Peace Park. And yet the floating of the lanterns still seemed unspoiled and moving.

Not everyone joined the crowds. Among those who conducted private ceremonies of their own were the children of the Folded Crane Club. Marching through the streets, they chanted a famous poem about the bomb: "Give me back my father, give me back my mother . . ." Then they withdrew to a secluded river bank. After they had floated their lanterns, one teenage girl broke down and would not stop sobbing. Lifton learned that her brother, a *hibakusha,* had died of leukemia four years previously. The club's adult mentor ran up to the psychiatrist and shouted, "Please let them know about these things in America!"

* * *

Day One

Mrs. Sakae Ito, the peace worker and town counselor from suburban Yano, also shuns the circus atmosphere of the launching ceremony. Every year she makes her own lantern and launches it from a lonely spot near her favorite tree. As her light floats downriver she prays for the souls of those coworkers whom she could not pull alive from the rubble of the houses they were all supposed to wreck near the Tsurumi Bridge on that distant August 6. Her heart is not at peace. Nearly forty years after the bombing she still bears a deep personal hatred for Harry Truman for having perpetrated the *ayamachi,* the great mistake.

Twenty-Eight

Edward Teller Takes All

To the power elite in Washington, the bomb looked like a boon, not a mistake. The weapon was elevated to the status of a prime public asset, and the struggle over its control escalated into a political confrontation. The devastating consequences of its radiation aftereffects remained covered up. And Groves was the icon of nuclear energy.

When the general delivered an accounting of his wartime mission before a new U.S. Senate Special Committee on Atomic Energy on November 28 and 29, 1945, the senators congratulated him for his "splendid management job" and his "great work." Deferentially they accepted his pontifical responses to their inquiries.

One senator asked what would happen to a prototypical casualty of radiation. "He can have enough so that he will be killed instantly," Groves testified. "He can have a smaller amount which will cause him to die rather soon, as I understand it from the doctors, without undue suffering. In fact, they say it is a very pleasant way to die." No one questioned this outrageous untruth.

The refusal to face the reality of radiation hazards was beginning to endanger American military personnel, and among the handful of specialists who became alarmed was the normally unflappable Colonel Stafford Warren, the ranking physician whom Groves had entrusted with the investigation of casualties in Hiroshima. Barely returned from Japan, the doctor was appointed chief of the Radiological Safety Section for the Crossroads atomic tests. It became a

345

personal crossroads for Warren; later he said he would "never want to go through the experience again."

In July of 1946 one million tons of radioactive water sprayed U.S. Navy vessels that had been abandoned to become targets for the tests in a lagoon off the Bikini Atolls. "The nature and extent of the contamination was completely unexpected," according to an official report, yet contingents of the 42,000 servicemen at the scene were ordered to decontaminate the ships under conditions that Warren called "extremely dangerous." Sailors slept on contaminated decks wearing only shorts. In some "hot spots" radioactivity remained "in excess of one hundred times tolerance."

The disaster was kept quiet for nearly forty years,* but after months of analyzing the effects of the military's "hairy-chested" disdain for safety, Dr. Warren concluded that the true horror was something else: radiation hazards were still *terra incognita*—except for the realization that the risks were many times more serious than anyone had suspected.

On January 19, 1947, the doctor spelled out his nightmare in a top-secret memorandum to his superior officer, Deke Parsons, who had at last pocketed his promotion to admiral, the reward for his contributions to the Hiroshima bomb. Warren recalled that most wartime estimates of allowable radiation tolerances had been "extrapolations," and he reminded Parsons: "We have had experience with such guesses, for they have been wrong by large and dangerous amounts." Little had been learned since then, the doctor pointed out, so he suggested that attempts to fix new standards of tolerances be abandoned. "They would hardly be worth the paper they were printed on," he wrote.

Once he had returned to civilian life as a professor at the University of Rochester School of Medicine, Warren felt it was time to initiate the public into the meaning of the Crossroads experience. He drafted a speech that concluded: "Inhabited areas so contaminated

---

* In 1983, two years after Warren's death, relevant classified documents came to light among his private papers in the library of the University of California at Los Angeles. They were discovered by a Navy veteran of the Crossroads tests who had become research director of the National Association of Atomic Veterans. The group was taking legal action against the Veterans Administration because the agency was stonewalling requests of ailing Crossroads survivors for medical care.

would have to be abandoned. This and all the rest that goes with it makes war intolerable. Outlawing the bomb is not the answer. War itself must be prevented."

In a memorandum to Groves, the doctor suggested that it would be best to volunteer this astounding news before "one of your favorite columnists" pinned the blame on the military so aggressively that "the effect on public relations will be difficult to combat." He requested permission to deliver a series of talks beginning with a meeting of two hundred medical students at Massachusetts General Hospital in Boston. For Groves, this threat to military tranquillity, if not security, was intolerable. He denied the required clearance at once by phone.

The general's dictatorship was approaching its end, however. Although he mobilized protracted political conspiracies on Capitol Hill, he lost his battle to keep control of atomic development in military hands, specifically his own. President Truman and the politicians handed the delicate new job to a civilian Atomic Energy Commission under David E. Lilienthal, the respected former chairman of the Tennessee Valley Authority.

Furious, Groves resisted the takeover like a military commander facing ouster from a fortress of his own loving creation. He stumped the country making speeches claiming total credit for ending the war. "Goddamit, general, let some other people sing your praises," one of his favorite personal assistants told him. Groves would not listen. "Every sentence in his speeches would start with 'I,' " this officer recalled. "I would change it to 'they.' He changed it back."

The relative inexperience and idealism of the new civilian AEC commissioners sent the general's egomania soaring. But at bottom his fury was intensely personal. He confided to one of the commissioners that he felt like a mother hen watching strangers take all her chicks. So he bad-mouthed the AEC through scathing memoranda and press leaks and feuded with Lilienthal as he dueled with Leo Szilard.*

"Mr. Lilienthal had made it very plain that he wanted no advice

---

* The general's campaign against Szilard continued into the postwar period. In a secret memo dated July 8, 1946, Groves vetoed the award of a "Certificate of Appreciation for Civilian War Service" for which Szilard had been recommended. The general charged that Szilard was undeserving because he had displayed "lack of support, even approaching disloyalty, to his superiors."

of any kind from me," he said. "He thought I was the lowest kind of human being."

Lilienthal did have his fill of Groves. "He does not respond to anything, we have found by bitter experience, except sternness and stuffing things down his throat," the AEC chairman noted in his journal. Lilienthal went to the Pentagon to see General Eisenhower, who had succeeded General Marshall as Chief of Staff, and asked that Groves be fired as military liaison on nuclear matters. Eisenhower was reluctant.

"I understand Groves and I know what a problem he is," he told Lilienthal. "He is a problem for us over here too. He was a czar during the war and everything is a comedown for a man of this type. Yes, it is true that he has a lot of enemies over here because of the way he rode herd on everyone during the war. There are ways of getting things done that don't require humiliating people and making enemies of them. Say, don't I know what I am talking about; I worked with Montgomery! And Patton was much the same."

Ike shrewdly analyzed Groves: he would never change ("He was that way before he was put in charge of the atomic project"), but his unique and invaluable experience could be harnessed. "We ought to use him as long as he has anything to contribute," Eisenhower counseled; "we ought to pump him dry." And he instructed Lilienthal on how to tame Groves.

"Call him in once in a while and ask his advice about something inconsequential. Kid him a bit—keep it light. That's what I do when he comes in here with a face as long as this. I say, 'Do you think I like sitting at this desk after being in command of twelve million troops? Why, sometimes I would like to push this desk over and walk out of here and never come back. But I don't.' And so on. Make him feel he isn't the only one who has things that don't please him."

But Groves could not be placated and in September 1947 Eisenhower removed him from the Military Liaison Committee. The disgruntled dictator's guerrilla warfare nevertheless continued to alienate so many people—even his friends—that a meeting was called in mid-January 1948 to deal with "the Groves situation." He was to be forced out of his last sinecure, a spot in the Armed Forces Special Weapons Project Command. Vannevar Bush, James Conant, and

Robert Oppenheimer attended the conference. The deliberations were cut short when Groves, realizing what was brewing, announced that he would retire the following month to become a vice president of the Remington Rand Corporation.*

Infatuation with power—arrogance, basically—had been the Achilles' heel that brought Groves down. Lilienthal rejoiced in his diary: "The business of having Napoleon sit on Elba while his crew waited for 'The Day'—that at least will no longer be our trouble." And the AEC chairman celebrated by starting to use a Remington shaver.

Robert Oppenheimer, Groves's ill-matched wartime partner, basked as a saint of science during the early post-Hiroshima years. He was made director of that intellectual citadel the Institute for Advanced Study in Princeton. His ascetic face peered somberly from the cover of *Time*. His old friends bridled at his increasingly cozy references to his chum "George"—General George C. Marshall had become Secretary of State—but the policy makers in Washington soaked up his advice.

"He is worth living a lifetime, just to know that mankind has been able to produce such a being," AEC chairman Lilienthal rhapsodized. "We may have to wait another hundred years for the second one to come off the line."

Oppie continued to deliver apocalyptic pronouncements that were open to misinterpretation. At MIT he told an audience that "the physicists have known sin." At a White House meeting he burst out at Truman, "Mr. President, I have blood on my hands." It was generally assumed that he meant to express regret for his role in destroying Hiroshima and Nagasaki. Indeed, Truman told Dean Acheson, "Don't you bring that fellow around again. After all, all he did was make the bomb. I'm the guy who fired it off." Oppenheimer did not trouble to clarify that, to him, guilt, which he did feel, was not the same as regret, which he did not.

Truman's open resentment was short-lived—he valued Oppenheimer's expertise too much to banish him—but between 1949 and 1953 Oppie's arrogance infuriated his powerful enemies. He called the chief scientist of the Air Force "paranoid." He was "rude beyond

* Groves published his memoirs in 1962 and died in 1970, having outlived his enemy Szilard by six years.

belief" to the Air Force Secretary. And he incurred the undying hatred of the proud and devious Lewis L. Strauss.

The Wall Street financier had become a member of the AEC and eventually succeeded Lilienthal as chairman.* Ultraconservative, fiercely anti-Soviet, and paranoically suspicious on security questions, Strauss considered Oppenheimer disloyal and made certain with J. Edgar Hoover that the FBI kept him under close surveillance. Oppenheimer, in turn, detested Strauss. At a congressional hearing he denounced Strauss's security preoccupations as "morbid" and ridiculed him until laughter swept the chamber. Strauss never forgave. "There was a look of hatred here that you don't see very often in a man's face," David Lilienthal remembered.

Most unforgivable was Oppenheimer's failure to show immediate enthusiasm for the H-bomb. The weapon's earliest advocate, Edward Teller, was promoting his "beloved super" with noisy passion. Strauss and his partisans were eager to go ahead with its development, but the blue-ribbon General Advisory Committee of the AEC recommended against this step in a unanimous opinion. Its judgment was not written by the committee chairman, Oppenheimer, whose doubts were based on technical and strategic reservations, but by a member who appreciated less parochial aspects, James Conant, still president of Harvard.

"The extreme dangers to mankind inherent in the proposal wholly outweigh any military advantage," Conant warned. "A super bomb might become a weapon of genocide." An even stronger separate opinion, composed by two committee members who were also veterans of the Los Alamos mesa, Enrico Fermi and Isidor Rabi, branded the super "an evil thing," "wrong on fundamental ethical principles."

Irresistible events rescued Teller's pet project. Klaus Fuchs, whose grasp of the H-bomb was total, was arrested in London and confessed to spying for the Russians throughout the war and in the years since then. Teller was incensed. The possibility that he might be a personal loser in a new arms race further stirred what he later called "my almost desperate interest in the thermonuclear effort." And just

---

* Strauss also made so many enemies that the Senate refused to confirm his reappointment to a second term as AEC chairman.

about then, fortuitously, he and Stanislaw Ulam hit upon an ingenious technical trick that would make the "super" vastly cheaper to produce than had been feared—and much more compact for delivery.

Opposition collapsed. Oppenheimer, who had scoffed that the new weapon might have to be delivered "by ox cart," blessed Teller's breakthrough. He deemed it "technically so sweet that you could not argue." Truman gave the go-ahead. At Livermore, California, the government built a new laboratory for Teller to preside over the designing of the weapon. As Livermore's director, he functioned not only as the father of the "super" but as its permanent shepherd and as the godfather for generations of nuclear weapons not yet born.

Like Strauss, Teller could not forget old wounds. And as the political climate changed after Eisenhower was elected President in 1952, Edward's duel with Oppie, born in wartime jealousies at Los Alamos and kept alive by the fight over the H-bomb decision, was bound to enter a new phase.

Republican Senator Joseph R. McCarthy, the most irresponsible of the Communist hunters, acquired the power of a committee chairmanship and threatened to investigate Oppenheimer. FBI Director Hoover persuaded him to leave the case to Strauss, who was more determined than ever to purge Oppie. FBI agents helped by snooping for fresh dirt and Teller was one of their more rewarding sources. He told them details of how he thought Oppenheimer had conspired against the H-bomb and also dropped word that "in his youth Oppenheimer was troubled with some sort of physical or mental attacks which may have permanently affected him."

The case reached the critical stage in 1953, when another Strauss ally, William L. Borden, the recently retired executive director of the Joint Congressional Committee on Atomic Energy, moved Hoover into action by sending him a 25-count indictment charging that "more probably than not" Oppenheimer was "functioning as an espionage agent." The particulars involved little more than the charges General Groves had decided to ignore when he cleared Oppie during the war. Yet Strauss thought they justified the revocation of Oppenheimer's working papers—his security clearance.

Day One

. . .

A secret hearing before a three-man Personnel Security Board of the Atomic Energy Commission convened on April 12, 1954, in Room 2022 of AEC Building T-3, a shabby temporary structure on Constitution Avenue in downtown Washington. It was a memorable occasion because the board's proceedings would become as notorious as the persecution-by-government in the Dreyfus Affair of another time.

Two of Oppenheimer's judges had prejudged the case. Evidence was withheld from his lawyers; their conversations were bugged and tapped by the FBI. Errors of Oppenheimer's memory were treated as lies. His indiscretion with his former mistress, Jean Tatlock, and his attempts to shield friends and former students were ballooned into "evidence" of continuing Communist ties. His character witnesses were bullied and entrapped.

The Oppie loyalists made an extraordinary parade to the witness stand: Vannevar Bush, James Conant, Enrico Fermi, Isidor Rabi, Johnny von Neumann, David Lilienthal, Hans Bethe, John McCloy, Bob Bacher, Norman Ramsey, and many more—all testified in Oppenheimer's behalf. Even John Lansdale, Groves's crusty intelligence chief, vouched for him. Of the witnesses who knew him intimately, only Groves turned his back*—until Edward Teller got his turn.

Given the atmosphere of the McCarthy witchhunt era, no witness carried more weight than Teller, the director of Livermore, the voice of science within the Republican establishment; and Strauss had satisfied himself that Teller's testimony would spring no surprises.

A week before Teller's appearance before the Oppenheimer board, an AEC liaison officer who went to see him in Livermore found him eager to make the most of the "case." Teller said he hoped that "some way can be found to 'deepen the charges' to include a docu-

---

* Strauss, knowing that Groves had written Oppenheimer a glowing letter in 1950 reaffirming his belief in Oppie's loyalty, had worried about the general's testimony. But when Strauss questioned Groves before the hearing the general assured him: "If I am asked whether I think the Commission would be justified in clearing Dr. Oppenheimer, I will say 'no.' If I am asked if I think he is a security risk, I will say, 'yes.' " Testifying at the hearing, Groves noted that security standards had been tightened since he cleared Oppenheimer during the war and said, "I would not clear Dr. Oppenheimer if I were a member of the Commission."

mentation of the 'consistently bad advice' that Oppenheimer had given all the way back to the end of the war." And Teller agreed when the AEC agent said it was important to "unfrock him in his own church"—Teller called it the "Oppie machine"—so that the "Oppie men" would lose their influence on scientists who were needed to build the H-bomb but were reluctant to follow Teller.

Under questioning by a government attorney, Teller testified at the hearing as Strauss had hoped.

QUESTION: Do you or do you not believe that Dr. Oppenheimer is a security risk?

TELLER: In a great number of instances, I have seen Dr. Oppenheimer act—I understood that Dr. Oppenheimer acted—in a way which for me was exceedingly difficult to understand, and his actions frankly appeared to me confused and complicated. To this extent I feel I would like to see the vital interests of this country in hands which I understand better and therefore trust more. In this very limited sense I would like to express a feeling that I would feel personally more secure if public matters would rest in other hands . . . If it is a question of wisdom and judgment, as demonstrated by actions in 1945, then I would say one would be wiser not to grant clearance.

The board agreed. It said that it had found "no indication of disloyalty" but voted two to one to strip Oppenheimer of his security clearance "because of the proof of fundamental defects in his 'character.' "

He never fully recovered from the ordeal. When a friendly author suggested to him that the hearing had resembled a dry crucifixion, Oppie smiled a martyr's smile and replied, "You know, it wasn't so very dry. I can still feel the warm blood on my hands."

As he told Truman, he had bloodied his hands himself by building the Hiroshima and Nagasaki bombs. At his loyalty hearing the establishment had bloodied them again. It was a convenient metaphor for this master of metaphors, but it missed the point. As his friend Fermi sadly analyzed the debacle, Oppenheimer, like Groves, had been brought down largely by his personality, his arrogance, his belief that he could do no wrong.

Day One

To the end of his days Oppenheimer felt that he had committed no *ayamachi,* no error, when he built the bomb. He was dying of throat cancer* when he wrote to a former student: "What I have never done is to express regret for doing what I did and could at Los Alamos."

Many of Oppenheimer's friends felt that Edward Teller had destroyed himself along with Oppie at the security hearings. They were wrong.

Some weeks after the AEC rendered judgment, Teller visited Los Alamos and spotted a familiar face in the dining room of the central building. It was Bob Christie, an old physicist friend; the two men and their families had once shared an apartment. Teller left his table to greet Christie with hand outstretched. Christie looked at the hand and turned away. Teller staggered back to his table, but the shock of the rejection was too much. He returned to his room and cried.

In subsequent years he suffered more rebuffs. Some colleagues never forgave him. With many of them he was barely on speaking terms. But, like the blood on Oppenheimer's hands, feelings were rendered irrelevant by the times, and the irrepressible Teller knew it.

What mattered was the power of the bomb, bigger bombs, smaller bombs, more bombs, thousands of them, tens of thousands, more ingenious ways to test them, hide them, deploy them, pinpoint them onto target cities. This came to be called "deterrence," and to the players of power poker in Washington, presidents like Richard Nixon and Ronald Reagan, Teller's passion for the manifold guises of "deterrence" was attractive. He cheered them with his jolly exuberance, his message that things were not so bad if only American deterrence could be kept more powerful than Soviet deterrence.

And so, like Oppenheimer, Teller found no need for regret. In the 1960s he allowed that a peaceful demonstration should have preceded the dropping of the Hiroshima bomb. It was a playful concession, for he made plain at the same time that he considered nuclear arms synonymous with progress. "To abstain from progress

* The letter, to David Bohm, who had had to leave the country because of his alleged Communist history, was written in 1966. Oppenheimer died on February 18, 1967, at the age of sixty-two at Princeton, his Elba.

is a medieval idea," he explained. "I am in favor of any advance in knowledge or any development of the greater power of man."

With the years more of Teller's restraints fell away. In 1975 he called Oppenheimer "a secret Red." In the 1980s he agitated for space weapons that most of his old Los Alamos coworkers derided as "star wars" fantasies. And he insisted that the deadliness of nuclear weapons was being much exaggerated, that their horror was actually "a dangerous myth." Why, he had heard that three days after the bombing the streetcars were running again in Hiroshima.*

* The Hiroshima newspaper *Chugoku Shimbun* reported that eighteen streetcars and five buses had been restored to service to cope with a daily passenger load of 42,000, but this was as of November 5, three months after the bombing.

Part 8
Today

Twenty-Nine

The New Hiroshima

When I arrived in Hiroshima nearly forty years after the bombing, Teller's claim looked plausible. Somehow I had not expected to face a city without apparent blemish except for the ruptured A-Bomb Dome.

Because of my advance reading, it felt eerie to drive in a taxi, with the driver wearing immaculate white gloves, through a district as gleaming and built up as downtown Palo Alto, California, knowing that this had once been the East Drill Field with its rows of dying and dead.

In the Fukuya department store, where even the resilient Dr. Hachiya had been unable to stomach the temporary quarantine ward, I could have ordered made-to-measure men's shirts in dozens of fabrics and styles.

And strolling across the new Aioi T-Bridge, the aiming point of the *Enola Gay,* on my first Sunday, I came across one of the mayor's assistants wearing a jeans suit with a denim hat at a cocky angle. He greeted me cheerfully but had no time for extended conversation. He was busy fishing off the bridge with his two small sons, who were squirming with excitement.

Unprepared for so much normality, I was even more startled by Hiroshima's love affair with everything American: the gaily colored T-shirts all over the streets, with their legends in English, messages like "Good American Spirit" and "Oregon As We Like It"; the giggly schoolgirls jamming into a Baskin-Robbins ice-cream place. The general opulence surprised me too. The Cafe Konzerthaus Mozart with its extraordinarily authentic Austrian pastries *mit Schlag* turned out to be part of a chain owned by local businessmen; there were five of their Mozart cafés in Hiroshima.

The extent of the preoccupation with peace (*heiwa*) also surprised me. And yet: Where but in Hiroshima was it appropriate to have a Peace Diner or a Peace Demolition Company? But when I became one of the 1.2 million annual visitors to the Peace Museum I learned that the exhibits of bent coins, remnants of burned clothing, and the photographs of the gruesomely injured victims invariably produced strong reactions from Americans. The artifacts accuse. Some visitors were ashamed and wept. Some felt angry and wrote in the visitors' book that they remembered Pearl Harbor.

I was shaken by the museum's stark and graphic reconstruction of the event. Then I felt defensive and wanted to tell someone, "Hey, I wasn't here! I was fighting the Nazis in Europe at the time. I had nothing to do with this. Don't hold this against me, OK?" But didn't I share responsibility, somehow, for what happened here? Perhaps. Even more, I resented something that was not in the museum at all: recognition that the bombing did end the war, thereby saving lives, American and Japanese; that it had hardly been the unprovoked war crime depicted by the museum display and the English-language commentary; that the exigencies of war loosened morality on both sides. It troubled me that the museum made no effort to connect the bombing to the context of its time. But then: Was my resentment a copout, an excuse to justify the inexcusable? Probably, probably.

As I interviewed survivors in the following weeks I found that the recuperative powers of Edward Teller's streetcars were meaningless. The presence of the great *ayamachi,* the mistake, was palpable. Hiroshi Oda, the omnipresent director of my "business hotel," the Silk Plaza, shared his experiences as a twenty-four-year-old lieutenant in the barracks 800 yards from the hypocenter. How lucky he had been! All his hair had fallen out, skin hemorrhages had dotted his legs, but he had been ill for only four months and recovered completely.

Oda, the smiling greeter of tourists, seemed a cheerful survivor. Most others I talked with were not. When Susumu Desaki, now a television executive, described how he found his mother on the East Drill Ground when he was ten years old, my male interpreter broke down. When Motoji Maeoka told how he burned corpses for three days when he was a nineteen-year-old policeman, tears flooded his creased, fleshy face and would not stop. Maeoka had recently retired after serving thirty-five years as a detective on the Hiroshima police force. For these people the sixth of August, 1945, was still not over.

The bombing also was not history for Akira Kondo when I met him in the white calm of the A-Bomb Hospital. Its 170 beds were still reserved for patients like him, victims of the first nuclear explosion over a live target. A fifty-nine-year-old electrical engineer, Kondo had been hospitalized frequently. Too weak to work for the past decade, he spent much of his time reflecting on the event that had enfeebled him. He wore an immaculately pressed blue-and-white-checked kimono and smiled pleasantly.

At 8:15 a.m. on August 6, 1945, he said, he had been knocked against a wall 1.1 mile distant from the blast point, the hypocenter. Not visibly injured, he had gone into the city to help evacuate the wounded. Suddenly, a week later, his life changed forever. He vomited and lost his appetite and energy. His gums and bowels began to bleed. About half his hair fell out. He was bedfast and listless for six months and never regained his once excellent health.

Although many people suffered from the same symptoms and often died of them, it was weeks before even the doctors learned what ailed Kondo. "Acute radiation effect" was the diagnosis entered into his medical records, but everyone said how lucky he was. He survived. He was not even burned.

He would not be so lucky again, he told me. The number of nuclear weapons was too enormous now. They were in too many hands and becoming ever more efficient. There was sure to be another war, Kondo said; this time nobody would survive.

I asked him whether the world had learned anything from Hiroshima.

"No," he said, and shrugged.

Thirty

"Real Estate Is a Sound Investment Here"

When I met Victor Weisskopf in 1983 in the cozy clutter of his 120-year-old home in Cambridge, Massachusetts, he was asking himself the same question.

The fortieth-anniversary reunion of his World War II physicist colleagues was coming up at the Los Alamos National Laboratory. At seventy-four, retired from his professorship in physics at the Massachusetts Institute of Technology, he was eager to see them once more, the enthusiasts with whom he had built the bomb on their Magic Mountain. But he was not at all certain that he wanted to attend formal festivities. It sounded embarrassing.

"Viki" Weisskopf still thought they had done right to build their gadget. Everything had looked so different then! Hitler seemed to be leading in the race for the bomb, and once he was defeated, the Japanese resisted so fanatically that Weisskopf—gentle, funny, full of the charm of his native Vienna—thought it might require ten bombs to subdue them, if not the fifty that others had in mind.

While he had worked on calculating the effects of nuclear blasts, he was infinitely more interested in preventing their baby from being stillborn, a dud.

By 1983 Weisskopf had long been one of the scientists most active in the peace movement, and he could hardly believe the plans for the reunion. It was to be a clubby get-together of old grads. Talk of weapons was taboo. Nobody was supposed to mention the

362

crazy arithmetic of the American nuclear stockpile that was making Los Alamos prosper: *a hundred times greater than needed to destroy humanity, one standard bomb capable of wiping out 1200 Hiroshimas.*

It occurred to Weisskopf that he was in a position to change the hear-no-evil, see-no-evil plans of the Los Alamos administration chiefs and to administer a jolt. His stature and popularity had prompted them to ask that he deliver the banquet address. He decided to accept, but he would surprise them and talk about the craziness being perpetuated by his alma mater. The depth of the nuclear madness had to be understood, especially in this setting. "A virulent case of collective mental disease"—that's what he called it in the speech he began to write.

Crazy. That, Weisskopf believed, was also the word for the contemporary Los Alamos as he and his fellow veterans gathered there for their celebration in April. They found themselves in a sleek, expanding city of 20,000 new nuclear enthusiasts, some 7000 of them working in its high-tech industry: nuclear death. They spent $350 million in tax money annually, much of it to invent increasingly sophisticated new weapons. First they had built a stockpile of A-bombs, then the H-bomb, more recently the warheads for Minuteman and Cruise missiles. Now they were working—"the bastards," said Weisskopf to a friend—on President Reagan's scenario for war in space. The craziness seemed permanent and profitable.

"Real estate is a sound investment here," boasted the laboratory's recruiting brochure.

Weisskopf and 110 of his colleagues saw no reminders of the wartime transience they had left behind. They remembered shabby barracks and muddy dirt roads with no sidewalks. Now they found 30 square miles of cheerful modern laboratory and administration buildings, broad four-lane avenues, a hotel with an addition going up, a private 80-bed hospital, 38 doctors (including two psychiatrists), a McDonald's, a Knights of Columbus building with bingo Wednesday nights at 7:30, many new subdivisions and still more condominiums under construction. The only shortage was parking space.

Reunion proceedings opened in a glow of nostalgia. The most

lionized of the alumni was former Captain James F. Nolan, M.D., the obstetrician who had delivered so many of the scientists' children on the mesa during the war. The patriarch of the assembly, Isidor Rabi, eighty-five, the round and owlish Nobel laureate whom all remembered as Oppenheimer's gruff senior adviser, delivered a wistful reminiscence that he titled "We Meant So Well."

By the last evening, some of the pride was turning into embarrassment. Rabi captured the mood when Bill Moyers, interviewing him for CBS television, asked him what he thought of Los Alamos today. "An abomination," snapped the old gentleman, reverting to type. "We should have put this thing to rest thirty years ago at least. I feel sorrow that the place still exists."

The final cocktail party at Fuller Lodge, the stately old log building where they had held their dances during the war, broke up at about 7:30. And as the aged veterans of the bomb walked with their wives across the street to the Community Building and their banquet, they saw the pond facing Oppenheimer Drive shimmering with the light of candles placed along the banks by peace demonstrators.

Most of the protesters standing along the scientists' route were silent. A few called out the slogan painted on their placards by Ed Grothus, a Los Alamos businessman: "One Bomb Is Too Many." Some of the scientists recognized Grothus. Years ago he had worked on the H-bomb prototype as a machinist in the C-Shop. He had since turned into one of the town's few peace heretics.

Many in the scientists' procession too had long ago changed their minds about the bomb. Hans Bethe, the German-born Nobelist who had been head of the Theoretical Division and Weisskopf's boss during the war, thought he was a wrong man to be picketed. His heart was with the demonstrators. "They didn't know how many of us were on their side," he told me later. Some of the marchers called to the placard bearers: "We're with you!" Viki Weisskopf, appalled that his presence in the procession might be misinterpreted as an endorsement of hawkish views, stepped out of the ranks of his friends and handed the demonstrators copies of the speech he was about to deliver.

Rising to face his peers after dinner, he told them: "Do not condemn the demonstrators in front of our building. Some of their slogans may be simplistic, but they express the revulsion at the craziest arms race in history." He felt proud, as he told me, to see himself cast in the role once occupied by Leo Szilard: the conscience of the scientists.

By no means the conscience of all the scientists, however.

The gulf splitting the banquet group was wide and Dr. Paul Olum was made uncomfortably aware of it as he circulated from table to table. Olum, president of the University of Oregon, shared the views of Weisskopf and Bethe, his wartime comrades in the Theoretical Division. But Viki's speech was not enough for Olum. He wanted the group to go formally on record for disarmament and was soliciting signatures to a statement he had drafted. Though the wording was less militant than Olum's personal feelings would have dictated—to some, the manifesto seemed no more radical than an endorsement of motherhood—only 70 of the 110 veterans agreed to sign it.

The focal point of Olum's opposition came from the table of Edward Teller, for whom there still could never be enough bombs to bedevil the hated Russians.* "This is the kind of thing that leads to war!" Teller shouted when he finished reading Olum's statement. He pounded on the dinner table. His famous Groucho Marx eyebrows were dancing.

Seventy signers out of 110. But the count at the banquet in Los Alamos was misleading. A few veterans had turned their backs totally and did not wish to dignify the occasion by their presence; they did not want to be counted. They were too disgusted with the state of the world, the stalemate that they had done so much to bring about, and some were saying so for the first time.

Seth Neddermeyer, seventy-five, one of the old-timers who stayed away, spoke up in an interview at his Seattle home a few days after the reunion. His achievement of plutonium implosion at Los Alamos had been pivotal. Now he was in anguish.

---

* Another notable document that Teller refused to sign was the patent application for the H-bomb. It was a protest of pride, not shame. His co-inventor, the Polish-born mathematician Stanislaw Ulam, had already affixed his own signature when the form was presented to Teller. "What is this?" he demanded, pointing to Ulam's name. "*I* am the inventor of the hydrogen bomb!"

Day One

"I get overwhelmed by a feeling of terrible guilt when I think about the history of the bomb," Neddermeyer said. Near tears, he wondered aloud: "This is what bugs me more than anything else—I don't remember having any strong feelings about [the bombings] at the time. I guess I just got caught up in the mindless hysteria."

Epilogue

Forty years ago our people plunged ahead without regard for the nuclear realities. Their successors are doing it yet. Every time the earth shakes under Nevada for another test, "progress" continues toward another new and "sweeter" weapon.

The pattern of redundant arming—along with the follies that invited the attack on Pearl Harbor, the escalation of the Vietnam War, the invasion of the Bay of Pigs, the litany of disasters throughout history—is chronic. All expose the same lack in the machinery that produces national judgment: reason.

American nuclear history shows that presidents are too easily captured by arms enthusiasts and too innocent of technical skills to evaluate technological novelty. But no expertise is required to recognize that the age of crazily costly and complex arms technology demands, to start with, a new regulatory mechanism: a tough, dispassionate body qualified to assess the flow of true realities and to keep voters informed, independently from the President, about the relative value and the true risks of available choices affecting national security as the alternatives emerge.

The authors of the Constitution could hardly have foreseen a time when inadequately informed judgments, made in a vacuum of secrecy, could plunge civilization into consequences not only cataclysmic but irreversible. When a man like James Conant believes that "a super bomb should never be produced," is not the public entitled to a conscious choice between short-term gain and long-term risk?

Hiroshima tells us that the issue is reason versus extinction—not American deterrence versus Soviet deterrence; not progress versus technological standstill. The nuclear dawn brought false promise, but the day is not done. Not as of this millisecond.

Notes

PAGE 18
troubled Ramsey?: N. F. Ramsey Oral History; N. F. Ramsey interviews
PAGE 19
it was: Groves, 201 file; Telephone Conversations, August 25
PAGE 20
and walking: Szilard, *His Version,* p. 17
PAGE 20
science fiction: Szilard, *His Version,* p. 16; Wells, p. 152
PAGE 21
"merest moonshine.": Szilard, *His Version,* p. 17
PAGE 21
in Berlin: Blumberg and Owens, p. 86
PAGE 21
and walk: Szilard, *His Version,* p. 19
PAGE 22
their profession: Moore, pp. 226–27
PAGE 23
understand physics: Moore, p. 234; Lapp, *Atoms and People,* pp. 14–15
PAGE 23
an envelope: Moore, pp. 266–67
PAGE 23
departing Bohr: Otto Frisch, Oral History

PAGE 24
months ago: Moore, p. 230
PAGE 24
handy soon: Szilard, *His Version,* p. 62
PAGE 25
High School.": C. L. Critchfield interview
PAGE 25
than ever: Blumberg and Owens, p. 67
PAGE 25
been repealed: B. J. O'Keefe interview
PAGE 26
he instructed: Moore, p. 234
PAGE 26
the experimentalists: Moore, p. 236; Blumberg and Owens, p. 84
PAGE 26
household lamp: Moore, pp. 235, 239
PAGE 26
for weeks: P. H. Abelson, L. W. Alvarez interviews
PAGE 27
at Caltech: Oppenheimer Letters, p. 207
PAGE 27
neutrons, yes: P. Morrison interview
PAGE 28
nearest hotel?": Blumberg and Owens, pp. 84–85

Day One

PAGE 29
of it.": Szilard, *His Version*, p. 22
PAGE 30
was possible: *Nation*, Nov. 22, 1945
PAGE 30
"code"—Hungarian: Blumberg and Owens, p. 87
PAGE 31
or what: Szilard, *His Version*, p. 56
PAGE 31
would cooperate: Moore, p. 256
PAGE 32*n*
in 1911: Irving, p. 41
PAGE 33
the Queen: Clark, p. 511
PAGE 33
"old fool,": Clark, p. 648
PAGE 34
"prehistory.": Hewlett and Anderson, p. 18
PAGE 35
to act: Lapp, "The Einstein Letter"
PAGE 37
requires action.": Finney, pp. 23–27; Hellman, pp. 73–80; Sachs, Testimony, Special Committee on Atomic Energy, pp. 553–73; Sachs, personal communication to R. E. Lapp, July 21, 1964
PAGE 37
downright upsetting: P. H. Abelson interview
PAGE 38
angry colonel: E. Teller and E. P. Wigner interviews
PAGE 38
taxpayers' dollars: Szilard, *His Version*, pp. 81–86
PAGE 40
uranium research: Irving, pp. 56, 68
PAGE 40
in Germany.": Clark, p. 679
PAGE 40
larger scale.": Clark, p. 681
PAGE 41
adopted country: Goodchild, p. 45; Blumberg and Owens, pp. 102–3
PAGE 41
speeded up: Szilard, *His Version*, p. 177
PAGE 42
like Briggs: Clark, pp. 684–85
PAGE 42
became annoyed: Sherwin, p. 36
PAGE 43
foreseeable future: Conant, p. 278

PAGE 44
so vigorously: M. E. L. Oliphant, personal communication
PAGE 44
sat stunned: Davis, p. 112
PAGE 45
Berkeley colleagues: Goodchild, p. 46
PAGE 45
would succeed: Libby, p. 91
PAGE 45
the world: Hewlett and Anderson, p. 44
PAGE 46
a name: Sherwin, p. 37; Hewlett and Anderson, pp. 45–46
PAGE 47
to assemble: Hewlett and Anderson, p. 47
PAGE 47
Sunday, December 7: Davis, pp. 119–20
PAGE 47
be King: Davis, pp. 116, 120
PAGE 48
May 26: Davis, p. 125; Szilard, *His Version*, p. 152; Wyden, "Why Hitler Didn't Drop the A-Bomb," p. 1G
PAGE 48
Nazi A-bombs: Szilard, *His Version*, p. 156; Libby, pp. 134–35
PAGE 49
arrogant personality: Davis, p. 127
PAGE 51
go ahead: Davis, pp. 129–31; Blumberg and Owens, pp. 116–18; Goodchild, pp. 53–54; E. Teller, R. Serber, H. A. Bethe interviews
PAGE 51
people go . . .": Libby, pp. 90–92; Compton, *Atomic Quest*, pp. 108–110
PAGE 52
Pearl Harbor: Compton, *Atomic Quest*, pp. 136–39; *New York Times* (by J. D. R. Bruckner), November 30, 1982, p. C-2; Fermi, L., p. 197; Conant, p. 289
PAGE 53
357 tons: Hewlett and Anderson, p. 44; Wattenberg, pp. 51–53
PAGE 54
production phase: Fermi, L., pp. 196–97

Notes

PAGE 54
against mankind: Szilard, *His Version,* p. 146; Conant, p. 144; Blumberg and Owens, p. 122

PAGE 54*n*
imminent danger: Compton, *Atomic Quest,* p. 139

PAGE 55
that thing.": Goodchild, pp. 55–56; Groves, *Now It Can Be Told,* p. 3

PAGE 56
Kenneth D. Nichols: Groves, *Now It Can Be Told,* pp. 4–5

PAGE 56
than probabilities.": Groueff, p. 9

PAGE 57
the son: Groueff, pp. 107–9

PAGE 57
scientists watched: R. Serber interview

PAGE 57
his eyes: A. W. Marks interview

PAGE 58
many bottlenecks: Groves, *Now It Can Be Told,* pp. 33–37; Groueff, pp. 50–51

PAGE 58*n*
me, Franklin: J. J. McCloy interview

PAGE 59
start moving: Groueff, pp. 14–15

PAGE 60
like that: Groueff, pp. 32–34; Groves, *Now It Can Be Told,* pp. 39–41

PAGE 60
military mind: Compton, *Atomic Quest,* p. 113

PAGE 61
on it: Groueff, pp. 35–39; Davis, p. 143; Goodchild, p. 64; Blumberg and Owens, p. 120

PAGE 61
asking Oppenheimer: Davis, pp. 143–44

PAGE 62
less alike: J. Wilson interview

PAGE 62
people's war.": Groueff, p. 42; R. R. Wilson interview

PAGE 63
Pied Piper: Davis, p. 144; Goodchild, p. 64; R. Serber, "The Early Years," in Isidor I. Rabi, ed., *Oppenheimer,* pp. 18–19

PAGE 63
than good: Goodchild, pp. 13, 17, 22

PAGE 63*n*
both names: R. Serber, C. L. Critchfield interviews

PAGE 64
ambition grew: Davis, p. 144

PAGE 65
for life: Goodchild, pp. 31, 35; R. Serber interview

PAGE 65
new ambition: Goodchild, pp. 36–40; R. Serber, P. Sherr, J. Wilson, E. McMillan interviews

PAGE 67
not Oppenheimer: Davis, pp. 144–47; Groueff, pp. 3, 40–44; Groves, *Now It Can Be Told,* pp. 60–63; Hewlett and Anderson, p. 228; Goodchild, p. 65

PAGE 67
it works: Groueff, p. 44

PAGE 69*n*
saw it: F. Oppenheimer interview

PAGE 69
the year: Hewlett and Anderson, p. 229; Groueff, pp. 64–66; Groves, *Now It Can Be Told,* pp. 64–67; Goodchild, p. 67; Dudley, pp. 2–5; McMillan, E. M., pp. 14–15; Manley, "A New Laboratory," p. 26; interview, E. McMillan

PAGE 70
think so: Hewlett and Anderson, pp. 114–15; Sherwin, p. 47

PAGE 71
at him: U.S. Atomic Energy Commission, Personnel Security Board, "In the Matter of J. Robert Oppenheimer" (Hearings), pp. 919, 921; P. H. Abelson, V. F. Weisskopf interviews

PAGE 71
for both: Goodchild, p. 32

PAGE 72
marry Kitty": Nelson, *American Radical,* p. 268

PAGE 72
than social: Nelson, *American Radical,* p. 269

PAGE 72
academic reputation: Goodchild, p. 32

PAGE 73
to Russia: Goodchild, pp. 69–70

PAGE 73
back door.": Goodchild, p. 92

PAGE 73
"photo reproduction.": Oppenheimer Hearings, p. 5
PAGE 74
Radiation Laboratory: Goodchild, p. 66
PAGE 74
whispers throughout: Nelson, *American Radical,* p. 265; transcript of telephone conversation, National Archives
PAGE 74*n*
engaged in.": Oppenheimer Hearings, p. 268; Nelson, p. 294
PAGE 75
a half.": Oppenheimer Hearings, p. 811
PAGE 76
committed suicide: Oppenheimer Hearings, pp. 153–54; Davis, p. 149; Goodchild, p. 90
PAGE 77
man's eyes?: Groves, *Now It Can Be Told,* p. 63; Goodchild, pp. 90–91
PAGE 77
with me.": Davis, p. 144
PAGE 77
be harvested: H. L. Anderson, R. E. Lapp interviews
PAGE 78
he said: C. L. Critchfield, H. D. Smyth interviews
PAGE 78
the duration: Groves draft, Secretary of War Henry L. Stimson to Attorney General, October 28, 1942, Groves Top Secret File, National Archives
PAGE 79
losing him.": Memorandum to the Officer in Charge, Counter Intelligence Corps, 24 January 1943, RG 77, National Archives
PAGE 80
vital information.": Groves to District Engineer, June 14, 1943, Groves Top Secret File, National Archives
PAGE 80
cooperate further: Goodchild, pp. 92–94
PAGE 80*n*
bad judgment: Goodchild, p. 241
PAGE 81
United States.": Oppenheimer Hearings, p. 274

PAGE 81
about Eltenton: Goodchild, pp. 95–96
PAGE 81
to him?: Goodchild, p. 94
PAGE 81
general's desk: Groueff, p. 249; R. Groves, J. O'Leary interviews
PAGE 82
was Oppenheimer: Oppenheimer Hearings, pp. 271, 266, 262; Davis, p. 155; A. W. Marks interview
PAGE 82
the drink: Davis, pp. 158–59
PAGE 82
the Party: Oppenheimer Hearings, pp. 260, 266
PAGE 82
could get.": Davis, pp. 156–57
PAGE 82
of help.": Oppenheimer Hearings, pp. 261, 263
PAGE 83
still operating.": Oppenheimer Hearings, pp. 871, 875
PAGE 83
a vacuum: Goodchild: pp. 95, 96, 98, 99
PAGE 84
the institute: Irving, pp. 101–2; Robert Jungk, *Brighter Than a Thousand Suns,* pp. 98–104
PAGE 85
German competition: Moore, pp. 290–93
PAGE 86
guided missiles: Irving, pp. 118–21
PAGE 86
save it.": Dower, p. 43; Pacific War Research Society, *The Day Man Lost,* pp. 20, 24; M. Takeuchi, S. Yokoyama interviews
PAGE 89
United States: Morehead, pp. 49–51, 71–73, 83–91; Hyde, p. 104
PAGE 90
furious pace: Golovin, pp. 36–44
PAGE 94
medical team: Wilson, R. R., pp. 41–42; R. R. Wilson, J. Wilson interviews
PAGE 94
hitherto impossible: Davis, pp. 161–162
PAGE 94
three hours: N. F. Ramsey interview

Notes

PAGE 95
go crazy.": Davis, p. 163

PAGE 95
reminisced later: Wilson, R. R., pp. 42–43; R. R. Wilson, R. F. Bacher interviews

PAGE 96
difficult people: Goodchild, pp. 72, 73; Hewlett and Anderson, p. 231; Groves, *Now It Can Be Told,* p. 197; Wilson, R. R., p. 45

PAGE 98
2000 yards: Davis, pp. 165–68; Goodchild, p. 80; R. Serber, J. H. Manley interviews

PAGE 99
of whiskey.": Davis, pp. 170–73; Goodchild, p. 82

PAGE 100n
became enraged: R. F. Bacher, N. F. Ramsey interviews

PAGE 101
be done.": Hewlett and Anderson, p. 238; Wilson, R. R., p. 45; R. R. Wilson, J. Wilson, A. W. Marks, H. L. Barnett, N. F. Ramsey interviews

PAGE 102
entire laboratory: Blumberg and Owens, pp. 126–36; Davis, pp. 177–80; H. A. Bethe, E. Teller interviews

PAGE 103
the beer: Goodchild, p. 100; Davis, p. 216; Blumberg and Owens, pp. 137, 456

PAGE 105
obstacles left: Hewlett and Anderson, pp. 246–47; Davis, pp. 117–120; Goodchild, pp. 100–104; Groueff, pp. 320–23

PAGE 109
use it.": Groves, *Now It Can Be Told,* pp. 200–206; Wyden, "Why Hitler Didn't Drop the A-Bomb," p. G1; Sherwin, p. 50; Irving, pp. 244, 245–47, 250, 252, 259–60; Goodchild, p. 111

PAGE 110
Los Alamos: Morehead, pp. 94–99; Hyde, pp. 105–7

PAGE 111
would help: Golovin, pp. 45–47

PAGE 112
locked up!": Conant, pp. 292–93; Goodchild, pp. 107, 118; Hewlett and Anderson, pp. 312–13, 248; R. F. Bacher, C. L. Critchfield interviews

PAGE 114
so despondent: E. McMillan, D. Hawkins, P. Sherr, J. Wilson, S. Barnett, N. F. Ramsey, R. F. Bacher interviews

PAGE 115
even Kitty: Goodchild, pp. 128, 288; P. Sherr interview

PAGE 116
had plans: Ulam, *Adventures,* p. 167; O'Keefe, p. 72; Smith, *A Peril,* pp. 6–7; Groueff, p. 211; Sherwin, p. 199; Moore, pp. 324, 328–29, 327, 330; Hewlett and Anderson, p. 316

PAGE 121
the meeting: Moore, pp. 333, 334, 338, 342; Gowing, pp. 354–55

PAGE 122
come again: Moore, p. 346; Smith, p. 9; Gowing, pp. 356–57

PAGE 126
was forthcoming.": Moore, pp. 347, 348–50, 351–53; Gowing, pp. 356–358; Sherwin, p. 98; Smith, *A Peril,* pp. 10–11; Hewlett and Anderson, pp. 327–30

PAGE 127
be present: Finney, pp. 24–25

PAGE 128
his successor: Hewlett and Anderson, p. 338; Clark, pp. 697–700; Moore, p. 362; Baker, p. 279

PAGE 129
FDR's desk: Giovannitti and Freed, p. 30

PAGE 131
Byrnes's oats: Sherwin, pp. 146, 148; Giovannitti and Freed, pp. 31, 32, 25–26, 28–29, 46; J. O'Leary interview

PAGE 132
acts meanly.": Hewlett and Anderson, pp. 342–43; Donovan, pp. 48–49; Sherwin, p. 150; R. G. Arneson, J. A. Volpe, F. C. Pogue, J. J. McCloy interviews

PAGE 135
the war: Sherwin, pp. 162–64, 291–292; Giovannitti and Freed, pp. 49–51; Groueff, p. 331; Knebel and Bailey, "Secret Revealed," p. 20

PAGE 139
May 8: Clark, p. 705

Day One

PAGE 140
convincing: Sherwin, pp. 117–18
PAGE 140
Hans Bethe: H. A. Bethe interview
PAGE 140
"collective action.": Szilard, *His Version,* p. 190
PAGE 141
was dead: Szilard, *His Version,* pp. 182, 196–204, 206
PAGE 143
the laboratory: Szilard, *His Version,* pp. 182, 184; Giovannitti and Freed, p. 29
PAGE 144
sweet achievement: Byrnes, *Speaking Frankly,* p. 284; Giovannitti and Freed, p. 66; Sherwin, p. 169; Szilard, p. 185
PAGE 144
U.N. talks: Compton Memo to Nichols, June 4, 1945
PAGE 146
being heard: Smith, *A Peril,* pp. 30–33; Goodchild, p. 29; J. A. Volpe interview
PAGE 149
do that.": Hilts, p. 75; Else, "The Day After Trinity" (film script), pp. 37–38; Robert R. Wilson Oral History; R. R. Wilson, J. Wilson interviews
PAGE 149
that point.": Else, "The Day After Trinity," pp. 35–36; Hilts, p. 76
PAGE 150
friend's motives: R. F. Bacher interview
PAGE 151
serious analysis: I. I. Rabi interview
PAGE 151n
be minimized: Bernstein, J.
PAGE 151
big bang: K. T. Bainbridge Oral History; K. T. Bainbridge interview
PAGE 152
his mouth: Smith, *A Peril,* p. 62; Else, "The Day After Trinity," p. 54
PAGE 152
decision making: Smith, *A Peril,* p. 62; R. F. Bacher interview
PAGE 153
was that: N. F. Ramsey interview
PAGE 153
the subject: P. Morrison interview

PAGE 154
President Truman: Strauss, *Men and Decisions,* pp. 192–93; Giovannitti and Freed, p. 145
PAGE 154
the files: Knebel and Bailey, "Secret Revealed," pp. 20–21; Smith, *A Peril,* p. 39; Giovannitti and Freed, p. 67; Hewlett and Anderson, p. 355; Donovan, pp. 69–70
PAGE 155
who counted: Oliphant, personal communication; Davis, p. 142
PAGE 157
United States: Giovannitti and Freed, pp. 58–60, 62
PAGE 157n
human system": I. Janis interview; Morison, p. 620
PAGE 158
recalled later: Sherwin, p. 203; Giovannitti and Freed, p. 106; Smith, *A Peril,* p. 38
PAGE 159
he said: Sherwin, pp. 204–6; Hewlett and Anderson, pp. 356–57; Giovannitti and Freed, pp. 98–101; Compton, *Atomic Quest,* p. 237
PAGE 159n
such force.": Knebel and Bailey, "Secret Revealed," p. 23
PAGE 161
to fight: Donovan, p. 67; Compton, *Atomic Quest,* pp. 238–39; Giovannitti and Freed, p. 104
PAGE 164
lesser voices: Sherwin, pp. 208–9, 303; Hewlett and Anderson, pp. 358–60; Giovannitti and Freed, pp. 305, 109–10; Donovan, p. 68; R. G. Arneson interview
PAGE 166
of events.": Szilard, *His Version,* p. 186; Giovannitti and Freed, p. 111; Sherwin, p. 210–13; Smith, *A Peril,* pp. 42–46; Hewlett and Anderson, pp. 366–67; Compton, *Atomic Quest,* pp. 234–6
PAGE 168
out again.": Giovannitti and Freed, pp. 114–16; Sherwin, pp. 212–13; Smith, *A Peril,* p. 46
PAGE 168
Truman personally: Giovannitti and Freed, pp. 118–19

Notes

PAGE 171
the matter: Sherwin, pp. 304–5;
Giovannitti and Freed, pp. 120,
123; Compton, *Atomic Quest*,
p. 240; Smith, *A Peril*, p. 49;
Szilard, *His Version*, p. 215;
A. W. Marks, E. Teller interviews
PAGE 171*n*
not known: Davis, p. 182; E. Teller
interview
PAGE 174*n*
look ahead.": Toland, pp. 858–61;
Giovannitti and Freed, pp. 134–39;
Knebel and Bailey, "Secret Re-
vealed," p. 20; Leahy, p. 431;
Groves, *Now It Can Be Told*, pp.
271–72; Mee, p. 22; J. J. McCloy
interview
PAGE 175
the kill": Davis, p. 247
PAGE 175
perfunctory brushoff: Sherwin, pp.
215–17, 307; Giovannitti and
Freed, pp. 144–46; Bard, pp. 52–
53; Smith, *A Peril*, pp. 52–53;
A. K. Smith interview
PAGE 176
weapon—now!": Giovannitti and
Freed, pp. 162–64; Szilard, *His
Version*, p. 167; Compton, *Atomic
Quest*, p. 262
PAGE 177
issue is.": Smith, *A Peril*, pp. 54–55;
Szilard, *His Version*, p. 212; E. P.
Wigner, R. E. Lapp interviews
PAGE 179
its bottle: Sherwin, pp. 217–19;
Smith, *A Peril*, pp. 55–56; Blum-
berg and Owens, pp. 155–57; Tel-
ler, "Seven Hours of Reminis-
cences," p. 191; Teller with
Brown, pp. 13–14
PAGE 180*n*
the country.' ": Szilard, *His Version*,
pp. 187, 188, 214; Giovannitti and
Freed, pp. 167–69; Compton,
Atomic Quest, pp. 246–47; Knebel
and Bailey, "Secret Revealed," pp.
19–23
PAGE 185*n*
so far: Thomas and Witts, pp. 86–88,
108–10; Pacific War Research Society, *Longest Day*, pp. 101–2;
Toland, pp. 758–63; Giovannitti
and Freed, pp. 34–36

PAGE 185
suffer scars.": Tuve, Oral History
PAGE 187
was over: Pacific War Research Society, *Longest Day*, pp. 25–26, 49,
93–94; Dower, pp. 48, 49; Kojiro
Nishina, Yokoyama interviews
PAGE 189
my laboratory.": Irving, pp. 279,
282–85, 289–90; Groves, *Now It
Can Be Told*, pp. 234–44
PAGE 191
the war: Thomas and Witts, pp.
151–52; Spitzer, p. 15
PAGE 193
war work.": Groves, *Now It Can Be
Told*, pp. 258–61; Thomas and
Witts, pp. 10, 16, 22, 25, 33, 35–
37, 40, 75, 77–78, 95, 129, 131;
Marx, p. 81
PAGE 197
effects appreciably: Target Committee, notes of first, second, and
third meetings; interviews: H. A.
Bethe, J. A. Derry; W. Penney,
personal communication; Thomas
and Witts, p. 155
PAGE 199
it blindfolded.": Thomas and Witts,
pp. 158–61; Groves, *Now It Can
Be Told*, pp. 169, 272–75; Cary,
p. 11
PAGE 200
is life: Lifton, pp. 51–52
PAGE 202
called Trinity: Thomas and Witts,
pp. 62, 63, 97–98, 144–45, 166;
Committee for the Compilation of
Materials, pp. 23–24, 349–53; Pacific War Research Society, *Longest Day*, pp. 96, 97, 150; Kosakai,
pp. 46, 69; S. Desaki interview
PAGE 205*n*
the plant: Groueff, pp. 302, 307–
309; Feynman, pp. 119–22
PAGE 205
would work: Goodchild, pp. 149–50;
Groueff, pp. 324, 339, 357
PAGE 206*n*
unauthorized: Lapp, *Atoms and People*, pp. 57–61; Libby, pp. 202–4;
Hempelmann, "The Acute Radiation Syndrome" (Slotin is the
anonymous Case #3); Alsop and
Lapp, *Saturday Evening Post*,
March 6, 1954, pp. 25+

PAGE 208
bet zero: Goodchild, pp. 152–55; Groueff, pp. 344–45; Smith, *A Peril*, p. 9; Lamont, pp. 144–45; Laurence, "Atom Bomb Designers"

PAGE 209n
with it: Marks, p. 14

PAGE 210
of respect.": Goodchild, pp. 158–59; Lamont, p. 210; L. H. Hempelmann interview

PAGE 212
hundred miles: Lamont, pp. 210–12; Groueff, pp. 354–55; Goodchild, p. 161; Cahn, p. 74; J. H. Manley interview

PAGE 213n
scientists' pool: Smith, *A Peril*, p. 76; Groueff, p. 356; Lamont, p. 237; K. T. Bainbridge interview

PAGE 214
skin blisters: Lamont, pp. 238, 249–250, 252–53, 269–70; Smith, *A Peril*, p. 77; Else, "The Day After Trinity," p. 50; Goodchild, p. 162; Hirschfelder, p. 77; Weisskopf MS, pp. 14, 30, 31

PAGE 216
long afterward: Jette, p. 110; Lamont, p. 156; Feynman, p. 132; Groueff, p. 356; Else, "The Day After Trinity" script, p. 48; Paton

PAGE 217
suited him: C. L. Critchfield interview

PAGE 219
unique—outburst: Lamont, pp. 78, 79, 111, 112, 113, 229; Kistiakowsky, p. 60; K. Cohen, J. H. Manley, H. A. Bethe, R. F. Bacher, R. P. Feynman, J. Wilson interviews

PAGE 220n
and detonated: Morehead, pp. 101–102, 105–6; Hyde, pp. 109–11; Linschitz, "Science," pp. 1501–5

PAGE 223
new weapon: Ferrell, pp. 47, 49–50, 55; Giovannitti and Freed, p. 201; Donovan, p. 91

PAGE 224
world politics: Groves, *Now It Can Be Told*, pp. 303, 433; Ferrell, p. 55; Giovannitti and Freed,
p. 242; Stimson Diary, p. 31, July 21, 1945; p. 33, July 22, 1945

PAGE 226
climactic phase: Sherwin, p. 225; Giovannitti and Freed, pp. 222–24; Mee, p. 222; Ferrell, p. 54; Holloway, pp. 20, 22

PAGE 228
of paper.": Sherwin, pp. 235–36; Hewlett and Anderson, p. 395; Giovannitti and Freed, pp. 226–28, 239; Ferrell, p. 56; Stimson Diary, July 24, 1945, p. 39; Eisenhower, p. 443

PAGE 230
great trip: Giovannitti and Freed, pp. 248, 250, 254; Sherwin, p. 231; Donovan, pp. 95–96; G. Elsey interview

PAGE 234
the bombings: Pacific War Research Society, *Longest Day*, pp. 148–49, 155, 164–65, 185; Brooks, pp. 90–92, 96–97; Toland, pp. 25–26

PAGE 237
he reflected: Knebel and Bailey, *No High Ground*, pp. 131–33; Thomas and Witts, pp. 199, 200, 207–9; Groves, *Now It Can Be Told*, p. 306; Toland, p. 869; N. F. Ramsey, J. F. Nolan interviews

PAGE 237
code-named "Centerboard.": Laurence, *Dawn*, p. 199; Thomas and Witts, p. 195

PAGE 239
Enola Gay: Groves, *Now It Can Be Told*, pp. 312–13; Thomas and Witts, pp. 255–56, 259; Groves to George, 23 July, 1945; Groves to De Lany, August 17, 1945, Folder 5c, Groves Top Secret File, NA

PAGE 242
his control: Thomas and Witt, pp. 270–72, 277; Knebel and Bailey, *No High Ground*, pp. 146, 149–152; Groves, *Now It Can Be Told*, p. 317; Toland, pp. 874–75

PAGE 244
by poison: Thomas and Witt, 281–291; Knebel and Bailey, *No High Ground*, pp. 154–57; Tibbets, pp. 134+; Toland, pp. 874–76

PAGE 245
the bombing: Thomas and Witts, p. 335; Toland, p. 878

Notes

PAGE 247
we done?": Thomas and Witts, pp. 293–99, 301–2, 304–9; Tibbets, p. 136; Marx, pp. 134–36, 143, 167–73

PAGE 254n
bring upstairs: Pacific War Research Society, *Longest Day,* pp. 234, 238–39

PAGE 255
would die: Committee for the Compilation, pp. 6, 118, 353; Kosakai, p. 28; K. Horibe, M. Furuta interviews

PAGE 256
it stood: K. Horibe interview

PAGE 257n
the blast: Lifton, pp. 553–54

PAGE 257
tear down: Ishida, pp. 227–37; S. Ito interview

PAGE 258
the river: M. Matsubara interview

PAGE 259
lingering radiation: F. Morishita interview

PAGE 261
cannot win.": T. Teramae interview

PAGE 262
to all: M. Maeoka interview

PAGE 264
about it: Hamai, pp. 3–4, 9–10, 17–18, 20–21; Lifton, R. J., *Death in Life,* pp. 211–15; Pacific War Research Society, *Longest Day,* pp. 281–82; F. Hamai, J. Hamai interviews

PAGE 265
need help: Hachiya, pp. 76–79

PAGE 266
the facts: Pacific War Research Society, *Longest Day,* pp. 269–70, 284–85

PAGE 266
not leaving: K. Horibe interview

PAGE 269
it there: T. Okimoto interview

PAGE 272n
as remedies: Committee for the Compilation, p. 532

PAGE 272
they survived: S. Desaki interview

PAGE 273
generation later: F. Hamai interview

PAGE 274
drifted away: F. Ono, A. Kuramoto, M. Tamura, F. Garnett, M. Maeoka interviews

PAGE 279
dying daily: Hachiya, pp. 15, 20–21, 25, 26, 31, 32, 51, 57, 63, 65, 69; Hersey, p. 67

PAGE 281
American A-Bomb: *Boston Globe,* Nov. 3, 1975; Bernstein, B. J., "Unraveling a Mystery," p. 19; N. Fukui, M. L. Zapf interviews

PAGE 286
torn apart.": Groves, *Now It Can Be Told,* pp. 319–23; Knebel and Bailey, *No High Ground,* pp. 216–17

PAGE 288
this earth.": Knebel and Bailey, *No High Ground,* pp. 215, 217; Hewlett and Anderson, p. 402; Manchester, p. 291; Groves, *Now It Can Be Told,* pp. 324, 328, 329, 330

PAGE 289
ever made: Knebel and Bailey, *No High Ground,* pp. 228–31; Donovan, p. 96; G. Elsey interview

PAGE 290
9 p.m.: Cohen, p. 21; Goodchild, p. 167; Smith, *A Peril,* pp. 76–77; Oppenheimer Letters, p. 292; Else, Trinity TV script, p. 59; A. W. Marks, R. F. Bacher, A. K. Smith interviews

PAGE 291
did it.": Hahn, D., p. 185; Groves, *Now It Can Be Told,* pp. 333–34, 338; Hahn, O., p. 170

PAGE 292
coming automatically: Knebel and Bailey, *No High Ground,* pp. 208, 219; Groves, *Now It Can Be Told,* pp. 341–42; Giovannitti and Freed, p. 271; N. F. Ramsey interview

PAGE 293
any explaining.": Groves, *Now It Can Be Told,* p. 344; Norman F. Ramsey Oral History, July 19, 1960, pp. 166–68; N. F. Ramsey interview

PAGE 294n
bomb there: Trumbull (entire book)

PAGE 294
the runway: Groves, *Now It Can Be Told,* pp. 342–43; Committee for the Compilation, p. 367

Day One

PAGE 294
a beast . . .": Clark, p. 708; Hiebert, p. 237; Szilard, *His Version,* p. 231; Donovan, pp. 96–97

PAGE 295
the Japanese: Groves, *Now It Can Be Told,* pp. 352–53

PAGE 298
under way.": Knebel and Bailey, *No High Ground,* pp. 188–91, 200; Toland, pp. 889, 894; Butow, p. 151; Committee for the Compilation, p. 22

PAGE 299
next day: Nishina Memorial Foundation; S. Yokoyama, K. Niizuma interviews

PAGE 302
was not: Brooks, pp. 169, 171; Takayama, pp. 127–29; Pacific War Research Society, *Japan's Longest Day,* pp. 31–35; Toland, pp. 912–916; Giovannitti and Freed, pp. 278–79

PAGE 303
they could: K. Niizuma, S. Yokoyama, T. Kitagawa interviews

PAGE 306
please rise . . .": Toland, pp. 918, 919, 922, 935, 936–37, 939, 944, 945, 946, 949, 951–52, 958, 959; Giovannitti and Freed, pp. 293, 303; Pacific War Research Society, *Japan's Longest Day,* pp. 216–17, 286, 327

PAGE 307
had fallen: S. Yokoyama interview

PAGE 308
wrote later: Hamai, pp. 21, 22, 45–46

PAGE 309
her bed: M. Tomasawa, M. Yamaoka interviews

PAGE 311
to rest: Hachiya, pp. 81–83, 125

PAGE 313
good health: I. Ito, K. Horibe, T. Teramae interviews

PAGE 314
from there: Hamai, pp. 27, 31, 49

PAGE 314
would die: G. Ouchi interview

PAGE 316
near starvation: Hachiya, p. 159, Junod, p. 265; Committee for the Compilation, p. 533

PAGE 318
happening there: Hiebert, p. 28; Cousins, *Present Tense,* p. 127

PAGE 319
their turn: Junod, pp. 261–62; Manchester, p. 448; C. J. Sams, P. Morrison interviews

PAGE 321
for decades: Lawrence, "Visit to Hiroshima," Committee for the Compilation, p. 15; Burchett, p. 113

PAGE 325
been understood.": Lang, *From Hiroshima,* pp. 41–42, 46, 47, 50; Junod, pp. 262–63, 265, 270–71; *Japan Times,* September 12, 1945; *New York Times,* September 13, 1945, p. 4; Gannon, pp. 15, 18; J. F. Nolan, C. Sams, P. Morrison interviews

PAGES 325–26n
Hirschfelder, pp. 87–88; Finch interview

PAGE 327
nearly twenty-five years: *New York Times,* Sept. 19, p. 5; Manchester, p. 510; Compton, *Atomic Quest,* pp. 244–45; Barnouw, p. 16; Jaffe, pp. 12, 14

PAGE 328
just beginning: Groves, *Now It Can Be Told,* pp. 367–72; General Headquarters (news release); S. Yokoyama, R. G. Arneson interviews

PAGE 330
wrote later: Hamai, pp. 54–55; Hatfield, p. 111; M. O. Hatfield interview

PAGE 332
of survival: Jungk, *Strahlen aus der Asche,* pp. 67–68, 95–97, 100, 108, 109, 114; Lifton, *Death in Life,* p. 213; J. D. Montgomery interview

PAGE 333
like Job: J. Hersey interview

PAGE 334
until 1949: Jungk, *Strahlen aus der Asche,* pp. 243–45; Lifton, *Death in Life,* pp. 327–38; Manchester, p. 510

PAGE 334n
the bomb.": Steinberg, p. 21; Lifton, *Death in Life,* p. 67

PAGE 335
never married: S. Imahori, I. Ito,
F. Morishita interviews
PAGE 335*n*
and debilitation: Lifton, p. 172
PAGE 336
the future: Cousins, *Present Tense,*
p. 325; Steinberg, pp. 72, 78; Rosenthal, p. 64; S. Imahori interview
PAGE 338
young lovers: Jungk, *Strahlen aus
der Asche,* pp. 252–57; 279–84,
287; Lifton, *Death in Life,* pp.
103–4, 133, 137, 141, 344–52;
S. Jablon interview
PAGE 339
another holocaust: Lifton, *Death in
Life,* p. 104; Coerr, p. 20; Lifton,
B. J.
PAGE 341
new life.": Jungk, *Strahlen aus der
Asche,* pp. 292–93; Hersey, pp. 3,
38–42, 111–12; Committee for the
Compilation, pp. 559, 565; Cousins, "Hiroshima," p. 10; Cousins,
Present Tense, pp. 324–52
PAGE 342*n*
so horrible": Clark, pp. 672, 671
PAGE 343
in America!": Lifton, *Death in Life,*
pp. 271, 271–79, 273–74, 284–85,
334, 540; Steinberg, pp. 21–22, 88;
Kosakai, p. 47
PAGE 344
great mistake: I. Ito interview
PAGE 347
by phone: International Radiation

Research and Training Institute;
Groves Testimony, November 28–
29, 1945; Warren to Meyers;
Warren to Groves; Warren to
Parsons
PAGE 347*n*
his superiors": Groves to Col. E. E.
Kirkpatrick, National Archives,
RG 77
PAGE 349
Remington shaver: Hewlett and An-
derson, p. 644; Lapp, *Atoms and
People,* p. 80; Libby, pp. 266–67,
270, 271; Herken, p. 243; J. A.
Volpe interview
PAGE 351
security clearance: Goodchild, pp.
178, 174, 180, 213, 201, 189,
214–15, 217–18
PAGE 355
in Hiroshima: Bernstein, B. J., "In
the Matter of," pp. 216, 230, 235,
252; Goodchild, pp. 254, 270, 286;
New York Times Magazine (by
William L. Laurence), August 1,
1965; *Reader's Digest* (by Edward
Teller), November 1982
PAGE 361
and shrugged: S. Fuji, H. Oda, S.
Desaki, M. Maeoka, A. Kondo
interviews
PAGE 366
mindless hysteria.": Paton; V. F.
Weisskopf, L. H. Hempelmann,
I. I. Rabi, E. Grothus, H. A.
Bethe, P. Olum interviews

Bibliography

Abelson, Philip H. "A Sport Played by Graduate Students," *Bulletin of the Atomic Scientists,* May 1974, pp. 48–52

Agnew, Harold M. "Early Impressions," *Bulletin of the Atomic Scientists,* December 1982, pp. 20–1

Alperovitz, Gar. *Atomic Diplomacy: Hiroshima and Potsdam* (New York: Simon and Schuster, 1965)

Alsop, Stewart, and Ralph E. Lapp. "The Strange Death of Louis Slotin," *Saturday Evening Post,* March 6, 1954

Alvarez, Luis W. "Berkeley: A Lab Like No Other," *Science and Public Affairs,* April 1974, pp. 18–23

———. *Ernest Orlando Lawrence, 1901–1958* (New York: Columbia University Press, paperback, 1970); Oral History, 1967, American Institute of Physics, New York

Anders, Roger M. "The Rosenberg Case Revisited: The Greenglass Testimony and the Protection of Atomic Secrets," *American Historical Review,* April 1978, pp. 388–400

Anderson, Herbert L. "Fermi, Szilard and Trinity," *Bulletin of the Atomic Scientists,* October 1974, pp. 40–7

Araki, Takeshi. "Public/Private Cooperation in Renewing Cities—The Rebirth of Hiroshima." Address at Japan-America Conference of Mayors and Chamber of Commerce Presidents, November 11, 1981, San Diego

Bainbridge, Kenneth T. "Prelude to Trinity," *Bulletin of the Atomic Scientists,* April 1975, pp. 42–6

———. "A Foul and Awesome Display," *Bulletin of the Atomic Scientists,* May 1975, pp. 40–6; Oral History, September 8, 1960, American Institute of Physics, New York

Baker, Liva. *Felix Frankfurter* (New York: Coward-McCann, 1969)

Baldwin, Hanson W. "The Strategic Need for the Bomb Question," in Paul R. Baker, ed., *The Atomic Bomb: The Great Decision* (New York: Holt Rinehart, 1968)

Bard, Ralph A. "War Was Really Won Before We Used A-Bomb," *U. S. News and World Report,* August 15, 1960, pp. 73–5

Barnaby, Frank. "The Effects of a Global Nuclear War: The Arsenals," *AMBIO* 11:2–3 (1982), pp. 76–83

Day One

Barnouw, Erik. "Columbia and the A-Bomb Film," *Columbia,* November 1982, pp. 13–5+

Batchelder, Robert C. *The Irreversible Decision* (New York: Macmillan, 1961)

Baxter, James Phinney III. *Scientists Against Time* (Cambridge, Mass.: MIT Press, 1968)

Berninger, Ernst H., ed. *Otto Hahn in Selbstzeugnissen und Bilddokumenten* (Hamburg: Rowohlt)

Bernstein, Barton J. "Doomsday II," *New York Times Magazine,* July 27, 1975, pp. 21+

———. "In the Matter of J. Robert Oppenheimer," *Historical Studies in the Physical Sciences* 12: Part 2 (1982), pp. 195–252

———. "Unraveling a Mystery: American POW's Killed at Hiroshima," *Foreign Service Journal,* October 1979, pp. 17–9+

———, ed. *The Atomic Bomb: The Critical Issues* (Boston: Little, Brown, 1976)

Bernstein, Barton J., and Allen J. Matusow. *The A-Bomb Decision in the Truman Administration, a Documentary History* (New York: Harper, 1966)

Bernstein, Jeremy. "I. I. Rabi" (profile), *New Yorker,* October 20, 1975, pp. 47–50.

Bethe, Hans A. "Comments on the History of the H-Bomb," *Los Alamos Science,* Fall 1982, pp. 43–53; Oral History, October 1966, American Institute of Physics, New York

Blumberg, Stanley A., and Gwinn Owens. *Energy and Conflict: The Life and Times of Edward Teller* (New York: Putnam, 1976)

Boffey, Philip M. "Radiation Risk May Be Higher than Thought," *New York Times,* July 26, 1983, pp. C1–2

Boston Globe. "Hiroshima Footnote: How Two Americans Died," by Charles L. Whipple, November 3, 1975, pp. 1+

Brode, Bernice. "Tales of Los Alamos," in Badash, Hirschfelder, Broida, eds., *Reminiscences of Los Alamos 1943–1945* (Boston: Reidel, 1980), pp. 133–59

Brooks, Lester. *Behind Japan's Surrender* (New York: McGraw-Hill, 1968)

Brown, Anthony Cave, and Charles B. Macdonald, eds. *The Secret History of the Atomic Bomb* (New York: Delta, 1977)

Brown, Richard H., and Van R. Halsey, eds. *Hiroshima, A Study in Science, Politics and the Ethics of War* (Menlo Park, Calif.: Addison-Wesley, 1970)

Bruckner, D. J. R. "The Day the Nuclear Age Was Born," *New York Times,* November 30, 1982, pp. C1–2

Buck, Pearl S. "The Bomb—Did We Have to Drop It?" *American Weekly,* March 8, 15, 22, 1959

Burchett, Wilfred. *At the Barricades* (New York: Times Books, 1981)

Burns, John F. "Comments by Soviet Marshal Point Up Public's War Jitters," *New York Times,* December 11, 1983, pp. 1+

Bush, Vannevar. *Pieces of the Action* (New York: Morrow, 1970)

Butow, Robert J. C. *Japan's Decision to Surrender* (Stanford, Calif.: Stanford University Press, paperback, 1954)

Byrnes, James F. *Speaking Frankly* (New York: Harper, 1947)

———. "We Were Anxious to Get the War Over," *U.S. News and World Report,* August 15, 1960, pp. 65–7

Cahn, Robert. "Behind the First A-Bomb," *Saturday Evening Post,* July 16, 1960, pp. 16+

Caldicott, Helen. *Nuclear Madness—What You Can Do* (New York: Bantam, 1980)

Cary, Otis. *Mr. Stimson's "Pet" City—The Sparing of Kyoto, 1945* (Kyoto: Doshisha University, Moonlight Series No. 3, December 1975)

Bibliography

Childs, Herbert. *An American Genius* (Ernest O. Lawrence) (New York: Dutton, 1968)

Church, Fermor, and Peggy Pond. *When Los Alamos Was a Ranch School* (Los Alamos, N. M.: Los Alamos Historical Society, 1974)

Clark, Ronald W. *Einstein: The Life and Times* (New York: Avon, paperback, 1971)

Cochran, Thomas B., et al. *Nuclear Weapons Datebook, Vol. I: U.S. Nuclear Forces and Capabilities* (Boston: Ballinger, 1984)

Coerr, Eleanor. *Sadako and the Thousand Paper Cranes* (New York: Putnam, 1977)

Cohen, Karl P. "Harold C. Urey, The War Years: 1939–1944." Contribution to biography in preparation by Professor Cohen, March 1983, Palo Alto, Calif.

Cohen, Sam. *The Truth about the Neutron Bomb* (New York: Morrow, 1983)

Cole, K. C. "Victor Weisskopf: Living for Beethoven and Quantum Mechanics," *Discover,* June 1983, pp. 48–54

Committee for the Compilation of Materials on Damage Caused by the Atomic Bombs in Hiroshima and Nagasaki. *Hiroshima and Nagasaki* (New York: Basic Books, 1981)

Compton, Arthur H. *Atomic Quest* (New York: Oxford, 1956)

———. Memo to K. D. Nichols re Szilard interview with J. Byrnes, June 4, 1945. MED File, Miscellaneous Reds, Folder 4, National Archives, RG 77

Conant, James B. *My Several Lives* (New York: Harper, 1970)

Cousins, Norman. "Hiroshima—Four Years Later," *Saturday Review,* September 17, 1949, pp. 8–10+

———. *Present Tense* (New York: McGraw-Hill, 1967)

Cox, Meg. "Art as Warning: The Unforgettable Fire," *Wall Street Journal,* August 27, 1982, p. 17

Craig, William. *The Fall of Japan* (New York: Dial Press, 1967)

Davis, Nuel Pharr. *Lawrence and Oppenheimer* (New York: Simon and Schuster, 1968)

Donovan, Robert J. *Conflict and Crisis* (New York: Norton, 1977)

Dower, J. W. "Science, Society, and the Japanese Atomic-Bomb Project During World War II," *Bulletin of Concerned Asian Scholars,* April–June, 1978, pp. 41–54

Dudley, John H. "Ranch School to Secret City," in Badash, Hirschfelder, Broida, eds., *Reminiscences of Los Alamos 1943–1945* (Boston: Reidel, 1980), pp. 1–11

Dyson, Freeman. *Disturbing the Universe* (New York: Harper, 1979)

———. "Reflections: Weapons and Hope," *New Yorker,* February 6, 1984, pp. 52–4, February 13, pp. 67–8, February 20, pp. 52–6, February 27, pp. 54–6

Eisenhower, Dwight D. *Crusade in Europe* (New York: Doubleday, 1948)

Else, Jon (producer and director). *"The Day After Trinity"* (film script), 1978. Distributed by Pyramid Films, Santa Monica, Calif.

English Department, Hiroshima Jogakuin High School, editor. *Summer Cloud, A-Bomb Experience of a Girls' School in Hiroshima* (Tokyo: San-Yu-Sha, undated)

Erskine, Hazel Gaudet. "The Polls: Atomic Weapons and Nuclear Energy," *Public Opinion Quarterly* 27 (Summer 1963), pp. 155–90

Fabin, Sky. *How Well We Meant* (transcript of 28-minute video documentary) (Immediate Family Productions: Santa Fe, N. M., 1983)

Feis, Herbert. *Between War and Peace: The Potsdam Conference* (Princeton: Princeton University Press, 1960)

Fermi, Enrico. My Observations During the Explosion at Trinity on July 16, 1945, Trinity Test Reports, File 319.1, National Archives

Fermi, Laura. *Atoms in the Family* (Chicago: University of Chicago Press, 1954)

Ferrell, Robert H., ed. *Off the Record: The Private Papers of Harry S. Truman* (New York: Penguin, paperback, 1980)

Feynman, Richard P. "Los Alamos from Below," in Badash, Hirschfelder, Broida, eds., *Reminiscences of Los Alamos 1943–1945* (Boston: Reidel, 1980), pp. 105–32

Finch, Stuart C. Hiroshima: "Immediate and Long-Range Medical Effects," in *Proceedings of the Symposium: The Role of the Academy in Addressing the Issues of Nuclear War* (Geneva, N.Y.: Hobart and William Smith Colleges, 1982)

———. "Occurrence of Cancer in Atomic Bomb Survivors," in Ruth Adams and Susan Cullen, eds., *The Final Epidemic* (Chicago: Educational Foundation for Nuclear Science, 1981)

Finch, Stuart C., and Iwao M. Moriyama. *The Delayed Effects of Radiation Exposure among Atomic Bomb Survivors, Hiroshima and Nagasaki, 1945–79* (Hiroshima: Radiation Effects Research Foundation, Technical Report TR 16–78, 1980)

Finney, Nat S. "How FDR Planned to Use the A-Bomb," *Look* 14:6 (March 14, 1950), pp. 23–7

Fleming, John A. "The Fifth Washington Conference on Theoretical Physics," *Scientific Monthly* XLVIII (March 1939), pp. 278–82

Forsberg, Randall. "A Bilateral Nuclear-Weapon Freeze," *Scientific American* 247:5 (November 1982), pp. 52–61

Frankfurter, Felix. Strictly Private S-1 File, Dr. Niels Bohr #19, National Archives

Friendly, Alfred. "New Age Within Grasp," *Washington Post,* March 20–March 27, 1946 (eight articles)

Frisch, Otto R. "How It All Began," *Physics Today,* November 1967, pp. 43–8

———. *Lise Meitner, 1878–1968.* Biographical Memoirs of Fellows of the Royal Society (London) 16 (1970), pp. 405–19; Oral History, May 1967, American Institute of Physics, New York

———. "Somebody Turned the Sun on with a Switch," *Science and Public Affairs,* April 1974, pp. 12–8

———. *What Little I Remember* (Cambridge, England: Cambridge University Press, 1979)

Gallup, George H. *The Gallup Poll: Public Opinion, 1935–1971* (New York: Random, 1971)

Gannon, William, ed. *The Effects of the Atomic Bombs on Hiroshima and Nagasaki, by The United States Strategic Bombing Survey* (Santa Fe: Gannon, 1973)

Geiger, H. Jack. "Illusion of Survival," in Ruth Adams and Susan Cullen, eds., *The Final Epidemic* (Chicago: Educational Foundation for Nuclear Science, 1981)

General Headquarters, United States Army Forces, Pacific, Public Relations Office. "U.S. Troops Destroy Jap Atomic Research Equipment" (press release), Tokyo, November 23, 1945

Gigon, Fernand. *Formula for Death* (New York: Roy, 1958)

Giovannitti, Len, and Fred Freed. *The Decision to Drop the Bomb* (New York: Coward-McCann, 1965)

Gofman, John W. *Radiation and Human Health* (San Francisco: Sierra Club, 1981)

Golovin, I. N. *I. V. Kurchatov* (Bloomington, Ind.: Selbstverlag Press, n.d.)

Goodchild, Peter. *J. Robert Oppenheimer, Shatterer of Worlds* (Boston: Houghton Mifflin, 1981)

Goudsmit, Samuel A. *Alsos* (New York: Schuman, 1947)

Bibliography

Gowing, Margaret. *Britain and Atomic Energy 1939–1945* (New York: St. Martin's, 1964)

Greenglass, David. Testimony quoted in "The Case of Morton Sobell: New Queries from the Defense," *Science,* September 1966, pp. 1501–5

Groueff, Stephane. *Manhattan Project* (Boston: Little, Brown, 1967)

Groves, Leslie R. Transcript of telephone conversations with Oppenheimer re Hiroshima, August 6, 1945; Groves 201, Telephone Conversations, RG 77, National Archives

———. Memorandum, Groves to Chief of Staff, 24 August 1945, "casualties from radiation unlikely," Folder 5B Top Secret Manhattan Project File, 1942–1946, National Archives

———. Memorandum of telephone conversation with Lt. Col. Rea, August 25, 1945, courtesy Barton J. Bernstein

———. Telephone conversation with George Kistiakowsky, August 25, 1945, re "hoax" of Japanese radiation broadcasts, Groves Top Secret Files, National Archives

———. Memorandum, Groves to District Engineer, Washington, July 8, 1946, EIDM-WL-26, National Archives; recommendation against military decoration for Leo Szilard

———. Testimony Before Hearings, Special Committee on Atomic Energy, U.S. Senate, 79th Congress, Part 5, November 28–29, 1945, pp. 32–71

———. *Now It Can Be Told* (New York: Harper, 1962)

Haberman, Clyde. "August in Japan: Hiroshima, Nagasaki and Baseball," *New York Times,* August 10, 1983, p. A2

———. "For Japan, 'Day After' Is No Match for Hiroshima," *New York Times,* January 6, 1984, p. A2

———. "Where the Atomic Age Began Life Is Workaday," *New York Times,* February 7, 1984, p. A2

Hachiya, Michihiko. *Hiroshima Diary.* Translated and edited by Warner Wells (Chapel Hill: University of North Carolina Press, 1955)

Hahn, Dietrich, ed. *Otto Hahn—Begruender des Atomzeitalters* (Munich: List)

Hahn, Otto. *Otto Hahn: My Life* (New York: Herder and Herder, 1970)

Hamai, Shinzo. *Mayor of the Atom-Bombed City* (Tokyo: Asahi Shinbun, 1967). In Japanese only.

Hamatani, Masaharu. "Research Approach to a Comprehensive Study of the Long-Term Human Effects of the Atomic Bomb," *Hitotsubashi Journal of Social Studies,* 13:1 (November 1981)

Hatfield, Mark O. *Between a Rock and a Hard Place* (Waco, Texas: Word Books, 1976)

Hawkins, David. *Project Y: The Los Alamos Story* (Los Angeles: Tomash, 1983)

Heisenberg, Werner. *Physics and Beyond* (New York: Harper, 1971)

Hellman, Geoffrey T. "The Contemporaneous Memoranda of Dr. Sachs," *New Yorker,* December 1, 1945, pp. 73–80

Hempelmann, Louis H., et al. "The Acute Radiation Syndrome: A Study of Nine Cases and a Review of the Problem," *Annals of Internal Medicine* 36:2 (February 1952), pp. 279–510

———. *A Twenty-Seven-Year Study of Selected Los Alamos Plutonium Workers* (Los Alamos: Los Alamos Scientific Laboratory, 1973)

Hendrix, Kathleen. "Hiroshima Survivor Feels Mission to Work for Peace" (Shigeko Sasamori), *Los Angeles Times,* December 1, 1982

Herken, Gregg. *The Winning Weapon* (New York: Knopf, 1980)

Hermann, Armin. *Werner Heisenberg, 1901–1975* (Bonn: Inter Nationes, 1976)

———. *The New Physics* (Munich: Heinz Moos, 1979)

Hersey, John. *Hiroshima* (New York: Bantam, paperback, 1946)

Hewlett, Richard G., and Oscar E. Anderson, Jr. *The New World, 1939/1946* (University Park, Penna.: Pennsylvania State University Press, 1962)

Hiebert, Erwin N. *The Impact of Atomic Energy* (Newton, Kans.: Faith and Life Press, 1961)

Hilts, Philip J. *Scientific Temperaments* (New York: Simon and Schuster, 1982)

Hirschfelder, Joseph. "The Scientific and Technological Miracle at Los Alamos," in Badash, Hirschfelder, Broida, eds., *Reminiscences of Los Alamos 1943–1945* (Boston: Reidel, 1980), pp. 67–88

Hoffmann, Frederic de. "Pure Science in the Service of Wartime Technology," *Bulletin of the Atomic Scientists,* January 1975

Holloway, David. *The Soviet Union and the Arms Race* (New Haven: Yale University Press, 1983)

Hyde, Montgomery. *The Atom Bomb Spies* (New York: Ballantine Books, paperback, 1980)

Ibuse, Masuji. *Black Rain* (novel) (Tokyo: Kodansha, paperback, 1969)

Imahori, Seiji, et al. *Hiroshima Steps Toward Peace.* Translated by Barbara Reynolds and Hiromasa Hanabusa (Hiroshima: Hiroshima Peace Culture Center, 1969)

International Radiation Research and Training Institute (IRRTI). "The Irradiation of Personnel During Operation Crossroads: An Evaluation Based on Official Documents, by Arjun Makhijani and David Albright"; Washington, May 1983, presented before House Veterans Affairs Committee, Washington, May 24, 1983

Irving, David. *The German Atomic Bomb* (New York: Simon and Schuster, 1967)

Ishida, Tadashi, ed. *A Call from Hiroshima and Nagasaki—Interim Reports of Hibakusha Surveys,* pp. 227–37 (Mrs. Sakae Ito) (Tokyo: Japan National Preparatory Committee, 1977)

Jablon, Seymour. "The Origin and Findings of the Atomic Bomb Casualty Commission," *Nuclear Safety,* 14:6 (November–December, 1973)

Jaffe, Susan. "Why the Bomb Didn't Hit Home," *Nuclear Times,* March 1983, pp. 10–5

Janis, Irving L. *Psychological Effects of the Atomic Attack on Japan* (Santa Monica: Rand, 1960)

————. *Victims of Groupthink* (Boston: Houghton Mifflin, 1972)

Japan Broadcasting Corporation (NHK), ed. *Unforgettable Fire* (New York: Pantheon, 1977)

Japan Radiation Research Society. "A Review of Thirty Years Study of Hiroshima and Nagasaki Atomic Bomb Survivors," Vol. 16 Suppl. (Chiba, Japan, September 1975)

Japanese Atomic Bomb Survivors (*Hibakusha*) writings of and about

Akiba, Tadatoshi. "Understanding Hibakusha," *Our World* 31:1 (1979), pp. 6–7

Francia, Luis H. "Hibakushas: Victims Then, Victims Now," *Village Voice,* January 18, 1983

Iwata, Eddie. "A-Bomb Survivors in U.S.," *Los Angeles Times,* p. I2, June 8, 1981

MacClarin, Wanda. "I'm One of the Lucky Ones," *Oakland Tribune/Today,* August 6, 1981

McConahay, Mary Jo. "First Person Nuclear," *Northern California Journal,* January 1983, pp. 43–7

Nakahara, Liz. "The Bomb and the Remembering," *Washington Post,* August 6, 1981, pp. C1+

National Committee for Atomic Bomb Survivors in the United States. *Amer-*

Bibliography

ican Atomic Bomb Survivors (San Francisco: Committee of Atomic Bomb Survivors in the United States of America, n.d.)

Perlman, David. "Japan A-Bombs Still Plague S.F. Survivors," *San Francisco Chronicle,* May 9, 1981, p. 32

Rockey, Linda. "A 'Survivor of the Light' Recalls Hiroshima Horror," *Seattle Post-Intelligencer,* May 22, 1981

Stroup, Dorothy A. "In the Shadow of Hiroshima," *San Francisco Sunday Examiner & Chronicle/California Living,* August 13, 1978, pp. 6–12

Tatsuno, Sheridan. "U.S. Refuses to Help Victims of Hiroshima and Nagasaki," *San Jose Mercury,* August 6, 1979

Vobejda, Barbara. "Team Here to Treat Blast Survivors," *Honolulu Advertiser,* May 26, 1981, p. A6

Jette, Eleanor. *Inside Box 1663* (Los Alamos, N. M.: Los Alamos Historical Society, paperback, 1977)

Jungk, Robert. *Brighter Than a Thousand Suns* (New York: Harcourt, 1958)

———. *Strahlen aus der Asche* (Bern: Scherz, 1959)

Junod, Marcel. *Warrior Without Weapons* (New York: MacMillan, 1951)

Kamidoi, Isoko. "Eyewitness on the Aioi Bridge," in *Burned by the Pika* (Hiroshima: Medical Cooperative of Hiroshima, 1978)

Kennedy, Edward M. Nuclear Freeze and Reductions Forum, U.S. Senate. Transcript of Hearings, March 22, 1982, Washington, pp. 1–139

Kennedy, Edward M., and Mark O. Hatfield. *Freeze!* (New York, Bantam, paperback, 1982)

Kevles, Daniel J. *The Physicists* (New York: Knopf, 1977)

Kistiakowsky, George B. "Reminiscences of War-Time Los Alamos," in Badash, Hirschfelder, Broida, eds., *Reminiscences of Los Alamos 1943–1945* (Boston: Reidel, 1980), pp. 49–65

Knebel, Fletcher, and Charles W. Bailey II. *No High Ground* (New York: Harper, 1960)

———. "Secret Revealed After 18 Years: The Fight Over the A-Bomb," *Look,* August 13, 1960, pp. 19–23

Kosakai, Yoshiteru. *Hiroshima Peace Reader* (Hiroshima: Hiroshima Peace Culture Foundation, 1980)

Kramish, Arnold. *Atomic Energy in the Soviet Union* (Stanford: Stanford University Press, 1959)

Kunetka, James W. *City of Fire* (Englewood Cliffs, N. J.: Prentice-Hall, 1979)

———. *Oppenheimer, the Years of Risk* (Englewood Cliffs, N. J.: Prentice-Hall, 1982)

Lamont, Lansing. *Day of Trinity* (New York: Atheneum, 1965)

Lang, Daniel. *From Hiroshima to the Moon* (New York: Simon and Schuster, 1959)

———. "The Top Top Secret" (A Reporter At Large), *New Yorker,* October 27, 1945, pp. 54–69

Lapp, Ralph E. *Atoms and People* (New York: Harper, 1956)

———. "The Einstein Letter that Started It All," *New York Times Magazine,* August 2, 1964, pp. 13+

———. *The New Priesthood* (New York: Harper, 1965)

Laurence, William L. *Dawn Over Zero* (New York: Knopf, 1946)

———. "Atom Bomb Designers Bet in '45 it Would Fizzle," *New York Times,* July 29, 1951

———. "An Historic Eyewitness Report on the Early Development and Testing of the A-Bomb," in *Hiroshima Plus 20* (New York: Delacorte, 1965), pp. 161–211

———. "Would You Make the Bomb Again?" *New York Times Magazine,* August 1, 1965, pp. 8+

Day One

Lawrence, Ernest O. Correspondence between Lawrence and Dr. Karl K. Darrow, re A-bomb demonstration option, August 1945, Bancroft Library, University of California, Berkeley

Lawrence, William H. "The Second New York Times Report of the Hiroshima Blast," in *Hiroshima Plus 20* (New York: Delacorte, 1965), pp. 155–60

———. "Visit to Hiroshima Proves It World's Most-Damaged City," *New York Times,* September 5, 1945, pp. 1+

Leahy, William D. *I Was There* (New York: Whittlesey House, 1950)

Libby, Leona Marshall. *The Uranium People* (New York: Crane Russak/Scribner, 1979)

Liebow, Averill A. *Encounter with Disaster* (New York: Norton, 1970)

Lifton, Betty Jean. "A Thousand Cranes," *Horn Book Magazine,* April 1963, pp. 211–7

Lifton, Betty Jean, and Eikoh Hosoe. *Return to Hiroshima* (New York: Kodansha, 1984, re-issue)

Lifton, Robert Jay. "Beyond Nuclear Numbing: A Call to Teach and Learn," in *Proceedings of the Symposium: The Role of the Academy in Addressing the Issues of Nuclear War* (Geneva, N.Y.: Hobart and William Smith Colleges, 1982)

———. *Death in Life* (New York: Random, 1967)

Linschitz, Henry. Deposition re David Greenglass, State of Massachusetts, County of Middlesex, United States versus Morton Sobell, August 17, 1966, unpublished

Los Alamos National Laboratory. The First Forty Years, brochure (Los Alamos, N. M.: Los Alamos National Laboratory, 1983), pp. 1–16

Los Alamos National Laboratory Fortieth Anniversary Reunion. Statement of Wartime Scientists. "Frightened for the Future of Humanity," *New York Times,* April 24, 1983, p. E21

Los Alamos Science 4:7 (Winter/Spring 1983), "The Evolution of the Laboratory"

Luft, Joseph, and W. M. Wheeler. "Reaction to John Hersey's 'Hiroshima,'" *Journal of Social Psychology,* August 1948, pp. 135–40

Manchester, William. *American Caesar* (Boston: Little, Brown, 1978)

Manley, John H. "Assembling the Wartime Labs," *Bulletin of the Atomic Scientists,* May 1974, pp. 42–8

———. "A New Laboratory is Born," in Badash, Hirschfelder, Broida, eds., *Reminiscences of Los Alamos 1943–1945* (Boston: Reidel, 1980), pp. 21–39

Margolick, David. "Law Panel Sees Atom Arms as Illegal," *New York Times,* June 7, 1982, p. B2

Mark, J. Carson. "Nuclear Weapons: Characteristics and Capabilities," in Ruth Adams and Susan Cullen, eds., *The Final Epidemic* (Chicago: Educational Foundation for Nuclear Science, 1981)

Marks, John. *The Search for the Manchurian Candidate* (New York: McGraw-Hill, 1980)

Marx, Joseph L. *Seven Hours to Zero* (New York: Putnam, 1967)

McMillan, Edwin M. "Early Days at Los Alamos," in Badash, Hirschfelder, Broida, eds., *Reminiscences of Los Alamos 1943–1945* (Boston: Reidel, 1980), pp. 13–9; Oral History, October 1972, American Institute of Physics, New York

McMillan, Elsie. "Outside the Inner Fence," in Badash, Hirschfelder, Broida, eds., *Reminiscences of Los Alamos 1943–1945* (Boston: Reidel, 1980), pp. 41–7

Mee, Charles L., Jr. *Meeting at Potsdam* (New York: Evans, 1975)

Meitner, Lise. "Looking Back," *Bulletin of the Atomic Scientists,* November 1963, pp. 2–7

Bibliography

Melanson, Philip H. "The Human Guinea Pigs at Bikini," *Nation,* July 9–16, 1983, pp. 33+

Mendelsohn, Everett. "The Historian Confronts the Bomb," in *Proceedings of the Symposium: The Role of the Academy in Addressing the Issues of Nuclear War* (Geneva, N.Y.: Hobart and William Smith Colleges, 1982)

Menninger, Karl. "The Suicidal Intention of Nuclear Armament," *Bulletin of the Menninger Clinic,* 47:4, 1983, pp. 325–53

Meyrowitz, Elliott L. "Are Nuclear Weapons Legal?," *Bulletin of the Atomic Scientists,* October 1983, pp. 49–52

Miller, Merle, and Abe Spitzer. *We Dropped the A-Bomb* (New York: Putnam, 1974)

Moore, Ruth. *Niels Bohr* (New York: Knopf, 1966)

Morehead, Alan. *The Traitors* (New York: Harper, 1952)

Morison, Elting E. *Turmoil and Tradition—A Study of the Life and Times of Henry L. Stimson* (Boston: Houghton Mifflin, 1960)

Morrison, Philip. Testimony, Special Committee on Atomic Energy, U.S. Senate, December 6, 1945, Part V, pp. 233–51; Oral History, February 1967, American Institute of Physics, New York

Morton, Louis. *The Decision to Use the Atomic Bomb in Command Decisions.* Edited by Kent Roberts Greenfield, Office of the Chief of Military History (Washington: U.S. Army, 1960)

Murphy, Bruce Allen. *The Brandeis/Frankfurter Connection* (New York: Oxford, 1982)

Naeve, Virginia, editor. *Friends of the Hibakusha* (Denver: Alan Swallow, 1964)

Nelson, Steve. *Steve Nelson, American Radical* (Pittsburgh: University of Pittsburgh Press, 1981)

———. Transcript of telephone conversation with "Joe" re Oppenheimer political background, in "Investigative" file, Leslie Groves Top Secret Papers, 1942–1943 (John Lansdale), National Archives

Nishina Memorial Foundation, ed. *The Atomic Bombs* (Tokyo: Kofusha Shoten, 1973)

Nizer, Louis. *The Implosion Conspiracy* (Garden City, N.Y.: Doubleday, 1973)

Oe, Kenzaburo. *Hiroshima Notes* (Tokyo: YMCA Press, 1981)

O'Keefe, Bernard J. *The Nuclear Hostages* (Boston: Houghton Mifflin, 1983)

Oliphant, M. E. L. "The Beginning: Chadwick and the Neutron," *Bulletin of the Atomic Scientists,* December 1982, pp. 14–7

———. Communications to the author, April 13, June 17, 1983

Oppenheimer, J. Robert. *Letters and Recollections,* see Smith, Alice Kimball

———. Security Hearings, see U.S. Atomic Energy Commission

Osada, Arata. *Children of the A-Bomb* (New York: Putnam, 1963)

Oughterson, Ashley W., and Shields Warren. *Medical Effects of the Atomic Bomb in Japan* (New York: McGraw-Hill, 1956)

Pacific War Research Society. *The Day Man Lost* (Tokyo: Kodansha, paperback, 1981), in English

———. *Japan's Longest Day* (Tokyo: Kodansha, paperback, 1968), in English

Paton, Dean. "Torment of an Honored Scientist" (Seth Neddermeyer), *Boston Globe,* April 27, 1983

Penney, William G. (Lord). Communications to the author, April 8, April 26, May 16, 1983

Penney, William G. (Lord), et al. *The Nuclear Explosive Yields at Hiroshima and Nagasaki* (London: Royal Society of London Philosophical Transactions, vol. 266, A.1177, 11 June, 1970), pp. 357–424

Peterson, Iver. "G. I. Deaths in Hiroshima A-Blast Reported," *New York Times,* August 23, 1979, p. 11

Poen, Monte M., ed. *Strictly Personal and Confidential—The Letters Harry Truman Never Mailed* (Boston: Little, Brown, 1982)

Powers, Thomas. *Thinking About the Next War* (New York: New American Library, paperback, 1982)

———. "Seeing the Light of Armageddon," *Rolling Stone,* April 29, 1982

Rabi, Isidor I. *Science: The Center of Culture* (New York: New American Library, 1970)

———, ed. *Oppenheimer* (New York: Scribner, 1969)

Rabinowitch, Eugene. "James Franck and Leo Szilard," *Bulletin of the Atomic Scientists,* October 1964, pp. 16–17+

Ramsey, Norman F. Oral History, July 1960, Columbia University Oral History Project

Reynolds, Earle. *The Forbidden Voyage* (New York: McKay, 1961)

Rosenthal, A. M. "Hiroshima Today," in *Hiroshima Plus 20* (New York: Delacorte, 1965)

Sachs, Alexander. "Early History, Atomic Project in Relation to President Roosevelt, 1939–1940" (unpublished MS), written August 8–9, 1945

———. Testimony, Special Committee on Atomic Energy, U.S. Senate, 79th Congress, Second Session, Part 5, February 15, 1946, pp. 553–73

Sagan, Carl. "The Nuclear Winter," *Parade,* October 30, 1983, pp. 4–7

Sagan, Carl, et al. "Nuclear Winter: Global Consequences of Multiple Nuclear Explosions," *Science,* December 1983, pp. 1283–1300

Sanders, David. *John Hersey* (New York: Twayne, 1967)

Schell, Jonathan. *The Fate of the Earth* (New York: Knopf, 1982)

Schlender, Brenton R. "Lacking an Emergency to Mobilize Around, Los Alamos Falters," *Wall Street Journal,* September 30, 1982, pp. 1+

Schoenberger, Walter Smith. *Decision of Destiny* (Columbus: Ohio University Press, 1969)

Serber, Robert. "The Early Years," see Rabi, I. *Oppenheimer*

Sherwin, Martin J. *A World Destroyed* (New York: Knopf, 1975)

Shimizu, Sakae. "Historical Sketch of the Scientific Field Survey in Hiroshima Several Days After the Atomic Bombing," *Bulletin of the Institute for Chemical Research* (Kyoto University) 60:2, 1982

Siemes, Father P. Eyewitness Account (Hiroshima), September 1945, Groves Top Secret Files, National Archives

Smith, Alice Kimball. "The Elusive Dr. Szilard," *Harper's,* July 1960, pp. 77–86

———. "Los Alamos: Focus of an Age," *Bulletin of the Atomic Scientists,* June 1970, pp. 15–20

———. *A Peril and a Hope* (Chicago: University of Chicago Press, 1965)

Smith, Alice Kimball, and Charles Weiner, eds. *Robert Oppenheimer, Letters and Recollections* (Cambridge, Mass.: Harvard University Press, 1980)

Smith, Cyril. "Some Recollections of Metallurgy at Los Alamos, 1943–5," *Journal of Nuclear Materials 100* (1981), pp. 3–10

Smyth, Henry DeWolf. *Atomic Energy* (The Smyth Report) (Washington: Government Printing Office, 1945)

Spitzer, Abe. See Miller, Merle

Steinberg, Rafael. *Postscript from Hiroshima* (New York: Random, 1966)

Stern, Philip M. *The Oppenheimer Case: Security on Trial* (New York: Harper, 1969)

Stimson, Henry L. "The Decision to Use the Atomic Bomb," *Harper's,* February 1947

———. Diary, May 1945–August 1945 (unpublished MS). Sterling Memorial Library, Yale University, New Haven, Conn.

Stimson, Henry L., and McGeorge Bundy, *On Active Service in Peace and War* (New York: Harper, 1948)

Bibliography

Strauss, Lewis L. "I Proposed Bombing an Uninhabited Area," *U.S. News and World Report*, August 15, 1960, pp. 71–3
———. *Men and Decisions* (Garden City, N.Y.: Doubleday, 1962)
Sutherland, John P. "The Story General Marshall Told Me," *U.S. News and World Report*, November 2, 1959, pp. 50–6
Szilard, Leo. U.S. Army, G-2 Report, to ACS, War Plans Division, Washington, October 1, 1940, Groves Top Secret Files, National Archives
———. Officer in Charge, CIC, surveillance report re Leo Szilard, Washington, June 24, 1943, 12 pp., Groves Top Secret Files, National Archives
———. Intelligence and Security Division. Manhattan District, Investigative Report, 1942–1945, Washington, March 12, 1945
———. "Top Secret" biographical sketch, War Department, June 1, 1945; Folder #12, Intelligence and Security, Groves Top Secret File, National Archives
———. "Truman Did Not Understand," *U.S. News and World Report*, August 15, 1960, pp. 68–9
———. "Are We on the Road to War?," *Congressional Record*, Senate, June 13, 1962, pp. 9565–8
———. *Leo Szilard: His Version of the Facts*, vol. 2. Spencer R. Weart and Gertrude Weiss Szilard, eds. (Cambridge: MIT Press, 1978)
Takayama, Hitoshi, ed. *Hiroshima in Memoriam and Today* (Hiroshima: BIC Co., paperback, 1979)
Target Committee. Notes on meetings, April 27, May 10, May 11, May 28, 1945. Groves Top Secret Files, Folder 5D, RG 77, National Archives
Teller, Edward. Bombing of Hiroshima "Was a Mistake," *U.S. News and World Report*, August 15, 1960, pp. 75–6
———. "Dangerous Myths About Nuclear Arms," *Reader's Digest*, November 1982, pp. 139–44
———. "Reagan's Courage," *New York Times*, March 30, 1983, p. A31
———. "Seven Hours of Reminiscences," *Los Alamos Science*, Winter/Spring 1983, pp. 190–5
Teller, Edward, with Allen Brown. *The Legacy of Hiroshima* (Garden City, N.Y.: Doubleday, 1962)
Thomas, Gordon, and Max Morgan Witts. *Enola Gay* (New York: Pocket Books, paperback, 1977)
Tibbets, Paul W., as told to Wesley Price. "How to Drop an Atom Bomb," *Saturday Evening Post*, June 8, 1946, pp. 134+
Time Magazine, August 9, 1971. "The Unmentioned Victims" (unsigned article about American POW victims of Hiroshima)
Toland, John. *The Rising Sun* (New York: Bantam, paperback, 1971)
Toyoda, Toshiyuki. "Scientists Look at Peace and Security," *Bulletin of the Atomic Scientists*, February 1984, pp. 16–31
Truman, Harry S. *Year of Decisions* (Garden City, N.Y.: Doubleday, 1955)
Trumbull, Robert. *Nine Who Survived Hiroshima and Nagasaki* (New York: Dutton, 1957)
Truslow, Edith C. *Manhattan District History—Nonscientific Aspects of Los Alamos Project Y, 1942–1946* (Los Alamos: Manhattan Engineer District History, no date)
Tuve, Merle. Oral history, May 1967, American Institute of Physics, New York
Ulam, Stanislaw M. *Adventures of a Mathematician* (New York: Scribner's, 1976)
Ulam, Stanislaw M., et al. "John von Neumann, 1903–1957," in *Perspectives in American History*, vol. II, 1968. Cambridge, Mass.: Charles Warren Center for Studies in American History
Ungar, Sanford J. "An American's Discomfort in Hiroshima," *Washington Post*, August 14, 1983

Day One

U.S. Atomic Energy Commission, Personnel Security Board, "In the Matter of
J. Robert Oppenheimer" (Hearings), Washington 1954
U.S. Strategic Bomb Survey, Reports, Pacific War: No. 3, *The Effects of
Atomic Bombs on Hiroshima and Nagasaki;* No. 13, *The Effects of Atomic
Bombs on Health and Medical Services in Hiroshima and Nagasaki;* No.
60, *The Effects of Air Attack on the City of Hiroshima;* No. 93, *Effects
of the Atomic Bomb on Hiroshima, Japan* (Washington: Government
Printing Office, 1945–1947)
Vallentin, Antonina. *The Drama of Albert Einstein* (New York: Doubleday,
1954)
Warren, Stafford L. Teletype CM-IN-7928, September 10, 1945, Warren to
Groves re Hiroshima radiation injuries, Groves Top Secret Files, National
Archives
————. Memorandum for Groves re safety talks on Bikini tests, October 9,
1946
————. Letter to Dr. William G. Meyers re irradiation of personnel at Bikini
tests, December 31, 1946
————. Memorandum to Admiral W. S. Parsons, re wartime radiation toler-
ances, January 18, 1947
————. *The Role of Radiation in the Development of the Atomic Bomb in
Radiology in World War II.* Edited by Kenneth D. A. Allen, Surgeon
General's Office (Washington: Medical Department of the U. S. Army,
1966), pp. 879–901
Wattenberg, Albert. "The Building of the First Chain Reaction Pile," *Bulletin
of the Atomic Scientists,* June 1974, pp. 51–7
Weart, Spencer R. *Scientists in Power* (Cambridge, Mass.: Harvard University
Press, 1979)
Weiner, Charles. "Retroactive Saber Rattling?," *Bulletin of the Atomic Scien-
tists,* April 1978, pp. 10–2
Weisskopf, Victor F. Banquet Speech at the Fortieth Anniversary Conference
of the Los Alamos National Laboratory, April 15, 1983
————. Autobiographical manuscript in progress; chapter on Los Alamos
Wells, H. G. *The World Set Free* (novel) (New York: Dutton, 1914)
Wigner, Eugene P. "A Conversation with Eugene Wigner," *Science,* August 10,
1973, pp. 527–33
Wilson, Jane. "The End of Youth and Innocence," *Bulletin of the Atomic Sci-
entists,* June 1975, pp. 12–4
Wilson, Robert R. "A Recruit for Los Alamos," *Bulletin of the Atomic Scien-
tists,* March 1975, pp. 41–7
Wolff, Anthony. "Twenty-Five Years with the Bomb—A Conversation with
Nobel-Prize Winner Eugene P. Wigner," *Look,* December 26, 1967, pp.
57–61
Wyden, Peter. "Why Hitler Didn't Drop the A-Bomb," *St. Louis Post-Dispatch,*
August 3, 1952
————. "The Hunt for Hitler's A-Bomb Project," *St. Louis Post-Dispatch,* Au-
gust 4, 1952
Yavenditti, Michael J. "John Hersey and the American Conscience: The Re-
ception of 'Hiroshima,'" *Pacific Historical Review,* October 1974, pp.
24–49
Yuzaki, Minoru. "Community Disorganization and Family Destruction due to
the Atomic Bomb Disaster in Hiroshima." Paper presented at XVIIIth
International Seminar of the Committee on Family Research, Roserberg
Castle, Sweden, June 16–9, 1980

Acknowledgments

To look back on the reconstruction of a record as complex as the one traced in these pages is to realize again one's utter dependence on the knowledge, time, and interminable good will of others—people who, almost without exception, were total strangers until very lately. I have been doing this kind of work for more than forty years, but the kindness of such strangers never fails to amaze and move me.

In the present project, my debt was magnified by my ignorance of physics and of the (to most Americans so abysmally unfamiliar) culture and language of Japan, not to speak of the emotions of people who were subjected to the world's first atomic bombing and, for the most part, had never shared their experiences with a Westerner.

Four specialized hoards of historical treasures were invaluable. At the National Archives in Washington, the sixty-plus bulging boxes containing the top-secret papers of General Groves and allied documents are only part of the feast. Archivist Edward J. Reese guided me through these files and introduced me to other remarkable material.

At the Hiroshima/Nagasaki Memorial Collection of the Wilmington College Peace Resource Center in Wilmington, Ohio, Earl and Helen Redding preside over a library of Japanese literature (in both Japanese and English) that is by far the most complete in the United States. The scope of this material is all but overwhelming and Mrs. Redding was a patient guide. The scientific literature on the effects of the Hiroshima and Nagasaki bombings (thirty-eight pages of fine print) is listed in the Japanese history, *Hiroshima and Nagasaki* (see below).

At the Center for History of Physics of the American Institute of Physics, in New York, Spencer R. Weart gave me access to the extraordinary files of oral histories recorded by just about every American nuclear physicist of historical interest. The Institute's science library operated by John Aubrey (as well as the Kline Library at Yale University) proved indispensable. Louise Hilland was the guide through the API's unique photo library.

At Los Alamos National Laboratory, archivist Alison Kerr supplied nuggets from the veritable ocean of records sequestered by the bomb builders.

The literature on nuclear weapons and Hiroshima is too enormous to be fully mastered by anyone. I did my best. Since I did not wish to drown the

Acknowledgments

text in footnotes, I have provided the most precise possible source notes. Of the books I found useful (see Bibliography), I have drawn on eight in particular. For the pre-Hiroshima period: *The New World,* by Richard G. Hewlett and Oscar E. Anderson, Jr., and *Leo Szilard: His Version of the Facts,* edited by Spencer R. Weart and Gertrude Weiss Szilard. For the efforts of the American scientists: *J. Robert Oppenheimer, Shatterer of Worlds,* by Peter Goodchild. For military aspects: *Now It Can be Told,* by Leslie R. Groves, and *Enola Gay,* by Gordon Thomas and Max Morgan Witts. For Hiroshima after the bombing: *Death in Life,* by Robert Jay Lifton, M.D., *The Day Man Lost,* by the Pacific War Research Society, and the exhaustive compilation *Hiroshima and Nagasaki,* by a group of Japanese scholars, the Committee for the Compilation of Materials on Damage Caused by the Atomic Bombs in Hiroshima and Nagasaki, published in Japan in 1979 and in the United States in 1981.

Historians who provided unique insights or data included Roger M. Anders, U.S. Department of Energy; Lawrence Badash, University of California (Santa Barbara); David Bradley, M.D., author of *No Place to Hide;* Barton J. Bernstein, Stanford University; Robert J. Donovan, historian of the Truman era; Lillian Hoddeson, University of Illinois; Vincent Jones, U.S. Army; Ralph Lapp, consultant on nuclear problems; Forrest C. Pogue, biographer of General George C. Marshall; Martin J. Sherwin, Tufts University; Alice Kimball Smith, historian and Los Alamos alumna; Charles Weiner, Massachusetts Institute of Technology.

My American and British interviewees—most of them scientists who worked at Los Alamos during World War II—included

Abelson, Philip H.	Krohn, Robert D.
*Alvarez, Luis W.	Lansdale, John
Anderson, Herbert L.	Lapp, Ralph E.
Arneson, R. Gordon	Lifton, Robert Jay (M.D.)
Bacher, Robert F.	Linschitz, Henry
Bainbridge, Kenneth T.	Manley, John H.
Barnett, Henry L. (M.D.)	Marks, Anne Wilson
Barnett, Shirley	McCloy, John J.
*Bethe, Hans A.	*McMillan, Edwin M.
Bundy, McGeorge	McMillan, Elsie
Christy, Robert F.	Metropolis, Nicholas
Cohen, Karl	Miller, Robert W. (M.D.)
Cousins, Norman	Montgomery, John D.
Critchfield, Charles L.	Morrison, Philip
Derry, John A.	Nolan, James F. (M.D.)
Dyson, Freeman	Oliphant, Sir M. E. L.
Elsey, George	(correspondence)
Feld, Bernard T.	O'Keefe, Bernard J.
*Feynman, Richard P.	O'Leary, Jean
Finch, Stuart C. (M.D.)	Olum, Paul
Fowler, William	Oppenheimer, Frank
Grothus, Edward	Penney, William G. (Lord)
Groves, Lieutenant General	(correspondence)
Richard	*Rabi, Isidor I.
Hatfield, Sen. Mark O.	Ramsey, Norman F.
Hawkins, David	Reynolds, Barbara
Hempelmann, Louis H. (M.D.)	Rotblat, Josef
Hersey, John	Sams, Crawford J. (M.D.)
Hewlett, Richard G.	Schreiber, Raemer
Higinbotham, William A.	Schull, William J. (correspondence)
Inglis, David R.	Serber, Robert

Acknowledgments

Sherr, Pat
Sherr, Rubby
Smith, Alice Kimball
Smith, Cyril S.
Smyth, Henry DeWolf
Teller, Edward
Ulam, Stanislaw M.

Volpe, Joseph A.
Weisskopf, Victor F.
*Wigner, Eugene P.
Wilson, Jane
Wilson, Robert R.
Zapf, Martin L.

* Nobel laureates

The following generously shared their expertise in advising me before my departure for the research in Japan: John Z. Bowers, M.D., Norman Cousins (who established my credentials with the Hiroshima leaders), Irving Janis, Seymour Jablon, Kanji Kuramoto, Kimuko Laskey, Wayne P. Lammers, Robert Jay Lifton, M.D., Osamu Masaoka, Edwin M. Reingold, Barbara Reynolds, Walter Sheridan, and Rafael Steinberg. Particularly valuable was the expertise of Mrs. Reynolds, acquired over the many years of her residence in Hiroshima and her involvement with its marvelously idealistic World Friendship Center, which she founded and operated for a long time.

Stuart C. Finch, M.D., clarified medical questions in Hiroshima as well as at his home in New Jersey.

Four new Japanese friends were indispensable among my guides in Hiroshima and require special thanks. Tomin Harada, M.D., led in the organization of the entire research effort. Minoru Yuzaki, professor of sociology at Hiroshima University, whose decades of painstaking detective work have given him encyclopedic knowledge of people and events closest to the hypocenter of the atomic explosion, identified and located the most critically important eyewitnesses and won their cooperation. Keiko Ogura arranged and administered the interviewing, the interpreting, and also the official contacts without which nothing moves in Japan. The irrepressible Mikimasa Maruyama was the principal research assistant.

In Tokyo, both during my stay in Japan and ever since, the meticulous Yasushi Matsushima was my cultural godfather and shrewd hunter of forgotten people and obscure facts. Professor Tadashi Ishida and his staff at Hitotsubashi University contributed the wealth of their decades of interviewing for the life histories of atomic bomb victims.

My principal interviewees in Hiroshima, Kyoto, and Tokyo were

Araki, Takeshi (Mayor)
Arisue, Seizo
Baba, Hatsue
Desaki, Susumu
Fuji, Shaw
Fukui, Nobuichi
Furuta, Masanobu
Hamai, Fumiko
Hamai, Junso
Hirano, Taro (M.D.)
Horibe, Katsuko
Hamamoto, Masue
Imahori, Seiji
Ishikawa, Hisato
Ito, Itsuro
Ito, Sakae
Jennings, Ginger
Jennings, Joe (Rev.)

Kamidoi, Isoko
Katsura, Tsurumi
Koyama, Ayao (M.D.)
Kuramoto, Atsushi (M.D.)
Kuramoto, Kiyoshi (M.D.)
Kurashige, Tatsuya
Kishida, Mitsugi
Kitagawa, Tetsuzo
Kobayashi, Iwakichi
Komatsue, Kikue
Kondo, Akira
Kuboura, Hiroto
Kuwabara, Chioko
Kurauchi, Hitoshi
Maeoka, Motoji
Masumoto, Kimiko
Masuoka, Teijiro
Matsubara, Miyoko

Day One

Morishita, Fumiko
Morita, Yushiyuki (M.D.)
Moritaki, Ichiro
Niizuma, Kiokazu
Oda, Hiroshi
Oda, Keizo
Ogame, Tsutomu
Okimoto, Tsuneo
Ouchi, Goro (M.D.)
Rappaport, M. E.
Reikaishi, Suwa
Sakuma, Kiyoshi
Sasami, Hanayo

Shimizu, Kiyoshi (M.D.)
Shimizu, Sakae
Shindo, Hiroshi
Takahashi, Akihiro
Takeuchi, Masashi
Takeuchi, Takeshi
Tamura, Masato
Teramae, Taeko
Wakaki, Shigetoshi
Yamaoka, Michiko
Yanagida, Hiroshi
Yokoyama, Sumi
Yoshika, Yutaka

Among former residents of Hiroshima whom I interviewed in the United States and Canada were

Akiba, Tadatoshi
Garnett, Florence
Honda, Mary
Jenkins, Kuniko
Kobayashi, Sally
Kuramoto, Kanji
Laskey, Kimuko
Niimoto, Yoshiako
Nishina, Kojiro

Ono, Fumi
Sasamori, Shigeko
Shinoda, Hisako
Suyeishi, Kazuze
Suzuki, Yoshiko
Tomasawa, Mitsuo
Yamada, Asubo (Sister)
Yamaoka, May

Leads to interviewees and other logistical support in Hiroshima came from Shaw Fuji, Toshiyuko Fukazaki, Yasutake Hirayama, Toru Kanai, Moriako Kawamura, Yasuo Miyazaki, Hiroshi Oda, Keiko Shoda, Katsukuni Tanaka, Akira Tashiro, Teizo Umeda, and Setsumi Wakabayashi.

The Hiroshima interpreters were: Tomoko Kondo, Yoko Nadamitsu, Kaori Seo, Kumiko Tahama, Michiko Tashiro, Chiyo Yoshida, and Mayumi Yoshida.

All interviewing was done between 1982 and 1984.

In the United States, the translations were sensitively done by Sekiko McDonald of the Sterling Library staff at Yale.

Elaine Seaton marshalled the library resources and supplied her usual canny editorial judgment and her much needed serenity.

At Simon and Schuster, Michael Korda, assisted by John Herman, massaged the manuscript into shape.

P.W.
Ridgefield, Connecticut
May 1984

Index

Index

Japanese Ministry of Education, 327, 333
Jemez Springs, N. M., as Project Y site, 68
Jeppson, Norris R., 244, 245, 246
Jews:
in concentration camps, 54n
Hiroshima Maidens aided by, 340
Joliot-Curie, Frédéric, 90, 108
J. Robert Oppenheimer—Shatterer of Worlds (Goodchild), 76n
Junod, Marcel, 318–19, 322, 324

Kaiser Wilhelm Institute, 20, 35, 40, 84–86, 188
Kapitza, Peter, 120–21, 123, 128n
Keitel, Wilhelm, 65
keloid scars, 335
Kennedy, Edward, 330n
Kennedy, John F., 130n
Kido, Marquis Koichi, 296–97
Kishida, Mitsugi, 278n
Kistiakowsky, George B. (Kisty), 45n, 46, 112
at Alamogordo test, 205, 206–7, 208, 209, 211, 212, 215–16
Kleinsorge, Father Wilhelm, 276n
Kokura Arsenal, as A-bomb target, 196, 228, 239, 293
Kondo, Akira, 361
Kremer, Simon Davidovich, 89
Kuramoto, Kanji, 273
Kurchatov, Igor Vasilevich, 89–90, 110–11, 226
Kyoto, as A-bomb target, 193, 195, 196, 197, 198, 227, 228

Lansdale, John, Jr., 63, 81–83, 352
Lapp, Ralph E., 177
Laurence, William L., 212, 213, 216, 319n
Lawrence, Ernest O., 64, 67, 71, 74, 76, 86, 95
demonstration alternative and, 154–155, 160–61, 170
Groves's first meeting with, 60–61
in initiation of A-bomb project, 44–45, 46, 47
on Interim Committee, 156, 159, 160–61, 163, 165, 168–71
Leahy, William D., 129, 173, 227n, 319–21, 324
LeMay, Curtis, 228n, 292
fire raids and, 164, 183–85, 231
Hiroshima bombing and, 199, 239

Levine, Stanley, 280
Lewis, Robert, 243, 247
Liebowitz, Benjamin, 30, 39
Lifton, Robert Jay, 338n, 341–42, 343
Lilienthal, David E., 347–48, 349, 350, 352
Lindberg, Charles, 35n
Little Boy, *see* uranium bomb
Los Alamos, N. M., laboratory (Project Y), 65–70, 93–105, 111–16, 147–53, 238
Bohr's arrival at, 115–16
compartmentalization vs. free flow of ideas at, 66, 97, 98–100
construction costs of, 68n
Delivery Group at, 16–17, 152, 191
demonstration alternative discussed at, 150–53, 216–17
fortieth-anniversary reunion at, 362–65
Gadget Division at, 113
Hiroshima bombing announced at, 289–90
housing at, 100n
implosion research at, 98–99, 102, 103–4, 111–12, 113, 116
Interim Committee science advisers' meeting at, 168–71, 174
Japanese reports of radiation sickness as concern at, 18–19
moral concerns expressed at, 147–149
Oppenheimer appointed director of, 66, 67
Oppenheimer's proposal for, 65–67
Ordnance Division at, 103
plutonium bomb tested by, *see* Alamogordo, N. M., Trinity test
population at, 68, 96
radiation hazards at, 210
schism between military and scientists at, 95, 100
scientists recruited for, 93–95
scientists to join army at, 67, 95
security concerns at, 16–17, 71–77, 80–83, 94n, 99–100, 109
Serber's briefing at, 97–98, 99
site chosen for, 68–69
startup of, 95–99
Szilard's antibomb petition at, 177–179
Target Committee meeting at, 195–196
Teller's dissatisfaction at, 101–2
Theoretical Division at, 101–2, 218

405

Index

PICTURE CREDITS